Family Maps
of
Guernsey County, Ohio
Deluxe Edition

With Homesteads, Roads, Waterways, Towns, Cemeteries, Railroads, and More

Family Maps

of

Guernsey County, Ohio

Deluxe Edition

With Homesteads, Roads, Waterways, Towns, Cemeteries, Railroads, and More

by Gregory A. Boyd, J.D.

Featuring **3** *Maps Per Township ...*

Arphax Publishing Co.
www.arphax.com

Family Maps of Guernsey County, Ohio, Deluxe Edition: With Homesteads, Roads, Waterways, Towns, Cemeteries, Railroads, and More.
by Gregory A. Boyd, J.D.

ISBN 1-4203-1532-3

Published by Arphax Publishing Co., 2210 Research Park Blvd., Norman, Oklahoma, USA 73069
www.arphax.com

First Edition

ATTENTION HISTORICAL & GENEALOGICAL SOCIETIES, UNIVERSITIES, COLLEGES, CORPORATIONS, FAMILY REUNION COORDINATORS, AND PROFESSIONAL ORGANIZATIONS: Quantity discounts are available on bulk purchases of this book. For information, please contact Arphax Publishing Co., at the address listed above, or at (405) 366-6181, or visit our web-site at www.arphax.com and contact us through the "Bulk Sales" link.

This book is dedicated to my wonderful family:

Vicki, Jordan, & Amy Boyd

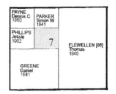

Contents

- Part I -

The Big Picture

- Part II -

Township Map Groups

(each Map Group contains a Patent Index, Patent Map, Road Map, & Historical Map)

Appendices

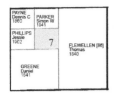

Preface

The quest for the discovery of my ancestors' origins, migrations, beliefs, and life-ways has brought me rewards that I could never have imagined. The *Family Maps* series of books is my first effort to share with historical and genealogical researchers, some of the tools that I have developed to achieve my research goals. I firmly believe that this effort will allow many people to reap the same sorts of treasures that I have.

Our Federal government's General Land Office of the Bureau of Land Management (the "GLO") has given genealogists and historians an incredible gift by virtue of its enormous database housed on its web-site at glorecords.blm.gov. Here, you can search for and find millions of parcels of land purchased by our ancestors in about thirty states.

This GLO web-site is one of the best FREE on-line tools available to family researchers. But, it is not for the faint of heart, nor is it for those unwilling or unable to to sift through and analyze the thousands of records that exist for most counties.

My immediate goal with this series is to spare you the hundreds of hours of work that it would take you to map the Land Patents for this county. Every Guernsey County homestead or land patent that I have gleaned from public GLO databases is mapped here. Consequently, I can usually show you in an instant, where your ancestor's land is located, as well as the names of nearby land-owners.

Originally, that was my primary goal. But after speaking to other genealogists, it became clear that there was much more that they wanted. Taking their advice set me back almost a full year, but I think you will agree it was worth the wait. Because now, you can learn so much more.

Now, this book answers these sorts of questions:

- Are there any variant spellings for surnames that I have missed in searching GLO records?
- Where is my family's traditional home-place?
- What cemeteries are near Grandma's house?
- My Granddad used to swim in such-and-such-Creek—where is that?
- How close is this little community to that one?
- Are there any other people with the same surname who bought land in the county?
- How about cousins and in-laws—did they buy land in the area?

And these are just for starters!

The rules for using the *Family Maps* books are simple, but the strategies for success are many. Some techniques are apparent on first use, but many are gained with time and experience. Please take the time to notice the roads, cemeteries, creek-names, family names, and unique first-names throughout the whole county. You cannot imagine what YOU might be the first to discover.

I hope to learn that many of you have answered age-old research questions within these pages or that you have discovered relationships previously not even considered. When these sorts of things happen to you, will you please let me hear about it? I would like nothing better. My contact information can always be found at www.arphax.com.

One more thing: please read the "How To Use This Book" chapter; it starts on the next page. This will give you the very best chance to find the treasures that lie within these pages.

My family and I wish you the very best of luck, both in life, and in your research.   Greg Boyd

How to Use This Book - A Graphical Summary

Part I
"The Big Picture"

Map A ▸ *Counties in the State*
Map B ▸ *Surrounding Counties*
Map C ▸ *Congressional Townships (Map Groups) in the County*
Map D ▸ *Cities & Towns in the County*
Map E ▸ *Cemeteries in the County*
Surnames in the County ▸ *Number of Land-Parcels for Each Surname*
Surname/Township Index ▸ *Directs you to Township Map Groups in Part II*

The Surname/Township Index can direct you to any number of **Township Map Groups**

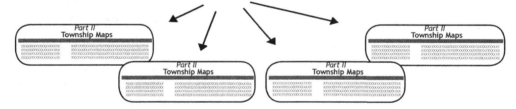

Part II
Township Map Groups
(1 for each Township in the County)

Each Township Map Group contains all four of of the following tools . . .

Land Patent Index ▸ *Every-name Index of Patents Mapped in this Township*
Land Patent Map ▸ *Map of Patents as listed in above Index*
Road Map ▸ *Map of Roads, City-centers, and Cemeteries in the Township*
Historical Map ▸ *Map of Railroads, Lakes, Rivers, Creeks, City-Centers, and Cemeteries*

Appendices

Appendix A ▸ *Congressional Authority enabling Patents within our Maps*
Appendix B ▸ *Section-Parts / Aliquot Parts (a comprehensive list)*
Appendix C ▸ *Multi-patentee Groups (Individuals within Buying Groups)*

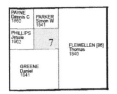

How to Use This Book

The two "Parts" of this *Family Maps* volume seek to answer two different types of questions. Part I deals with broad questions like: what counties surround Guernsey County, are there any ASHCRAFTs in Guernsey County, and if so, in which Townships or Maps can I find them? Ultimately, though, Part I should point you to a particular Township Map Group in Part II.

Part II concerns itself with details like: where exactly is this family's land, who else bought land in the area, and what roads and streams run through the land, or are located nearby. The Chart on the opposite page, and the remainder of this chapter attempt to convey to you the particulars of these two "parts", as well as how best to use them to achieve your research goals.

Part I
"The Big Picture"

Within Part I, you will find five "Big Picture" maps and two county-wide surname tools.

These include:

- Map A - Where Guernsey County lies within the state
- Map B - Counties that surround Guernsey County
- Map C - Congressional Townships of Guernsey County (+ Map Group Numbers)
- Map D - Cities & Towns of Guernsey County (with Index)
- Map E - Cemeteries of Guernsey County (with Index)
- Surnames in Guernsey County Patents (with Parcel-counts for each surname)
- Surname/Township Index (with Parcel-counts for each surname by Township)

The five "Big-Picture" Maps are fairly self-explanatory, yet should not be overlooked. This is particularly true of Maps "C", "D", and "E", all of which show Guernsey County and its Congressional Townships (and their assigned Map Group Numbers).

Let me briefly explain this concept of Map Group Numbers. These are a device completely of our own invention. They were created to help you quickly locate maps without having to remember the full legal name of the various Congressional Townships. It is simply easier to remember "Map Group 1" than a legal name like: "Township 9-North Range 6-West, 5th Principal Meridian." But the fact is that the TRUE legal name for these Townships IS terribly important. These are the designations that others will be familiar with and you will need to accurately record them in your notes. This is why both Map Group numbers AND legal descriptions of Townships are almost always displayed together.

Map "C" will be your first intoduction to "Map Group Numbers", and that is all it contains: legal Township descriptions and their assigned Map Group Numbers. Once you get further into your research, and more immersed in the details, you will likely want to refer back to Map "C" from time to time, in order to regain your bearings on just where in the county you are researching.

Remember, township boundaries are a completely artificial device, created to standardize land descriptions. But do not let them become a boundary in your mind when choosing which townships to research. Your relative's in-laws, children, cousins, siblings, and mamas and papas, might just as easily have lived in the township next to the one your grandfather lived in—rather than in the one where he actually lived. So Map "C" can be your guide to which other Townships/ Map Groups you likewise ought to analyze.

Of course, the same holds true for County lines; this is the purpose behind Map "B". It shows you surrounding counties that you may want to consider for further reserarch.

Map "D", the Cities and Towns map, is the first map with an index. Map "E" is the second (Cemeteries). Both, Maps "D" and "E" give you broad views of City (or Cemetery) locations in the County. But they go much further by pointing you toward pertinent Township Map Groups so you can locate the patents, roads, and waterways located near a particular city or cemetery.

Once you are familiar with these *Family Maps* volumes and the county you are researching, the "Surnames In Guernsey County" chapter (or its sister chapter in other volumes) is where you'll likely start your future research sessions. Here, you can quickly scan its few pages and see if anyone in the county possesses the surnames you are researching. The "Surnames in Guernsey County" list shows only two things: surnames and the number of parcels of land we have located for that surname in Guernsey County. But whether or not you immediately locate the surnames you are researching, please do not go any further without taking a few moments to scan ALL the surnames in these very few pages.

You cannot imagine how many lost ancestors are waiting to be found by someone willing to take just a little longer to scan the "Surnames In Guernsey County" list. Misspellings and typographical errors abound in most any index of this sort. Don't miss out on finding your Kinard that was written Rynard or Cox that was written Lox. If it looks funny or wrong, it very often is. And one of those little errors may well be your relative.

Now, armed with a surname and the knowledge that it has one or more entries in this book, you are ready for the "Surname/Township Index." Unlike the "Surnames In Guernsey County", which has only one line per Surname, the "Surname/ Township Index" contains one line-item for each Township Map Group in which each surname is found. In other words, each line represents a different Township Map Group that you will need to review.

Specifically, each line of the Surname/Township Index contains the following four columns of information:

1. Surname
2. Township Map Group Number (these Map Groups are found in Part II)
3. Parcels of Land (number of them with the given Surname within the Township)
4. Meridian/Township/Range (the legal description for this Township Map Group)

The key column here is that of the Township Map Group Number. While you should definitely record the Meridian, Township, and Range, you can do that later. Right now, you need to dig a little deeper. That Map Group Number tells you where in Part II that you need to start digging.

But before you leave the "Surname/Township Index", do the same thing that you did with the "Surnames in Guernsey County" list: take a moment to scan the pages of the Index and see if there are similarly spelled or misspelled surnames that deserve your attention. Here again, is an easy opportunity to discover grossly misspelled family names with very little effort. Now you are ready to turn to . . .

Part II
"Township Map Groups"

You will normally arrive here in Part II after being directed to do so by one or more "Map Group Numbers" in the Surname/Township Index of Part I.

Each Map Group represents a set of four tools dedicated to a single Congressional Township that is either wholly or partially within the county. If you are trying to learn all that you can about a particular family or their land, then these tools should usually be viewed in the order they are presented.

These four tools include:

1. a Land Patent Index
2. a Land Patent Map
3. a Road Map, and
4. an Historical Map

As I mentioned earlier, each grouping of this sort is assigned a Map Group Number. So, let's now move on to a discussion of the four tools that make up one of these Township Map Groups.

Land Patent Index

Each Township Map Group's Index begins with a title, something along these lines:

MAP GROUP 1: Index to Land Patents
Township 16-North Range 5-West (2ⁿᵈ PM)

The Index contains seven (7) columns. They are:

1. ID (a unique ID number for this Individual and a corresponding Parcel of land in this Township)
2. Individual in Patent (name)
3. Sec. (Section), and
4. Sec. Part (Section Part, or Aliquot Part)
5. Date Issued (Patent)
6. Other Counties (often means multiple counties were mentioned in GLO records, or the section lies within multiple counties).
7. For More Info . . . (points to other places within this index or elsewhere in the book where you can find more information)

While most of the seven columns are self-explanatory, I will take a few moments to explain the "Sec. Part." and "For More Info" columns.

The "Sec. Part" column refers to what surveryors and other land professionals refer to as an Aliquot Part. The origins and use of such a term mean little to a non-surveyor, and I have chosen to simply call these sub-sections of land what they are: a "Section Part". No matter what we call them, what we are referring to are things like a quarter-section or half-section or quarter-quarter-section. See Appendix "B" for most of the "Section Parts" you will come across (and many you will not) and what size land-parcel they represent.

The "For More Info" column of the Index may seem like a small appendage to each line, but please

recognize quickly that this is not so. And to understand the various items you might find here, you need to become familiar with the Legend that appears at the top of each Land Patent Index.

Here is a sample of the Legend . . .

LEGEND

"For More Info . . . " column

A = Authority (Legislative Act, See Appendix "A")
B = Block or Lot (location in Section unknown)
C = Cancelled Patent
F = Fractional Section
G = Group (Multi-Patentee Patent, see Appendix "C")
V = Overlaps another Parcel
R = Re-Issued (Parcel patented more than once)

Most parcels of land will have only one or two of these items in their "For More Info" columns, but when that is not the case, there is often some valuable information to be gained from further investigation. Below, I will explain what each of these items means to you you as a researcher.

A = Authority
(Legislative Act, See Appendix "A")
All Federal Land Patents were issued because some branch of our government (usually the U.S. Congress) passed a law making such a transfer of title possible. And therefore every patent within these pages will have an "A" item next to it in the index. The number after the "A" indicates which item in Appendix "A" holds the citation to the particular law which authorized the transfer of land to the public. As it stands, most of the Public Land data compiled and released by our government, and which serves as the basis for the patents mapped here, concerns itself with "Cash Sale" homesteads. So in some Counties, the law which authorized cash sales will be the primary, if not the only, entry in the Appendix.

B = Block or Lot (location in Section unknown)
A "B" designation in the Index is a tip-off that the EXACT location of the patent within the map is not apparent from the legal description. This Patent will nonetheless be noted within the proper

Section along with any other Lots purchased in the Section. Given the scope of this project (many states and many Counties are being mapped), trying to locate all relevant plats for Lots (if they even exist) and accurately mapping them would have taken one person several lifetimes. But since our primary goal from the onset has been to establish relationships between neighbors and families, very little is lost to this goal since we can still observe who all lived in which Section.

C = Cancelled Patent

A Cancelled Patent is just that: cancelled. Whether the original Patentee forfeited his or her patent due to fraud, a technicality, non-payment, or whatever, the fact remains that it is significant to know who received patents for what parcels and when. A cancellation may be evidence that the Patentee never physically re-located to the land, but does not in itself prove that point. Further evidence would be required to prove that. *See also*, Re-issued Patents, *below*.

F = Fractional Section

A Fractional Section is one that contains less than 640 acres, almost always because of a body of water. The exact size and shape of land-parcels contained in such sections may not be ascertainable, but we map them nonetheless. Just keep in mind that we are not mapping an actual parcel to scale in such instances. Another point to consider is that we have located some fractional sections that are not so designated by the Bureau of Land Management in their data. This means that not all fractional sections have been so identified in our indexes.

G = Group
(Multi-Patentee Patent, see Appendix "C")

A "G" designation means that the Patent was issued to a GROUP of people (Multi-patentees). The "G" will always be followed by a number. Some such groups were quite large and it was impractical if not impossible to display each individual in our maps without unduly affecting readability. EACH person in the group is named in the Index, but they won't all be found on the Map. You will find the name of the first person in such a Group

on the map with the Group number next to it, enclosed in [square brackets].

To find all the members of the Group you can either scan the Index for all people with the same Group Number or you can simply refer to Appendix "C" where all members of the Group are listed next to their number.

O = Overlaps another Parcel

An Overlap is one where PART of a parcel of land gets issued on more than one patent. For genealogical purposes, both transfers of title are important and both Patentees are mapped. If the ENTIRE parcel of land is re-issued, that is what we call it, a Re-Issued Patent (*see below*). The number after the "O" indicates the ID for the overlapping Patent(s) contained within the same Index. Like Re-Issued and Cancelled Patents, Overlaps may cause a map-reader to be confused at first, but for genealogical purposes, all of these parties' relationships to the underlying land is important, and therefore, we map them.

R = Re-Issued (Parcel patented more than once)

The label, "Re-issued Patent" describes Patents which were issued more than once for land with the EXACT SAME LEGAL DESCRIPTION. Whether the original patent was cancelled or not, there were a good many parcels which were patented more than once. The number after the "R" indicates the ID for the other Patent contained within the same Index that was for the same land. A quick glance at the map itself within the relevant Section will be the quickest way to find the other Patentee to whom the Parcel was transferred. They should both be mapped in the same general area.

I have gone to some length describing all sorts of anomalies either in the underlying data or in their representation on the maps and indexes in this book. Most of this will bore the most ardent reseracher, but I do this with all due respect to those researchers who will inevitably (and rightfully) ask: *"Why isn't so-and-so's name on the exact spot that the index says it should be?"*

In most cases it will be due to the existence of a Multi-Patentee Patent, a Re-issued Patent, a Cancelled Patent, or Overlapping Parcels named in separate Patents. I don't pretend that this discussion will answer every question along these lines, but I hope it will at least convince you of the complexity of the subject.

Not to despair, this book's companion web-site will offer a way to further explain "odd-ball" or errant data. Each book (County) will have its own web-page or pages to discuss such situations. You can go to www.arphax.com to find the relevant web-page for Guernsey County.

Land Patent Map

On the first two-page spread following each Township's Index to Land Patents, you'll find the corresponding Land Patent Map. And here lies the real heart of our work. For the first time anywhere, researchers will be able to observe and analyze, on a grand scale, most of the original land-owners for an area AND see them mapped in proximity to each one another.

We encourage you to make vigorous use of the accompanying Index described above, but then later, to abandon it, and just stare at these maps for a while. This is a great way to catch misspellings or to find collateral kin you'd not known were in the area.

Each Land Patent Map represents one Congressional Township containing approximately 36-square miles. Each of these square miles is labeled by an accompanying Section Number (1 through 36, in most cases). Keep in mind, that this book concerns itself solely with Guernsey County's patents. Townships which creep into one or more other counties will not be shown in their entirety in any one book. You will need to consult other books, as they become available, in order to view other countys' patents, cities, cemeteries, etc.

But getting back to Guernsey County: each Land Patent Map contains a Statistical Chart that looks like the following:

Township Statistics

Parcels Mapped	:	173
Number of Patents	:	163
Number of Individuals	:	152
Patentees Identified	:	151
Number of Surnames	:	137
Multi-Patentee Parcels	:	4
Oldest Patent Date	:	11/27/1820
Most Recent Patent	:	9/28/1917
Block/Lot Parcels	:	0
Parcels Re-Issued	:	3
Parcels that Overlap	:	8
Cities and Towns	:	6
Cemeteries	:	6

This information may be of more use to a social statistician or historian than a genealogist, but I think all three will find it interesting.

Most of the statistics are self-explanatory, and what is not, was described in the above discussion of the Index's Legend, but I do want to mention a few of them that may affect your understanding of the Land Patent Maps.

First of all, Patents often contain more than one Parcel of land, so it is common for there to be more Parcels than Patents. Also, the Number of Individuals will more often than not, not match the number of Patentees. A Patentee is literally the person or PERSONS named in a patent. So, a Patent may have a multi-person Patentee or a single-person patentee. Nonetheless, we account for all these individuals in our indexes.

On the lower-righthand side of the Patent Map is a Legend which describes various features in the map, including Section Boundaries, Patent (land) Boundaries, Lots (numbered), and Multi-Patentee Group Numbers. You'll also find a "Helpful Hints" Box that will assist you.

One important note: though the vast majority of Patents mapped in this series will prove to be reasonably accurate representations of their actual locations, we cannot claim this for patents lying along state and county lines, or waterways, or that have been platted (lots).

Shifting boundaries and sparse legal descriptions in the GLO data make this a reality that we have nonetheless tried to overcome by estimating these patents' locations the best that we can.

Road Map

On the two-page spread following each Patent Map you will find a Road Map covering the exact same area (the same Congressional Township).

For me, fully exploring the past means that every once in a while I must leave the library and travel to the actual locations where my ancestors once walked and worked the land. Our Township Road Maps are a great place to begin such a quest.

Keep in mind that the scaling and proportion of these maps was chosen in order to squeeze hundreds of people-names, road-names, and place-names into tinier spaces than you would traditionally see. These are not professional road-maps, and like any secondary genealogical source, should be looked upon as an entry-way to original sources—in this case, original patents and applications, professionally produced maps and surveys, etc.

Both our Road Maps and Historical Maps contain cemeteries and city-centers, along with a listing of these on the left-hand side of the map. I should note that I am showing you city center-points, rather than city-limit boundaries, because in many instances, this will represent a place where settlement began. This may be a good time to mention that many cemeteries are located on private property, Always check with a local historical or genealogical society to see if a particular cemetery is publicly accessible (if it is not obviously so). As a final point, look for your surnames among the road-names. You will often be surprised by what you find.

Historical Map

The third and final map in each Map Group is our attempt to display what each Township might have looked like before the advent of modern roads. In frontier times, people were usually more determined to settle near rivers and creeks than they were near roads, which were often few and far between. As was the case with the Road Map, we've included the same cemeteries and city-centers. We've also included railroads, many of which came along before most roads.

While some may claim "Historical Map" to be a bit of a misnomer for this tool, we settled for this label simply because it was almost as accurate as saying "Railroads, Lakes, Rivers, Cities, and Cemeteries," and it is much easier to remember.

In Closing . . .

By way of example, here is *A Really Good Way to Use a Township Map Group*. First, find the person you are researching in the Township's Index to Land Patents, which will direct you to the proper Section and parcel on the Patent Map. But before leaving the Index, scan all the patents within it, looking for other names of interest. Now, turn to the Patent Map and locate your parcels of land. Pay special attention to the names of patent-holders who own land surrounding your person of interest. Next, turn the page and look at the same Section(s) on the Road Map. Note which roads are closest to your parcels and also the names of nearby towns and cemeteries. Using other resources, you may be able to learn of kin who have been buried here, plus, you may choose to visit these cemeteries the next time you are in the area.

Finally, turn to the Historical Map. Look once more at the same Sections where you found your research subject's land. Note the nearby streams, creeks, and other geographical features. You may be surprised to find family names were used to name them, or you may see a name you haven't heard mentioned in years and years—and a new research possibility is born.

Many more techniques for using these *Family Maps* volumes will no doubt be discovered. If from time to time, you will navigate to Guernsey County's web-page at www.arphax.com (use the "Research" link), you can learn new tricks as they become known (or you can share ones you have employed). But for now, you are ready to get started. So, go, and good luck.

– Part I –

The Big Picture

Map A - Where Guernsey County, Ohio Lies Within the State

Legend

State Boundary

County Boundaries

Guernsey County, Ohio

Helpful Hints

1   We start with Map "A" which simply shows us where within the State this county lies.

2   Map "B" zooms in further to help us more easily identify surrounding Counties.

3   Map "C" zooms in even further to reveal the Congressional Townships that either lie within or intersect Guernsey County.

Map B - Guernsey County, Ohio and Surrounding Counties

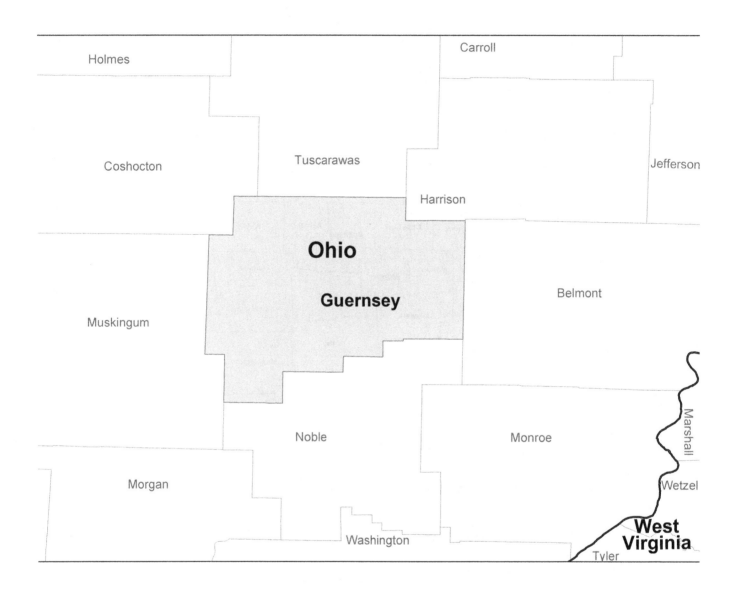

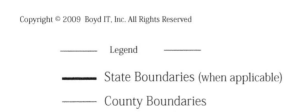

——— Legend ———

State Boundaries (when applicable)

County Boundaries

──── Helpful Hints ────

1 Many Patent-holders and their families settled across county lines. It is always a good idea to check nearby counties for your families.

2 Refer to Map "A" to see a broader view of where this County lies within the State, and Map "C" to see which Congressional Townships lie within Guernsey County.

Map C - Congressional Townships of Guernsey County, Ohio

Map Group 1 Township 4-N Range 4-W	**Map Group 2** Township 4-N Range 3-W	**Map Group 3** Township 4-N Range 2-W	**Map Group 4** Township 4-N Range 1-W	**Map Group 5** Township 11-N Range 7-W
Map Group 6 Township 3-N Range 4-W	**Map Group 7** Township 3-N Range 3-W	**Map Group 8** Township 3-N Range 2-W	**Map Group 9** Township 3-N Range 1-W	**Map Group 10** Township 10-N Range 7-W
Map Group 11 Township 2-N Range 4-W	**Map Group 12** Township 2-N Range 3-W	**Map Group 13** Township 2-N Range 2-W	**Map Group 14** Township 2-N Range 1-W	**Map Group 15** Township 9-N Range 7-W
Map Group 16 Township 1-N Range 4-W	**Map Group 17** Township 1-N Range 3-W	**Map Group 18** Township 1-N Range 2-W	**Map Group 19** Township 1-N Range 1-W	

Map Group 21
Township 8-N Range 9-W

Map Group 20
Township 9-N Range 10-W

— Legend —

□ Guernsey County, Ohio

□ Congressional Townships

— Helpful Hints —

1 Many Patent-holders and their families settled across county lines. It is always a good idea to check nearby counties for your families (See Map "B").

2 Refer to Map "A" to see a broader view of where this county lies within the State, and Map "B" for a view of the counties surrounding Guernsey County.

Map D Index: Cities & Towns of Guernsey County, Ohio

The following represents the Cities and Towns of Guernsey County (along with the corresponding Map Group in which each is found). Cities and Towns are displayed in both the Road and Historical maps in the Group.

City/Town	Map Group No.
Abledell	12
Antrim	9
Barton Manor	12
Birds Run	1
Birmingham	3
Black	12
Blacktop	18
Bluebell	20
Boden	6
Brady	8
Browns Heights	12
Buckeyeville	17
Buffalo	21
Byesville	18
Cambridge	12
Cassell	11
Cassellview	16
Cedar Hills	12
Center	13
Chestnut Grove Cottage Area	19
Claysville	16
Clio (historical)	8
College Hill	11
Colonial Heights	16
Coventry Estates	12
Craig	13
Cumberland	20
Derwent	21
Duch Addition	19
East Cambridge	12
East Shore Cottage Area	19
Eastmoor	12
Easton	14
Echo Point	19
Elizabethtown	14
Fairdale	12
Fairmont	12
Fairview	10
Fairview	21
Five Forks	12
Flat Ridge	6
Georgetown	12
Gibson	19
Greenwood	18
Guernsey	2
Helena	20
Henderson Heights	12
Hickory Grove Cottage Area	19
Ideal	18
Indian Camp	6
Jackson Special	17
Kimbolton	2
Kings Mine	18
Kipling	18
Londonderry	5
Lore City	18
Lucasburg	17
Mantua	6
Marysville	17

City/Town	Map Group No.
Meadow Village	12
Middlebourne	10
Morgan Manor	16
New Gottingen	19
North Salem	7
Northgate	12
Oakgrove	5
Oakwood	17
Odell	3
Old Washington	13
Oldham	12
Opperman	20
Pleasant City	21
Quaker City	15
Ridgewood Acres	11
Robins	18
Salesville	15
Seneca Lake Estates	19
Senecaville	18
Spencer Station	15
Spring Valley	17
Sunnymeade	12
Sycamore Hills	12
Toledoville (historical)	1
Tyner	7
Walhonding	21
Warrentown	13
West Shore Cottage Area	19
Winterset	9

Map D - Cities & Towns of Guernsey County, Ohio

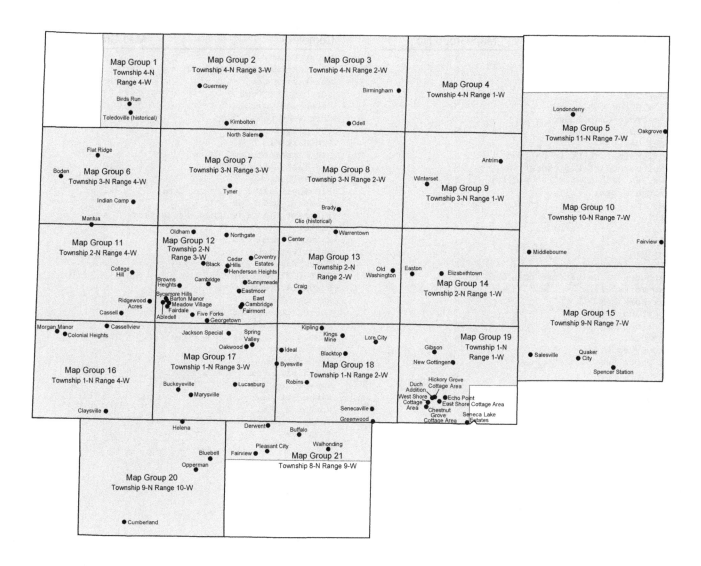

─── Legend ───

Guernsey County, Ohio

Congressional Townships

─── Helpful Hints ───

1 Cities and towns are marked only at their center-points as published by the USGS and/or NationalAtlas.gov. This often enables us to more closely approximate where these might have existed when first settled.

2 To see more specifically where these Cities & Towns are located within the county, refer to both the Road and Historical maps in the Map-Group referred to above. See also, the Map "D" Index on the opposite page.

Map E Index: Cemeteries of Guernsey County, Ohio

The following represents many of the Cemeteries of Guernsey County, along with the corresponding Township Map Group in which each is found. Cemeteries are displayed in both the Road and Historical maps in the Map Groups referred to below.

Cemetery	Map Group No.
Allen Cem.	8
Antrim Presbyterian Cem.	9
Banker Cem.	1
Barker Cem.	15
Battle Ridge Cem.	13
Beech Grove Chapel Cem.	17
Bells Cem.	7
Bethel Cem.	2
Bethel Methodist Episcopal Cem.	20
Bethel Methodist Protestant Cem.	18
Birds Run Methodist Episcopal Cem.	1
Birmingham Cem.	3
Bond Cem.	10
Buffalo Cem.	21
Bunfills Cem.	10
Carlisle Cem.	14
Cedar Cem.	16
Center Baptist Cem.	12
Chestnut Hill United Brethren Cem.	4
Clear Fork Cem.	3
Clear Fork Cem.	3
Cumberland Cem.	3
Cumberland Cem.	20
Darby Cem.	4
Earleys Cem.	2
East Union Cem.	16
Eldon Cem.	15
Elizabethtown Cem.	14
Engle Cem.	4
Enon Cem.	17
Fairview Cem.	10
Flat Ridge Cem.	3
Flat Ridge Cem.	6
Fletcher Cem.	15
Ford Cem.	11
Forney Cem.	1
Founders Cem.	12
Frame Number One Cem.	14
Friends Cem.	15
George Cem.	4
Gibson Station Cem.	19
Glenview Cem.	9
Greenlawn Cem.	15
Greenwood Cem.	17
Guernsey Memorial Gardens	12
Harmony Cem.	17
Hawthorne Cem.	6
Hopewell Methodist Episcopal Cem.	6
Irish Ridge Cem.	3
Jones Cem.	2
Kimbolton Cem.	7
Leatherwood Cem.	14
Lebanon Cem.	11
Lore City Cem.	18
McCleary Cem.	8
McCoy Cem.	10
McQuade Cem.	14
Morrow Cem.	6
Mount Calvary Cem.	12

Cemetery	Map Group No.
Mount Calvary Cem.	17
Mount Herman Cem.	6
Mount Zion Cem.	17
North Salem Cem.	7
Northfield Cem.	6
Northwood Cem.	12
Old City Cem.	12
Old Hartford Cem.	21
Old Kimbolton Cem.	2
Old Washington Cem.	13
Pisgah Cem.	10
Pleasant City Protestant Cem.	21
Pleasant Hill Cem.	8
Pleasant Hill Methodist Protestant	4
Quaker Cem.	5
Saint Michael Cem.	18
Saint Patricks Cem.	19
Salem Baptist Cem.	19
Salt Fork Baptist Cem.	10
Sandhill Cem.	19
Sarchet Run Cem.	11
Scotch Covenanter Cem.	5
Senecaville Cem.	18
Sigman Cem.	17
Sunset View Cem.	5
Township Cem.	2
Union Hill Cem.	1
Weaver Cem.	19
Winterset Cem.	9
Worthing Cem.	1
Yankee Point Cem.	5
Zion Cem.	16

Map E - Cemeteries of Guernsey County, Ohio

Map Group 1
Township 4-N Range 4-W
Union Hill
Forney
Banker
Birds Run Methodist Episcopal
Worthing

Map Group 2
Township 4-N Range 3-W
Earleys
Township
Bethel
Jones
Old Kimbolton

Map Group 3
Township 4-N Range 2-W
Flat Ridge
Cumberland
Irish Ridge Birmingham
Clear Fork
Clear Fork

Map Group 4
Township 4-N Range 1-W
George
Engle
Pleasant Hill Methodist Protestant
Chestnut Hill United Brethren
Darby

Map Group 5
Township 11-N Range 7-W
Scotch Covenanter
Sunset View
Quaker
Yankee Point

Map Group 6
Township 3-N Range 4-W
Flat Ridge
Northfield
Mount Herman
Morrow
Hawthorne
Hopewell Methodist Episcopal

Map Group 7
Township 3-N Range 3-W
Kimbolton
North Salem
Bells

Map Group 8
Township 3-N Range 2-W
McCleary
Pleasant Hill
Allen

Map Group 9
Township 3-N Range 1-W
Antrim Presbyterian
Winterset
Glenview

Map Group 10
Township 10-N Range 7-W
Bond
Bunfills McCoy
Salt Fork Baptist
Pisgah
Fairview

Map Group 11
Township 2-N Range 4-W
Lebanon
Ford

Map Group 12
Township 2-N Range 3-W
Center Baptist
Northwood
Founders Old City Guernsey Memorial Gardens
Mount Calvary

Map Group 13
Township 2-N Range 2-W
Old Washington
Battle Ridge

Map Group 14
Township 2-N Range 1-W
Carlisle
Elizabethtown
McQuade
Frame Number One
Leatherwood

Map Group 15
Township 9-N Range 7-W
Fletcher
Greenlawn
Friends
Barker
Eldon

Map Group 16
Township 1-N Range 4-W
East Union
Zion
Cedar

Map Group 17
Township 1-N Range 3-W
Sigman
Beech Grove Chapel
Mount Calvary
Greenwood
Enon
Mount Zion
Harmony

Map Group 18
Township 1-N Range 2-W
Lore City
Bethel Saint Michael
Methodist Protestant
Senecaville

Map Group 19
Township 1-N Range 1-W
Weaver
Gibson Station
Saint Patricks
Sandhill
Salem Baptist

Map Group 20
Township 9-N Range 10-W
Bethel Methodist Episcopal
Cumberland

Map Group 21
Township 8-N Range 9-W
Buffalo
Old Hartford
Pleasant City Protestant

Legend

☐ Guernsey County, Ohio

☐ Congressional Townships

Copyright © 2009 Boyd IT, Inc. All Rights Reserved

Helpful Hints

1 Cemeteries are marked at locations as published by the USGS and/or NationalAtlas.gov.

2 To see more specifically where these Cemeteries are located, refer to the Road & Historical maps in the Map-Group referred to above. See also, the Map "E" Index on the opposite page to make sure you don't miss any of the Cemeteries located within this Congressional township.

Surnames in Guernsey County, Ohio Patents

The following list represents the surnames that we have located in Guernsey County, Ohio Patents and the number of parcels that we have mapped for each one. Here is a quick way to determine the existence (or not) of Patents to be found in the subsequent indexes and maps of this volume.

Surname	# of Land Parcels	Surname	# of Land Parcels	Surname	# of Land Parcels	Surname	# of Land Parcels
ACHESON	10	BOGLE	9	COATES	1	DYSON	1
ADAIR	3	BOND	3	COCHRAN	2	EAGLETON	1
ADAMS	3	BOONE	2	COCKRAN	1	ECKELBERY	2
AIKIN	1	BOSTON	1	COLE	1	EDIE	2
AIKINS	2	BOTTS	2	COLEMAN	4	ELLIOTT	1
AKIN	1	BOWERS	1	COLES	1	EMERSON	3
ALLEN	3	BOYCE	1	COLLINS	2	ENGLE	1
ANDERSON	6	BOYD	12	CONAN	1	ENTROT	1
ANNETT	2	BOYLE	1	CONANN	1	EVANS	9
ARBUCKLE	2	BRACKIN	1	CONDON	2	EWINGS	1
ARCHER	4	BRADEN	1	CONNER	2	FARRA	2
ARMSTRONG	4	BRADFORD	1	COOK	6	FERBACK	1
ASHER	1	BRADING	1	COOPER	1	FERBRACH	1
ASKIN	1	BRADSHAW	2	COPELAND	1	FERBRACHE	8
ASKINS	1	BRASHEAR	1	CORBET	3	FERGUSON	2
ATCHESON	1	BRATSHAW	1	CORNELIUS	1	FERRELL	1
ATCHISON	2	BRATTON	3	CORTRIGHT	1	FIELD	3
ATKINSON	3	BREWER	1	COULTER	6	FINLEY	6
ATKISON	1	BRILL	4	COWAN	2	FISHELL	1
ATTWOOD	1	BRITTON	5	COWDEN	2	FISHER	3
ATWOOD	1	BROOM	1	COWEL	1	FITZPATRICK	1
AYERS	2	BROWN	9	COWGILL	1	FLEMING	1
AZBILL	2	BRUSH	28	COX	5	FLING	1
BAIRD	4	BRUSHAL	1	CRAIG	2	FORD	5
BAKER	1	BRYAN	1	CRAWFORD	5	FORDYCE	1
BANKS	1	BRYANT	1	CREIGHTON	2	FOREACRE	1
BARBER	1	BRYSON	2	CROSBY	1	FOREMAN	1
BARKHURST	2	BUCHANAN	6	CROSS	1	FORREST	1
BARNDOLLAR	1	BUCKINGHAM	18	CROW	3	FORSYTHE	3
BARNES	2	BUNNEL	1	CULBERTSON	3	FOSTER	4
BARTON	1	BURNSIDE	2	CULLEN	3	FOULKE	1
BAUM	3	BURT	6	CULLY	1	FOX	2
BAXTER	1	BURTON	1	CULVER	1	FOY	1
BAY	4	BYE	4	CUMMING	1	FRAME	4
BEAHAM	1	CAEIRNS	1	DARRAUGH	1	FRANEY	1
BEAL	14	CALDWELL	2	DAVIES	1	FRAZER	1
BEALE	1	CALLANTINE	1	DAVIS	8	FRAZIER	2
BEALL	1	CALLENDINE	1	DAVOULT	1	FREEMAN	1
BEATTY	26	CAMP	2	DAWSON	1	FREY	1
BEEMER	2	CAMPBELL	6	DAY	1	FRY	2
BEETLY	1	CARLILE	2	DAYTON	1	FULLER	11
BELL	17	CARMICHAEL	1	DE LARUE	2	FULTON	1
BELLEW	1	CAROTHERS	1	DEAN	1	FURNEY	8
BELT	3	CARPENTER	2	DEEREN	2	GALAGHER	2
BENJAMIN	1	CARR	1	DELARUE	1	GALAWAY	1
BEVARD	5	CARRELL	1	DELONG	1	GALLATIN	1
BEYMER	4	CARROTHERS	1	DENNIS	5	GALLENTINE	1
BEYNOR	1	CARRY	1	DENNISON	2	GALLIWAY	2
BICHARD	1	CARTER	6	DEPEW	3	GALLOWAY	1
BICKHAM	2	CARUTHERS	2	DEW	2	GANSON	2
BIERCE	1	CASSIDY	1	DILDINE	1	GANT	2
BIGGS	16	CEASAR	1	DISALLUMS	3	GARDINER	1
BIGHAM	2	CHALFANT	1	DOUGLASS	7	GASKILL	1
BIGLEY	2	CHANDLER	3	DOWNEY	1	GASS	1
BIRD	1	CHANEY	1	DRAKE	4	GAURNER	1
BISHOP	2	CHAPMAN	1	DRYDEN	2	GENTZLER	3
BIXLER	1	CLARK	10	DUFF	19	GEORGE	1
BLACK	2	CLARKE	2	DUFFEY	5	GIBSON	16
BLACKSHIRE	1	CLARY	4	DUFFY	1	GILL	3
BLAIR	11	CLEGG	3	DUKE	1	GILLASPIE	1
BLISS	2	CLEMENTS	1	DULL	1	GILLESPIE	4
BOGGS	1	COARTS	1	DUNCAN	1	GILLET	1

Surname	# of Land Parcels	Surname	# of Land Parcels	Surname	# of Land Parcels	Surname	# of Land Parcels
GILPEN	1	HOLLAND	1	LENFESTY	1	MCCUNE	4
GILPIN	5	HOLT	1	LENT	1	MCDONALD	5
GIST	1	HONEYWELDS	1	LETT	1	MCDONNELL	2
GOINGS	2	HOSACK	3	LEWIS	3	MCDOWEL	1
GOMBAR	1	HOWARD	1	LINCH	1	MCDOWELL	3
GOODDE	1	HUFF	4	LINDLEY	2	MCDOWL	1
GOODERL	1	HUFFMAN	7	LINDSEY	1	MCELHEREN	1
GOSSET	1	HUGHES	1	LINGENFELTER	1	MCELROY	2
GOWENS	2	HUGHS	2	LISLE	1	MCGOWAN	2
GRACEY	1	HUNT	2	LITTLE	11	MCGREW	1
GRAHAM	10	HUNTER	7	LLEWELLYN	1	MCGUIRE	2
GRAY	2	HURBERT	1	LOGAN	4	MCILVAIN	2
GREEN	1	HUTCHESON	1	LONG	4	MCILYAR	4
GREENLAND	1	HUTCHINSON	2	LONGSTRETH	1	MCKEE	10
GREGORY	1	HYDE	2	LONGWORTH	2	MCKINNEY	2
GRIER	1	INGLEHART	2	LOURY	1	MCKINNIE	1
GRIFFIN	5	IRWIN	1	LOVE	3	MCKNIGHT	1
GRIFFITH	3	ISRAEL	1	LOWRY	3	MCLAUGHLIN	2
GRIMES	10	JACKSON	3	LUCCOCK	2	MCMICHAEL	1
GROVE	2	JACOBY	1	LUCK	1	MCMILLAN	1
GUNN	1	JAMES	1	LUCY	1	MCMILLEN	1
HAGAN	3	JENKINS	2	LUPER	1	MCMULLAN	2
HAGEN	1	JOHNSON	18	LYANS	1	MCMULLEN	5
HAGER	1	JOHNSTON	12	LYLE	1	MCMULLIN	1
HAINELINE	1	JONES	15	LYNCH	1	MCNAIR	1
HAINS	2	JORDON	3	LYONS	1	MCNEELY	1
HALE	1	KANADY	1	MACKEY	4	MCVICKER	1
HALL	11	KARR	7	MADDIN	1	MCWILLIAMS	6
HALLY	1	KEARNES	1	MAGEE	2	MEDEARIS	3
HAMILTON	6	KEARNS	1	MAGNESS	1	MEHAFFEY	7
HAMMERSLEY	2	KEEN	4	MALOY	4	MEHAFFY	1
HAMMOND	3	KELL	9	MANYPENNY	1	MEHOFFY	1
HANNA	1	KELLEY	1	MAPLE	7	MESKIMEN	1
HANNAH	1	KELLS	2	MARDIS	2	MILLER	16
HARDING	1	KELLY	1	MARINER	1	MILLIGAN	2
HARDISTY	3	KENNEDY	7	MARKEE	1	MILLIKEN	1
HARR	1	KENNEY	1	MARLATT	3	MILNER	1
HARRIS	1	KERSHAW	2	MARLOW	3	MILONE	3
HARRISS	1	KESTER	2	MARQUAND	4	MIRES	1
HART	2	KILBRIDE	1	MARSH	1	MISKIMEN	12
HARTLEY	3	KIMBLE	8	MARSHAL	1	MISKIMENS	3
HARTMAN	5	KING	1	MARSHALL	3	MISKIMIN	2
HARVERT	1	KINKEAD	9	MARTIN	7	MISKIMINS	3
HATCHER	3	KIRKPATRICK	1	MASTERS	3	MITCHELL	8
HATFIELD	1	KLINE	1	MASTIN	1	MOLAND	2
HAVER	1	KNAPP	1	MATHERS	1	MOLLOY	1
HAWES	3	KREIDER	4	MATHEWS	1	MONTGOMERY	1
HAWS	4	LACKEY	1	MATTHEWS	1	MOOR	1
HAWTHORN	4	LAFOLLETT	2	MAXWELL	3	MOORE	8
HAYES	1	LAKE	2	MCALHENEY	1	MOORES	1
HAYS	2	LANE	1	MCBRIDE	2	MORGAN	2
HEANS	1	LANGLOIS	1	MCBURNEY	1	MORRIS	4
HECKEL	1	LANING	3	MCCALL	1	MORRISON	9
HEDGE	8	LANNING	7	MCCANN	1	MORROW	7
HELANNEN	1	LARISON	1	MCCARTNEY	14	MORTON	3
HELLYER	2	LAUGHLAND	1	MCCLUNEY	2	MULLEN	1
HENDEN	2	LAUGHLIN	1	MCCOLLUM	2	MURPHY	1
HENDERSON	1	LAURENCE	2	MCCOMB	1	NEEDLER	1
HENRY	7	LAW	1	MCCONAUGHY	3	NEELEY	1
HERST	2	LAWRENCE	4	MCCONKEY	2	NEIL	1
HESHER	1	LAZEARE	2	MCCONN	1	NEILL	1
HESKETT	1	LE PEDRIN	1	MCCONNAUGHEY	1	NELSON	2
HIBBS	1	LEACH	4	MCCORMICK	1	NEVIN	3
HILGER	1	LEAMON	1	MCCOUGHY	1	NEWBURN	1
HILL	3	LEARD	1	MCCOY	2	NEWELL	4
HILLARD	1	LEE	1	MCCRACKEN	4	NEWLAND	2
HINELINE	1	LEECH	7	MCCREARY	1	NEWNOM	3
HISKETT	4	LEEPER	3	MCCROSSON	1	NICHOLS	1
HOFFMAN	1	LEMON	1	MCCULLEY	5	NICHOLSON	2
HOLCOMB	2	LENFESTEY	1	MCCULLOUGH	4	NICKEL	1

Surname	# of Land Parcels	Surname	# of Land Parcels	Surname	# of Land Parcels	Surname	# of Land Parcels
NOBLE	2	ROLLINS	1	STULE	1	WHITCRAFT	4
NORMAN	2	ROOSE	1	STULL	1	WHITE	5
NORRIS	2	ROSE	6	STURGES	53	WHITEHILL	2
NORTHGRAVES	1	ROSS	2	SUIT	1	WHITTEN	2
NOURSE	4	ROWEN	1	SUNAFRANK	1	WIER	2
OBNEY	1	RUBART	1	SUTTON	1	WIERS	1
OCALLIS	2	RUSSELL	3	SWAIM	2	WILEY	2
OGIER	6	RUTLEDGE	2	SWEARINGEN	2	WILKIN	2
OHARA	1	RYAN	1	SWISHER	1	WILKINSON	1
OLDHAM	3	SANDERS	1	SWYHART	1	WILLIAMS	8
OLIVER	2	SARCHET	3	TALBUT	1	WILLIS	3
ONG	1	SAVELY	2	TAYLOR	5	WILLSON	3
ORR	4	SAVIERS	1	TEEL	2	WILSON	13
OVERLEY	1	SCHOOLEY	1	TEMPLE	1	WINE	3
PADGITT	1	SCHWYHART	2	TERREL	1	WINEBURNER	1
PALMER	4	SCOTT	12	TETIRICK	1	WINN	1
PARISH	1	SECRIST	1	THARP	1	WIRICK	1
PARKE	1	SELDERS	1	THOMAS	7	WISCARVER	4
PARRISH	2	SHAFFER	2	THOMPSON	15	WISCORVER	1
PATRICK	2	SHARP	1	TIMMONS	1	WIYRICK	1
PATTERSON	16	SHEELEY	1	TINGLE	1	WOLFORD	2
PAXTON	7	SHEELY	1	TOBIN	4	WOOD	1
PAYLOR	1	SHERAR	1	TONER	2	WOODGET	1
PEACH	1	SHERRARD	2	TOOL	1	WOODROW	1
PEDWIN	1	SHIPLEY	1	TOPHAND	1	WOODS	2
PEOPLES	1	SHOFF	5	TORODE	1	WOODSIDE	2
PEREGO	3	SHRIVER	8	TOWNSEND	1	YARNEL	1
PERRY	4	SIGHTS	2	TOWNSHEND	1	YATES	3
PETERS	2	SIGMAN	1	TRACE	1	YOUNG	3
PHILIPS	1	SILLS	3	TROTT	1	ZIMMERMAN	3
PHILLIPS	7	SIMKINS	1	TRUSLER	5		
PICKERING	3	SIMMERMAN	1	TULLOUGH	2		
PLEMLINE	1	SIMPSON	1	TURKLE	2		
POLAND	2	SINES	2	TURNEY	3		
POOLE	1	SLASON	1	UNDERHILL	1		
PORTER	2	SLATER	1	VAMPELT	1		
POUNDS	2	SMALLY	1	VAN CAMPEN	1		
POWEL	1	SMITH	31	VAN HORNE	1		
PRATT	1	SNODGRASS	1	VANCUREN	2		
PRESLEY	2	SNOW	1	VANDVORT	1		
PRESTLY	1	SOLINGER	2	VANSICKEL	1		
PRIOR	1	SPAID	2	VERNON	4		
PULLEY	2	SPARKS	1	VERREY	1		
RANKIN	3	SPEERS	1	VOLKERT	1		
RANNELLS	1	SPENCER	2	VOORHES	3		
RAY	2	SPICER	1	WADE	2		
REA	2	SPILMAN	1	WAGONER	1		
READ	1	SPRAGUE	2	WAGSTAFF	6		
REAVES	1	STACKEY	1	WALGAMOTT	3		
REDMAN	1	STACKHOUSE	1	WALKER	3		
REED	5	STANBERRY	1	WALLACE	1		
REEVES	1	STANBERY	55	WALLER	8		
REILY	3	STARKEY	2	WALTERS	2		
RENNER	1	STEELL	1	WARD	1		
RICE	3	STEETH	1	WARDAN	1		
RICH	1	STEPHENS	2	WARDEN	13		
RIGDEN	1	STEVENS	4	WARNICK	3		
RIGGS	3	STEVENSON	1	WARRACK	1		
RISHER	3	STEWART	16	WATERS	1		
ROBB	3	STIERS	2	WEBSTER	3		
ROBBINS	3	STIGLER	1	WEIR	4		
ROBE	1	STILES	3	WELCH	1		
ROBERT	4	STINER	1	WELKER	1		
ROBERTS	2	STOCKDALE	4	WELLS	2		
ROBERTSON	6	STOKELY	5	WENTWORTH	1		
ROBINS	14	STRAHL	2	WERDEN	1		
ROBINSON	6	STRAKE	1	WEST	3		
RODGERS	3	STROIN	1	WHARTON	2		
ROGERS	1	STRONG	5	WHEELER	1		
ROLINGSON	1	STUART	2	WHITAKER	3		

Surname/Township Index

This Index allows you to determine which *Township Map Group(s)* contain individuals with the following surnames. Each *Map Group* has a corresponding full-name index of all individuals who obtained patents for land within its Congressional township's borders. After each index you will find the Patent Map to which it refers, and just thereafter, you can view the township's Road Map and Historical Map, with the latter map displaying streams, railroads, and more.

So, once you find your Surname here, proceed to the Index at the beginning of the **Map Group** indicated below.

Surname	Map Group	Parcels of Land	Meridian/Township/Range
ACHESON	**6**	10	U.S. Military Survey 3-N 4-W
ADAIR	**3**	3	U.S. Military Survey 4-N 2-W
ADAMS	**8**	2	U.S. Military Survey 3-N 2-W
" "	**1**	1	U.S. Military Survey 4-N 4-W
AIKIN	**17**	1	U.S. Military Survey 1-N 3-W
AIKINS	**20**	2	Ohio River Survey 9-N 10-W
AKIN	**17**	1	U.S. Military Survey 1-N 3-W
ALLEN	**8**	2	U.S. Military Survey 3-N 2-W
" "	**17**	1	U.S. Military Survey 1-N 3-W
ANDERSON	**3**	2	U.S. Military Survey 4-N 2-W
" "	**2**	2	U.S. Military Survey 4-N 3-W
" "	**15**	1	Ohio River Survey 9-N 7-W
" "	**18**	1	U.S. Military Survey 1-N 2-W
ANNETT	**11**	2	U.S. Military Survey 2-N 4-W
ARBUCKLE	**17**	2	U.S. Military Survey 1-N 3-W
ARCHER	**20**	4	Ohio River Survey 9-N 10-W
ARMSTRONG	**8**	3	U.S. Military Survey 3-N 2-W
" "	**19**	1	U.S. Military Survey 1-N 1-W
ASHER	**20**	1	Ohio River Survey 9-N 10-W
ASKIN	**19**	1	U.S. Military Survey 1-N 1-W
ASKINS	**12**	1	U.S. Military Survey 2-N 3-W
ATCHESON	**6**	1	U.S. Military Survey 3-N 4-W
ATCHISON	**6**	2	U.S. Military Survey 3-N 4-W
ATKINSON	**2**	2	U.S. Military Survey 4-N 3-W
" "	**6**	1	U.S. Military Survey 3-N 4-W
ATKISON	**6**	1	U.S. Military Survey 3-N 4-W
ATTWOOD	**6**	1	U.S. Military Survey 3-N 4-W
ATWOOD	**6**	1	U.S. Military Survey 3-N 4-W
AYERS	**17**	1	U.S. Military Survey 1-N 3-W
" "	**8**	1	U.S. Military Survey 3-N 2-W
AZBILL	**17**	2	U.S. Military Survey 1-N 3-W
BAIRD	**2**	3	U.S. Military Survey 4-N 3-W
" "	**8**	1	U.S. Military Survey 3-N 2-W
BAKER	**19**	1	U.S. Military Survey 1-N 1-W
BANKS	**1**	1	U.S. Military Survey 4-N 4-W
BARBER	**13**	1	U.S. Military Survey 2-N 2-W
BARKHURST	**10**	2	Ohio River Survey 10-N 7-W
BARNDOLLAR	**16**	1	U.S. Military Survey 1-N 4-W
BARNES	**8**	2	U.S. Military Survey 3-N 2-W
BARTON	**3**	1	U.S. Military Survey 4-N 2-W
BAUM	**19**	3	U.S. Military Survey 1-N 1-W
BAXTER	**5**	1	Ohio River Survey 11-N 7-W
BAY	**15**	3	Ohio River Survey 9-N 7-W
" "	**20**	1	Ohio River Survey 9-N 10-W

Surname	Map Group	Parcels of Land	Meridian/Township/Range		
BEAHAM	**13**	1	U.S. Military Survey	2-N	2-W
BEAL	**3**	8	U.S. Military Survey	4-N	2-W
" "	**2**	6	U.S. Military Survey	4-N	3-W
BEALE	**2**	1	U.S. Military Survey	4-N	3-W
BEALL	**15**	1	Ohio River Survey	9-N	7-W
BEATTY	**1**	16	U.S. Military Survey	4-N	4-W
" "	**17**	6	U.S. Military Survey	1-N	3-W
" "	**12**	3	U.S. Military Survey	2-N	3-W
" "	**19**	1	U.S. Military Survey	1-N	1-W
BEEMER	**8**	2	U.S. Military Survey	3-N	2-W
BEETLY	**17**	1	U.S. Military Survey	1-N	3-W
BELL	**7**	7	U.S. Military Survey	3-N	3-W
" "	**17**	3	U.S. Military Survey	1-N	3-W
" "	**11**	2	U.S. Military Survey	2-N	4-W
" "	**4**	2	U.S. Military Survey	4-N	1-W
" "	**2**	2	U.S. Military Survey	4-N	3-W
" "	**18**	1	U.S. Military Survey	1-N	2-W
BELLEW	**20**	1	Ohio River Survey	9-N	10-W
BELT	**8**	3	U.S. Military Survey	3-N	2-W
BENJAMIN	**1**	1	U.S. Military Survey	4-N	4-W
BEVARD	**2**	3	U.S. Military Survey	4-N	3-W
" "	**14**	1	U.S. Military Survey	2-N	1-W
" "	**9**	1	U.S. Military Survey	3-N	1-W
BEYMER	**13**	4	U.S. Military Survey	2-N	2-W
BEYNOR	**13**	1	U.S. Military Survey	2-N	2-W
BICHARD	**17**	1	U.S. Military Survey	1-N	3-W
BICKHAM	**13**	2	U.S. Military Survey	2-N	2-W
BIERCE	**17**	1	U.S. Military Survey	1-N	3-W
BIGGS	**8**	10	U.S. Military Survey	3-N	2-W
" "	**19**	3	U.S. Military Survey	1-N	1-W
" "	**12**	3	U.S. Military Survey	2-N	3-W
BIGHAM	**18**	1	U.S. Military Survey	1-N	2-W
" "	**11**	1	U.S. Military Survey	2-N	4-W
BIGLEY	**2**	2	U.S. Military Survey	4-N	3-W
BIRD	**2**	1	U.S. Military Survey	4-N	3-W
BISHOP	**20**	2	Ohio River Survey	9-N	10-W
BIXLER	**9**	1	U.S. Military Survey	3-N	1-W
BLACK	**19**	1	U.S. Military Survey	1-N	1-W
" "	**13**	1	U.S. Military Survey	2-N	2-W
BLACKSHIRE	**19**	1	U.S. Military Survey	1-N	1-W
BLAIR	**13**	6	U.S. Military Survey	2-N	2-W
" "	**12**	3	U.S. Military Survey	2-N	3-W
" "	**11**	2	U.S. Military Survey	2-N	4-W
BLISS	**17**	1	U.S. Military Survey	1-N	3-W
" "	**6**	1	U.S. Military Survey	3-N	4-W
BOGGS	**7**	1	U.S. Military Survey	3-N	3-W
BOGLE	**7**	7	U.S. Military Survey	3-N	3-W
" "	**6**	2	U.S. Military Survey	3-N	4-W
BOND	**20**	2	Ohio River Survey	9-N	10-W
" "	**10**	1	Ohio River Survey	10-N	7-W
BOONE	**5**	2	Ohio River Survey	11-N	7-W
BOSTON	**8**	1	U.S. Military Survey	3-N	2-W
BOTTS	**18**	2	U.S. Military Survey	1-N	2-W
BOWERS	**1**	1	U.S. Military Survey	4-N	4-W
BOYCE	**3**	1	U.S. Military Survey	4-N	2-W
BOYD	**9**	3	U.S. Military Survey	3-N	1-W
" "	**8**	3	U.S. Military Survey	3-N	2-W
" "	**17**	1	U.S. Military Survey	1-N	3-W
" "	**16**	1	U.S. Military Survey	1-N	4-W
" "	**13**	1	U.S. Military Survey	2-N	2-W

Surname	Map Group	Parcels of Land	Meridian/Township/Range
BOYD (Cont'd)	6	1	U.S. Military Survey 3-N 4-W
" "	4	1	U.S. Military Survey 4-N 1-W
" "	2	1	U.S. Military Survey 4-N 3-W
BOYLE	7	1	U.S. Military Survey 3-N 3-W
BRACKIN	8	1	U.S. Military Survey 3-N 2-W
BRADEN	11	1	U.S. Military Survey 2-N 4-W
BRADFORD	11	1	U.S. Military Survey 2-N 4-W
BRADING	11	1	U.S. Military Survey 2-N 4-W
BRADSHAW	7	2	U.S. Military Survey 3-N 3-W
BRASHEAR	4	1	U.S. Military Survey 4-N 1-W
BRATSHAW	2	1	U.S. Military Survey 4-N 3-W
BRATTON	3	3	U.S. Military Survey 4-N 2-W
BREWER	3	1	U.S. Military Survey 4-N 2-W
BRILL	15	3	Ohio River Survey 9-N 7-W
" "	2	1	U.S. Military Survey 4-N 3-W
BRITTON	2	3	U.S. Military Survey 4-N 3-W
" "	7	2	U.S. Military Survey 3-N 3-W
BROOM	6	1	U.S. Military Survey 3-N 4-W
BROWN	20	2	Ohio River Survey 9-N 10-W
" "	11	2	U.S. Military Survey 2-N 4-W
" "	6	2	U.S. Military Survey 3-N 4-W
" "	5	1	Ohio River Survey 11-N 7-W
" "	17	1	U.S. Military Survey 1-N 3-W
" "	4	1	U.S. Military Survey 4-N 1-W
BRUSH	6	13	U.S. Military Survey 3-N 4-W
" "	1	10	U.S. Military Survey 4-N 4-W
" "	17	3	U.S. Military Survey 1-N 3-W
" "	7	2	U.S. Military Survey 3-N 3-W
BRUSHAL	1	1	U.S. Military Survey 4-N 4-W
BRYAN	3	1	U.S. Military Survey 4-N 2-W
BRYANT	13	1	U.S. Military Survey 2-N 2-W
BRYSON	17	2	U.S. Military Survey 1-N 3-W
BUCHANAN	6	4	U.S. Military Survey 3-N 4-W
" "	3	2	U.S. Military Survey 4-N 2-W
BUCKINGHAM	6	6	U.S. Military Survey 3-N 4-W
" "	20	4	Ohio River Survey 9-N 10-W
" "	2	3	U.S. Military Survey 4-N 3-W
" "	18	1	U.S. Military Survey 1-N 2-W
" "	13	1	U.S. Military Survey 2-N 2-W
" "	8	1	U.S. Military Survey 3-N 2-W
" "	7	1	U.S. Military Survey 3-N 3-W
" "	1	1	U.S. Military Survey 4-N 4-W
BUNNEL	8	1	U.S. Military Survey 3-N 2-W
BURNSIDE	5	2	Ohio River Survey 11-N 7-W
BURT	20	2	Ohio River Survey 9-N 10-W
" "	17	2	U.S. Military Survey 1-N 3-W
" "	21	1	Ohio River Survey 8-N 9-W
" "	18	1	U.S. Military Survey 1-N 2-W
BURTON	20	1	Ohio River Survey 9-N 10-W
BYE	18	4	U.S. Military Survey 1-N 2-W
CAEIRNS	20	1	Ohio River Survey 9-N 10-W
CALDWELL	10	1	Ohio River Survey 10-N 7-W
" "	2	1	U.S. Military Survey 4-N 3-W
CALLANTINE	2	1	U.S. Military Survey 4-N 3-W
CALLENDINE	9	1	U.S. Military Survey 3-N 1-W
CAMP	16	2	U.S. Military Survey 1-N 4-W
CAMPBELL	6	2	U.S. Military Survey 3-N 4-W
" "	10	1	Ohio River Survey 10-N 7-W
" "	18	1	U.S. Military Survey 1-N 2-W
" "	13	1	U.S. Military Survey 2-N 2-W

Surname	Map Group	Parcels of Land	Meridian/Township/Range
CAMPBELL (Cont'd)	**8**	1	U.S. Military Survey 3-N 2-W
CARLILE	**9**	2	U.S. Military Survey 3-N 1-W
CARMICHAEL	**2**	1	U.S. Military Survey 4-N 3-W
CAROTHERS	**10**	1	Ohio River Survey 10-N 7-W
CARPENTER	**5**	1	Ohio River Survey 11-N 7-W
" "	**2**	1	U.S. Military Survey 4-N 3-W
CARR	**2**	1	U.S. Military Survey 4-N 3-W
CARRELL	**17**	1	U.S. Military Survey 1-N 3-W
CARROTHERS	**10**	1	Ohio River Survey 10-N 7-W
CARRY	**17**	1	U.S. Military Survey 1-N 3-W
CARTER	**19**	3	U.S. Military Survey 1-N 1-W
" "	**2**	2	U.S. Military Survey 4-N 3-W
" "	**20**	1	Ohio River Survey 9-N 10-W
CARUTHERS	**19**	2	U.S. Military Survey 1-N 1-W
CASSIDY	**8**	1	U.S. Military Survey 3-N 2-W
CEASAR	**3**	1	U.S. Military Survey 4-N 2-W
CHALFANT	**15**	1	Ohio River Survey 9-N 7-W
CHANDLER	**2**	2	U.S. Military Survey 4-N 3-W
" "	**4**	1	U.S. Military Survey 4-N 1-W
CHANEY	**2**	1	U.S. Military Survey 4-N 3-W
CHAPMAN	**17**	1	U.S. Military Survey 1-N 3-W
CLARK	**6**	4	U.S. Military Survey 3-N 4-W
" "	**18**	3	U.S. Military Survey 1-N 2-W
" "	**20**	1	Ohio River Survey 9-N 10-W
" "	**17**	1	U.S. Military Survey 1-N 3-W
" "	**4**	1	U.S. Military Survey 4-N 1-W
CLARKE	**8**	2	U.S. Military Survey 3-N 2-W
CLARY	**15**	4	Ohio River Survey 9-N 7-W
CLEGG	**13**	3	U.S. Military Survey 2-N 2-W
CLEMENTS	**11**	1	U.S. Military Survey 2-N 4-W
COARTS	**13**	1	U.S. Military Survey 2-N 2-W
COATES	**4**	1	U.S. Military Survey 4-N 1-W
COCHRAN	**11**	1	U.S. Military Survey 2-N 4-W
" "	**6**	1	U.S. Military Survey 3-N 4-W
COCKRAN	**6**	1	U.S. Military Survey 3-N 4-W
COLE	**13**	1	U.S. Military Survey 2-N 2-W
COLEMAN	**17**	3	U.S. Military Survey 1-N 3-W
" "	**8**	1	U.S. Military Survey 3-N 2-W
COLES	**15**	1	Ohio River Survey 9-N 7-W
COLLINS	**17**	2	U.S. Military Survey 1-N 3-W
CONAN	**8**	1	U.S. Military Survey 3-N 2-W
CONANN	**8**	1	U.S. Military Survey 3-N 2-W
CONDON	**15**	1	Ohio River Survey 9-N 7-W
" "	**18**	1	U.S. Military Survey 1-N 2-W
CONNER	**20**	1	Ohio River Survey 9-N 10-W
" "	**17**	1	U.S. Military Survey 1-N 3-W
COOK	**2**	4	U.S. Military Survey 4-N 3-W
" "	**6**	1	U.S. Military Survey 3-N 4-W
" "	**1**	1	U.S. Military Survey 4-N 4-W
COOPER	**5**	1	Ohio River Survey 11-N 7-W
COPELAND	**9**	1	U.S. Military Survey 3-N 1-W
CORBET	**6**	2	U.S. Military Survey 3-N 4-W
" "	**8**	1	U.S. Military Survey 3-N 2-W
CORNELIUS	**6**	1	U.S. Military Survey 3-N 4-W
CORTRIGHT	**3**	1	U.S. Military Survey 4-N 2-W
COULTER	**16**	3	U.S. Military Survey 1-N 4-W
" "	**6**	3	U.S. Military Survey 3-N 4-W
COWAN	**7**	2	U.S. Military Survey 3-N 3-W
COWDEN	**20**	2	Ohio River Survey 9-N 10-W
COWEL	**6**	1	U.S. Military Survey 3-N 4-W

Surname	Map Group	Parcels of Land	Meridian/Township/Range
COWGILL	**1**	1	U.S. Military Survey 4-N 4-W
COX	**17**	2	U.S. Military Survey 1-N 3-W
" "	**5**	1	Ohio River Survey 11-N 7-W
" "	**9**	1	U.S. Military Survey 3-N 1-W
" "	**8**	1	U.S. Military Survey 3-N 2-W
CRAIG	**17**	2	U.S. Military Survey 1-N 3-W
CRAWFORD	**8**	4	U.S. Military Survey 3-N 2-W
" "	**2**	1	U.S. Military Survey 4-N 3-W
CREIGHTON	**6**	2	U.S. Military Survey 3-N 4-W
CROSBY	**13**	1	U.S. Military Survey 2-N 2-W
CROSS	**3**	1	U.S. Military Survey 4-N 2-W
CROW	**7**	2	U.S. Military Survey 3-N 3-W
" "	**20**	1	Ohio River Survey 9-N 10-W
CULBERTSON	**3**	2	U.S. Military Survey 4-N 2-W
" "	**6**	1	U.S. Military Survey 3-N 4-W
CULLEN	**6**	3	U.S. Military Survey 3-N 4-W
CULLY	**7**	1	U.S. Military Survey 3-N 3-W
CULVER	**20**	1	Ohio River Survey 9-N 10-W
CUMMING	**16**	1	U.S. Military Survey 1-N 4-W
DARRAUGH	**11**	1	U.S. Military Survey 2-N 4-W
DAVIES	**18**	1	U.S. Military Survey 1-N 2-W
DAVIS	**6**	6	U.S. Military Survey 3-N 4-W
" "	**12**	1	U.S. Military Survey 2-N 3-W
" "	**4**	1	U.S. Military Survey 4-N 1-W
DAVOULT	**3**	1	U.S. Military Survey 4-N 2-W
DAWSON	**2**	1	U.S. Military Survey 4-N 3-W
DAY	**8**	1	U.S. Military Survey 3-N 2-W
DAYTON	**9**	1	U.S. Military Survey 3-N 1-W
DE LARUE	**17**	2	U.S. Military Survey 1-N 3-W
DEAN	**20**	1	Ohio River Survey 9-N 10-W
DEEREN	**20**	1	Ohio River Survey 9-N 10-W
" "	**17**	1	U.S. Military Survey 1-N 3-W
DELARUE	**17**	1	U.S. Military Survey 1-N 3-W
DELONG	**19**	1	U.S. Military Survey 1-N 1-W
DENNIS	**17**	4	U.S. Military Survey 1-N 3-W
" "	**20**	1	Ohio River Survey 9-N 10-W
DENNISON	**17**	2	U.S. Military Survey 1-N 3-W
DEPEW	**19**	3	U.S. Military Survey 1-N 1-W
DEW	**6**	2	U.S. Military Survey 3-N 4-W
DILDINE	**2**	1	U.S. Military Survey 4-N 3-W
DISALLUMS	**6**	3	U.S. Military Survey 3-N 4-W
DOUGLASS	**7**	4	U.S. Military Survey 3-N 3-W
" "	**2**	3	U.S. Military Survey 4-N 3-W
DOWNEY	**20**	1	Ohio River Survey 9-N 10-W
DRAKE	**7**	2	U.S. Military Survey 3-N 3-W
" "	**2**	2	U.S. Military Survey 4-N 3-W
DRYDEN	**5**	2	Ohio River Survey 11-N 7-W
DUFF	**6**	19	U.S. Military Survey 3-N 4-W
DUFFEY	**3**	2	U.S. Military Survey 4-N 2-W
" "	**2**	2	U.S. Military Survey 4-N 3-W
" "	**8**	1	U.S. Military Survey 3-N 2-W
DUFFY	**8**	1	U.S. Military Survey 3-N 2-W
DUKE	**17**	1	U.S. Military Survey 1-N 3-W
DULL	**7**	1	U.S. Military Survey 3-N 3-W
DUNCAN	**5**	1	Ohio River Survey 11-N 7-W
DYSON	**13**	1	U.S. Military Survey 2-N 2-W
EAGLETON	**13**	1	U.S. Military Survey 2-N 2-W
ECKELBERY	**6**	1	U.S. Military Survey 3-N 4-W
" "	**1**	1	U.S. Military Survey 4-N 4-W
EDIE	**2**	2	U.S. Military Survey 4-N 3-W

Surname	Map Group	Parcels of Land	Meridian/Township/Range
ELLIOTT	**20**	1	Ohio River Survey 9-N 10-W
EMERSON	**19**	3	U.S. Military Survey 1-N 1-W
ENGLE	**4**	1	U.S. Military Survey 4-N 1-W
ENTROT	**19**	1	U.S. Military Survey 1-N 1-W
EVANS	**20**	2	Ohio River Survey 9-N 10-W
" "	**13**	2	U.S. Military Survey 2-N 2-W
" "	**6**	2	U.S. Military Survey 3-N 4-W
" "	**2**	2	U.S. Military Survey 4-N 3-W
" "	**7**	1	U.S. Military Survey 3-N 3-W
EWINGS	**13**	1	U.S. Military Survey 2-N 2-W
FARRA	**15**	2	Ohio River Survey 9-N 7-W
FERBACK	**12**	1	U.S. Military Survey 2-N 3-W
FERBRACH	**12**	1	U.S. Military Survey 2-N 3-W
FERBRACHE	**6**	8	U.S. Military Survey 3-N 4-W
FERGUSON	**12**	1	U.S. Military Survey 2-N 3-W
" "	**6**	1	U.S. Military Survey 3-N 4-W
FERRELL	**3**	1	U.S. Military Survey 4-N 2-W
FIELD	**19**	3	U.S. Military Survey 1-N 1-W
FINLEY	**21**	4	Ohio River Survey 8-N 9-W
" "	**13**	2	U.S. Military Survey 2-N 2-W
FISHELL	**20**	1	Ohio River Survey 9-N 10-W
FISHER	**20**	1	Ohio River Survey 9-N 10-W
" "	**17**	1	U.S. Military Survey 1-N 3-W
" "	**3**	1	U.S. Military Survey 4-N 2-W
FITZPATRICK	**1**	1	U.S. Military Survey 4-N 4-W
FLEMING	**13**	1	U.S. Military Survey 2-N 2-W
FLING	**19**	1	U.S. Military Survey 1-N 1-W
FORD	**13**	2	U.S. Military Survey 2-N 2-W
" "	**8**	2	U.S. Military Survey 3-N 2-W
" "	**11**	1	U.S. Military Survey 2-N 4-W
FORDYCE	**16**	1	U.S. Military Survey 1-N 4-W
FOREACRE	**19**	1	U.S. Military Survey 1-N 1-W
FOREMAN	**21**	1	Ohio River Survey 8-N 9-W
FORREST	**6**	1	U.S. Military Survey 3-N 4-W
FORSYTHE	**6**	3	U.S. Military Survey 3-N 4-W
FOSTER	**20**	1	Ohio River Survey 9-N 10-W
" "	**19**	1	U.S. Military Survey 1-N 1-W
" "	**6**	1	U.S. Military Survey 3-N 4-W
" "	**2**	1	U.S. Military Survey 4-N 3-W
FOULKE	**15**	1	Ohio River Survey 9-N 7-W
FOX	**17**	2	U.S. Military Survey 1-N 3-W
FOY	**12**	1	U.S. Military Survey 2-N 3-W
FRAME	**2**	3	U.S. Military Survey 4-N 3-W
" "	**18**	1	U.S. Military Survey 1-N 2-W
FRANEY	**8**	1	U.S. Military Survey 3-N 2-W
FRAZER	**8**	1	U.S. Military Survey 3-N 2-W
FRAZIER	**11**	1	U.S. Military Survey 2-N 4-W
" "	**7**	1	U.S. Military Survey 3-N 3-W
FREEMAN	**17**	1	U.S. Military Survey 1-N 3-W
FREY	**17**	1	U.S. Military Survey 1-N 3-W
FRY	**17**	2	U.S. Military Survey 1-N 3-W
FULLER	**1**	6	U.S. Military Survey 4-N 4-W
" "	**2**	3	U.S. Military Survey 4-N 3-W
" "	**7**	1	U.S. Military Survey 3-N 3-W
" "	**3**	1	U.S. Military Survey 4-N 2-W
FULTON	**11**	1	U.S. Military Survey 2-N 4-W
FURNEY	**2**	7	U.S. Military Survey 4-N 3-W
" "	**1**	1	U.S. Military Survey 4-N 4-W
GALAGHER	**6**	2	U.S. Military Survey 3-N 4-W
GALAWAY	**16**	1	U.S. Military Survey 1-N 4-W

Surname	Map Group	Parcels of Land	Meridian/Township/Range
GALLATIN	**8**	1	U.S. Military Survey 3-N 2-W
GALLENTINE	**3**	1	U.S. Military Survey 4-N 2-W
GALLIWAY	**17**	2	U.S. Military Survey 1-N 3-W
GALLOWAY	**15**	1	Ohio River Survey 9-N 7-W
GANSON	**1**	2	U.S. Military Survey 4-N 4-W
GANT	**6**	2	U.S. Military Survey 3-N 4-W
GARDINER	**10**	1	Ohio River Survey 10-N 7-W
GASKILL	**2**	1	U.S. Military Survey 4-N 3-W
GASS	**17**	1	U.S. Military Survey 1-N 3-W
GAURNER	**1**	1	U.S. Military Survey 4-N 4-W
GENTZLER	**7**	3	U.S. Military Survey 3-N 3-W
GEORGE	**15**	1	Ohio River Survey 9-N 7-W
GIBSON	**2**	9	U.S. Military Survey 4-N 3-W
" "	**7**	3	U.S. Military Survey 3-N 3-W
" "	**8**	2	U.S. Military Survey 3-N 2-W
" "	**1**	2	U.S. Military Survey 4-N 4-W
GILL	**21**	1	Ohio River Survey 8-N 9-W
" "	**20**	1	Ohio River Survey 9-N 10-W
" "	**7**	1	U.S. Military Survey 3-N 3-W
GILLASPIE	**8**	1	U.S. Military Survey 3-N 2-W
GILLESPIE	**8**	3	U.S. Military Survey 3-N 2-W
" "	**3**	1	U.S. Military Survey 4-N 2-W
GILLET	**9**	1	U.S. Military Survey 3-N 1-W
GILPEN	**18**	1	U.S. Military Survey 1-N 2-W
GILPIN	**2**	3	U.S. Military Survey 4-N 3-W
" "	**18**	2	U.S. Military Survey 1-N 2-W
GIST	**11**	1	U.S. Military Survey 2-N 4-W
GOINGS	**20**	2	Ohio River Survey 9-N 10-W
GOMBAR	**12**	1	U.S. Military Survey 2-N 3-W
GOODDE	**7**	1	U.S. Military Survey 3-N 3-W
GOODERL	**19**	1	U.S. Military Survey 1-N 1-W
GOSSET	**15**	1	Ohio River Survey 9-N 7-W
GOWENS	**20**	2	Ohio River Survey 9-N 10-W
GRACEY	**10**	1	Ohio River Survey 10-N 7-W
GRAHAM	**3**	3	U.S. Military Survey 4-N 2-W
" "	**2**	3	U.S. Military Survey 4-N 3-W
" "	**15**	2	Ohio River Survey 9-N 7-W
" "	**17**	2	U.S. Military Survey 1-N 3-W
GRAY	**17**	1	U.S. Military Survey 1-N 3-W
" "	**9**	1	U.S. Military Survey 3-N 1-W
GREEN	**18**	1	U.S. Military Survey 1-N 2-W
GREENLAND	**13**	1	U.S. Military Survey 2-N 2-W
GREGORY	**2**	1	U.S. Military Survey 4-N 3-W
GRIER	**15**	1	Ohio River Survey 9-N 7-W
GRIFFIN	**7**	2	U.S. Military Survey 3-N 3-W
" "	**10**	1	Ohio River Survey 10-N 7-W
" "	**17**	1	U.S. Military Survey 1-N 3-W
" "	**2**	1	U.S. Military Survey 4-N 3-W
GRIFFITH	**10**	2	Ohio River Survey 10-N 7-W
" "	**4**	1	U.S. Military Survey 4-N 1-W
GRIMES	**3**	7	U.S. Military Survey 4-N 2-W
" "	**20**	2	Ohio River Survey 9-N 10-W
" "	**2**	1	U.S. Military Survey 4-N 3-W
GROVE	**1**	2	U.S. Military Survey 4-N 4-W
GUNN	**8**	1	U.S. Military Survey 3-N 2-W
HAGAN	**17**	1	U.S. Military Survey 1-N 3-W
" "	**8**	1	U.S. Military Survey 3-N 2-W
" "	**1**	1	U.S. Military Survey 4-N 4-W
HAGEN	**9**	1	U.S. Military Survey 3-N 1-W
HAGER	**15**	1	Ohio River Survey 9-N 7-W

Surname	Map Group	Parcels of Land	Meridian/Township/Range
HAINELINE	**20**	1	Ohio River Survey 9-N 10-W
HAINS	**20**	1	Ohio River Survey 9-N 10-W
" "	**11**	1	U.S. Military Survey 2-N 4-W
HALE	**6**	1	U.S. Military Survey 3-N 4-W
HALL	**6**	4	U.S. Military Survey 3-N 4-W
" "	**15**	3	Ohio River Survey 9-N 7-W
" "	**17**	2	U.S. Military Survey 1-N 3-W
" "	**2**	1	U.S. Military Survey 4-N 3-W
" "	**1**	1	U.S. Military Survey 4-N 4-W
HALLY	**20**	1	Ohio River Survey 9-N 10-W
HAMILTON	**20**	2	Ohio River Survey 9-N 10-W
" "	**5**	1	Ohio River Survey 11-N 7-W
" "	**6**	1	U.S. Military Survey 3-N 4-W
" "	**2**	1	U.S. Military Survey 4-N 3-W
" "	**1**	1	U.S. Military Survey 4-N 4-W
HAMMERSLEY	**7**	1	U.S. Military Survey 3-N 3-W
" "	**1**	1	U.S. Military Survey 4-N 4-W
HAMMOND	**20**	1	Ohio River Survey 9-N 10-W
" "	**11**	1	U.S. Military Survey 2-N 4-W
" "	**7**	1	U.S. Military Survey 3-N 3-W
HANNA	**17**	1	U.S. Military Survey 1-N 3-W
HANNAH	**5**	1	Ohio River Survey 11-N 7-W
HARDING	**2**	1	U.S. Military Survey 4-N 3-W
HARDISTY	**2**	2	U.S. Military Survey 4-N 3-W
" "	**3**	1	U.S. Military Survey 4-N 2-W
HARR	**20**	1	Ohio River Survey 9-N 10-W
HARRIS	**2**	1	U.S. Military Survey 4-N 3-W
HARRISS	**7**	1	U.S. Military Survey 3-N 3-W
HART	**6**	1	U.S. Military Survey 3-N 4-W
" "	**2**	1	U.S. Military Survey 4-N 3-W
HARTLEY	**15**	3	Ohio River Survey 9-N 7-W
HARTMAN	**20**	4	Ohio River Survey 9-N 10-W
" "	**16**	1	U.S. Military Survey 1-N 4-W
HARVERT	**2**	1	U.S. Military Survey 4-N 3-W
HATCHER	**2**	2	U.S. Military Survey 4-N 3-W
" "	**3**	1	U.S. Military Survey 4-N 2-W
HATFIELD	**20**	1	Ohio River Survey 9-N 10-W
HAVER	**8**	1	U.S. Military Survey 3-N 2-W
HAWES	**1**	2	U.S. Military Survey 4-N 4-W
" "	**6**	1	U.S. Military Survey 3-N 4-W
HAWS	**20**	2	Ohio River Survey 9-N 10-W
" "	**17**	2	U.S. Military Survey 1-N 3-W
HAWTHORN	**6**	4	U.S. Military Survey 3-N 4-W
HAYES	**15**	1	Ohio River Survey 9-N 7-W
HAYS	**15**	1	Ohio River Survey 9-N 7-W
" "	**13**	1	U.S. Military Survey 2-N 2-W
HEANS	**11**	1	U.S. Military Survey 2-N 4-W
HECKEL	**17**	1	U.S. Military Survey 1-N 3-W
HEDGE	**6**	5	U.S. Military Survey 3-N 4-W
" "	**7**	2	U.S. Military Survey 3-N 3-W
" "	**2**	1	U.S. Military Survey 4-N 3-W
HELANNEN	**8**	1	U.S. Military Survey 3-N 2-W
HELLYER	**6**	2	U.S. Military Survey 3-N 4-W
HENDEN	**2**	2	U.S. Military Survey 4-N 3-W
HENDERSON	**8**	1	U.S. Military Survey 3-N 2-W
HENRY	**17**	5	U.S. Military Survey 1-N 3-W
" "	**8**	2	U.S. Military Survey 3-N 2-W
HERST	**12**	1	U.S. Military Survey 2-N 3-W
" "	**11**	1	U.S. Military Survey 2-N 4-W
HESHER	**1**	1	U.S. Military Survey 4-N 4-W

Surname	Map Group	Parcels of Land	Meridian/Township/Range
HESKETT	**20**	1	Ohio River Survey 9-N 10-W
HIBBS	**5**	1	Ohio River Survey 11-N 7-W
HILGER	**13**	1	U.S. Military Survey 2-N 2-W
HILL	**13**	1	U.S. Military Survey 2-N 2-W
" "	**12**	1	U.S. Military Survey 2-N 3-W
" "	**3**	1	U.S. Military Survey 4-N 2-W
HILLARD	**6**	1	U.S. Military Survey 3-N 4-W
HINELINE	**20**	1	Ohio River Survey 9-N 10-W
HISKETT	**20**	2	Ohio River Survey 9-N 10-W
" "	**17**	1	U.S. Military Survey 1-N 3-W
" "	**3**	1	U.S. Military Survey 4-N 2-W
HOFFMAN	**3**	1	U.S. Military Survey 4-N 2-W
HOLCOMB	**6**	2	U.S. Military Survey 3-N 4-W
HOLLAND	**20**	1	Ohio River Survey 9-N 10-W
HOLT	**15**	1	Ohio River Survey 9-N 7-W
HONEYWELDS	**1**	1	U.S. Military Survey 4-N 4-W
HOSACK	**7**	3	U.S. Military Survey 3-N 3-W
HOWARD	**8**	1	U.S. Military Survey 3-N 2-W
HUFF	**20**	2	Ohio River Survey 9-N 10-W
" "	**19**	1	U.S. Military Survey 1-N 1-W
" "	**13**	1	U.S. Military Survey 2-N 2-W
HUFFMAN	**8**	5	U.S. Military Survey 3-N 2-W
" "	**9**	2	U.S. Military Survey 3-N 1-W
HUGHES	**4**	1	U.S. Military Survey 4-N 1-W
HUGHS	**21**	1	Ohio River Survey 8-N 9-W
" "	**3**	1	U.S. Military Survey 4-N 2-W
HUNT	**18**	1	U.S. Military Survey 1-N 2-W
" "	**2**	1	U.S. Military Survey 4-N 3-W
HUNTER	**16**	7	U.S. Military Survey 1-N 4-W
HURBERT	**1**	1	U.S. Military Survey 4-N 4-W
HUTCHESON	**7**	1	U.S. Military Survey 3-N 3-W
HUTCHINSON	**5**	2	Ohio River Survey 11-N 7-W
HYDE	**13**	2	U.S. Military Survey 2-N 2-W
INGLEHART	**1**	2	U.S. Military Survey 4-N 4-W
IRWIN	**13**	1	U.S. Military Survey 2-N 2-W
ISRAEL	**18**	1	U.S. Military Survey 1-N 2-W
JACKSON	**6**	2	U.S. Military Survey 3-N 4-W
" "	**11**	1	U.S. Military Survey 2-N 4-W
JACOBY	**13**	1	U.S. Military Survey 2-N 2-W
JAMES	**15**	1	Ohio River Survey 9-N 7-W
JENKINS	**17**	1	U.S. Military Survey 1-N 3-W
" "	**8**	1	U.S. Military Survey 3-N 2-W
JOHNSON	**20**	8	Ohio River Survey 9-N 10-W
" "	**3**	3	U.S. Military Survey 4-N 2-W
" "	**15**	2	Ohio River Survey 9-N 7-W
" "	**16**	2	U.S. Military Survey 1-N 4-W
" "	**14**	1	U.S. Military Survey 2-N 1-W
" "	**2**	1	U.S. Military Survey 4-N 3-W
" "	**1**	1	U.S. Military Survey 4-N 4-W
JOHNSTON	**3**	7	U.S. Military Survey 4-N 2-W
" "	**1**	2	U.S. Military Survey 4-N 4-W
" "	**13**	1	U.S. Military Survey 2-N 2-W
" "	**11**	1	U.S. Military Survey 2-N 4-W
" "	**2**	1	U.S. Military Survey 4-N 3-W
JONES	**20**	7	Ohio River Survey 9-N 10-W
" "	**6**	4	U.S. Military Survey 3-N 4-W
" "	**2**	3	U.S. Military Survey 4-N 3-W
" "	**1**	1	U.S. Military Survey 4-N 4-W
JORDON	**20**	3	Ohio River Survey 9-N 10-W
KANADY	**1**	1	U.S. Military Survey 4-N 4-W

Surname	Map Group	Parcels of Land	Meridian/Township/Range
KARR	**17**	6	U.S. Military Survey 1-N 3-W
" "	**20**	1	Ohio River Survey 9-N 10-W
KEARNES	**8**	1	U.S. Military Survey 3-N 2-W
KEARNS	**8**	1	U.S. Military Survey 3-N 2-W
KEEN	**8**	2	U.S. Military Survey 3-N 2-W
" "	**1**	2	U.S. Military Survey 4-N 4-W
KELL	**13**	4	U.S. Military Survey 2-N 2-W
" "	**6**	2	U.S. Military Survey 3-N 4-W
" "	**20**	1	Ohio River Survey 9-N 10-W
" "	**8**	1	U.S. Military Survey 3-N 2-W
" "	**7**	1	U.S. Military Survey 3-N 3-W
KELLEY	**17**	1	U.S. Military Survey 1-N 3-W
KELLS	**20**	2	Ohio River Survey 9-N 10-W
KELLY	**16**	1	U.S. Military Survey 1-N 4-W
KENNEDY	**3**	3	U.S. Military Survey 4-N 2-W
" "	**17**	2	U.S. Military Survey 1-N 3-W
" "	**7**	2	U.S. Military Survey 3-N 3-W
KENNEY	**20**	1	Ohio River Survey 9-N 10-W
KERSHAW	**13**	2	U.S. Military Survey 2-N 2-W
KESTER	**15**	2	Ohio River Survey 9-N 7-W
KILBRIDE	**6**	1	U.S. Military Survey 3-N 4-W
KIMBLE	**3**	6	U.S. Military Survey 4-N 2-W
" "	**8**	1	U.S. Military Survey 3-N 2-W
" "	**2**	1	U.S. Military Survey 4-N 3-W
KING	**2**	1	U.S. Military Survey 4-N 3-W
KINKEAD	**7**	9	U.S. Military Survey 3-N 3-W
KIRKPATRICK	**9**	1	U.S. Military Survey 3-N 1-W
KLINE	**17**	1	U.S. Military Survey 1-N 3-W
KNAPP	**13**	1	U.S. Military Survey 2-N 2-W
KREIDER	**1**	4	U.S. Military Survey 4-N 4-W
LACKEY	**8**	1	U.S. Military Survey 3-N 2-W
LAFOLLETT	**21**	2	Ohio River Survey 8-N 9-W
LAKE	**8**	2	U.S. Military Survey 3-N 2-W
LANE	**13**	1	U.S. Military Survey 2-N 2-W
LANGLOIS	**20**	1	Ohio River Survey 9-N 10-W
LANING	**8**	1	U.S. Military Survey 3-N 2-W
" "	**3**	1	U.S. Military Survey 4-N 2-W
" "	**2**	1	U.S. Military Survey 4-N 3-W
LANNING	**3**	4	U.S. Military Survey 4-N 2-W
" "	**2**	2	U.S. Military Survey 4-N 3-W
" "	**4**	1	U.S. Military Survey 4-N 1-W
LARISON	**2**	1	U.S. Military Survey 4-N 3-W
LAUGHLAND	**13**	1	U.S. Military Survey 2-N 2-W
LAUGHLIN	**18**	1	U.S. Military Survey 1-N 2-W
LAURENCE	**18**	1	U.S. Military Survey 1-N 2-W
" "	**1**	1	U.S. Military Survey 4-N 4-W
LAW	**11**	1	U.S. Military Survey 2-N 4-W
LAWRENCE	**6**	3	U.S. Military Survey 3-N 4-W
" "	**9**	1	U.S. Military Survey 3-N 1-W
LAZEARE	**20**	2	Ohio River Survey 9-N 10-W
LE PEDRIN	**20**	1	Ohio River Survey 9-N 10-W
LEACH	**1**	3	U.S. Military Survey 4-N 4-W
" "	**2**	1	U.S. Military Survey 4-N 3-W
LEAMON	**16**	1	U.S. Military Survey 1-N 4-W
LEARD	**13**	1	U.S. Military Survey 2-N 2-W
LEE	**6**	1	U.S. Military Survey 3-N 4-W
LEECH	**6**	4	U.S. Military Survey 3-N 4-W
" "	**7**	2	U.S. Military Survey 3-N 3-W
" "	**2**	1	U.S. Military Survey 4-N 3-W
LEEPER	**7**	2	U.S. Military Survey 3-N 3-W

Surname	Map Group	Parcels of Land	Meridian/Township/Range
LEEPER (Cont'd)	8	1	U.S. Military Survey 3-N 2-W
LEMON	16	1	U.S. Military Survey 1-N 4-W
LENFESTEY	9	1	U.S. Military Survey 3-N 1-W
LENFESTY	12	1	U.S. Military Survey 2-N 3-W
LENT	6	1	U.S. Military Survey 3-N 4-W
LETT	20	1	Ohio River Survey 9-N 10-W
LEWIS	2	2	U.S. Military Survey 4-N 3-W
" "	1	1	U.S. Military Survey 4-N 4-W
LINCH	6	1	U.S. Military Survey 3-N 4-W
LINDLEY	20	1	Ohio River Survey 9-N 10-W
" "	11	1	U.S. Military Survey 2-N 4-W
LINDSEY	6	1	U.S. Military Survey 3-N 4-W
LINGENFELTER	15	1	Ohio River Survey 9-N 7-W
LISLE	11	1	U.S. Military Survey 2-N 4-W
LITTLE	3	9	U.S. Military Survey 4-N 2-W
" "	8	2	U.S. Military Survey 3-N 2-W
LLEWELLYN	20	1	Ohio River Survey 9-N 10-W
LOGAN	5	2	Ohio River Survey 11-N 7-W
" "	4	2	U.S. Military Survey 4-N 1-W
LONG	17	2	U.S. Military Survey 1-N 3-W
" "	2	2	U.S. Military Survey 4-N 3-W
LONGSTRETH	2	1	U.S. Military Survey 4-N 3-W
LONGWORTH	17	2	U.S. Military Survey 1-N 3-W
LOURY	3	1	U.S. Military Survey 4-N 2-W
LOVE	1	3	U.S. Military Survey 4-N 4-W
LOWRY	18	2	U.S. Military Survey 1-N 2-W
" "	3	1	U.S. Military Survey 4-N 2-W
LUCCOCK	7	1	U.S. Military Survey 3-N 3-W
" "	2	1	U.S. Military Survey 4-N 3-W
LUCK	6	1	U.S. Military Survey 3-N 4-W
LUCY	8	1	U.S. Military Survey 3-N 2-W
LUPER	8	1	U.S. Military Survey 3-N 2-W
LYANS	17	1	U.S. Military Survey 1-N 3-W
LYLE	20	1	Ohio River Survey 9-N 10-W
LYNCH	6	1	U.S. Military Survey 3-N 4-W
LYONS	6	1	U.S. Military Survey 3-N 4-W
MACKEY	11	3	U.S. Military Survey 2-N 4-W
" "	20	1	Ohio River Survey 9-N 10-W
MADDIN	5	1	Ohio River Survey 11-N 7-W
MAGEE	16	2	U.S. Military Survey 1-N 4-W
MAGNESS	1	1	U.S. Military Survey 4-N 4-W
MALOY	6	4	U.S. Military Survey 3-N 4-W
MANYPENNY	6	1	U.S. Military Survey 3-N 4-W
MAPLE	1	4	U.S. Military Survey 4-N 4-W
" "	6	2	U.S. Military Survey 3-N 4-W
" "	20	1	Ohio River Survey 9-N 10-W
MARDIS	2	2	U.S. Military Survey 4-N 3-W
MARINER	19	1	U.S. Military Survey 1-N 1-W
MARKEE	6	1	U.S. Military Survey 3-N 4-W
MARLATT	1	3	U.S. Military Survey 4-N 4-W
MARLOW	3	3	U.S. Military Survey 4-N 2-W
MARQUAND	7	3	U.S. Military Survey 3-N 3-W
" "	1	1	U.S. Military Survey 4-N 4-W
MARSH	15	1	Ohio River Survey 9-N 7-W
MARSHAL	20	1	Ohio River Survey 9-N 10-W
MARSHALL	15	2	Ohio River Survey 9-N 7-W
" "	20	1	Ohio River Survey 9-N 10-W
MARTIN	8	3	U.S. Military Survey 3-N 2-W
" "	2	3	U.S. Military Survey 4-N 3-W
" "	3	1	U.S. Military Survey 4-N 2-W

Surname	Map Group	Parcels of Land	Meridian/Township/Range
MASTERS	9	2	U.S. Military Survey 3-N 1-W
" "	10	1	Ohio River Survey 10-N 7-W
MASTIN	18	1	U.S. Military Survey 1-N 2-W
MATHERS	7	1	U.S. Military Survey 3-N 3-W
MATHEWS	7	1	U.S. Military Survey 3-N 3-W
MATTHEWS	7	1	U.S. Military Survey 3-N 3-W
MAXWELL	17	2	U.S. Military Survey 1-N 3-W
" "	4	1	U.S. Military Survey 4-N 1-W
MCALHENEY	2	1	U.S. Military Survey 4-N 3-W
MCBRIDE	19	2	U.S. Military Survey 1-N 1-W
MCBURNEY	19	1	U.S. Military Survey 1-N 1-W
MCCALL	12	1	U.S. Military Survey 2-N 3-W
MCCANN	18	1	U.S. Military Survey 1-N 2-W
MCCARTNEY	2	12	U.S. Military Survey 4-N 3-W
" "	7	1	U.S. Military Survey 3-N 3-W
" "	3	1	U.S. Military Survey 4-N 2-W
MCCLUNEY	16	1	U.S. Military Survey 1-N 4-W
" "	12	1	U.S. Military Survey 2-N 3-W
MCCOLLUM	13	2	U.S. Military Survey 2-N 2-W
MCCOMB	5	1	Ohio River Survey 11-N 7-W
MCCONAUGHY	17	3	U.S. Military Survey 1-N 3-W
MCCONKEY	6	2	U.S. Military Survey 3-N 4-W
MCCONN	13	1	U.S. Military Survey 2-N 2-W
MCCONNAUGHEY	2	1	U.S. Military Survey 4-N 3-W
MCCORMICK	15	1	Ohio River Survey 9-N 7-W
MCCOUGHY	17	1	U.S. Military Survey 1-N 3-W
MCCOY	21	1	Ohio River Survey 8-N 9-W
" "	17	1	U.S. Military Survey 1-N 3-W
MCCRACKEN	11	2	U.S. Military Survey 2-N 4-W
" "	7	1	U.S. Military Survey 3-N 3-W
" "	3	1	U.S. Military Survey 4-N 2-W
MCCREARY	18	1	U.S. Military Survey 1-N 2-W
MCCROSSON	17	1	U.S. Military Survey 1-N 3-W
MCCULLEY	7	2	U.S. Military Survey 3-N 3-W
" "	6	2	U.S. Military Survey 3-N 4-W
" "	8	1	U.S. Military Survey 3-N 2-W
MCCULLOUGH	8	4	U.S. Military Survey 3-N 2-W
MCCUNE	2	2	U.S. Military Survey 4-N 3-W
" "	7	1	U.S. Military Survey 3-N 3-W
" "	1	1	U.S. Military Survey 4-N 4-W
MCDONALD	6	4	U.S. Military Survey 3-N 4-W
" "	17	1	U.S. Military Survey 1-N 3-W
MCDONNELL	2	2	U.S. Military Survey 4-N 3-W
MCDOWEL	12	1	U.S. Military Survey 2-N 3-W
MCDOWELL	6	2	U.S. Military Survey 3-N 4-W
" "	13	1	U.S. Military Survey 2-N 2-W
MCDOWL	12	1	U.S. Military Survey 2-N 3-W
MCELHEREN	6	1	U.S. Military Survey 3-N 4-W
MCELROY	5	1	Ohio River Survey 11-N 7-W
" "	17	1	U.S. Military Survey 1-N 3-W
MCGOWAN	6	2	U.S. Military Survey 3-N 4-W
MCGREW	3	1	U.S. Military Survey 4-N 2-W
MCGUIRE	6	2	U.S. Military Survey 3-N 4-W
MCILVAIN	15	1	Ohio River Survey 9-N 7-W
" "	16	1	U.S. Military Survey 1-N 4-W
MCILYAR	11	4	U.S. Military Survey 2-N 4-W
MCKEE	17	6	U.S. Military Survey 1-N 3-W
" "	2	3	U.S. Military Survey 4-N 3-W
" "	7	1	U.S. Military Survey 3-N 3-W
MCKINNEY	17	1	U.S. Military Survey 1-N 3-W

Surname	Map Group	Parcels of Land	Meridian/Township/Range
MCKINNEY (Cont'd)	4	1	U.S. Military Survey 4-N 1-W
MCKINNIE	5	1	Ohio River Survey 11-N 7-W
MCKNIGHT	11	1	U.S. Military Survey 2-N 4-W
MCLAUGHLIN	14	1	U.S. Military Survey 2-N 1-W
" "	3	1	U.S. Military Survey 4-N 2-W
MCMICHAEL	11	1	U.S. Military Survey 2-N 4-W
MCMILLAN	7	1	U.S. Military Survey 3-N 3-W
MCMILLEN	2	1	U.S. Military Survey 4-N 3-W
MCMULLAN	7	2	U.S. Military Survey 3-N 3-W
MCMULLEN	6	3	U.S. Military Survey 3-N 4-W
" "	7	1	U.S. Military Survey 3-N 3-W
" "	3	1	U.S. Military Survey 4-N 2-W
MCMULLIN	13	1	U.S. Military Survey 2-N 2-W
MCNAIR	17	1	U.S. Military Survey 1-N 3-W
MCNEELY	15	1	Ohio River Survey 9-N 7-W
MCVICKER	21	1	Ohio River Survey 8-N 9-W
MCWILLIAMS	3	4	U.S. Military Survey 4-N 2-W
" "	18	1	U.S. Military Survey 1-N 2-W
" "	8	1	U.S. Military Survey 3-N 2-W
MEDEARIS	19	3	U.S. Military Survey 1-N 1-W
MEHAFFEY	11	7	U.S. Military Survey 2-N 4-W
MEHAFFY	11	1	U.S. Military Survey 2-N 4-W
MEHOFFY	11	1	U.S. Military Survey 2-N 4-W
MESKIMEN	6	1	U.S. Military Survey 3-N 4-W
MILLER	7	7	U.S. Military Survey 3-N 3-W
" "	2	3	U.S. Military Survey 4-N 3-W
" "	19	2	U.S. Military Survey 1-N 1-W
" "	10	1	Ohio River Survey 10-N 7-W
" "	13	1	U.S. Military Survey 2-N 2-W
" "	8	1	U.S. Military Survey 3-N 2-W
" "	6	1	U.S. Military Survey 3-N 4-W
MILLIGAN	8	2	U.S. Military Survey 3-N 2-W
MILLIKEN	7	1	U.S. Military Survey 3-N 3-W
MILNER	2	1	U.S. Military Survey 4-N 3-W
MILONE	2	3	U.S. Military Survey 4-N 3-W
MIRES	7	1	U.S. Military Survey 3-N 3-W
MISKIMEN	1	11	U.S. Military Survey 4-N 4-W
" "	2	1	U.S. Military Survey 4-N 3-W
MISKIMENS	2	2	U.S. Military Survey 4-N 3-W
" "	1	1	U.S. Military Survey 4-N 4-W
MISKIMIN	6	2	U.S. Military Survey 3-N 4-W
MISKIMINS	6	2	U.S. Military Survey 3-N 4-W
" "	1	1	U.S. Military Survey 4-N 4-W
MITCHELL	1	4	U.S. Military Survey 4-N 4-W
" "	7	3	U.S. Military Survey 3-N 3-W
" "	2	1	U.S. Military Survey 4-N 3-W
MOLAND	15	2	Ohio River Survey 9-N 7-W
MOLLOY	17	1	U.S. Military Survey 1-N 3-W
MONTGOMERY	2	1	U.S. Military Survey 4-N 3-W
MOOR	3	1	U.S. Military Survey 4-N 2-W
MOORE	3	4	U.S. Military Survey 4-N 2-W
" "	20	2	Ohio River Survey 9-N 10-W
" "	14	1	U.S. Military Survey 2-N 1-W
" "	4	1	U.S. Military Survey 4-N 1-W
MOORES	3	1	U.S. Military Survey 4-N 2-W
MORGAN	18	1	U.S. Military Survey 1-N 2-W
" "	8	1	U.S. Military Survey 3-N 2-W
MORRIS	17	4	U.S. Military Survey 1-N 3-W
MORRISON	15	3	Ohio River Survey 9-N 7-W
" "	8	2	U.S. Military Survey 3-N 2-W

Surname	Map Group	Parcels of Land	Meridian/Township/Range
MORRISON (Cont'd)	**6**	2	U.S. Military Survey 3-N 4-W
" "	**1**	2	U.S. Military Survey 4-N 4-W
MORROW	**6**	7	U.S. Military Survey 3-N 4-W
MORTON	**8**	3	U.S. Military Survey 3-N 2-W
MULLEN	**20**	1	Ohio River Survey 9-N 10-W
MURPHY	**1**	1	U.S. Military Survey 4-N 4-W
NEEDLER	**21**	1	Ohio River Survey 8-N 9-W
NEELEY	**12**	1	U.S. Military Survey 2-N 3-W
NEIL	**3**	1	U.S. Military Survey 4-N 2-W
NEILL	**1**	1	U.S. Military Survey 4-N 4-W
NELSON	**17**	1	U.S. Military Survey 1-N 3-W
" "	**7**	1	U.S. Military Survey 3-N 3-W
NEVIN	**17**	3	U.S. Military Survey 1-N 3-W
NEWBURN	**3**	1	U.S. Military Survey 4-N 2-W
NEWELL	**7**	4	U.S. Military Survey 3-N 3-W
NEWLAND	**20**	1	Ohio River Survey 9-N 10-W
" "	**17**	1	U.S. Military Survey 1-N 3-W
NEWNOM	**17**	3	U.S. Military Survey 1-N 3-W
NICHOLS	**10**	1	Ohio River Survey 10-N 7-W
NICHOLSON	**17**	2	U.S. Military Survey 1-N 3-W
NICKEL	**5**	1	Ohio River Survey 11-N 7-W
NOBLE	**12**	2	U.S. Military Survey 2-N 3-W
NORMAN	**1**	2	U.S. Military Survey 4-N 4-W
NORRIS	**11**	1	U.S. Military Survey 2-N 4-W
" "	**1**	1	U.S. Military Survey 4-N 4-W
NORTHGRAVES	**8**	1	U.S. Military Survey 3-N 2-W
NOURSE	**17**	4	U.S. Military Survey 1-N 3-W
OBNEY	**17**	1	U.S. Military Survey 1-N 3-W
OCALLIS	**13**	2	U.S. Military Survey 2-N 2-W
OGIER	**20**	5	Ohio River Survey 9-N 10-W
" "	**17**	1	U.S. Military Survey 1-N 3-W
OHARA	**19**	1	U.S. Military Survey 1-N 1-W
OLDHAM	**7**	2	U.S. Military Survey 3-N 3-W
" "	**12**	1	U.S. Military Survey 2-N 3-W
OLIVER	**4**	2	U.S. Military Survey 4-N 1-W
ONG	**9**	1	U.S. Military Survey 3-N 1-W
ORR	**3**	3	U.S. Military Survey 4-N 2-W
" "	**6**	1	U.S. Military Survey 3-N 4-W
OVERLEY	**15**	1	Ohio River Survey 9-N 7-W
PADGITT	**9**	1	U.S. Military Survey 3-N 1-W
PALMER	**2**	4	U.S. Military Survey 4-N 3-W
PARISH	**20**	1	Ohio River Survey 9-N 10-W
PARKE	**8**	1	U.S. Military Survey 3-N 2-W
PARRISH	**20**	2	Ohio River Survey 9-N 10-W
PATRICK	**6**	2	U.S. Military Survey 3-N 4-W
PATTERSON	**13**	4	U.S. Military Survey 2-N 2-W
" "	**3**	4	U.S. Military Survey 4-N 2-W
" "	**7**	3	U.S. Military Survey 3-N 3-W
" "	**2**	3	U.S. Military Survey 4-N 3-W
" "	**20**	1	Ohio River Survey 9-N 10-W
" "	**12**	1	U.S. Military Survey 2-N 3-W
PAXTON	**20**	3	Ohio River Survey 9-N 10-W
" "	**17**	1	U.S. Military Survey 1-N 3-W
" "	**16**	1	U.S. Military Survey 1-N 4-W
" "	**11**	1	U.S. Military Survey 2-N 4-W
" "	**3**	1	U.S. Military Survey 4-N 2-W
PAYLOR	**2**	1	U.S. Military Survey 4-N 3-W
PEACH	**1**	1	U.S. Military Survey 4-N 4-W
PEDWIN	**17**	1	U.S. Military Survey 1-N 3-W
PEOPLES	**4**	1	U.S. Military Survey 4-N 1-W

Surname	Map Group	Parcels of Land	Meridian/Township/Range
PEREGO	**15**	3	Ohio River Survey 9-N 7-W
PERRY	**19**	3	U.S. Military Survey 1-N 1-W
" "	**20**	1	Ohio River Survey 9-N 10-W
PETERS	**18**	2	U.S. Military Survey 1-N 2-W
PHILIPS	**3**	1	U.S. Military Survey 4-N 2-W
PHILLIPS	**7**	2	U.S. Military Survey 3-N 3-W
" "	**2**	2	U.S. Military Survey 4-N 3-W
" "	**20**	1	Ohio River Survey 9-N 10-W
" "	**19**	1	U.S. Military Survey 1-N 1-W
" "	**1**	1	U.S. Military Survey 4-N 4-W
PICKERING	**8**	3	U.S. Military Survey 3-N 2-W
PLEMLINE	**8**	1	U.S. Military Survey 3-N 2-W
POLAND	**2**	2	U.S. Military Survey 4-N 3-W
POOLE	**16**	1	U.S. Military Survey 1-N 4-W
PORTER	**9**	1	U.S. Military Survey 3-N 1-W
" "	**8**	1	U.S. Military Survey 3-N 2-W
POUNDS	**9**	2	U.S. Military Survey 3-N 1-W
POWEL	**4**	1	U.S. Military Survey 4-N 1-W
PRATT	**19**	1	U.S. Military Survey 1-N 1-W
PRESLEY	**7**	1	U.S. Military Survey 3-N 3-W
" "	**2**	1	U.S. Military Survey 4-N 3-W
PRESTLY	**2**	1	U.S. Military Survey 4-N 3-W
PRIOR	**13**	1	U.S. Military Survey 2-N 2-W
PULLEY	**10**	1	Ohio River Survey 10-N 7-W
" "	**8**	1	U.S. Military Survey 3-N 2-W
RANKIN	**6**	3	U.S. Military Survey 3-N 4-W
RANNELLS	**20**	1	Ohio River Survey 9-N 10-W
RAY	**2**	1	U.S. Military Survey 4-N 3-W
" "	**1**	1	U.S. Military Survey 4-N 4-W
REA	**7**	2	U.S. Military Survey 3-N 3-W
READ	**4**	1	U.S. Military Survey 4-N 1-W
REAVES	**2**	1	U.S. Military Survey 4-N 3-W
REDMAN	**3**	1	U.S. Military Survey 4-N 2-W
REED	**21**	1	Ohio River Survey 8-N 9-W
" "	**18**	1	U.S. Military Survey 1-N 2-W
" "	**6**	1	U.S. Military Survey 3-N 4-W
" "	**4**	1	U.S. Military Survey 4-N 1-W
" "	**1**	1	U.S. Military Survey 4-N 4-W
REEVES	**12**	1	U.S. Military Survey 2-N 3-W
REILY	**8**	3	U.S. Military Survey 3-N 2-W
RENNER	**10**	1	Ohio River Survey 10-N 7-W
RICE	**13**	3	U.S. Military Survey 2-N 2-W
RICH	**13**	1	U.S. Military Survey 2-N 2-W
RIGDEN	**6**	1	U.S. Military Survey 3-N 4-W
RIGGS	**18**	2	U.S. Military Survey 1-N 2-W
" "	**21**	1	Ohio River Survey 8-N 9-W
RISHER	**3**	3	U.S. Military Survey 4-N 2-W
ROBB	**12**	2	U.S. Military Survey 2-N 3-W
" "	**2**	1	U.S. Military Survey 4-N 3-W
ROBBINS	**20**	2	Ohio River Survey 9-N 10-W
" "	**17**	1	U.S. Military Survey 1-N 3-W
ROBE	**18**	1	U.S. Military Survey 1-N 2-W
ROBERT	**17**	2	U.S. Military Survey 1-N 3-W
" "	**12**	2	U.S. Military Survey 2-N 3-W
ROBERTS	**17**	1	U.S. Military Survey 1-N 3-W
" "	**7**	1	U.S. Military Survey 3-N 3-W
ROBERTSON	**7**	3	U.S. Military Survey 3-N 3-W
" "	**6**	2	U.S. Military Survey 3-N 4-W
" "	**2**	1	U.S. Military Survey 4-N 3-W
ROBINS	**20**	13	Ohio River Survey 9-N 10-W

Surname	Map Group	Parcels of Land	Meridian/Township/Range
ROBINS (Cont'd)	**17**	1	U.S. Military Survey 1-N 3-W
ROBINSON	**8**	3	U.S. Military Survey 3-N 2-W
" "	**18**	2	U.S. Military Survey 1-N 2-W
" "	**20**	1	Ohio River Survey 9-N 10-W
RODGERS	**2**	3	U.S. Military Survey 4-N 3-W
ROGERS	**19**	1	U.S. Military Survey 1-N 1-W
ROLINGSON	**8**	1	U.S. Military Survey 3-N 2-W
ROLLINS	**12**	1	U.S. Military Survey 2-N 3-W
ROOSE	**20**	1	Ohio River Survey 9-N 10-W
ROSE	**2**	4	U.S. Military Survey 4-N 3-W
" "	**15**	1	Ohio River Survey 9-N 7-W
" "	**11**	1	U.S. Military Survey 2-N 4-W
ROSS	**3**	2	U.S. Military Survey 4-N 2-W
ROWEN	**13**	1	U.S. Military Survey 2-N 2-W
RUBART	**1**	1	U.S. Military Survey 4-N 4-W
RUSSELL	**20**	1	Ohio River Survey 9-N 10-W
" "	**19**	1	U.S. Military Survey 1-N 1-W
" "	**17**	1	U.S. Military Survey 1-N 3-W
RUTLEDGE	**6**	2	U.S. Military Survey 3-N 4-W
RYAN	**9**	1	U.S. Military Survey 3-N 1-W
SANDERS	**19**	1	U.S. Military Survey 1-N 1-W
SARCHET	**7**	3	U.S. Military Survey 3-N 3-W
SAVELY	**17**	2	U.S. Military Survey 1-N 3-W
SAVIERS	**3**	1	U.S. Military Survey 4-N 2-W
SCHOOLEY	**4**	1	U.S. Military Survey 4-N 1-W
SCHWYHART	**7**	1	U.S. Military Survey 3-N 3-W
" "	**2**	1	U.S. Military Survey 4-N 3-W
SCOTT	**20**	4	Ohio River Survey 9-N 10-W
" "	**17**	2	U.S. Military Survey 1-N 3-W
" "	**8**	2	U.S. Military Survey 3-N 2-W
" "	**6**	2	U.S. Military Survey 3-N 4-W
" "	**15**	1	Ohio River Survey 9-N 7-W
" "	**11**	1	U.S. Military Survey 2-N 4-W
SECRIST	**21**	1	Ohio River Survey 8-N 9-W
SELDERS	**17**	1	U.S. Military Survey 1-N 3-W
SHAFFER	**1**	2	U.S. Military Survey 4-N 4-W
SHARP	**20**	1	Ohio River Survey 9-N 10-W
SHEELEY	**2**	1	U.S. Military Survey 4-N 3-W
SHEELY	**1**	1	U.S. Military Survey 4-N 4-W
SHERAR	**6**	1	U.S. Military Survey 3-N 4-W
SHERRARD	**11**	2	U.S. Military Survey 2-N 4-W
SHIPLEY	**4**	1	U.S. Military Survey 4-N 1-W
SHOFF	**2**	2	U.S. Military Survey 4-N 3-W
" "	**1**	2	U.S. Military Survey 4-N 4-W
" "	**17**	1	U.S. Military Survey 1-N 3-W
SHRIVER	**20**	5	Ohio River Survey 9-N 10-W
" "	**17**	3	U.S. Military Survey 1-N 3-W
SIGHTS	**7**	2	U.S. Military Survey 3-N 3-W
SIGMAN	**18**	1	U.S. Military Survey 1-N 2-W
SILLS	**2**	3	U.S. Military Survey 4-N 3-W
SIMKINS	**2**	1	U.S. Military Survey 4-N 3-W
SIMMERMAN	**6**	1	U.S. Military Survey 3-N 4-W
SIMPSON	**11**	1	U.S. Military Survey 2-N 4-W
SINES	**20**	1	Ohio River Survey 9-N 10-W
" "	**17**	1	U.S. Military Survey 1-N 3-W
SLASON	**13**	1	U.S. Military Survey 2-N 2-W
SLATER	**17**	1	U.S. Military Survey 1-N 3-W
SMALLY	**17**	1	U.S. Military Survey 1-N 3-W
SMITH	**2**	7	U.S. Military Survey 4-N 3-W
" "	**3**	5	U.S. Military Survey 4-N 2-W

Surname	Map Group	Parcels of Land	Meridian/Township/Range
SMITH (Cont'd)	**4**	4	U.S. Military Survey 4-N 1-W
" "	**15**	3	Ohio River Survey 9-N 7-W
" "	**17**	3	U.S. Military Survey 1-N 3-W
" "	**1**	3	U.S. Military Survey 4-N 4-W
" "	**18**	2	U.S. Military Survey 1-N 2-W
" "	**20**	1	Ohio River Survey 9-N 10-W
" "	**9**	1	U.S. Military Survey 3-N 1-W
" "	**8**	1	U.S. Military Survey 3-N 2-W
" "	**7**	1	U.S. Military Survey 3-N 3-W
SNODGRASS	**6**	1	U.S. Military Survey 3-N 4-W
SNOW	**13**	1	U.S. Military Survey 2-N 2-W
SOLINGER	**6**	2	U.S. Military Survey 3-N 4-W
SPAID	**21**	2	Ohio River Survey 8-N 9-W
SPARKS	**1**	1	U.S. Military Survey 4-N 4-W
SPEERS	**8**	1	U.S. Military Survey 3-N 2-W
SPENCER	**16**	2	U.S. Military Survey 1-N 4-W
SPICER	**4**	1	U.S. Military Survey 4-N 1-W
SPILMAN	**20**	1	Ohio River Survey 9-N 10-W
SPRAGUE	**6**	2	U.S. Military Survey 3-N 4-W
STACKEY	**8**	1	U.S. Military Survey 3-N 2-W
STACKHOUSE	**1**	1	U.S. Military Survey 4-N 4-W
STANBERRY	**6**	1	U.S. Military Survey 3-N 4-W
STANBERY	**2**	11	U.S. Military Survey 4-N 3-W
" "	**6**	10	U.S. Military Survey 3-N 4-W
" "	**17**	9	U.S. Military Survey 1-N 3-W
" "	**1**	9	U.S. Military Survey 4-N 4-W
" "	**20**	5	Ohio River Survey 9-N 10-W
" "	**7**	4	U.S. Military Survey 3-N 3-W
" "	**21**	2	Ohio River Survey 8-N 9-W
" "	**3**	2	U.S. Military Survey 4-N 2-W
" "	**18**	1	U.S. Military Survey 1-N 2-W
" "	**11**	1	U.S. Military Survey 2-N 4-W
" "	**8**	1	U.S. Military Survey 3-N 2-W
STARKEY	**8**	2	U.S. Military Survey 3-N 2-W
STEELL	**16**	1	U.S. Military Survey 1-N 4-W
STEETH	**7**	1	U.S. Military Survey 3-N 3-W
STEPHENS	**17**	2	U.S. Military Survey 1-N 3-W
STEVENS	**17**	2	U.S. Military Survey 1-N 3-W
" "	**20**	1	Ohio River Survey 9-N 10-W
" "	**16**	1	U.S. Military Survey 1-N 4-W
STEVENSON	**11**	1	U.S. Military Survey 2-N 4-W
STEWART	**7**	10	U.S. Military Survey 3-N 3-W
" "	**12**	2	U.S. Military Survey 2-N 3-W
" "	**10**	1	Ohio River Survey 10-N 7-W
" "	**17**	1	U.S. Military Survey 1-N 3-W
" "	**8**	1	U.S. Military Survey 3-N 2-W
" "	**2**	1	U.S. Military Survey 4-N 3-W
STIERS	**19**	2	U.S. Military Survey 1-N 1-W
STIGLER	**19**	1	U.S. Military Survey 1-N 1-W
STILES	**8**	3	U.S. Military Survey 3-N 2-W
STINER	**2**	1	U.S. Military Survey 4-N 3-W
STOCKDALE	**8**	2	U.S. Military Survey 3-N 2-W
" "	**5**	1	Ohio River Survey 11-N 7-W
" "	**9**	1	U.S. Military Survey 3-N 1-W
STOKELY	**13**	4	U.S. Military Survey 2-N 2-W
" "	**17**	1	U.S. Military Survey 1-N 3-W
STRAHL	**17**	2	U.S. Military Survey 1-N 3-W
STRAKE	**20**	1	Ohio River Survey 9-N 10-W
STROIN	**3**	1	U.S. Military Survey 4-N 2-W
STRONG	**17**	4	U.S. Military Survey 1-N 3-W

Surname	Map Group	Parcels of Land	Meridian/Township/Range
STRONG (Cont'd)	**21**	1	Ohio River Survey 8-N 9-W
STUART	**18**	2	U.S. Military Survey 1-N 2-W
STULE	**16**	1	U.S. Military Survey 1-N 4-W
STULL	**8**	1	U.S. Military Survey 3-N 2-W
STURGES	**2**	21	U.S. Military Survey 4-N 3-W
" "	**6**	9	U.S. Military Survey 3-N 4-W
" "	**1**	9	U.S. Military Survey 4-N 4-W
" "	**3**	7	U.S. Military Survey 4-N 2-W
" "	**7**	3	U.S. Military Survey 3-N 3-W
" "	**17**	2	U.S. Military Survey 1-N 3-W
" "	**20**	1	Ohio River Survey 9-N 10-W
" "	**8**	1	U.S. Military Survey 3-N 2-W
SUIT	**11**	1	U.S. Military Survey 2-N 4-W
SUNAFRANK	**11**	1	U.S. Military Survey 2-N 4-W
SUTTON	**9**	1	U.S. Military Survey 3-N 1-W
SWAIM	**2**	2	U.S. Military Survey 4-N 3-W
SWEARINGEN	**1**	2	U.S. Military Survey 4-N 4-W
SWISHER	**7**	1	U.S. Military Survey 3-N 3-W
SWYHART	**7**	1	U.S. Military Survey 3-N 3-W
TALBUT	**13**	1	U.S. Military Survey 2-N 2-W
TAYLOR	**8**	2	U.S. Military Survey 3-N 2-W
" "	**17**	1	U.S. Military Survey 1-N 3-W
" "	**9**	1	U.S. Military Survey 3-N 1-W
" "	**3**	1	U.S. Military Survey 4-N 2-W
TEEL	**20**	2	Ohio River Survey 9-N 10-W
TEMPLE	**2**	1	U.S. Military Survey 4-N 3-W
TERREL	**2**	1	U.S. Military Survey 4-N 3-W
TETIRICK	**8**	1	U.S. Military Survey 3-N 2-W
THARP	**17**	1	U.S. Military Survey 1-N 3-W
THOMAS	**18**	3	U.S. Military Survey 1-N 2-W
" "	**5**	1	Ohio River Survey 11-N 7-W
" "	**15**	1	Ohio River Survey 9-N 7-W
" "	**8**	1	U.S. Military Survey 3-N 2-W
" "	**7**	1	U.S. Military Survey 3-N 3-W
THOMPSON	**2**	8	U.S. Military Survey 4-N 3-W
" "	**15**	2	Ohio River Survey 9-N 7-W
" "	**3**	2	U.S. Military Survey 4-N 2-W
" "	**21**	1	Ohio River Survey 8-N 9-W
" "	**19**	1	U.S. Military Survey 1-N 1-W
" "	**18**	1	U.S. Military Survey 1-N 2-W
TIMMONS	**13**	1	U.S. Military Survey 2-N 2-W
TINGLE	**17**	1	U.S. Military Survey 1-N 3-W
TOBIN	**2**	3	U.S. Military Survey 4-N 3-W
" "	**3**	1	U.S. Military Survey 4-N 2-W
TONER	**11**	2	U.S. Military Survey 2-N 4-W
TOOL	**2**	1	U.S. Military Survey 4-N 3-W
TOPHAND	**8**	1	U.S. Military Survey 3-N 2-W
TORODE	**17**	1	U.S. Military Survey 1-N 3-W
TOWNSEND	**15**	1	Ohio River Survey 9-N 7-W
TOWNSHEND	**17**	1	U.S. Military Survey 1-N 3-W
TRACE	**6**	1	U.S. Military Survey 3-N 4-W
TROTT	**9**	1	U.S. Military Survey 3-N 1-W
TRUSLER	**6**	5	U.S. Military Survey 3-N 4-W
TULLOUGH	**20**	2	Ohio River Survey 9-N 10-W
TURKLE	**10**	2	Ohio River Survey 10-N 7-W
TURNEY	**2**	2	U.S. Military Survey 4-N 3-W
" "	**1**	1	U.S. Military Survey 4-N 4-W
UNDERHILL	**12**	1	U.S. Military Survey 2-N 3-W
VAMPELT	**8**	1	U.S. Military Survey 3-N 2-W
VAN CAMPEN	**8**	1	U.S. Military Survey 3-N 2-W

Surname	Map Group	Parcels of Land	Meridian/Township/Range
VAN HORNE	**20**	1	Ohio River Survey 9-N 10-W
VANCUREN	**17**	2	U.S. Military Survey 1-N 3-W
VANDVORT	**20**	1	Ohio River Survey 9-N 10-W
VANSICKEL	**7**	1	U.S. Military Survey 3-N 3-W
VERNON	**13**	4	U.S. Military Survey 2-N 2-W
VERREY	**17**	1	U.S. Military Survey 1-N 3-W
VOLKERT	**2**	1	U.S. Military Survey 4-N 3-W
VOORHES	**6**	2	U.S. Military Survey 3-N 4-W
" "	**11**	1	U.S. Military Survey 2-N 4-W
WADE	**2**	2	U.S. Military Survey 4-N 3-W
WAGONER	**3**	1	U.S. Military Survey 4-N 2-W
WAGSTAFF	**6**	6	U.S. Military Survey 3-N 4-W
WALGAMOTT	**2**	2	U.S. Military Survey 4-N 3-W
" "	**1**	1	U.S. Military Survey 4-N 4-W
WALKER	**9**	2	U.S. Military Survey 3-N 1-W
" "	**7**	1	U.S. Military Survey 3-N 3-W
WALLACE	**17**	1	U.S. Military Survey 1-N 3-W
WALLER	**17**	4	U.S. Military Survey 1-N 3-W
" "	**16**	4	U.S. Military Survey 1-N 4-W
WALTERS	**3**	2	U.S. Military Survey 4-N 2-W
WARD	**11**	1	U.S. Military Survey 2-N 4-W
WARDAN	**7**	1	U.S. Military Survey 3-N 3-W
WARDEN	**7**	10	U.S. Military Survey 3-N 3-W
" "	**6**	2	U.S. Military Survey 3-N 4-W
" "	**18**	1	U.S. Military Survey 1-N 2-W
WARNICK	**3**	3	U.S. Military Survey 4-N 2-W
WARRACK	**9**	1	U.S. Military Survey 3-N 1-W
WATERS	**6**	1	U.S. Military Survey 3-N 4-W
WEBSTER	**15**	3	Ohio River Survey 9-N 7-W
WEIR	**6**	4	U.S. Military Survey 3-N 4-W
WELCH	**8**	1	U.S. Military Survey 3-N 2-W
WELKER	**1**	1	U.S. Military Survey 4-N 4-W
WELLS	**10**	1	Ohio River Survey 10-N 7-W
" "	**11**	1	U.S. Military Survey 2-N 4-W
WENTWORTH	**8**	1	U.S. Military Survey 3-N 2-W
WERDEN	**7**	1	U.S. Military Survey 3-N 3-W
WEST	**20**	2	Ohio River Survey 9-N 10-W
" "	**13**	1	U.S. Military Survey 2-N 2-W
WHARTON	**20**	2	Ohio River Survey 9-N 10-W
WHEELER	**2**	1	U.S. Military Survey 4-N 3-W
WHITAKER	**3**	2	U.S. Military Survey 4-N 2-W
" "	**8**	1	U.S. Military Survey 3-N 2-W
WHITCRAFT	**15**	4	Ohio River Survey 9-N 7-W
WHITE	**1**	2	U.S. Military Survey 4-N 4-W
" "	**13**	1	U.S. Military Survey 2-N 2-W
" "	**11**	1	U.S. Military Survey 2-N 4-W
" "	**3**	1	U.S. Military Survey 4-N 2-W
WHITEHILL	**8**	2	U.S. Military Survey 3-N 2-W
WHITTEN	**18**	2	U.S. Military Survey 1-N 2-W
WIER	**6**	2	U.S. Military Survey 3-N 4-W
WIERS	**17**	1	U.S. Military Survey 1-N 3-W
WILEY	**18**	1	U.S. Military Survey 1-N 2-W
" "	**8**	1	U.S. Military Survey 3-N 2-W
WILKIN	**5**	2	Ohio River Survey 11-N 7-W
WILKINSON	**18**	1	U.S. Military Survey 1-N 2-W
WILLIAMS	**17**	4	U.S. Military Survey 1-N 3-W
" "	**1**	3	U.S. Military Survey 4-N 4-W
" "	**12**	1	U.S. Military Survey 2-N 3-W
WILLIS	**8**	3	U.S. Military Survey 3-N 2-W
WILLSON	**17**	2	U.S. Military Survey 1-N 3-W

Surname	Map Group	Parcels of Land	Meridian/Township/Range
WILLSON (Cont'd)	**2**	1	U.S. Military Survey 4-N 3-W
WILSON	**17**	4	U.S. Military Survey 1-N 3-W
" "	**2**	3	U.S. Military Survey 4-N 3-W
" "	**7**	2	U.S. Military Survey 3-N 3-W
" "	**6**	2	U.S. Military Survey 3-N 4-W
" "	**1**	2	U.S. Military Survey 4-N 4-W
WINE	**9**	3	U.S. Military Survey 3-N 1-W
WINEBURNER	**15**	1	Ohio River Survey 9-N 7-W
WINN	**20**	1	Ohio River Survey 9-N 10-W
WIRICK	**13**	1	U.S. Military Survey 2-N 2-W
WISCARVER	**6**	4	U.S. Military Survey 3-N 4-W
WISCORVER	**6**	1	U.S. Military Survey 3-N 4-W
WIYRICK	**7**	1	U.S. Military Survey 3-N 3-W
WOLFORD	**19**	2	U.S. Military Survey 1-N 1-W
WOOD	**15**	1	Ohio River Survey 9-N 7-W
WOODGET	**10**	1	Ohio River Survey 10-N 7-W
WOODROW	**17**	1	U.S. Military Survey 1-N 3-W
WOODS	**13**	1	U.S. Military Survey 2-N 2-W
" "	**2**	1	U.S. Military Survey 4-N 3-W
WOODSIDE	**19**	2	U.S. Military Survey 1-N 1-W
YARNEL	**8**	1	U.S. Military Survey 3-N 2-W
YATES	**17**	3	U.S. Military Survey 1-N 3-W
YOUNG	**15**	1	Ohio River Survey 9-N 7-W
" "	**8**	1	U.S. Military Survey 3-N 2-W
" "	**6**	1	U.S. Military Survey 3-N 4-W
ZIMMERMAN	**6**	3	U.S. Military Survey 3-N 4-W

– Part II –

Township Map Groups

Map Group 1: Index to Land Patents

Township 4-North Range 4-West (U.S. Military Survey)

After you locate an individual in this Index, take note of the Section and Section Part then proceed to the Land Patent map on the pages immediately following. You should have no difficulty locating the corresponding parcel of land.

The "For More Info" Column will lead you to more information about the underlying Patents. See the *Legend* at right, and the "How to Use this Book" chapter, for more information.

<table>
<tr><td colspan="2" align="center">LEGEND</td></tr>
<tr><td colspan="2" align="center">"For More Info . . . " column</td></tr>
<tr><td>A</td><td>= Authority (Legislative Act, See Appendix "A")</td></tr>
<tr><td>B</td><td>= Block or Lot (location in Section unknown)</td></tr>
<tr><td>C</td><td>= Cancelled Patent</td></tr>
<tr><td>F</td><td>= Fractional Section</td></tr>
<tr><td>G</td><td>= Group (Multi-Patentee Patent, see Appendix "C")</td></tr>
<tr><td>V</td><td>= Overlaps another Parcel</td></tr>
<tr><td>R</td><td>= Re-Issued (Parcel patented more than once)</td></tr>
</table>

(A & G items require you to look in the Appendixes referred to above. All other Letter-designations followed by a number require you to locate line-items in this index that possess the ID number found after the letter).

ID	Individual in Patent	Sec.	Sec. Part	Date Issued	Other Counties	For More Info . . .
90	ADAMS, Mordecai	22	E½SW	1823-08-20		A1
96	BANKS, Samuel	9	SWSE	1840-11-10		A1
138	BEATTY, Zaccheus A	3	23	1807-12-05	Coshocton	A2
139	" "	3	24	1807-12-05	Coshocton	A2
145	" "	3	7	1807-12-05	Coshocton	A2
146	" "	3	9	1808-04-27	Coshocton	A2
131	" "	3	10	1808-05-03	Coshocton	A2
132	" "	3	11	1808-05-03	Coshocton	A2
137	" "	3	22	1808-05-03	Coshocton	A2
144	" "	3	6	1808-05-03	Coshocton	A2
133	" "	3	12	1808-08-20	Coshocton	A2
136	" "	3	21	1808-08-20	Coshocton	A2
140	" "	3	25	1808-08-20	Coshocton	A2
143	" "	3	5	1808-09-27	Coshocton	A2
141	" "	3	26	1808-10-01	Coshocton	A2
134	" "	3	15	1812-07-09	Coshocton	A2
135	" "	3	18	1812-07-09	Coshocton	A2
142	" "	3	4	1815-04-15	Coshocton	A2
47	BENJAMIN, James	23	NENE	1844-07-10	Coshocton	A1
88	BOWERS, Martin	3	38	1838-09-01	Coshocton	A1
21	BRUSH, Daniel	2	NWSW	1835-09-14		A1 G16
36	" "	1	W½SW	1837-08-05		A1 G53
23	" "	18	NWSE	1837-08-05	Coshocton	A1 G15
22	" "	18	SWSE	1837-08-05	Coshocton	A1 G11
37	" "	2	E½SE	1837-08-05		A1 G53
18	" "	21	SWNW	1837-08-05		A1
20	" "	22	SWSW	1837-08-05		A1 G13
17	" "	20	NWSE	1837-11-07		A1
19	" "	1	NESW	1840-11-10		A1 G19
16	" "	1	W½NE	1840-11-10		A1
61	BRUSHAL, John F	9	NESE	1844-07-10		A1
11	BUCKINGHAM, Alvah	2	E½NE	1840-11-10		A1
94	COOK, Robert	11	N½NW	1840-11-10		A1
79	COWGILL, Joseph	23	SENE	1840-10-10	Coshocton	A1
28	ECKELBERY, George	3	17	1840-10-10	Coshocton	A1
64	FITZPATRICK, Bernard	3	30	1840-11-10	Coshocton	A1 G49
1	FULLER, Abel	11	SWNW	1837-08-15		A1
25	FULLER, Elijah	10	SWNE	1840-10-10		A1
81	FULLER, Joseph	22	NWNW	1837-04-10		A1
80	" "	18	SESE	1837-08-05	Coshocton	A1
113	FULLER, Thomas R	23	NWNE	1835-09-30	Coshocton	A1
22	" "	18	SWSE	1837-08-05	Coshocton	A1 G11
26	FURNEY, Frederick	1	SENE	1837-08-10		A1
92	GANSON, Philip	3	36	1837-04-10	Coshocton	A1
91	" "	3	29	1837-08-10	Coshocton	A1
62	GAURNER, John	3	31	1837-08-15	Coshocton	A1

ID	Individual in Patent	Sec.	Sec. Part	Date Issued	Other Counties	For More Info . . .
123	GIBSON, William	21	E½NW	1829-06-01		A1
122	" "	20	NESW	1837-04-10		A1
82	GROVE, Joseph	13	E½NE	1840-11-10	Coshocton	A1
83	" "	13	SENW	1840-11-10	Coshocton	A1
124	HAGAN, William	10	SWNW	1840-11-10		A1
63	HALL, John	3	27	1838-09-01	Coshocton	A1
84	HAMILTON, Joseph	10	SESE	1840-11-10		A1
43	HAMMERSLEY, Isaac	2	SWSW	1835-09-08		A1
119	HAWES, Welles	2	NESW	1840-10-10		A1
120	" "	9	NWNE	1840-10-10		A1 G48
45	HESHER, Jacob	1	S½SE	1844-07-10		A1
7	HONEYWELDS, Albert	9	NWSW	1840-10-10		A1
15	HURBERT, Conrad	1	NESE	1853-12-15		A1
5	INGLEHART, Adam	9	E½NE	1844-07-10		A1
6	" "	9	SWNE	1844-07-10		A1
110	JOHNSON, Charles	10	NESW	1840-11-10		A1 G104
48	JOHNSTON, James	3	39	1837-08-10	Coshocton	A1
95	JOHNSTON, Robert	3	34	1840-11-10	Coshocton	A1
20	JONES, Hugh	22	SWSW	1837-08-05		A1 G13
64	KANADY, John	3	30	1840-11-10	Coshocton	A1 G49
59	KEEN, Jesse	23	NESE	1840-10-10	Coshocton	A1
60	" "	23	SWSE	1840-10-10	Coshocton	A1
36	KREIDER, Henry	1	W½SW	1837-08-05		A1 G53
37	" "	2	E½SE	1837-08-05		A1 G53
35	" "	1	SWNW	1844-07-10		A1
89	KREIDER, Mary	1	NWSE	1840-11-10		A1
65	LAURENCE, John	3	3	1835-04-30	Coshocton	A1
13	LEACH, Andrew	3	2	1835-04-30	Coshocton	A1
112	LEACH, Thomas	8	NENE	1835-10-05	Coshocton	A1 G56
111	" "	3	35	1840-11-10	Coshocton	A1 G54
78	LEWIS, Jonathan	3	40	1837-04-10	Coshocton	A1
49	LOVE, James	13	NENW	1842-08-01	Coshocton	A1
50	" "	13	W½NE	1842-08-01	Coshocton	A1
66	LOVE, John	3	37	1840-11-10	Coshocton	A1
87	MAGNESS, Levi	23	SWNE	1849-04-10	Coshocton	A1
3	MAPLE, Abraham	12	SENW	1835-09-23		A1
2	" "	12	NENW	1835-10-05		A1
125	MAPLE, William	22	SWNW	1837-04-10		A1
23	MAPLE, William B	18	NWSE	1837-08-05	Coshocton	A1 G15
4	MARLATT, Abraham	2	NWNW	1837-08-15		A1
21	MARLATT, John	2	NWSW	1835-09-14		A1 G16
67	" "	2	SWNW	1837-08-05		A1
101	MARQUAND, Solomon	9	NENW	1838-09-01		A1
51	MCCUNE, James	3	NE	1837-08-10	Coshocton	A1
34	MISKIMEN, Harrison	12	SENE	1840-11-10		A1
58	MISKIMEN, James	8	W½SW	1823-08-20	Coshocton	A1
56	" "	8	W½NE	1826-10-02	Coshocton	A1
53	" "	18	NESE	1835-04-30	Coshocton	A1
57	" "	8	W½SE	1837-08-05	Coshocton	A1
54	" "	8	E½SE	1840-10-10	Coshocton	A1
55	" "	8	SENE	1840-10-10	Coshocton	A1
52	" "	1	E½NW	1844-07-10		A1
68	MISKIMEN, John	10	W½SW	1840-11-10		A1
126	MISKIMEN, William	13	W½NW	1823-08-20	Coshocton	A1
127	" "	8	E½SW	1826-10-02	Coshocton	A1
44	MISKIMENS, Isaac	20	E½SE	1837-08-10		A1
40	MISKIMINS, Hilliary	22	NWSW	1835-04-21		A1
9	MITCHELL, Alexander	20	SWSW	1837-04-10		A1
8	" "	20	SWSE	1837-08-15		A1
30	MITCHELL, George	12	W½SW	1829-04-01		A1
29	" "	10	SWSE	1840-11-10		A1
10	MORRISON, Alexander	3	1	1840-10-10	Coshocton	A1
85	MORRISON, Joseph	11	E½NE	1840-10-10		A1
111	MURPHY, Michael	3	35	1840-11-10	Coshocton	A1 G54
129	NEILL, William	3	28	1837-04-10	Coshocton	A1 G69
120	NORMAN, Benjamin B	9	NWNE	1840-10-10		A1 G48
97	NORMAN, Samuel	2	SWNE	1840-10-10		A1
86	NORRIS, Joseph	12	W½NW	1840-10-10		A1
69	PEACH, John	10	NESE	1844-07-10		A1
31	PHILLIPS, George	3	16	1840-11-10	Coshocton	A1
114	RAY, Thomas	20	W½NE	1837-04-10		A1
130	REED, William	21	NWNW	1837-08-02		A1
117	RUBART, Vincent	22	E½NW	1821-09-08		A1

ID	Individual in Patent	Sec.	Sec. Part	Date Issued	Other Counties	For More Info . . .
99	SHAFFER, Christopher	2	E½NW	1840-11-10		A1 G78
99	SHAFFER, Samuel	2	E½NW	1840-11-10		A1 G78
98	"	2	NWNE	1840-11-10		A1
14	SHEELY, Christian	12	E½SE	1823-08-20		A1
93	SHOFF, Philip	20	SESW	1835-10-05		A1
118	SHOFF, Washington	20	NWSW	1837-08-02		A1
46	SMITH, Jacob	9	SESW	1840-11-10		A1
121	SMITH, William C	3	8	1837-11-07	Coshocton	A1
128	SMITH, William N	10	SENW	1837-11-07		A1
19	SPARKS, Eli	1	NESW	1840-11-10		A1 G19
12	STACKHOUSE, Amos	3	14	1811-02-20	Coshocton	A2
42	STANBERY, Howard	9	SESE	1840-11-10		A1
41	" "	9	SENW	1844-07-10		A1
129	STANBERY, Jonas	3	28	1837-04-10	Coshocton	A1 G69
75	" "	2	W½SE	1837-08-15		A1
77	" "	9	W½NW	1838-09-01		A1
72	" "	11	NWNE	1840-11-10		A1
73	" "	12	NWSE	1840-11-10		A1
74	" "	12	W½NE	1840-11-10		A1
76	" "	3	33	1840-11-10	Coshocton	A1
110	STURGES, Solomon	10	NESW	1840-11-10		A1 G104
102	" "	1	SESW	1844-07-10		A1
103	" "	10	E½NE	1844-07-10		A1
104	" "	10	NENW	1844-07-10		A1
105	" "	10	NWNE	1844-07-10		A1
106	" "	10	NWSE	1844-07-10		A1
107	" "	10	SESW	1844-07-10		A1
108	" "	12	NENE	1844-07-10		A1
109	" "	9	NESW	1844-07-10		A1
115	SWEARINGEN, Thomas	23	NWSE	1838-09-01	Coshocton	A1
116	" "	23	SESE	1838-09-01	Coshocton	A1
27	TURNEY, Frederick	1	NENE	1837-04-10		A1
70	WALGAMOTT, John	20	E½NE	1832-04-02		A1
24	WELKER, David	3	32	1837-08-15	Coshocton	A1
32	WHITE, George	11	SENW	1840-11-10		A1
33	" "	11	SWNE	1840-11-10		A1
71	WILLIAMS, John	3	19	1837-08-05	Coshocton	A1
112	WILLIAMS, Samuel	8	NENE	1835-10-05	Coshocton	A1 G56
100	" "	2	SESW	1837-04-10		A1
38	WILSON, Henry	12	E½SW	1835-04-02		A1
39	" "	12	SWSE	1835-04-30		A1

Patent Map

T4-N R4-W
U.S. Military Survey Meridian

Map Group 1

Township Statistics

Parcels Mapped	:	146
Number of Patents	:	136
Number of Individuals	:	93
Patentees Identified	:	95
Number of Surnames	:	71
Multi-Patentee Parcels	:	14
Oldest Patent Date	:	12/5/1807
Most Recent Patent	:	12/15/1853
Block/Lot Parcels	:	38
Parcels Re - Issued	:	0
Parcels that Overlap	:	0
Cities and Towns	:	2
Cemeteries	:	5

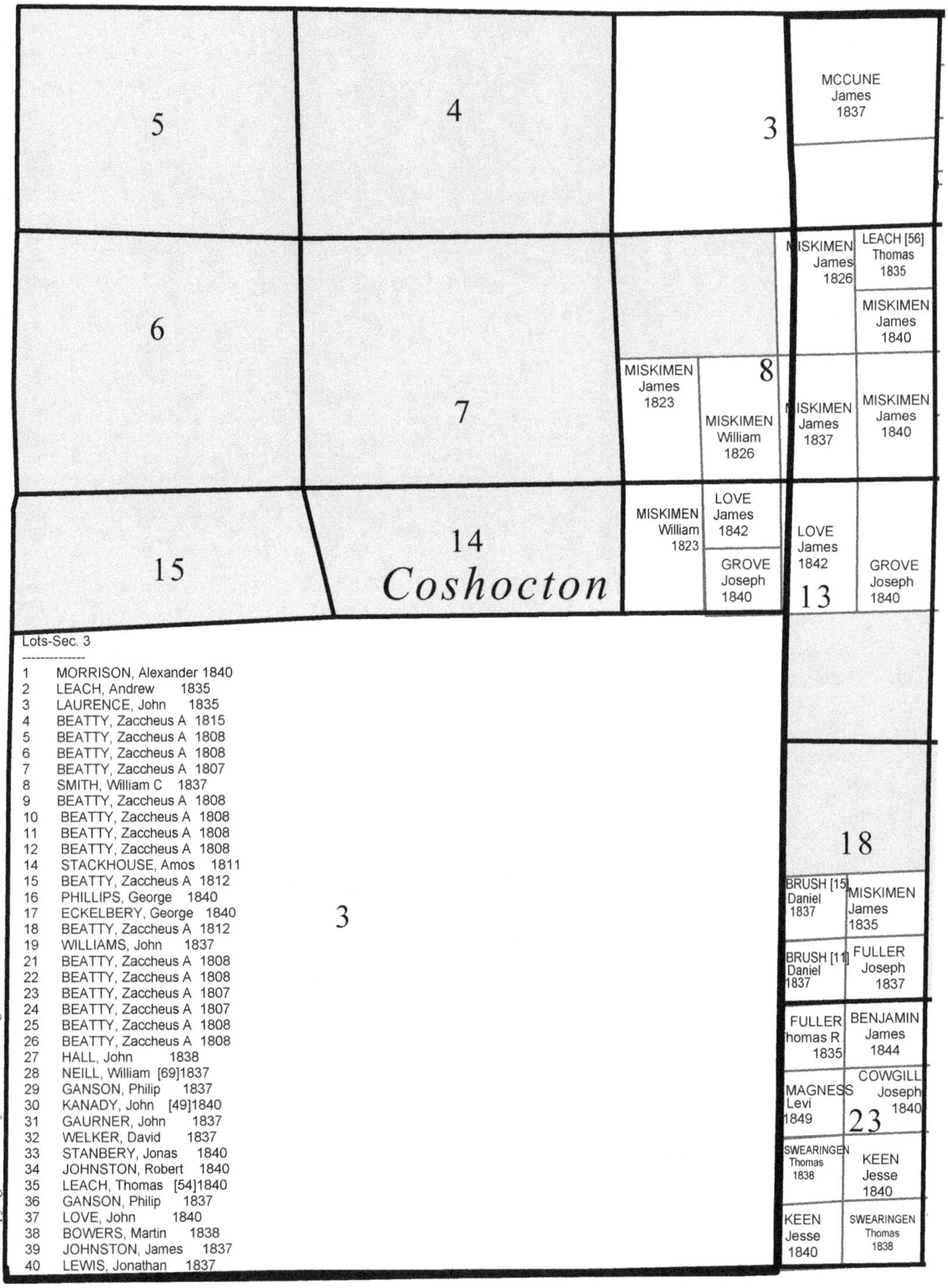

Map grid (top to bottom, left to right):

Row 1: 5 | 4 | 3 | MCCUNE James 1837

Row 2 / 3: 6 | 7 | MISKIMEN James 1823 | 8 MISKIMEN William 1826 | MISKIMEN James 1826 / LEACH [56] Thomas 1835 / MISKIMEN James 1840 / MISKIMEN James 1837 / MISKIMEN James 1840

Row: 15 | 14 *Coshocton* | MISKIMEN William 1823 | LOVE James 1842 / GROVE Joseph 1840 | LOVE James 1842 13 / GROVE Joseph 1840

3

18

BRUSH [15] Daniel 1837 | MISKIMEN James 1835
BRUSH [11] Daniel 1837 | FULLER Joseph 1837
FULLER Thomas R 1835 | BENJAMIN James 1844
MAGNESS Levi 1849 | COWGILL Joseph 1840 23
SWEARINGEN Thomas 1838 | KEEN Jesse 1840
KEEN Jesse 1840 | SWEARINGEN Thomas 1838

Lots-Sec. 3

1	MORRISON, Alexander	1840
2	LEACH, Andrew	1835
3	LAURENCE, John	1835
4	BEATTY, Zaccheus A	1815
5	BEATTY, Zaccheus A	1808
6	BEATTY, Zaccheus A	1808
7	BEATTY, Zaccheus A	1807
8	SMITH, William C	1837
9	BEATTY, Zaccheus A	1808
10	BEATTY, Zaccheus A	1808
11	BEATTY, Zaccheus A	1808
12	BEATTY, Zaccheus A	1808
14	STACKHOUSE, Amos	1811
15	BEATTY, Zaccheus A	1812
16	PHILLIPS, George	1840
17	ECKELBERY, George	1840
18	BEATTY, Zaccheus A	1812
19	WILLIAMS, John	1837
21	BEATTY, Zaccheus A	1808
22	BEATTY, Zaccheus A	1808
23	BEATTY, Zaccheus A	1807
24	BEATTY, Zaccheus A	1807
25	BEATTY, Zaccheus A	1808
26	BEATTY, Zaccheus A	1808
27	HALL, John	1838
28	NEILL, William [69]	1837
29	GANSON, Philip	1837
30	KANADY, John [49]	1840
31	GAURNER, John	1837
32	WELKER, David	1837
33	STANBERY, Jonas	1840
34	JOHNSTON, Robert	1840
35	LEACH, Thomas [54]	1840
36	GANSON, Philip	1837
37	LOVE, John	1840
38	BOWERS, Martin	1838
39	JOHNSTON, James	1837
40	LEWIS, Jonathan	1837

3

Map Grid

Section 2
- MARLATT Abraham 1837
- SHAFFER Samuel 1840
- BUCKINGHAM Alvah 1840
- SHAFFER [78] Samuel 1840
- MARLATT John 1837
- NORMAN Samuel 1840
- BRUSH [16] Daniel 1835
- HAWES Welles 1840
- 2
- KREIDER [53] Henry 1837
- HAMMERSLEY Isaac 1835
- WILLIAMS Samuel 1837
- STANBERY Jonas 1837

Section 1
- KREIDER Henry 1844
- MISKIMEN James 1844
- BRUSH Daniel 1840
- TURNEY Frederick 1837
- FURNEY Frederick 1837
- 1
- BRUSH [19] Daniel 1840
- KREIDER Mary 1840
- HURBERT Conrad 1853
- KREIDER [53] Henry 1837
- STURGES Solomon 1844
- HESHER Jacob 1844

Section 9
- STANBERY Jonas 1838
- MARQUAND Solomon 1838
- HAWES [48] Welles 1840
- INGLEHART Adam 1844
- STANBERY Howard 1844
- INGLEHART Adam 1844
- HONEYWELDS Albert 1840
- STURGES Solomon 1844
- 9
- BRUSHAL John F 1844
- SMITH Jacob 1840
- BANKS Samuel 1840
- STANBERY Howard 1840

Section 10
- STURGES Solomon 1844
- STURGES Solomon 1844
- HAGAN William 1840
- SMITH William N 1837
- FULLER Elijah 1840
- 10
- STURGES Solomon 1844
- MISKIMEN John 1840
- STURGES [104] Solomon 1840
- STURGES Solomon 1844
- PEACH John 1844
- STURGES Solomon 1844
- MITCHELL George 1840
- HAMILTON Joseph 1840

Section 12
- NORRIS Joseph 1840
- MAPLE Abraham 1835
- STURGES Solomon 1844
- MAPLE Abraham 1835
- STANBERY Jonas 1840
- MISKIMEN Harrison 1840
- 12
- MITCHELL George 1829
- WILSON Henry 1835
- STANBERY Jonas 1840
- WILSON Henry 1835
- SHEELY Christian 1823

Section 11
- COOK Robert 1840
- STANBERY Jonas 1840
- MORRISON Joseph 1840
- FULLER Abel 1837
- WHITE George 1840
- WHITE George 1840
- 11

Guernsey

19

Section 20
- WALGAMOTT John 1832
- RAY Thomas 1837
- SHOFF Washington 1837
- GIBSON William 1837
- BRUSH Daniel 1837
- 20
- MITCHELL Alexander 1837
- SHOFF Philip 1835
- MITCHELL Alexander 1837
- MISKIMENS Isaac 1837

Section 22
- FULLER Joseph 1837
- RUBART Vincent 1821
- MAPLE William 1837
- 22
- MISKIMINS Hilliary 1835
- ADAMS Mordecai 1823
- BRUSH [13] Daniel 1837

Section 21
- REED William 1837
- BRUSH Daniel 1837
- GIBSON William 1829
- 21

Helpful Hints

1. This Map's INDEX can be found on the preceding pages.

2. Refer to Map "C" to see where this Township lies within Guernsey County, Ohio.

3. Numbers within square brackets [ ] denote a multi-patentee land parcel (multi-owner). Refer to Appendix "C" for a full list of members in this group.

4. Areas that look to be crowded with Patentees usually indicate multiple sales of the same parcel (Re-issues) or Overlapping parcels. See this Township's Index for an explanation of these and other circumstances that might explain "odd" groupings of Patentees on this map.

Legend

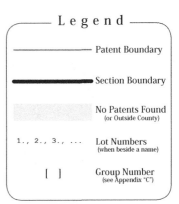

— Patent Boundary

— Section Boundary

No Patents Found (or Outside County)

1., 2., 3., ...   Lot Numbers (when beside a name)

[ ]   Group Number (see Appendix "C")

Road Map

T4-N R4-W
U.S. Military Survey Meridian

Map Group 1

Cities & Towns
Birds Run
Toledoville (historical)

Cemeteries
Banker Cemetery
Birds Run Methodist
Episcopal Cemetery
Forney Cemetery
Union Hill Cemetery
Worthing Cemetery

5

4

3

6

7

8

15

14

13

Coshocton

18

3

23

Twp Hwy 121

Worthing Rd

Bates Rd

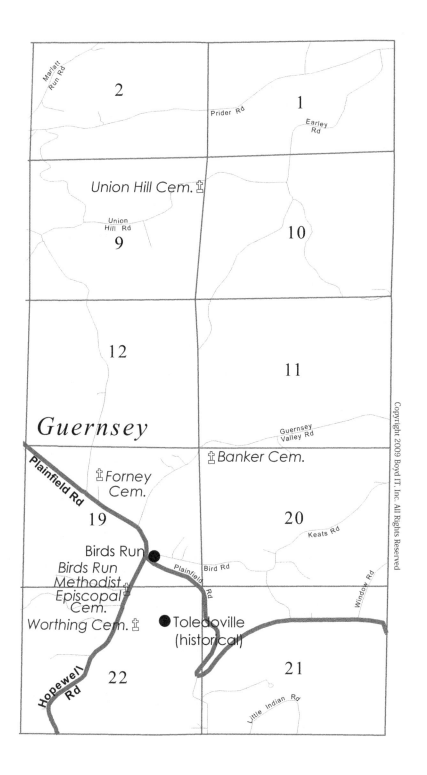

Marlatt Run Rd

2

Prider Rd

1

Earley Rd

Union Hill Cem. ⚱

Union Hill Rd

9

10

12

11

Guernsey

Guernsey Valley Rd

Plainfield Rd

⚱ Banker Cem.

⚱ Forney Cem.

19

20

Keats Rd

Birds Run ●

Birds Run Methodist Episcopal Cem. ⚱

Plainfield Bird Rd

Plainfield Rd

Window Rd

Worthing Cem. ⚱

● Toledoville (historical)

Hopewell Rd

22

21

Little Indian Rd

Helpful Hints

1. This road map has a number of uses, but primarily it is to help you: a) find the present location of land owned by your ancestors (at least the general area), b) find cemeteries and city-centers, and c) estimate the route/roads used by Census-takers & tax-assessors.

2. If you plan to travel to Guernsey County to locate cemeteries or land parcels, please pick up a modern travel map for the area before you do. Mapping old land parcels on modern maps is not as exact a science as you might think. Just the slightest variations in public land survey coordinates, estimates of parcel boundaries, or road-map deviations can greatly alter a map's representation of how a road either does or doesn't cross a particular parcel of land.

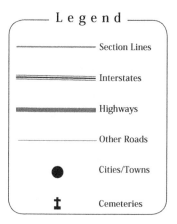

Legend

———————	Section Lines
≡≡≡≡≡≡	Interstates
▬▬▬▬▬	Highways
———————	Other Roads
●	Cities/Towns
⚱	Cemeteries

Scale: Section = 1 mile X 1 mile
(generally, with some exceptions)

Historical Map

T4-N R4-W
U.S. Military Survey Meridian

Map Group 1

Cities & Towns
Birds Run
Toledoville (historical)

Cemeteries
Banker Cemetery
Birds Run Methodist
 Episcopal Cemetery
Forney Cemetery
Union Hill Cemetery
Worthing Cemetery

5

4

3

6

7

8

Coshocton

15

14

13

3

18

23

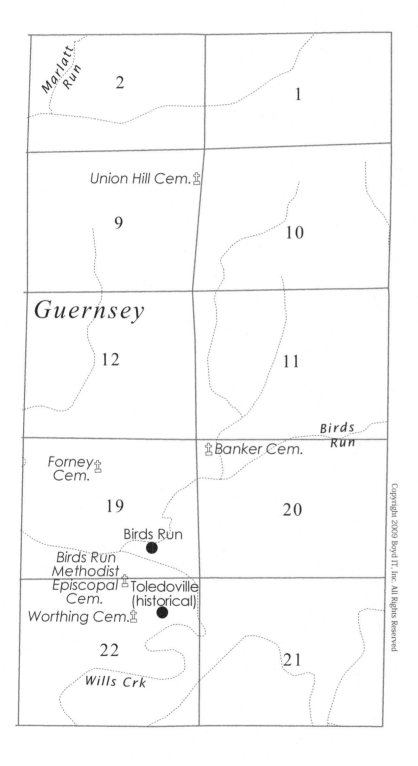

Helpful Hints

1. This Map takes a different look at the same Congressional Township displayed in the preceding two maps. It presents features that can help you better envision the historical development of the area: a) Water-bodies (lakes & ponds), b) Water-courses (rivers, streams, etc.), c) Railroads, d) City/ town center-points (where they were oftentimes located when first settled), and e) Cemeteries.

2. Using this "Historical" map in tandem with this Township's Patent Map and Road Map, may lead you to some interesting discoveries. You will often find roads, towns, cemeteries, and waterways are named after nearby landowners: sometimes those names will be the ones you are researching. See how many of these research gems you can find here in Guernsey County.

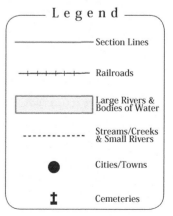

Legend

———————	Section Lines
+–+–+–+–+	Railroads
▭	Large Rivers & Bodies of Water
- - - - - - - -	Streams/Creeks & Small Rivers
●	Cities/Towns
✝	Cemeteries

Scale: Section = 1 mile X 1 mile
(there are some exceptions)

Map Group 2: Index to Land Patents

Township 4-North Range 3-West (U.S. Military Survey)

After you locate an individual in this Index, take note of the Section and Section Part then proceed to the Land Patent map on the pages immediately following. You should have no difficulty locating the corresponding parcel of land.

The "For More Info" Column will lead you to more information about the underlying Patents. See the *Legend* at right, and the "How to Use this Book" chapter, for more information.

```
                        LEGEND
                "For More Info . . . " column
A = Authority (Legislative Act, See Appendix "A")
B = Block or Lot (location in Section unknown)
C = Cancelled Patent
F = Fractional Section
G = Group (Multi-Patentee Patent, see Appendix "C")
V = Overlaps another Parcel
R = Re-Issued (Parcel patented more than once)

(A & G items require you to look in the Appendixes referred
to above. All other Letter-designations followed by a number
require you to locate line-items in this index that possess
the ID number found after the letter).
```

ID	Individual in Patent	Sec.	Sec. Part	Date Issued	Other Counties	For More Info . . .
185	ANDERSON, George	2	SWSW	1835-04-21		A1
186	"	9	NWNW	1835-04-21		A1
239	ATKINSON, John	5	NENW	1835-09-23		A1 R183
240	"	7	SWSW	1837-11-07		A1
241	BAIRD, John	11	E½NE	1837-08-02		A1
243	"	11	SWNE	1837-08-02		A1
242	"	11	NWNE	1837-11-07		A1
189	BEAL, George	8	W½SE	1832-04-02		A1
187	"	11	NESW	1840-10-10		A1
188	"	11	SESE	1840-10-10		A1
211	BEAL, Isaac	8	E½SE	1832-07-02		A1
235	BEAL, Jeremiah	8	W½NW	1835-09-14		A1
244	BEAL, John	10	E½SE	1832-04-02		A1
190	BEALE, George	11	NESE	1835-09-08		A1
302	BELL, Joseph	19	SE	1823-08-20		A1
303	"	20	SWSW	1838-09-01		A1
297	BEVARD, Jonathan	18	NENE	1835-09-30		A1 R374
335	BEVARD, Samuel	18	NWNW	1837-08-05		A1
334	"	17	NENE	1837-11-07		A1
370	BIGLEY, Thomas W	15	NENE	1838-09-01		A1
371	"	6	SESE	1838-09-01		A1
245	BIRD, John	5	NWNE	1838-09-01		A1
220	BOYD, James	16	SWSE	1840-11-10		A1
300	BRATSHAW, Joseph B	6	NESW	1840-11-10		A1
259	BRILL, John L	9	E½NW	1832-08-01		A1
221	BRITTON, James	18	SENW	1837-04-10		A1
330	BRITTON, Robert	18	NESE	1835-04-21		A1
329	"	12	SENE	1837-11-07		A1
153	BUCKINGHAM, Alvah	4	W½SE	1837-08-05		A1
152	"	1	SWSW	1837-08-10		A1
154	"	7	W½NE	1837-08-10		A1
312	CALDWELL, Levi	4	SENW	1844-07-10		A1
199	CALLANTINE, Henry	3	NENW	1838-09-01		A1
232	CARMICHAEL, James	5	NWNW	1835-09-23		A1 G66
195	CARPENTER, George W	2	NWNW	1837-04-10		A1
247	CARR, John	13	E½NW	1840-10-10		A1
156	CARTER, Andrew	19	NWSW	1844-07-10		A1
378	CARTER, William A	2	W½NE	1832-04-02		A1
213	CHANDLER, Isaac H	4	NENW	1837-11-07		A1
214	"	4	SWNE	1837-11-07		A1
379	CHANEY, William	4	NWNW	1840-11-10		A1
182	COOK, Ellis	3	SESE	1835-09-14		A1 G34 V155
180	"	2	NWSW	1835-09-30		A1
181	"	2	SWNW	1835-09-30		A1
331	COOK, Robert	25	NWSE	1840-11-10		A1
209	CRAWFORD, Hugh	14	SWNE	1837-04-10		A1

ID	Individual in Patent	Sec.	Sec. Part	Date Issued	Other Counties	For More Info . . .
313	DAWSON, Levi	13	NESE	1840-11-10		A1
295	DILDINE, Harmon	18	N½SW	1840-11-10		A1 G83
168	DOUGLASS, David	25	SWSE	1837-04-10		A1
336	DOUGLASS, Samuel	12	E½SE	1827-12-20		A1
337	" "	25	E½SE	1837-08-02		A1
380	DRAKE, William	21	NWSW	1837-04-10		A1
381	" "	21	SWSE	1837-04-10		A1
382	DUFFEY, William	16	NESE	1838-09-01		A1
383	" "	18	SESE	1838-09-01		A1
332	EDIE, Rosanna	3	NWSW	1835-04-30		A1
333	" "	4	NESE	1835-04-30		A1
159	EVANS, Benjamin	1	NWNW	1837-08-10		A1
246	EVANS, John C	1	E½SW	1837-04-10		A1
164	FOSTER, Christian	8	E½NW	1835-04-02		A1
251	FRAME, John	24	W½NE	1826-05-01		A1
250	" "	18	SWSW	1835-04-21		A1
384	FRAME, William	17	SESW	1837-08-05		A1
179	FULLER, Ellet	10	NWNE	1835-09-14		A1
237	FULLER, Johiel	10	NENE	1835-04-30		A1
238	" "	10	SWNE	1835-04-30		A1
149	FURNEY, Abraham	17	W½NW	1825-08-06		A1
147	" "	14	E½NW	1827-06-01		A1
148	" "	17	NENW	1837-08-10		A1
252	FURNEY, John	15	SENE	1840-11-10		A1
253	" "	6	NENW	1840-11-10		A1
359	" "	6	SENW	1844-07-10		A1 G100
296	FURNEY, Solomon	17	SWNE	1844-07-10		A1 G85
162	GASKILL, Charles	3	SWSW	1835-09-14		A1
192	GIBSON, George	22	E½NW	1829-04-01		A1
191	" "	19	SESW	1835-10-05		A1
222	GIBSON, James	23	W½SW	1837-04-10		A1
361	GIBSON, John	22	SWNW	1835-09-08		A1 G101
362	" "	23	SENE	1835-09-08		A1 G101
360	" "	22	SESE	1835-10-05		A1 G101
387	GIBSON, William	23	W½NE	1823-08-20		A1
385	" "	11	W½NW	1827-06-01		A1
386	" "	22	SWSE	1837-08-05		A1
177	GILPIN, Elijah	1	NWSW	1835-09-08		A1
178	" "	1	SWNW	1835-09-08		A1
388	GILPIN, William	13	E½SW	1835-09-08		A1
224	GRAHAM, James	20	E½NW	1826-04-03		A1
223	" "	11	SESW	1837-08-05		A1
389	GRAHAM, William	20	W½NE	1823-08-20		A1
254	GREGORY, John	10	E½NW	1837-08-15		A1
372	GRIFFIN, Thomas W	3	SWNW	1837-08-15		A1
212	GRIMES, Isaac	11	W½SE	1835-04-02		A1
255	HALL, John	4	W½SW	1840-11-10		A1 G45
304	HAMILTON, Joseph	6	SWSW	1840-11-10		A1
377	HARDING, Wesley	2	NENW	1844-07-10		A1
343	HARDISTY, Solomon	1	E½NE	1832-04-02		A1
375	HARDISTY, Warren M	1	E½SE	1835-04-02		A1
218	HARRIS, Jacob	15	W½NW	1835-10-05		A1
219	HART, Jacob	7	W½SE	1832-07-02		A1
166	HARVERT, Coonrod	17	SENE	1844-07-10		A1
257	HATCHER, John	1	W½NE	1835-09-08		A1
256	" "	1	SENW	1835-09-23		A1
217	HEDGE, Israel	13	W½SW	1826-06-16		A1
310	HENDEN, Joshua	13	E½NE	1837-11-07		A1
311	" "	13	NWNE	1837-11-07		A1
184	HUNT, Garner	7	E½NE	1830-12-01		A1
364	JOHNSON, Thomas	17	SWSW	1844-07-10		A1
258	JOHNSTON, John	10	NWSE	1840-10-10		A1
157	JONES, Asbury	2	SENW	1838-09-01		A1
161	JONES, Charles G	8	SESW	1844-07-10		A1
225	JONES, James L	8	NWSW	1844-07-10		A1
376	KIMBLE, Washington	10	SENE	1838-09-01		A1
236	KING, Job S	3	W½SE	1835-10-05		A1
260	LANING, John	17	NWSW	1837-08-10		A1
227	LANNING, James	17	SENW	1844-07-10		A1
226	" "	17	NWNE	1844-12-10		A1
365	LARISON, Thomas	22	NWSE	1840-10-10		A1
366	LEACH, Thomas	16	SESE	1842-08-01		A1 G55
367	LEECH, Thomas	12	SWNW	1842-08-01		A1 G59

ID	Individual in Patent	Sec.	Sec. Part	Date Issued	Other Counties	For More Info . . .
298	LEWIS, Jonathan	4	SESE	1835-09-14		A1
368	LEWIS, Thomas	22	E½NE	1835-04-02		A1
163	LONG, Charles	2	E½NE	1832-07-02		A1
167	LONG, Daniel	2	E½SW	1832-08-01		A1
228	LONGSTRETH, James	6	W½SE	1837-11-07		A1
318	LUCCOCK, Naphtali	23	E½SW	1831-06-01		A1
339	MARDIS, Samuel	7	E½SW	1835-09-23		A1
392	MARDIS, William	14	NWNW	1840-11-10		A1
261	MARTIN, John	21	NESE	1835-09-08		A1
262	" "	21	SESE	1837-08-10		A1
393	MARTIN, William	21	E½SW	1832-07-02		A1
197	McALHENEY, Hamilton	12	N½NE	1840-11-10		A1
169	MCCARTNEY, David	18	SENE	1837-08-02		A1
170	" "	23	NENE	1837-11-07		A1
200	MCCARTNEY, Henry	11	W½SW	1835-04-02		A1
202	" "	20	NESW	1837-08-02		A1
203	" "	20	NWSW	1837-08-10		A1
204	" "	20	SESW	1837-08-10		A1
201	" "	20	E½NE	1844-07-10		A1
396	MCCARTNEY, William	19	W½NE	1824-04-17		A1
397	" "	20	W½NW	1829-04-01		A1
394	" "	19	E½NE	1832-04-02		A1
363	" "	19	SENW	1835-09-08		A1 G105
395	" "	19	NENW	1835-09-30		A1
367	MCCONNAUGHEY, David P	12	SWNW	1842-08-01		A1 G59
210	MCCUNE, Hugh	21	E½NW	1837-08-10		A1
182	MCCUNE, James	3	SESE	1835-09-14		A1 G34 V155
263	MCDONNELL, John	3	NWNW	1837-04-10		A1
264	" "	4	SENE	1837-04-10		A1
229	MCKEE, James	15	E½NW	1840-10-10		A1
230	" "	5	NENE	1844-07-10		A1
231	" "	5	SENE	1844-07-10		A1
398	MCMILLEN, William	10	SWSE	1837-08-15		A1
248	MILLER, John F	14	SENE	1837-08-10		A1
249	" "	9	SESE	1837-08-10		A1
399	MILLER, William	8	SENE	1835-04-30		A1
175	MILNER, Edward	10	SWSW	1840-10-10		A1
158	MILONE, Barnabus	9	W½SE	1832-07-02		A1
171	MILONE, David	9	NESE	1835-10-05		A1
265	MILONE, John	9	W½NE	1832-04-02		A1
232	MISKIMEN, James	5	NWNW	1835-09-23		A1 G66
215	MISKIMENS, Isaac	5	NESW	1835-04-30		A1
216	" "	5	SENW	1835-04-30		A1
198	MITCHELL, Hanse	12	W½SE	1827-06-01		A1
317	MONTGOMERY, Mitchel L	17	S½SE	1840-11-10		A1
193	PALMER, George	5	SWSE	1837-08-15		A1
194	" "	6	NWNE	1837-08-15		A1
266	PALMER, John	5	NWSE	1844-07-10		A1
267	" "	5	SWNE	1844-07-10		A1
268	PATTERSON, John	21	NWNW	1835-09-08		A1
269	" "	21	SWNW	1837-04-10		A1
340	PATTERSON, Samuel	22	NESE	1840-11-10		A1
366	PAYLOR, Samuel	16	SESE	1842-08-01		A1 G55
270	PHILLIPS, John	10	E½SW	1827-06-01		A1
271	" "	11	E½NW	1829-04-01		A1
391	POLAND, William H	8	W½NE	1832-04-02		A1
390	" "	8	NENE	1837-08-05		A1
305	PRESLEY, Joseph	21	SWSW	1837-08-10		A1
306	PRESTLY, Joseph	21	NWSE	1837-04-10		A1
369	RAY, Thomas	12	SW	1829-04-01		A1
196	REAVES, Hallowell	9	NESW	1844-07-10		A1
233	ROBB, James	16	W½SW	1829-05-01		A1
341	ROBERTSON, Samuel	16	E½SW	1829-06-01		A1
272	RODGERS, John	6	E½NE	1840-11-10		A1
273	" "	7	NWSW	1840-11-10		A1
274	" "	7	SWNW	1840-11-10		A1
276	ROSE, John	14	SESE	1835-09-23		A1
275	" "	14	NESE	1837-04-10		A1
373	ROSE, Thompson	13	SESE	1835-09-14		A1
374	" "	18	NENE	1835-09-14		A1 R297
307	SCHWYHART, Joseph	17	N½SE	1838-09-01		A1
165	SHEELEY, Christian	16	NENE	1837-04-10		A1
326	SHOFF, Philip	3	E½SW	1844-07-10		A1

ID	Individual in Patent	Sec.	Sec. Part	Date Issued	Other Counties	For More Info . . .
327	SHOFF, Philip (Cont'd)	3	SENW	1844-07-10		A1
172	SILLS, David	22	NWNW	1837-04-10		A1
205	SILLS, Henry	18	NWSE	1837-04-10		A1
299	SILLS, Jonathan	18	SWNE	1837-08-02		A1
155	SIMKINS, Amos	3	E½SE	1832-07-02		A1 V182
234	SMITH, James	8	NESW	1835-04-21		A1
301	SMITH, Joseph B	9	NENE	1837-08-15		A1
319	SMITH, Nathaniel	2	NESE	1837-04-10		A1
320	" "	2	SESE	1837-04-10		A1
322	" "	9	SWNW	1837-04-10		A1
321	" "	8	SWSW	1840-10-10		A1
401	SMITH, Wilson	7	NESE	1835-04-30		A1
207	STANBERY, Howard	18	NENW	1838-09-01		A1
208	" "	5	SWNW	1840-11-10		A1
290	STANBERY, Jonas	16	SWNW	1838-09-01		A1
288	" "	16	SENE	1840-10-10		A1
291	" "	16	W½NE	1840-10-10		A1
295	" "	18	N½SW	1840-11-10		A1 G83
289	" "	16	SENW	1844-07-10		A1
296	" "	17	SWNE	1844-07-10		A1 G85
292	" "	4	NWNE	1844-07-10		A1
293	" "	5	E½SE	1844-07-10		A1
294	" "	6	NESE	1844-07-10		A1
277	STEWART, John	19	SWSW	1837-04-10		A1
324	STINER, Nicholas	14	W½SE	1827-06-01		A1
206	STURGES, Hezekiah	4	E½SW	1837-11-07		A1
363	STURGES, Solomon	19	SENW	1835-09-08		A1 G105
361	" "	22	SWNW	1835-09-08		A1 G101
362	" "	23	SENE	1835-09-08		A1 G101
360	" "	22	SESE	1835-10-05		A1 G101
344	" "	12	NWNW	1844-07-10		A1
345	" "	16	NWSE	1844-07-10		A1
346	" "	17	NESW	1844-07-10		A1
347	" "	18	SESE	1844-07-10		A1
348	" "	18	SWSE	1844-07-10		A1
349	" "	22	W½NE	1844-07-10		A1
350	" "	3	NENE	1844-07-10		A1
351	" "	3	W½NE	1844-07-10		A1
352	" "	4	SWNW	1844-07-10		A1
353	" "	5	W½SW	1844-07-10		A1
354	" "	6	NWSW	1844-07-10		A1
359	" "	6	SENW	1844-07-10		A1 G100
355	" "	6	SESW	1844-07-10		A1
356	" "	6	SWNE	1844-07-10		A1
357	" "	6	W½NW	1844-07-10		A1
358	" "	7	NWNW	1844-07-10		A1
315	SWAIM, Matthias M	14	NENE	1840-10-10		A1
316	" "	7	SESE	1840-10-10		A1
176	TEMPLE, Edward	13	W½SE	1828-01-30		A1
160	TERREL, Calvin	15	W½NE	1838-09-01		A1
150	THOMPSON, Abraham	13	W½NW	1835-09-08		A1
283	THOMPSON, John	9	W½SW	1835-09-08		A1
278	" "	1	W½SE	1835-09-23		A1
281	" "	12	NENW	1835-09-23		A1
282	" "	9	SENE	1835-09-23		A1
279	" "	10	NWNW	1837-11-07		A1
280	" "	10	NWSW	1840-10-10		A1
314	THOMPSON, Martin	10	SWNW	1835-09-30		A1
284	TOBIN, John	12	SENW	1837-08-15		A1
285	" "	12	SWNE	1837-08-15		A1
323	TOBIN, Nathaniel	9	SESW	1837-11-07		A1
286	TOOL, John	1	NENW	1835-10-05		A1
151	TURNEY, Abraham	14	SWNW	1838-09-01		A1
183	TURNEY, Frederick	5	NENW	1837-04-10		A1 R239
325	VOLKERT, Peter	18	SWNW	1844-07-10		A1
309	WADE, Joseph	19	W½NW	1835-09-08		A1
308	" "	13	SWNE	1837-11-07		A1
173	WALGAMOTT, David	16	NENW	1835-09-23		A1
287	WALGAMOTT, John	16	NWNW	1835-04-21		A1
328	WHEELER, Rezin	2	W½SE	1832-07-02		A1
338	WILLSON, Samuel M	4	NENE	1835-04-30		A1
174	WILSON, David	7	E½NW	1837-11-07		A1
400	WILSON, William	19	NESW	1837-04-10		A1

ID	Individual in Patent	Sec.	Sec. Part	Date Issued	Other Counties	For More Info . . .
255	WILSON, William M	4	W½SW	1840-11-10		A1 G45
342	WOODS, Samuel	14	NWNE	1837-04-10		A1

Patent Map

T4-N R3-W
U.S. Military Survey Meridian

Map Group 2

Township Statistics

Parcels Mapped	:	255
Number of Patents	:	253
Number of Individuals	:	168
Patentees Identified	:	166
Number of Surnames	:	120
Multi-Patentee Parcels	:	12
Oldest Patent Date	:	8/20/1823
Most Recent Patent	:	12/10/1844
Block/Lot Parcels	:	0
Parcels Re - Issued	:	2
Parcels that Overlap	:	2
Cities and Towns	:	2
Cemeteries	:	5

Section 5

MISKIMEN [66] James 1835 | ATKINSON John 1835 / TURNEY Frederick 1837 | BIRD John 1838 | MCKEE James 1844

STANBERY Howard 1840 | MISKIMENS Isaac 1835 | PALMER John 1844 | MCKEE James 1844

STURGES Solomon 1844 | MISKIMENS Isaac 1835 / PALMER John 1844 | STANBERY Jonas 1844

PALMER George

Section 4

CHANEY William 1840 | CHANDLER Isaac H 1837 | STANBERY Jonas 1844 | WILLSON Samuel M 1835

STURGES Solomon 1844 | CALDWELL Levi 1844 | CHANDLER Isaac H 1837 | MCDONNELL John 1837

HALL [45] John 1840 | STURGES Hezekiah 1837 | BUCKINGHAM Alvah 1837

Section 3

MCDONNELL John 1837 | CALLANTINE Henry 1838 | | STURGES Solomon 1844

GRIFFIN Thomas W 1837 | SHOFF Philip 1844 | STURGES Solomon 1844

EDIE Rosanna 1835 | EDIE Rosanna 1835 | SHOFF Philip 1844 | KING Job S 1835

LEWIS Jonathan 1835 | GASKILL Charles 1835

STURGES Solomon 1844 | SIMKINS Amos 1832 | COOK [34] Ellis 1835

Section 6

FURNEY John 1840 | PALMER George 1837 | RODGERS John 1840

STURGES Solomon 1844 | STURGES [100] Solomon 1844 / STURGES Solomon 1844

STURGES Solomon 1844 | BRATSHAW Joseph B 1840 | STANBERY Jonas 1844

HAMILTON Joseph 1840 | LONGSTRETH James 1837 / STURGES Solomon 1844 | BIGLEY Thomas W 1838

Section 7

STURGES Solomon 1844 | WILSON David 1837 | BUCKINGHAM Alvah 1837

RODGERS John 1840 | | HUNT Garner 1830

RODGERS John 1840 | MARDIS Samuel 1835 | HART Jacob 1832

ATKINSON John 1837

Section 8

BEAL Jeremiah 1835 | FOSTER Christian 1835 | POLAND William H 1832 | POLAND William H 1837

MILLER William 1835

SMITH Wilson 1835 | JONES James L 1844 | SMITH James 1835 | BEAL George 1832

SWAIM Matthias M 1840 | SMITH Nathaniel 1840 | JONES Charles G 1844 | BEAL Isaac 1832

Section 15

MCKEE James 1840 | BIGLEY Thomas W 1838 | MARDIS William 1840

HARRIS Jacob 1835 | TERREL Calvin 1838 | FURNEY John 1840 | TURNEY Abraham 1838

Section 14

WOODS Samuel 1837 | SWAIM Matthias M 1840

FURNEY Abraham 1827 | CRAWFORD Hugh 1837 | MILLER John F 1837

STINER Nicholas 1827 | ROSE John 1837 | ROSE John 1835

Section 13

THOMPSON Abraham 1835 | CARR John 1840 | HENDEN Joshua 1837 | HENDEN Joshua 1837

WADE Joseph 1837

HEDGE Israel 1826 | GILPIN William 1835 | TEMPLE Edward 1828 | DAWSON Levi 1840

ROSE Thompson 1835

Section 16

WALGAMOTT John 1835 | WALGAMOTT David 1835 | STANBERY Jonas 1840 | SHEELEY Christian 1837

STANBERY Jonas 1838 | STANBERY Jonas 1844 | STANBERY Jonas 1840

ROBB James 1829 | ROBERTSON Samuel 1829 | STURGES Solomon 1844 | DUFFEY William 1838

BOYD James 1840 | LEACH [55] Thomas 1842

Section 17

FURNEY Abraham 1825 | FURNEY Abraham 1837 | LANNING James 1844 | BEVARD Samuel 1837

LANNING James 1844 | STANBERY [85] Jonas 1844 | HARVERT Coonrod 1844

LANING John 1837 | STURGES Solomon 1844 | SCHWYHART Joseph 1838

JOHNSON Thomas 1844 | FRAME William 1837 | MONTGOMERY Mitchel L 1840

Section 18

BEVARD Samuel 1837 | STANBERY Howard 1838 | | BEVARD Jonathan 1835 / ROSE Thompson 1835

VOLKERT Peter 1844 | BRITTON James 1837 | SILLS Jonathan 1837 | MCCARTNEY David 1837

STANBERY [83] Jonas 1840 | SILLS Henry 1837 | BRITTON Robert 1835

FRAME John 1835 | STURGES Solomon 1844 | STURGES Solomon 1844 | DUFFEY William 1838

Section 25

COOK Robert 1840 | DOUGLASS Samuel 1837

DOUGLASS David 1837

Section 24

FRAME John 1826

Section 23

GIBSON William 1823 | MCCARTNEY David 1837 / STURGES [101] Solomon 1835

GIBSON James 1837 | LUCCOCK Naphtali 1831

CARPENTER George W 1837	HARDING Wesley 1844	CARTER William A 1832	LONG Charles 1832	EVANS Benjamin 1837	TOOL John 1835	HATCHER John 1835	HARDISTY Solomon 1832
COOK Ellis 1835	JONES Asbury 1838	**2**		GILPIN Elijah 1835	HATCHER John 1835		
COOK Ellis 1835	LONG Daniel 1832	WHEELER Rezin 1832	SMITH Nathaniel 1837	GILPIN Elijah 1835	EVANS John C 1837	THOMPSON John 1835	HARDISTY Warren M 1835
ANDERSON George 1835			SMITH Nathaniel 1837	BUCKINGHAM Alvah 1837			
ANDERSON George 1835	BRILL John L 1832	MILONE John 1832	SMITH Joseph B 1837	THOMPSON John 1837	GREGORY John 1837	FULLER Ellet 1835	FULLER Johiel 1835
SMITH Nathaniel 1837			THOMPSON John 1835	THOMPSON Martin 1835		FULLER Johiel 1835	KIMBLE Washington 1838
THOMPSON John 1835	REAVES Hallowell 1844	MILONE Barnabus 1832	MILONE David 1835	THOMPSON John 1840	PHILLIPS John 1827	JOHNSTON John 1840	BEAL John 1832
	TOBIN Nathaniel 1837		MILLER John F 1837	MILNER Edward 1840		MCMILLEN William 1837	
STURGES Solomon 1844	THOMPSON John 1835	MCALHENEY Hamilton 1840		GIBSON William 1827	PHILLIPS John 1829	BAIRD John 1837	BAIRD John 1837
LEECH [59] Thomas 1842	TOBIN John 1837	TOBIN John 1837	BRITTON Robert 1837			BAIRD John 1837	
12		MITCHELL Hanse 1827	DOUGLASS Samuel 1827		BEAL George 1840	GRIMES Isaac 1835	BEALE George 1835
RAY Thomas 1829				MCCARTNEY Henry 1835	GRAHAM James 1837		BEAL George 1840
WADE Joseph 1835	MCCARTNEY William 1835	MCCARTNEY William 1824	MCCARTNEY William 1832	MCCARTNEY William 1829	GRAHAM James 1826	GRAHAM William 1823	MCCARTNEY Henry 1844
	STURGES [105] Solomon 1835					**20**	
CARTER Andrew 1844	WILSON William 1837	**19**	BELL Joseph 1823	MCCARTNEY Henry 1837	MCCARTNEY Henry 1837		
STEWART John 1837	GIBSON George 1835			BELL Joseph 1838	MCCARTNEY Henry 1837		
SILLS David 1837	GIBSON George 1829	STURGES Solomon 1844	LEWIS Thomas 1835	PATTERSON John 1835			
STURGES [101] Solomon 1835				PATTERSON John 1837	MCCUNE Hugh 1837	**21**	
	LARISON Thomas 1840	PATTERSON Samuel 1840	DRAKE William 1837	MARTIN William 1832	PRESTLY Joseph 1837	MARTIN John 1835	
22	GIBSON William 1837	STURGES [101] Solomon 1835	PRESLEY Joseph 1837		DRAKE William 1837	MARTIN John 1837	

Helpful Hints

1. This Map's INDEX can be found on the preceding pages.

2. Refer to Map "C" to see where this Township lies within Guernsey County, Ohio.

3. Numbers within square brackets [ ] denote a multi-patentee land parcel (multi-owner). Refer to Appendix "C" for a full list of members in this group.

4. Areas that look to be crowded with Patentees usually indicate multiple sales of the same parcel (Re-issues) or Overlapping parcels. See this Township's Index for an explanation of these and other circumstances that might explain "odd" groupings of Patentees on this map.

Legend

———	Patent Boundary
▬▬▬	Section Boundary
	No Patents Found (or Outside County)
1., 2., 3., ...	Lot Numbers (when beside a name)
[ ]	Group Number (see Appendix "C")

Scale: Section = 1 mile X 1 mile (generally, with some exceptions)

Road Map

T4-N R3-W
U.S. Military Survey Meridian

Map Group 2

Cities & Towns
Guernsey
Kimbolton

Cemeteries
Bethel Cemetery
Earleys Cemetery
Jones Cemetery
Old Kimbolton Cemetery
Township Cemetery

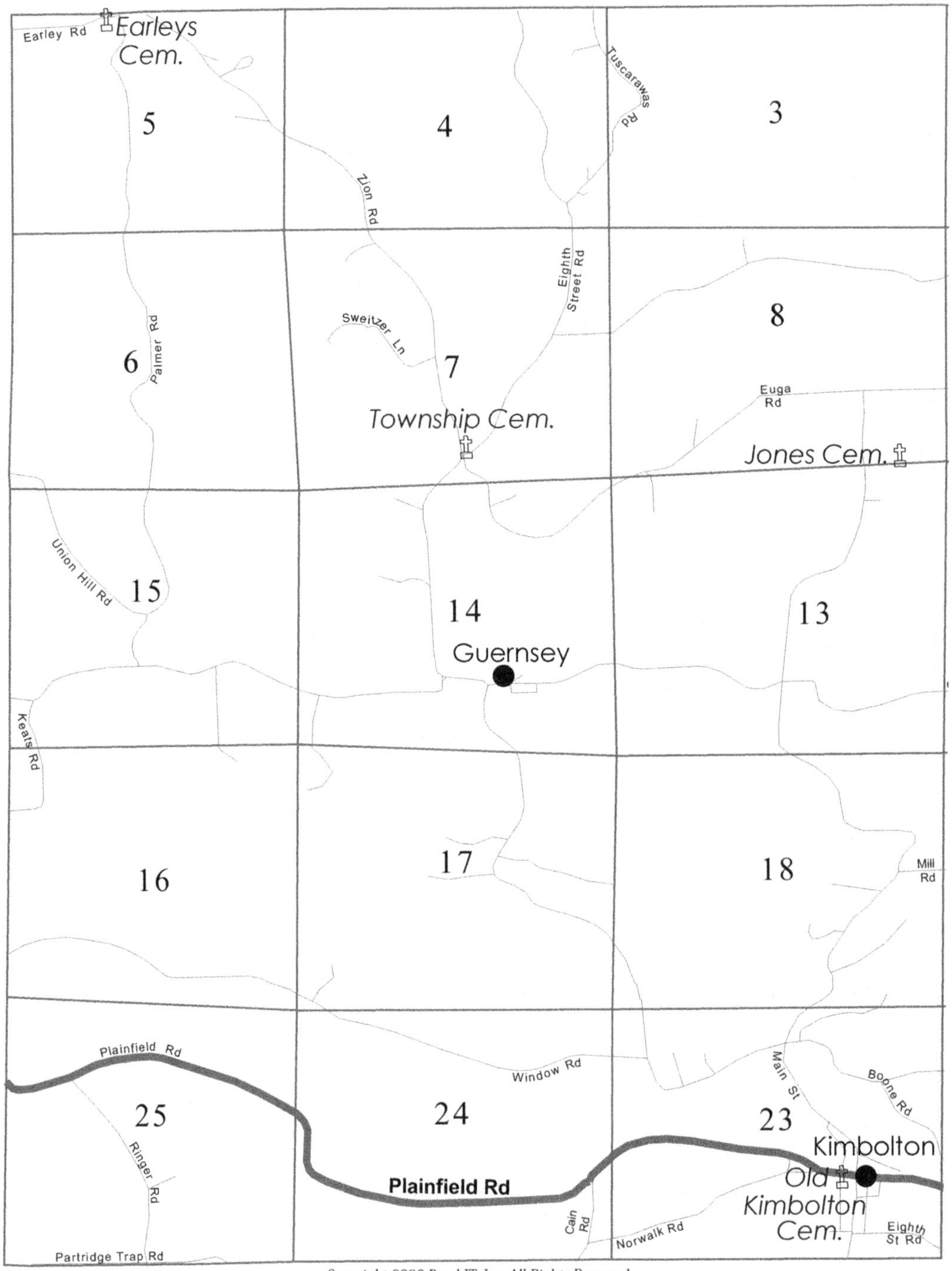

Earley Rd — Earleys Cem.

5   4   3

Tuscarawas Rd

Zion Rd

6   7   8

Palmer Rd

Sweitzer Ln

Eighth Street Rd

Township Cem.

Euga Rd

Jones Cem.

Union Hill Rd

15   14   13

Guernsey

Keats Rd

16   17   18

Mill Rd

Plainfield Rd

Window Rd

Main St

Boone Rd

25   24   23

Kimbolton

Plainfield Rd

Old Kimbolton Cem.

Ringer Rd

Cain Rd

Norwalk Rd

Eighth St Rd

Partridge Trap Rd

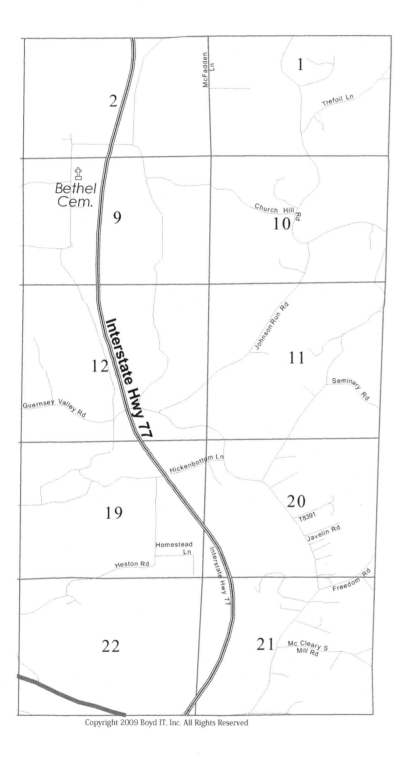

Helpful Hints

1. This road map has a number of uses, but primarily it is to help you: a) find the present location of land owned by your ancestors (at least the general area), b) find cemeteries and city-centers, and c) estimate the route/roads used by Census-takers & tax-assessors.

2. If you plan to travel to Guernsey County to locate cemeteries or land parcels, please pick up a modern travel map for the area before you do. Mapping old land parcels on modern maps is not as exact a science as you might think. Just the slightest variations in public land survey coordinates, estimates of parcel boundaries, or road-map deviations can greatly alter a map's representation of how a road either does or doesn't cross a particular parcel of land.

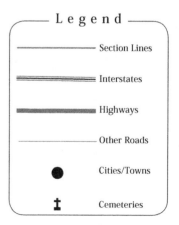

Legend

— Section Lines

— Interstates

— Highways

— Other Roads

● Cities/Towns

� Cemeteries

Scale: Section = 1 mile X 1 mile
(generally, with some exceptions)

Historical Map

T4-N R3-W
U.S. Military Survey Meridian

Map Group 2

Guernsey
Kimbolton

Cemeteries
Bethel Cemetery
Earleys Cemetery
Jones Cemetery
Old Kimbolton Cemetery
Township Cemetery

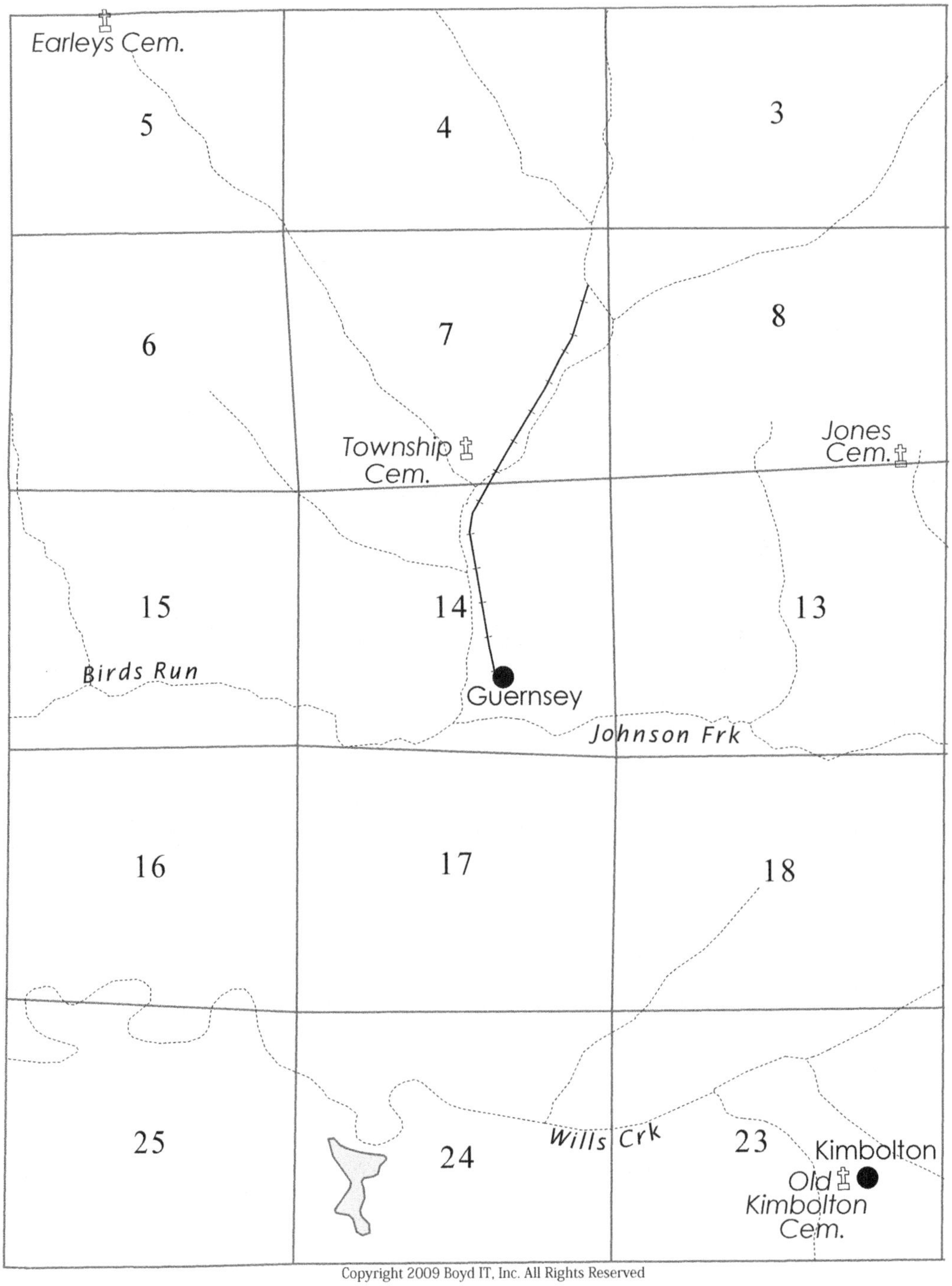

Earleys Cem.

5

4

3

6

7

8

Township Cem.

Jones Cem.

15

14

13

Birds Run

Guernsey

Johnson Frk

16

17

18

25

24

Wills Crk

23

Kimbolton

Old Kimbolton Cem.

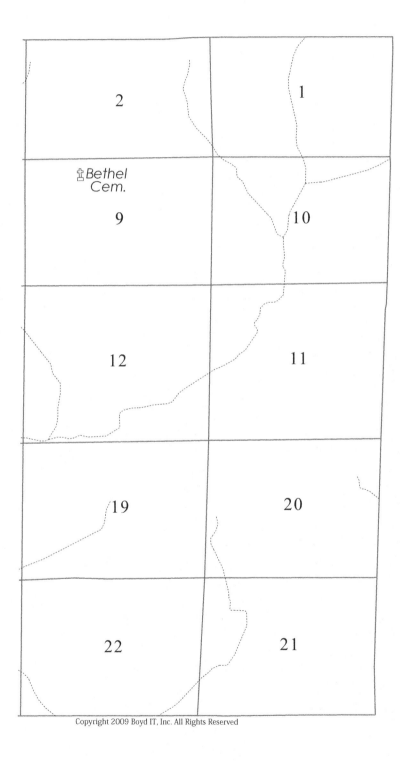

2	1
♱*Bethel Cem.* 9	10
12	11
19	20
22	21

Helpful Hints

1. This Map takes a different look at the same Congressional Township displayed in the preceding two maps. It presents features that can help you better envision the historical development of the area: a) Water-bodies (lakes & ponds), b) Water-courses (rivers, streams, etc.), c) Railroads, d) City/town center-points (where they were oftentimes located when first settled), and e) Cemeteries.

2. Using this "Historical" map in tandem with this Township's Patent Map and Road Map, may lead you to some interesting discoveries. You will often find roads, towns, cemeteries, and waterways are named after nearby landowners: sometimes those names will be the ones you are researching. See how many of these research gems you can find here in Guernsey County.

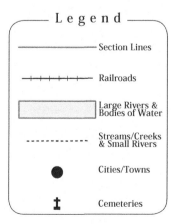

Legend

————————	Section Lines
┼┼┼┼┼┼	Railroads
▭	Large Rivers & Bodies of Water
– – – – – –	Streams/Creeks & Small Rivers
●	Cities/Towns
♱	Cemeteries

Scale: Section = 1 mile X 1 mile
(there are some exceptions)

Map Group 3: Index to Land Patents

Township 4-North Range 2-West (U.S. Military Survey)

After you locate an individual in this Index, take note of the Section and Section Part then proceed to the Land Patent map on the pages immediately following. You should have no difficulty locating the corresponding parcel of land.

The "For More Info" Column will lead you to more information about the underlying Patents. See the *Legend* at right, and the "How to Use this Book" chapter, for more information.

```
┌─────────────────────────────────────────────────────────┐
│                      LEGEND                             │
│           "For More Info . . ." column                  │
│  A = Authority (Legislative Act, See Appendix "A")      │
│  B = Block or Lot (location in Section unknown)         │
│  C = Cancelled Patent                                   │
│  F = Fractional Section                                 │
│  G = Group (Multi-Patentee Patent, see Appendix "C")    │
│  V = Overlaps another Parcel                            │
│  R = Re-Issued (Parcel patented more than once)         │
│                                                         │
│  (A & G items require you to look in the Appendixes     │
│  referred to above. All other Letter-designations       │
│  followed by a number require you to locate line-items  │
│  in this index that possess the ID number found after   │
│  the letter).                                           │
└─────────────────────────────────────────────────────────┘
```

ID	Individual in Patent	Sec.	Sec. Part	Date Issued	Other Counties	For More Info . . .
507	ADAIR, Rebecca	15	E½NW	1837-08-15		A1
508	ADAIR, Robert	5	NESW	1837-08-15		A1
509	" "	5	SWSW	1837-08-15		A1
440	ANDERSON, Grafton	17	NWNW	1837-11-07		A1
534	ANDERSON, William	15	E½NE	1828-08-20		A1
535	BARTON, William	4	W½NW	1834-07-16		A1
424	BEAL, Elias	6	W½SE	1831-02-10		A1
432	BEAL, George	6	E½SW	1830-12-01		A1
542	" "	18	NENW	1835-09-08		A1 G52
443	BEAL, Isaac	2	W½NE	1825-08-06		A1
462	BEAL, John	13	W½SW	1828-08-20		A1
463	" "	6	W½SW	1832-04-02		A1
500	BEAL, Nicholas	3	W½SW	1832-08-01		A1
536	BEAL, William	15	SWNW	1835-09-23		A1 R484
428	BOYCE, Francis	24	NESE	1835-10-05		A1
421	BRATTON, Edward	24	W½NE	1826-04-01		A1
452	BRATTON, James	18	W½SW	1824-04-17		A1
537	BRATTON, William	18	S½NW	1837-08-05		A1
444	BREWER, Isaac	4	E½NW	1832-04-02		A1
416	BRYAN, David	20	W½SE	1825-08-06		A1
417	BUCHANAN, David	20	E½SE	1832-04-02		A1
526	BUCHANAN, Thomas	15	NWNW	1835-09-30		A1
464	CEASAR, John	24	NENW	1838-09-01		A1 V435
538	CORTRIGHT, William	15	NESW	1837-04-05		A1
436	CROSS, George H	7	SWNW	1835-09-23		A1
410	CULBERTSON, Benjamin	14	SENW	1837-11-07		A1
411	" "	14	W½NW	1837-11-07		A1
525	DAVOULT, William	4	NWSW	1835-09-08		A1 G98
454	DUFFEY, James	22	W½SE	1829-05-01		A1
453	" "	15	SESW	1835-09-08		A1
491	FERRELL, Margaret	6	W½NE	1828-08-20		A1
418	FISHER, David	5	NWNW	1837-04-10		A1
450	FULLER, Jacob	16	SWNE	1837-11-07	'	A1
461	GALLENTINE, Jeremiah	17	SWNW	1835-09-23		A1
455	GILLESPIE, James	24	W½NW	1832-04-02		A1
413	GRAHAM, Charles	15	W½SW	1829-04-01		A1
414	GRAHAM, Christopher	6	E½NE	1826-10-02		A1
539	GRAHAM, William	5	W½SE	1826-04-01		A1
435	GRIMES, George	24	E½NW	1829-06-01		A1 V464
434	" "	16	SE	1835-04-02		A1
433	" "	15	SWSE	1835-10-05		A1
447	GRIMES, Isaac	25	E½NE	1831-02-10		A1
446	" "	16	NWNE	1835-04-21		A1
445	" "	16	E½NE	1835-09-23		A1
492	GRIMES, Mary E	14	NENW	1835-09-23		A1
490	HARDISTY, Lewis	5	NWSW	1837-04-10		A1

ID	Individual in Patent	Sec.	Sec. Part	Date Issued	Other Counties	For More Info . . .
501	HATCHER, Obadiah	5	W½NE	1832-07-02		A1
409	HILL, Arthur	5	E½NW	1835-09-08		A1
456	HISKETT, James	5	E½NE	1827-06-01		A1
437	HOFFMAN, George	21	NWSE	1835-04-30		A1
518	HUGHS, Sarah	18	NE	1821-09-08		A1
412	JOHNSON, Catherine	7	SWSE	1835-09-23		A1
493	JOHNSON, Mary	6	E½NW	1831-06-01		A1
527	JOHNSON, Thomas	6	E½SE	1840-10-10		A1
467	JOHNSTON, John	14	W½NE	1835-04-02		A1
465	" "	14	NENE	1835-09-14		A1
471	" "	7	SESE	1835-09-14		A1
466	" "	14	SENE	1840-10-10		A1
468	" "	4	SWSW	1840-10-10		A1
470	" "	7	NESE	1840-10-10		A1
469	" "	5	SWNW	1840-11-10		A1
498	KENNEDY, Moses W	17	E½NE	1837-08-15		A1
499	" "	18	NWNW	1837-11-07		A1
497	" "	14	SESE	1838-09-01		A1
407	KIMBLE, Adam	21	SWSE	1835-04-30		A1
532	KIMBLE, Washington	16	NWNW	1835-04-21		A1
533	" "	17	NWSE	1837-08-05		A1
540	KIMBLE, William	13	NESW	1835-04-21		A1
541	" "	13	SESW	1835-04-21		A1
542	" "	18	NENW	1835-09-08		A1 G52
485	LANING, Joseph	23	E½NW	1829-06-01		A1
426	LANNING, Ezekiel	23	W½NW	1825-08-06		A1
448	LANNING, Isaac M	16	E½NW	1835-04-02		A1
451	LANNING, Jacob	8	E½NE	1828-05-30		A1
510	LANNING, Robert H	23	E½SE	1829-04-01		A1
408	LITTLE, Archibald	19	W½SW	1825-08-06		A1
423	LITTLE, Edward	12	SWSE	1835-09-14		A1
422	" "	12	NWSE	1837-08-15		A1
429	LITTLE, Francis	19	E½SW	1831-02-10		A1
430	" "	19	NWSE	1837-04-10		A1
431	" "	19	SWSE	1837-08-05		A1
544	LITTLE, William	19	E½NE	1825-08-06		A1
545	" "	19	E½SE	1825-08-06		A1
543	" "	14	W½SE	1828-02-20		A1
472	LOURY, John	17	E½SE	1826-06-16		A1
473	LOWRY, John	17	SWSE	1835-04-21		A1
505	MARLOW, Peter	8	E½NW	1826-04-01		A1
506	" "	8	W½NE	1829-04-01		A1
504	" "	3	SESW	1835-04-21		A1
474	MARTIN, John	25	W½SW	1823-08-20		A1
441	MCCARTNEY, Henry	16	SWSW	1835-09-14		A1
546	MCCRACKEN, William	17	E½SW	1831-02-10		A1
427	MCGREW, Findley B	8	W½SW	1831-02-10		A1
503	MCLAUGHLIN, Patrick	6	W½NW	1832-04-02		A1
486	MCMULLEN, Joseph	24	W½SE	1824-04-17		A1
415	MCWILLIAMS, Daniel	25	SWSE	1837-04-10		A1
512	MCWILLIAMS, Robert	25	NWSE	1835-04-30		A1
511	" "	25	E½SE	1835-09-14		A1
513	" "	25	SWNE	1840-11-10		A1
516	MOOR, Samuel	4	E½SW	1829-06-01		A1
442	MOORE, Hezekiah	7	NWNW	1837-08-05		A1
515	MOORE, Samuel L	3	W½NW	1825-03-10		A1
528	MOORE, Thomas	7	E½NE	1831-02-10		A1
529	" "	8	W½NW	1831-02-10		A1
530	MOORES, Thomas	7	W½NE	1830-12-01		A1
457	NEIL, James	21	E½SW	1835-04-02		A1
531	NEWBURN, Thomas	17	NWSW	1835-09-30		A1
494	ORR, Mathew	17	W½NE	1828-07-30		A1
495	" "	7	E½SW	1835-09-08		A1
496	ORR, Matthew	17	E½NW	1831-02-10		A1
419	PATTERSON, David	16	NESW	1842-08-01		A1
420	" "	16	SWNW	1842-08-01		A1
438	PATTERSON, George	25	NENW	1835-09-23		A1
439	" "	25	NWNW	1835-09-23		A1
517	PAXTON, Samuel	24	E½NE	1821-09-08		A1
550	PHILIPS, Zephaniah L	24	SESE	1835-09-23		A1
514	REDMAN, Robert	5	SESW	1837-08-10		A1
402	RISHER, Abraham	2	E½SW	1835-04-02		A1
403	" "	3	NESW	1835-09-14		A1

ID	Individual in Patent	Sec.	Sec. Part	Date Issued	Other Counties	For More Info . . .
404	RISHER, Abraham (Cont'd)	3	NWNE	1835-09-14		A1
458	ROSS, James	2	E½NE	1827-09-20		A1
475	ROSS, John	3	E½NW	1835-04-02		A1
476	SAVIERS, John	21	E½SE	1830-12-01		A1
459	SMITH, James	17	SWSW	1837-08-15		A1
477	SMITH, John	8	E½SW	1831-02-10		A1
478	" "	8	SE	1831-02-10		A1
548	SMITH, William N	15	E½SE	1832-04-02		A1
547	" "	14	W½SW	1835-04-02		A1
483	STANBERY, Jonas	15	NWSE	1844-07-10		A1
484	" "	15	SWNW	1844-07-10		A1 R536
460	STROIN, James	18	E½SW	1823-08-20		A1
525	STURGES, Solomon	4	NWSW	1835-09-08		A1 G98
524	" "	5	NESE	1835-09-08		A1
521	" "	25	E½SW	1837-08-15		A1
523	" "	25	S½NW	1837-08-15		A1
519	" "	16	NWSW	1842-08-01		A1
520	" "	16	SESW	1842-08-01		A1
522	" "	25	NWNE	1842-08-01		A1
487	TAYLOR, Joseph	4	W½SE	1831-07-01		A1
406	THOMPSON, Abraham	7	W½SW	1831-06-01		A1
405	" "	15	NWNE	1835-09-08		A1
449	TOBIN, Isaac	14	NESE	1835-09-23		A1
479	WAGONER, John	3	SWNE	1835-04-21		A1
489	WALTERS, Joseph	4	NE	1837-08-05		A1
488	" "	4	E½SE	1837-08-10		A1
480	WARNICK, John	7	NENW	1835-09-23		A1
481	" "	7	NWSE	1835-09-23		A1
482	" "	7	SENW	1840-11-10		A1
502	WHITAKER, Obed	22	E½SE	1825-03-10		A1
549	WHITAKER, William	21	W½SW	1830-12-01		A1
425	WHITE, Elisha	5	SESE	1837-08-10		A1

Patent Map

T4-N R2-W
U.S. Military Survey Meridian

Map Group 3

Township Statistics

Parcels Mapped	:	149
Number of Patents	:	148
Number of Individuals	:	103
Patentees Identified	:	104
Number of Surnames	:	70
Multi-Patentee Parcels	:	2
Oldest Patent Date	:	9/8/1821
Most Recent Patent	:	7/10/1844
Block/Lot Parcels	:	0
Parcels Re - Issued	:	1
Parcels that Overlap	:	2
Cities and Towns	:	2
Cemeteries	:	6

Section 5: FISHER David 1837; JOHNSTON John 1840; HILL Arthur 1835; HATCHER Obadiah 1832; HISKETT James 1827; HARDISTY Lewis 1837; ADAIR Robert 1837; GRAHAM William 1826; STURGES Solomon 1835; ADAIR Robert 1837; REDMAN Robert 1837; WHITE Elisha 1837

Section 4: BARTON William 1834; BREWER Isaac 1832; WALTERS Joseph 1837; STURGES [98] Solomon 1835; MOOR Samuel 1829; TAYLOR Joseph 1831; WALTERS Joseph 1837; JOHNSTON John 1840

Section 3: MOORE Samuel L 1825; ROSS John 1835; RISHER Abraham 1835; WAGONER John 1835; BEAL Nicholas 1832; RISHER Abraham 1835; MARLOW Peter 1835

Section 6: MCLAUGHLIN Patrick 1832; JOHNSON Mary 1831; FERRELL Margaret 1828; BEAL John 1832; BEAL George 1830; BEAL Elias 1831; JOHNSON Thomas 1840

Section 7: GRAHAM Christopher 1826; MOORE Hezekiah 1837; WARNICK John 1835; CROSS George H 1835; WARNICK John 1840; THOMPSON Abraham 1831; ORR Mathew 1835

Section 8: MOORES Thomas 1830; MOORE Thomas 1831; MOORE Thomas 1831; WARNICK John 1835; JOHNSTON John 1840; JOHNSON Catherine 1835; JOHNSTON John 1835; MCGREW Findley B 1831; SMITH John 1831; MARLOW Peter 1826; MARLOW Peter 1829; LANNING Jacob 1828; SMITH John 1831

Section 15: BUCHANAN Thomas 1835; ADAIR Rebecca 1837; THOMPSON Abraham 1835; ANDERSON William 1828; STANBERY William 1835; BEAL Jonas 1844; GRAHAM Charles 1829; CORTRIGHT William 1837; STANBERY Jonas 1844; DUFFEY James 1835; GRIMES George 1835; SMITH William N 1832

Section 14: GRIMES Mary E 1835; CULBERTSON Benjamin 1837; JOHNSTON John 1835; CULBERTSON Benjamin 1837; JOHNSTON John 1835; JOHNSTON John 1840; SMITH William N 1835; LITTLE William 1828; TOBIN Isaac 1835; KENNEDY Moses W 1838

Section 13: BEAL John 1828; KIMBLE William 1835; KIMBLE William 1835

Section 16: KIMBLE Washington 1835; LANNING Isaac M 1835; GRIMES Isaac 1835; GRIMES Isaac 1835; PATTERSON David 1842; FULLER Jacob 1837; STURGES Solomon 1842; PATTERSON David 1842; GRIMES George 1835; MCCARTNEY Henry 1835; STURGES Solomon 1842

Section 17: ANDERSON Grafton 1837; ORR Matthew 1831; ORR Mathew 1828; KENNEDY Moses W 1837; GALLENTINE Jeremiah 1835; NEWBURN Thomas 1835; MCCRACKEN William 1831; KIMBLE Washington 1837; LOURY John 1826; SMITH James 1837; LOWRY John 1835

Section 18: KENNEDY Moses W 1837; KIMBLE [52] William 1835; BRATTON William 1837; HUGHS Sarah 1821; BRATTON James 1824; STROIN James 1823

Section 25: PATTERSON George 1835; PATTERSON George 1835; STURGES Solomon 1842; GRIMES Isaac 1831; STURGES Solomon 1837; MCWILLIAMS Robert 1840; MARTIN John 1823; STURGES Solomon 1837; MCWILLIAMS Robert 1835; MCWILLIAMS Daniel 1837; MCWILLIAMS Robert 1835

Section 24: GILLESPIE James 1832; CEASAR John 1838; BRATTON Edward 1826; PAXTON Samuel 1821; GRIMES George 1829; MCMULLEN Joseph 1824; BOYCE Francis 1835; PHILIPS Zephaniah L 1835

Section 23: LANNING Ezekiel 1825; LANING Joseph 1829; LANNING Robert H 1829

2	BEAL Isaac 1825	ROSS James 1827	**1**
	RISHER Abraham 1835		

9	**10**

12	**11**
LITTLE Edward 1837	
LITTLE Edward 1835	

19	LITTLE William 1825	**20**
LITTLE Archibald 1825	LITTLE Francis 1831	LITTLE Francis 1837 / LITTLE Francis 1837	LITTLE William 1825	BRYAN David 1825	BUCHANAN David 1832

22	WHITAKER Obed 1825	WHITAKER William 1830	**21**
DUFFEY James 1829		NEIL James 1835	HOFFMAN George 1835 / KIMBLE Adam 1835	SAVIERS John 1830

Copyright 2009 Boyd IT, Inc. All Rights Reserved

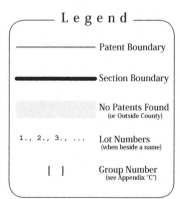

L e g e n d

———— Patent Boundary

━━━━ Section Boundary

No Patents Found (or Outside County)

1., 2., 3., ... Lot Numbers (when beside a name)

[ ] Group Number (see Appendix "C")

Scale: Section = 1 mile X 1 mile (generally, with some exceptions)

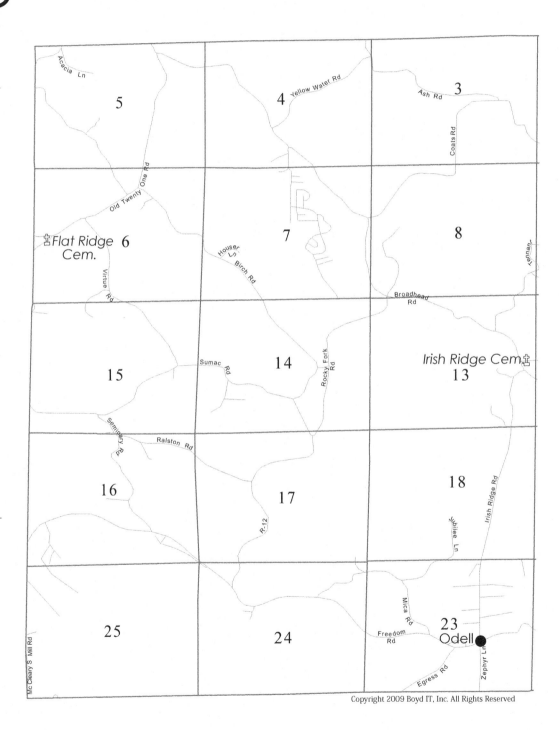

Road Map

T4-N R2-W
U.S. Military Survey Meridian

Map Group 3

Cities & Towns
Birmingham
Odell

Cemeteries
Birmingham Cemetery
Clear Fork Cemetery
Clear Fork Cemetery
Cumberland Cemetery
Flat Ridge Cemetery
Irish Ridge Cemetery

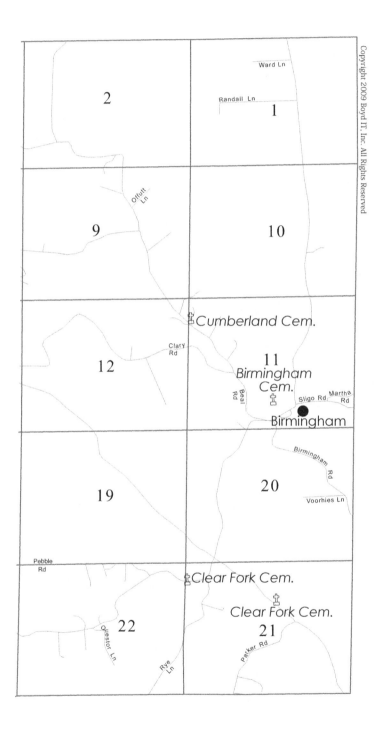

Helpful Hints

1. This road map has a number of uses, but primarily it is to help you: a) find the present location of land owned by your ancestors (at least the general area), b) find cemeteries and city-centers, and c) estimate the route/roads used by Census-takers & tax-assessors.

2. If you plan to travel to Guernsey County to locate cemeteries or land parcels, please pick up a modern travel map for the area before you do. Mapping old land parcels on modern maps is not as exact a science as you might think. Just the slightest variations in public land survey coordinates, estimates of parcel boundaries, or road-map deviations can greatly alter a map's representation of how a road either does or doesn't cross a particular parcel of land.

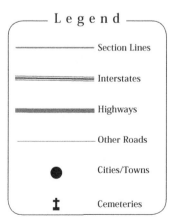

Legend

———————	Section Lines
═══════	Interstates
———————	Highways
———————	Other Roads
●	Cities/Towns
✝	Cemeteries

Scale: Section = 1 mile X 1 mile
(generally, with some exceptions)

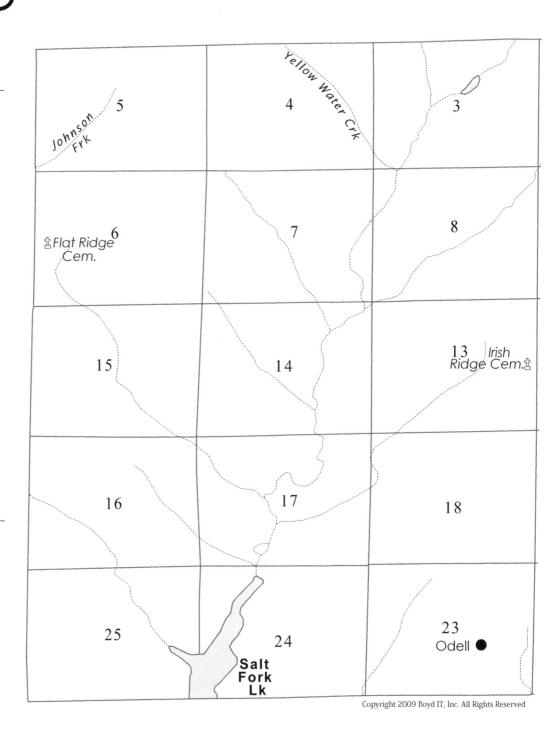

Historical Map

T4-N R2-W
U.S. Military Survey Meridian

Map Group 3

Cities & Towns
Birmingham
Odell

Cemeteries
Birmingham Cemetery
Clear Fork Cemetery
Clear Fork Cemetery
Cumberland Cemetery
Flat Ridge Cemetery
Irish Ridge Cemetery

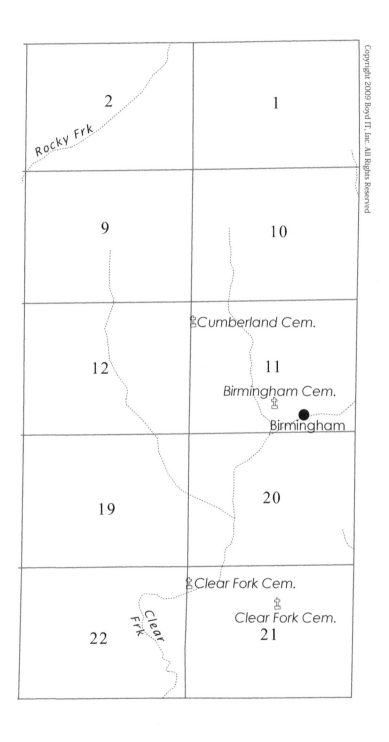

Helpful Hints

1. This Map takes a different look at the same Congressional Township displayed in the preceding two maps. It presents features that can help you better envision the historical development of the area: a) Water-bodies (lakes & ponds), b) Water-courses (rivers, streams, etc.), c) Railroads, d) City/ town center-points (where they were oftentimes located when first settled), and e) Cemeteries.

2. Using this "Historical" map in tandem with this Township's Patent Map and Road Map, may lead you to some interesting discoveries. You will often find roads, towns, cemeteries, and waterways are named after nearby landowners: sometimes those names will be the ones you are researching. See how many of these research gems you can find here in Guernsey County.

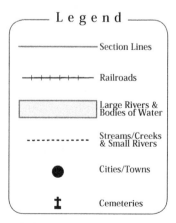

Scale: Section = 1 mile X 1 mile
(there are some exceptions)

Map Group 4: Index to Land Patents

Township 4-North Range 1-West (U.S. Military Survey)

After you locate an individual in this Index, take note of the Section and Section Part then proceed to the Land Patent map on the pages immediately following. You should have no difficulty locating the corresponding parcel of land.

The "For More Info" Column will lead you to more information about the underlying Patents. See the *Legend* at right, and the "How to Use this Book" chapter, for more information.

ID	Individual in Patent	Sec.	Sec. Part	Date Issued	Other Counties	For More Info . . .
571	BELL, Robert	22	E½SE	1831-06-01		A1
570	" "	21	E½SW	1835-04-02		A1
574	BOYD, Samuel	20	W½SW	1825-03-10		A1
568	BRASHEAR, Otho	5	W½NE	1832-10-10		A1
560	BROWN, John	21	NE	1821-09-08		A1
576	CHANDLER, Spencer	4	W½NE	1831-02-10		A1
555	CLARK, Alexander	3	E½NE	1835-04-02		A1
567	COATES, Lewis	15	NW	1829-04-01		A1
554	DAVIS, Abner	4	E½NE	1831-02-10		A1
566	ENGLE, Levi	3	W½NE	1831-02-10		A1
579	GRIFFITH, William	9	E½SW	1832-04-02		A1
551	HUGHES, Aaron	6	E½NE	1828-07-30		A1
561	LANNING, John	6	SW	1828-07-30		A1
557	LOGAN, Edward	22	W½SE	1826-04-03		A1
558	LOGAN, James	21	E½SE	1826-04-03		A1
572	MAXWELL, Robert	25	NW	1829-04-01		A1
575	MCKINNEY, Samuel F	20	W½SE	1832-04-02		A1
569	MOORE, Peter	9	NW	1826-05-01		A1
577	OLIVER, Thomas	25	E½NE	1832-04-02		A1
578	" "	25	W½NE	1835-09-08		A1
580	PEOPLES, William J	16	W½NW	1830-12-01		A1
553	POWEL, Abel	2	SE	1827-06-01		A1
562	READ, John	3	W½SE	1832-04-02		A1
573	REED, Robert	21	W½SW	1827-12-20		A1
564	SCHOOLEY, Joseph	2	W½SW	1830-12-01		A1
556	SHIPLEY, Amon	21	W½SE	1832-04-02		A1
552	SMITH, Aaron	2	SESW	1835-09-08		A1
559	SMITH, Jesse	8	E½NE	1832-04-02		A1
563	SMITH, Joseph R	8	W½NE	1832-07-02		A1
581	SMITH, William	2	W½NE	1835-04-02		A1
565	SPICER, Joseph	2	NESW	1835-04-21		A1

Patent Map

T4-N R1-W
U.S. Military Survey Meridian

Map Group 4

Township Statistics

Parcels Mapped	:	31
Number of Patents	:	31
Number of Individuals	:	29
Patentees Identified	:	29
Number of Surnames	:	25
Multi-Patentee Parcels	:	0
Oldest Patent Date	:	9/8/1821
Most Recent Patent	:	9/8/1835
Block/Lot Parcels	:	0
Parcels Re - Issued	:	0
Parcels that Overlap	:	0
Cities and Towns	:	0
Cemeteries	:	5

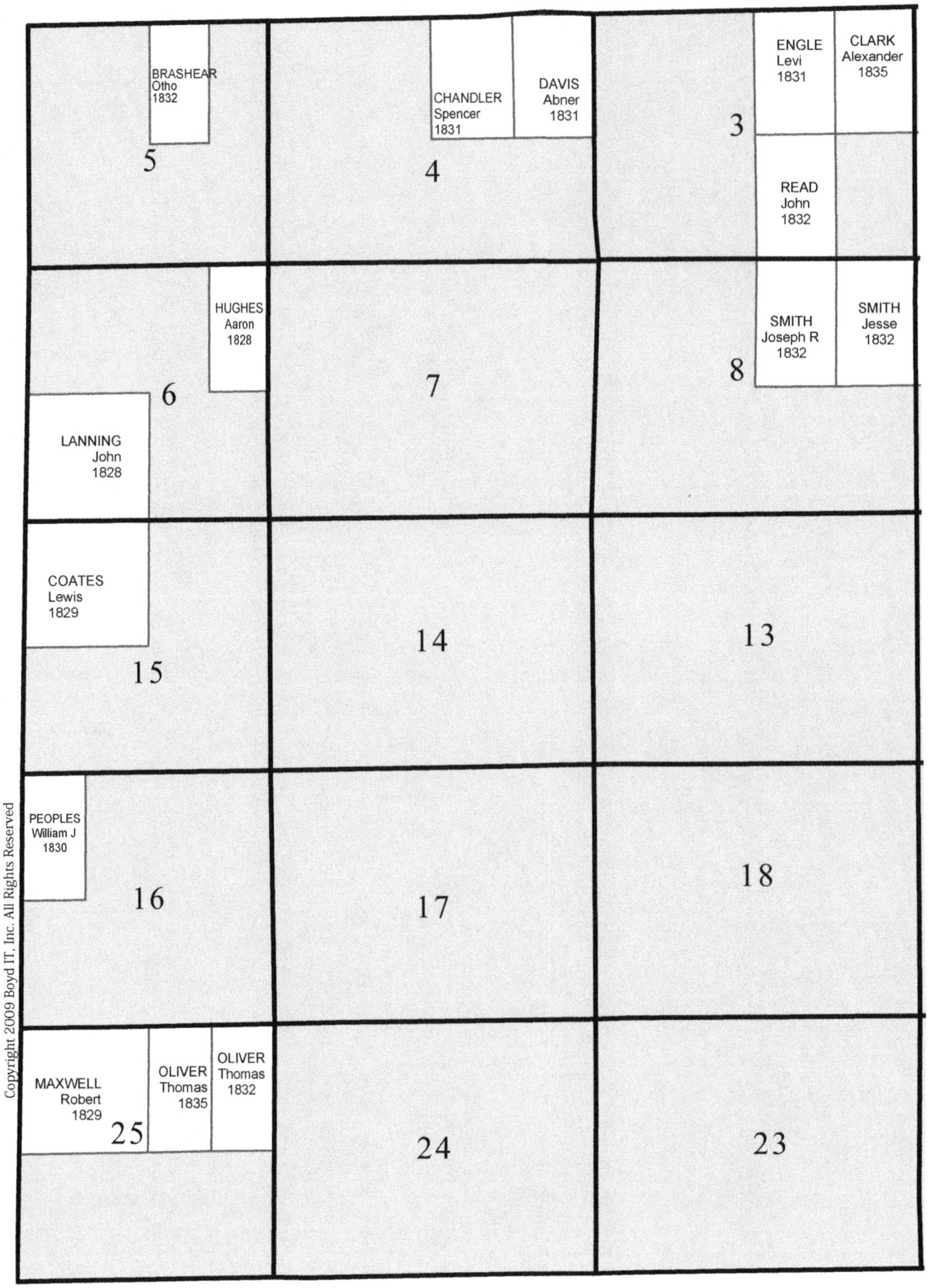

BRASHEAR
Otho
1832

5

CHANDLER
Spencer
1831

DAVIS
Abner
1831

4

3

ENGLE
Levi
1831

CLARK
Alexander
1835

READ
John
1832

HUGHES
Aaron
1828

6

7

8

SMITH
Joseph R
1832

SMITH
Jesse
1832

LANNING
John
1828

COATES
Lewis
1829

15

14

13

PEOPLES
William J
1830

16

17

18

MAXWELL
Robert
1829

25

OLIVER
Thomas
1835

OLIVER
Thomas
1832

24

23

2 SMITH William 1835	**1**
SCHOOLEY Joseph 1830 SPICER Joseph 1835 SMITH Aaron 1835 POWEL Abel 1827	
9 MOORE Peter 1826 GRIFFITH William 1832	**10**
12	**11**
19	**20** BOYD Samuel 1825 MCKINNEY Samuel F 1832
22 LOGAN Edward 1826 BELL Robert 1831	**21** BROWN John 1821 REED Robert 1827 BELL Robert 1835 SHIPLEY Amon 1832 LOGAN James 1826

Helpful Hints

1. This Map's INDEX can be found on the preceding pages.

2. Refer to Map "C" to see where this Township lies within Guernsey County, Ohio.

3. Numbers within square brackets [ ] denote a multi-patentee land parcel (multi-owner). Refer to Appendix "C" for a full list of members in this group.

4. Areas that look to be crowded with Patentees usually indicate multiple sales of the same parcel (Re-issues) or Overlapping parcels. See this Township's Index for an explanation of these and other circumstances that might explain "odd" groupings of Patentees on this map.

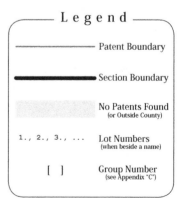

Legend

————————	Patent Boundary
▬▬▬▬▬▬▬▬	Section Boundary
▨▨▨▨▨	No Patents Found (or Outside County)
1., 2., 3., ...	Lot Numbers (when beside a name)
[ ]	Group Number (see Appendix "C")

Scale: Section = 1 mile X 1 mile
(generally, with some exceptions)

Road Map

T4-N R1-W
U.S. Military Survey Meridian

Map Group 4

Cities & Towns
None

Cemeteries
Chestnut Hill United Brethren
  Cemetery
Darby Cemetery
Engle Cemetery
George Cemetery
Pleasant Hill Methodist
  Protestant Cemetery

Newton Rd

Roby Rd

Speck Rd

3

✝ Engle Cem.

4

5

Seldom Seen Ln

Moccasin Rd

✝ George Cem.

Readman Rd SE

6

7

8

Sligo Rd

Martha Rd

15

14

Hines Rd

Watkins Ln

13

Detour

✝ Darby Cem.

16

Turkey Run Rd

Tanglewood Ln

17

18

Jeffers Ln

Daggs Ln

Hickory Hollow Rd

Grapevine Rd

25

Tattle Rd

24

Acorn Rd

23

Sugartree Rd

Tuttle Rd

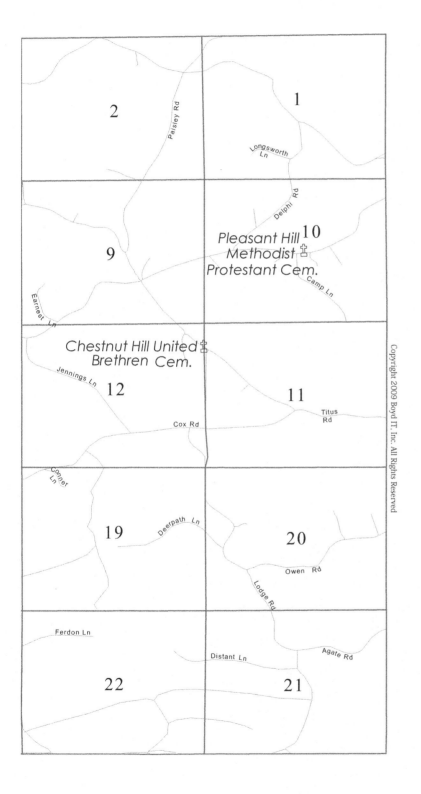

2

1

Paisley Rd

Longsworth Ln

Delphi Rd

Pleasant Hill 10
Methodist ☥
Protestant Cem.

9

Camp Ln

Earnest Ln

Chestnut Hill United ☥
Brethren Cem.

Jennings Ln 12

11

Cox Rd

Titus Rd

Comet Ln

Deerpath Ln

19

20

Owen Rd

Lodge Rd

Ferdon Ln

Distant Ln

Agate Rd

22

21

Helpful Hints

1. This road map has a number of uses, but primarily it is to help you: a) find the present location of land owned by your ancestors (at least the general area), b) find cemeteries and city-centers, and c) estimate the route/roads used by Census-takers & tax-assessors.

2. If you plan to travel to Guernsey County to locate cemeteries or land parcels, please pick up a modern travel map for the area before you do. Mapping old land parcels on modern maps is not as exact a science as you might think. Just the slightest variations in public land survey coordinates, estimates of parcel boundaries, or road-map deviations can greatly alter a map's representation of how a road either does or doesn't cross a particular parcel of land.

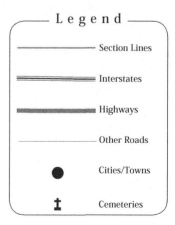

L e g e n d

———————— Section Lines

━━━━━━━━ Interstates

━━━━━━━━ Highways

———————— Other Roads

● Cities/Towns

☥ Cemeteries

Scale: Section = 1 mile X 1 mile
(generally, with some exceptions)

Historical Map

T4-N R1-W
U.S. Military Survey Meridian

Map Group 4

Cities & Towns
None

Cemeteries
Chestnut Hill United Brethren
  Cemetery
Darby Cemetery
Engle Cemetery
George Cemetery
Pleasant Hill Methodist
  Protestant Cemetery

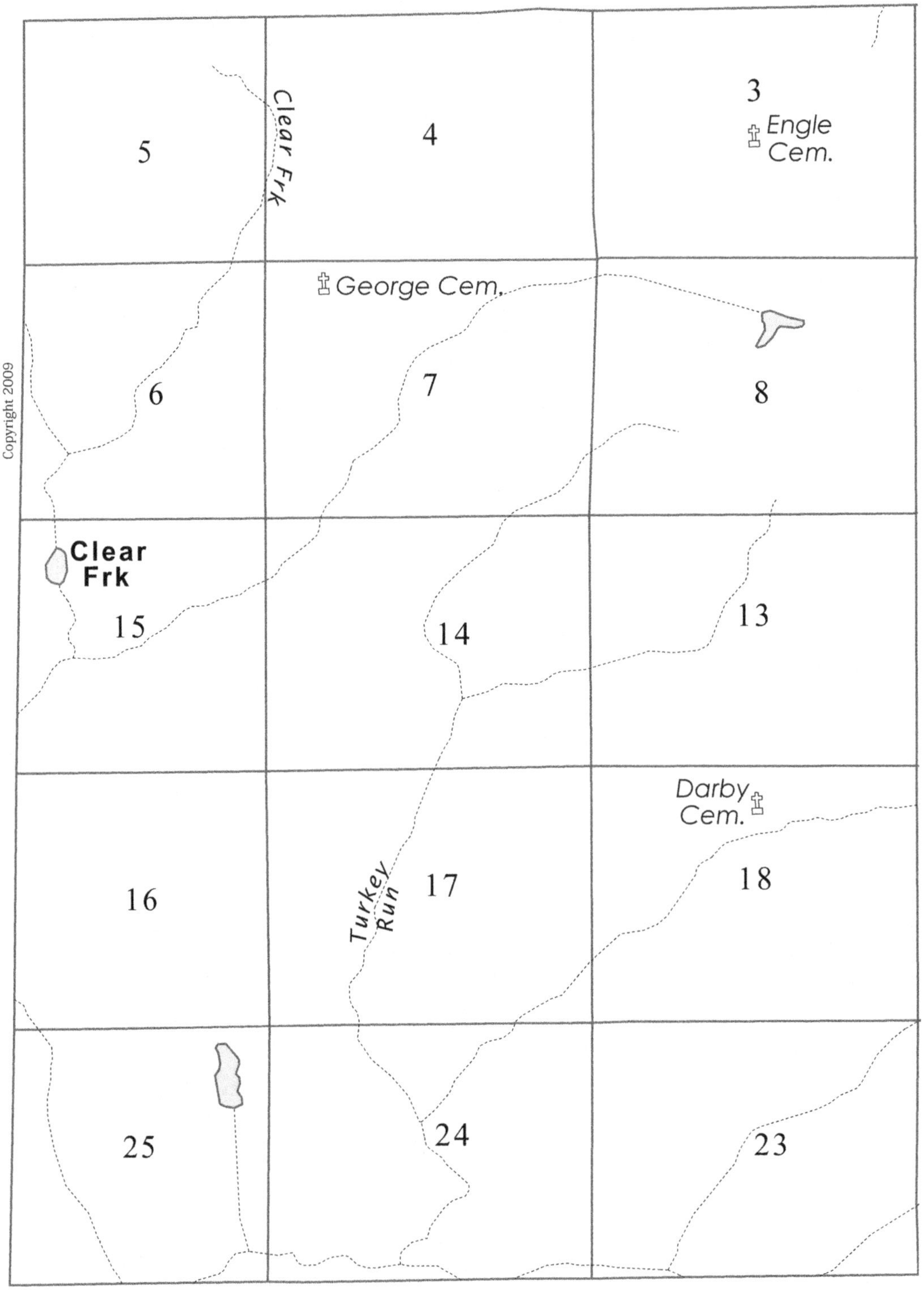

Copyright 2009

5	*Clear Frk* / 4	3 / Engle Cem.
6	George Cem. / 7	8
Clear Frk / 15	14	13
16	Turkey Run / 17	Darby Cem. / 18
25	24	23

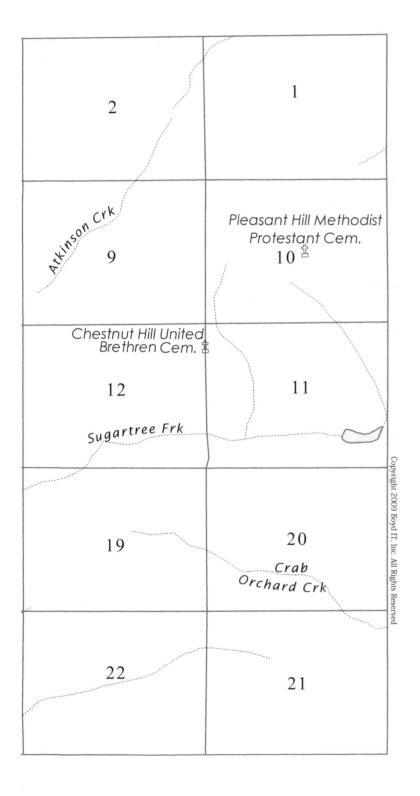

Helpful Hints

1. This Map takes a different look at the same Congressional Township displayed in the preceding two maps. It presents features that can help you better envision the historical development of the area: a) Water-bodies (lakes & ponds), b) Water-courses (rivers, streams, etc.), c) Railroads, d) City/town center-points (where they were oftentimes located when first settled), and e) Cemeteries.

2. Using this "Historical" map in tandem with this Township's Patent Map and Road Map, may lead you to some interesting discoveries. You will often find roads, towns, cemeteries, and waterways are named after nearby landowners: sometimes those names will be the ones you are researching. See how many of these research gems you can find here in Guernsey County.

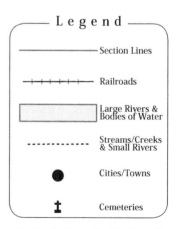

Scale: Section = 1 mile X 1 mile
(there are some exceptions)

Map Group 5: Index to Land Patents

Township 11-North Range 7-West (Ohio River Survey)

After you locate an individual in this Index, take note of the Section and Section Part then proceed to the Land Patent map on the pages immediately following. You should have no difficulty locating the corresponding parcel of land.

The "For More Info" Column will lead you to more information about the underlying Patents. See the *Legend* at right, and the "How to Use this Book" chapter, for more information.

```
                          LEGEND
              "For More Info . . . " column
A = Authority (Legislative Act, See Appendix "A")
B = Block or Lot (location in Section unknown)
C = Cancelled Patent
F = Fractional Section
G = Group  (Multi-Patentee Patent, see Appendix "C")
V = Overlaps another Parcel
R = Re-Issued (Parcel patented more than once)

(A & G items require you to look in the Appendixes referred
to above. All other Letter-designations followed by a number
require you to locate line-items in this index that possess
the ID number found after the letter).
```

ID	Individual in Patent	Sec.	Sec. Part	Date Issued	Other Counties	For More Info . . .
599	BAXTER, Robert	15	E½NW	1826-05-30		A1
598	BOONE, Richard	20	W½SW	1826-05-20		A1
597	" "	13	W½NW	1826-10-06		A1
587	BROWN, John	13	E½NW	1821-10-02		A1
606	BURNSIDE, William	15	W½NW	1823-09-10		A1
607	" "	21	E½NE	1823-09-10		A1
589	CARPENTER, John	27	SW	1966-09-19		A1
582	COOPER, Caleb	15	SE	1826-05-30		A1
596	COX, Noah	32	W½SW	1821-10-02		A1
601	DRYDEN, Samuel	15	E½SW	1824-05-06		A1
602	" "	15	W½SW	1826-05-30		A1
584	DUNCAN, James	15	W½NE	1824-05-06		A1
595	HAMILTON, Joseph	13	W½NE	1826-06-23		A1
588	HANNAH, John C	21	SE	1823-09-01		A1
608	HIBBS, William	15	E½NE	1829-04-02		A1
585	HUTCHINSON, James	21	E½SW	1830-11-01		A1
586	" "	21	W½SW	1830-11-01		A1
590	LOGAN, John	21	W½NW	1825-08-10		A1
609	LOGAN, William	32	NW	1825-08-10		A1
600	MADDIN, Robert	32	E½SW	1827-12-10		A1
583	MCCOMB, Hugh	8	W½SW	1826-05-20		A1
591	MCELROY, John	13	E½SW	1830-12-01		A1
603	MCKINNIE, Samuel F	27	W½SE	1830-12-01		A1
604	NICKEL, Thomas	21	W½NE	1823-09-10		A1
592	STOCKDALE, John	31	E½NE	1828-06-12		A1
594	THOMAS, Jonathan	21	E½NW	1824-10-20		A1
593	WILKIN, John	13	W½SW	1826-05-20		A1
605	WILKIN, Thomas	14	E½SE	1827-08-10		A1

Township Statistics

Parcels Mapped	:	28
Number of Patents	:	28
Number of Individuals	:	24
Patentees Identified	:	24
Number of Surnames	:	22
Multi-Patentee Parcels	:	0
Oldest Patent Date	:	10/2/1821
Most Recent Patent	:	9/19/1966
Block/Lot Parcels	:	0
Parcels Re - Issued	:	0
Parcels that Overlap	:	0
Cities and Towns	:	2
Cemeteries	:	4

Note: the area contained in this map amounts to far less than a full Township. Therefore, its contents are completely on this single page (instead of a "normal" 2-page spread).

Legend

———— Patent Boundary

▬▬▬▬ Section Boundary

No Patents Found (or Outside County)

1., 2., 3., ... Lot Numbers (when beside a name)

[ ] Group Number (see Appendix "C")

Scale: Section = 1 mile X 1 mile (generally, with some exceptions)

Map parcels

31

32
COX Noah 1821
MADDIN Robert 1827
LOGAN William 1825
STOCKDALE John 1828

33

25

26

27
CARPENTER John 1966
MCKINNIE Samuel F 1830

19

20
BOONE Richard 1826

21
HUTCHINSON James 1830
LOGAN John 1825
HUTCHINSON Jonathan 1830
THOMAS Jonathan 1824
HUTCHINSON John C 1823
HANNAH 1823
NICKEL Thomas 1823
BURNSIDE William 1823

13
WILKIN John 1826
BOONE Richard 1826
MCELROY John 1830
BROWN John 1821
HAMILTON Joseph 1826

14
WILKIN Thomas 1827
MCCOMB Hugh 1826

15
BURNSIDE William 1823
DRYDEN Samuel 1826
BAXTER Robert 1826
DRYDEN Samuel 1824
DUNCAN James 1824
COOPER Caleb 1826
HIBBS William 1829

7

8

9

1

2

3

Road Map

T11-N R7-W
Ohio River Survey Meridian

Map Group 5

Note: the area contained in this map amounts to far less than a full Township. Therefore, its contents are completely on this single page (instead of a "normal" 2-page spread).

Cities & Towns

Londonderry
Oakgrove

Cemeteries

Quaker Cemetery
Scotch Covenanter Cemetery
Sunset View Cemetery
Yankee Point Cemetery

Legend

———— Section Lines

═══════ Interstates

━━━━━━ Highways

———— Other Roads

● Cities/Towns

† Cemeteries

Scale: Section = 1 mile X 1 mile
(generally, with some exceptions)

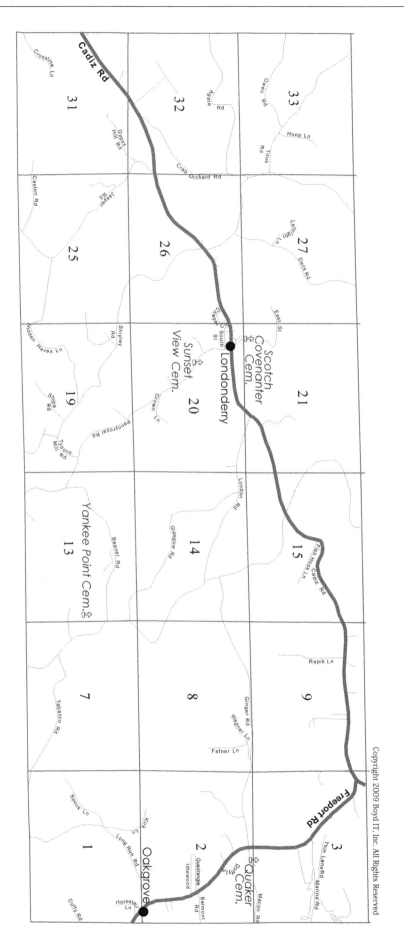

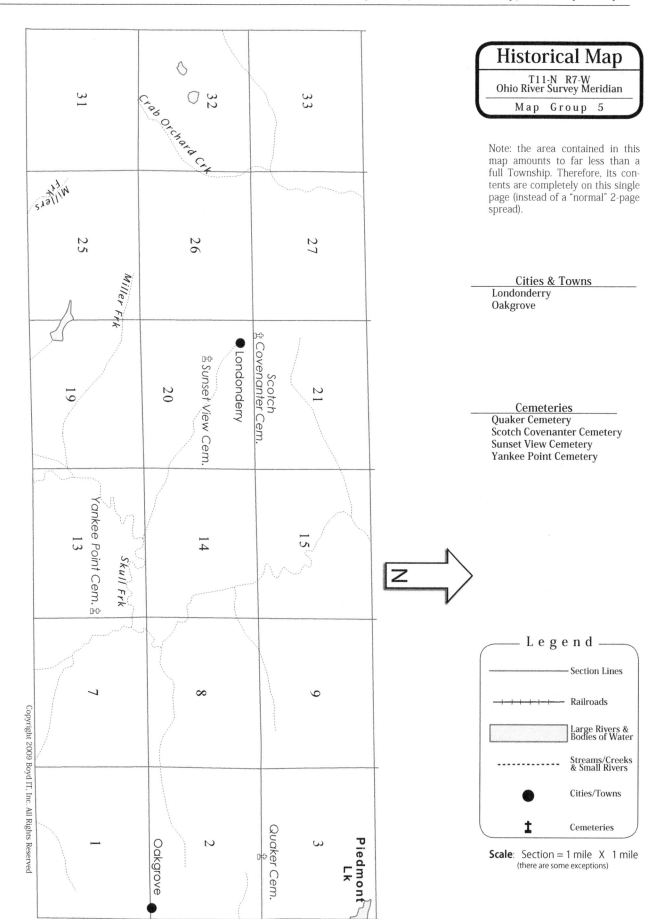

Historical Map
T11-N R7-W
Ohio River Survey Meridian
Map Group 5

Note: the area contained in this map amounts to far less than a full Township. Therefore, its contents are completely on this single page (instead of a "normal" 2-page spread).

Cities & Towns
Londonderry
Oakgrove

Cemeteries
Quaker Cemetery
Scotch Covenanter Cemetery
Sunset View Cemetery
Yankee Point Cemetery

N

Legend
——— Section Lines
+-+-+-+- Railroads
Large Rivers & Bodies of Water
- - - - - Streams/Creeks & Small Rivers
● Cities/Towns
✝ Cemeteries

Scale: Section = 1 mile X 1 mile
(there are some exceptions)

Map Group 6: Index to Land Patents

Township 3-North Range 4-West (U.S. Military Survey)

After you locate an individual in this Index, take note of the Section and Section Part then proceed to the Land Patent map on the pages immediately following. You should have no difficulty locating the corresponding parcel of land.

The "For More Info" Column will lead you to more information about the underlying Patents. See the *Legend* at right, and the "How to Use this Book" chapter, for more information.

```
                    LEGEND
        "For More Info . . . " column
A = Authority (Legislative Act, See Appendix "A")
B = Block or Lot (location in Section unknown)
C = Cancelled Patent
F = Fractional Section
G = Group (Multi-Patentee Patent, see Appendix "C")
V = Overlaps another Parcel
R = Re-Issued (Parcel patented more than once)

(A & G items require you to look in the Appendixes referred
to above. All other Letter-designations followed by a number
require you to locate line-items in this index that possess
the ID number found after the letter).
```

ID	Individual in Patent	Sec.	Sec. Part	Date Issued	Other Counties	For More Info . . .
647	ACHESON, David R	25	SENW	1835-09-08		A1
684	ACHESON, James	25	SENE	1835-09-08		A1
716	ACHESON, John	18	E½SW	1832-04-02		A1
717	" "	25	NWNW	1835-09-30		A1
718	" "	5	NESW	1837-04-10		A1
719	" "	5	SESW	1837-11-07		A1
770	ACHESON, John R	5	NWSE	1840-10-10		A1 G79
771	" "	5	SWSE	1840-10-10		A1 G79
796	ACHESON, Robert	5	SENW	1837-04-10		A1
797	" "	5	SWNE	1837-04-10		A1 R639
648	ATCHESON, David R	25	W½NE	1835-04-02		A1
642	ATCHISON, David	4	SWNW	1837-08-15		A1
643	" "	5	SENE	1837-08-15		A1
798	ATKINSON, Robert	2	NENE	1837-11-07		A1
685	ATKISON, James	8	NWSW	1842-08-01		A1
618	ATTWOOD, Cornelius	8	SESW	1840-10-10		A1 G24
628	ATWOOD, Cornelius	13	NENW	1838-09-01		A1
830	BLISS, Washington	13	S½NE	1840-11-10		A1
803	BOGLE, Samuel	20	E½SE	1826-06-16		A1
804	" "	20	W½SE	1827-12-20		A1
721	BOYD, John	22	SW	1825-03-10		A1
668	BROOM, Hugh	8	NENE	1837-11-07		A1
620	BROWN, John	3	SENE	1837-04-10		A1 G25
722	" "	3	NENE	1837-08-05		A1
639	BRUSH, Daniel	5	SWNE	1835-09-14		A1 G9 R797
637	" "	9	SWSW	1835-09-14		A1 G20
638	" "	2	SESW	1837-08-05		A1 G14
630	" "	2	SENE	1838-09-01		A1
641	" "	9	SENW	1838-09-01		A1 G18
640	" "	8	NWSE	1840-10-10		A1 G10
634	" "	4	N½NW	1842-08-01		A1
629	" "	19	SWSW	1844-07-10		A1
631	" "	3	NENW	1844-07-10		A1
632	" "	3	NWNE	1844-07-10		A1
633	" "	3	W½NW	1844-07-10		A1
635	" "	4	S½NE	1844-07-10		A1
636	" "	6	E½SW	1844-07-10		A1
723	BUCHANAN, John	25	NENE	1837-04-10		A1
724	" "	25	NENW	1837-04-10		A1
725	" "	25	SWNW	1837-04-10		A1
726	" "	5	N½NE	1840-10-10		A1
621	BUCKINGHAM, Alvah	19	SESE	1835-10-05		A1 G26
622	" "	13	NESE	1837-04-10		A1 G27
617	" "	2	SENW	1837-04-10		A1
620	" "	3	SENE	1837-04-10		A1 G25
619	" "	7	SWNW	1837-08-10		A1 G30

ID	Individual in Patent	Sec.	Sec. Part	Date Issued	Other Counties	For More Info . . .
618	BUCKINGHAM, Alvah (Cont'd)	8	SESW	1840-10-10		A1 G24
727	CAMPBELL, John	4	NWSE	1844-08-01		A1
832	CAMPBELL, William	5	NWNW	1844-08-01		A1
728	CLARK, John	13	E½SW	1823-08-20		A1
816	" "	13	NWSE	1835-09-08		A1 G97
817	" "	13	NWSW	1835-09-08		A1 G97
833	CLARK, William	12	SWNW	1835-04-21		A1
834	COCHRAN, William	21	E½SE	1821-09-08		A1
835	COCKRAN, William	21	NWSE	1835-09-23		A1
799	COOK, Robert	1	SWSE	1840-11-10		A1
792	CORBET, Peter	19	SWSE	1837-08-15		A1
793	" "	22	NWSE	1837-08-15		A1
836	CORNELIUS, William	14	SESW	1844-07-10		A1
686	COULTER, James	16	NESE	1837-11-07		A1
688	" "	17	W½SW	1837-11-07		A1
687	" "	17	SESW	1840-10-10		A1
627	COWEL, Christopher	14	NENW	1840-11-10		A1
838	CREIGHTON, William	7	E½SE	1826-10-02		A1
837	" "	4	E½SE	1831-02-10		A1
839	CULBERTSON, William	23	W½NW	1825-03-10		A1
689	CULLEN, James	20	E½SW	1828-01-30		A1
690	" "	20	W½SW	1831-02-10		A1
621	CULLEN, William	19	SESE	1835-10-05		A1 G26
625	DAVIS, Benjamin	11	E½SW	1844-07-10		A1 G35
626	" "	20	NWNE	1844-07-10		A1 G35
678	DAVIS, Jabez	19	NESE	1840-11-10		A1
679	" "	19	SESW	1840-11-10		A1
729	DAVIS, John	10	NWNE	1844-07-10		A1
730	" "	10	SENW	1844-07-10		A1
644	DEW, David	4	SWSE	1837-08-15		A1
739	" "	7	NWNE	1840-11-10		A1 G43
819	DISALLUMS, John	12	E½NW	1835-09-08		A1 G36
731	" "	12	NWNW	1835-09-23		A1
732	" "	9	SESW	1840-10-10		A1
819	DISALLUMS, Thomas	12	E½NW	1835-09-08		A1 G36
613	DUFF, Alexander	7	W½SE	1835-10-05		A1
612	" "	13	NWNW	1837-08-15		A1
831	" "	14	NENE	1840-10-10		A1 G47
623	DUFF, Andrew	3	SWSW	1835-04-30		A1
624	" "	7	NENE	1837-08-15		A1
740	DUFF, David	7	SWNE	1840-11-10		A1 G44
650	DUFF, George	17	SWSE	1838-09-01		A1
639	DUFF, James	5	SWNE	1835-09-14		A1 G9 R797
691	" "	6	SWNE	1835-09-30		A1
734	DUFF, John	18	E½NE	1832-04-02		A1
735	" "	7	NWSW	1835-09-14		A1
733	" "	17	NWNE	1837-08-15		A1
787	DUFF, Oliver	18	W½SW	1828-05-30		A1
786	" "	18	SWNW	1837-08-15		A1
788	DUFF, Oliver E	8	NENW	1837-08-10		A1
789	" "	8	NWNW	1840-11-10		A1
818	DUFF, Robert	3	SWNE	1835-09-08		A1 G99
800	" "	8	SWSW	1837-04-10		A1
840	DUFF, William	24	W½NE	1832-04-02		A1
651	ECKELBERY, George	4	N½SE	1838-09-01		A1
822	EVANS, David	7	SENE	1844-07-10		A1 G58
823	" "	8	SWNW	1844-07-10		A1 G58
682	FERBRACHE, Jacob N	12	NESW	1837-08-10		A1
683	" "	12	W½SW	1837-08-10		A1
754	FERBRACHE, John S	8	NWNE	1840-10-10		A1
756	" "	9	NWSW	1840-10-10		A1
757	" "	9	W½NW	1840-10-10		A1
755	" "	8	SENE	1840-11-10		A1
758	" "	9	NESW	1840-11-10		A1 G37
820	FERBRACHE, Thomas	20	W½NW	1838-09-01		A1
692	FERGUSON, James	18	E½SE	1823-08-20		A1
640	FORREST, Thomas S	8	NWSE	1840-10-10		A1 G10
736	FORSYTHE, John	24	E½SW	1831-02-10		A1
737	" "	24	W½SW	1831-02-10		A1
821	FORSYTHE, Thomas	24	S½NW	1835-09-30		A1
773	FOSTER, Jonathan	8	NESW	1840-11-10		A1
670	GALAGHER, Hugh	21	SWSE	1837-04-10		A1
669	" "	21	NENE	1837-08-05		A1

ID	Individual in Patent	Sec.	Sec. Part	Date Issued	Other Counties	For More Info . . .
794	GANT, Richard	20	E½NE	1837-08-15		A1
795	" "	20	SWNE	1838-09-01		A1
674	HALE, Isaiah B	9	NENW	1840-12-31		A1 G42
738	HALL, John	21	NENW	1837-08-15		A1
739	" "	7	NWNE	1840-11-10		A1 G43
740	" "	7	SWNE	1840-11-10		A1 G44
841	HALL, William	10	E½SW	1844-07-10		A1
622	HAMILTON, William	13	NESE	1837-04-10		A1 G27
663	HART, Howard	13	S½NW	1840-10-10		A1
831	HAWES, Welles	14	NENE	1840-10-10		A1 G47
693	HAWTHORN, James	16	W½SE	1830-12-01		A1
744	HAWTHORN, John M	16	NESW	1837-04-10		A1
746	" "	16	SESW	1838-09-01		A1
745	" "	16	SESE	1844-07-10		A1
610	HEDGE, Aaron	1	NESE	1837-04-10		A1
676	HEDGE, Israel	1	NWSW	1837-04-10		A1
677	" "	1	SWNW	1837-04-10		A1
675	" "	1	E½NW	1837-08-15		A1
776	HEDGE, Joseph	1	NESW	1837-04-10		A1
741	HELLYER, John	11	SENE	1844-07-10		A1
842	HELLYER, William	8	SWSE	1844-07-10		A1
829	HILLARD, Thurston	4	39	1805-01-10		A2
694	HOLCOMB, James	15	NENW	1844-07-10		A1
695	" "	15	W½NW	1844-07-10		A1
661	JACKSON, Hosea	10	NWSW	1844-07-10		A1
662	" "	11	W½NW	1844-07-10		A1
649	JONES, Enoch	22	E½NE	1827-06-01		A1
671	JONES, Hugh	2	SWNW	1835-09-08		A1
696	JONES, James	8	SENW	1835-09-08		A1
809	JONES, Sarah	10	SWNE	1852-07-01		A1
805	KELL, Samuel	14	SWSW	1844-07-10		A1 G51
806	" "	15	S½SW	1844-07-10		A1 G51
783	KILBRIDE, Michael	7	SENW	1844-07-10		A1
681	LAWRENCE, Jacob	2	W½SE	1832-07-02		A1
638	" "	2	SESW	1837-08-05		A1 G14
680	" "	2	SESE	1837-08-10		A1
807	LEE, Samuel	24	W½SE	1832-04-02		A1
825	LEECH, Thomas	15	NESW	1844-07-10		A1 G61
822	" "	7	SENE	1844-07-10		A1 G58
824	" "	8	SWNE	1844-07-10		A1 G60
823	" "	8	SWNW	1844-07-10		A1 G58
779	LENT, Ludlow	13	NENE	1835-10-05		A1
697	LINCH, James	14	NWNW	1837-04-10		A1
742	LINDSEY, John	18	NWNW	1840-10-10		A1
826	LUCK, Thomas	6	W½NW	1844-07-10		A1 G62
743	LYNCH, John	14	SWNW	1835-09-08		A1
698	LYONS, James	22	E½SE	1830-12-01		A1
616	MALOY, Alford	6	SENE	1844-07-10		A1
699	MALOY, James	5	NENW	1844-07-10		A1
700	" "	5	SWNW	1844-07-10		A1
843	MALOY, William	6	SWSW	1844-07-10		A1
654	MANYPENNY, George W	2	NWNW	1838-09-01		A1
673	MAPLE, Isaac	21	W½NW	1830-12-01		A1
672	" "	21	SENW	1835-09-08		A1
701	MARKEE, James	10	NENW	1844-07-10		A1
702	MCCONKEY, James	17	SENW	1840-11-10		A1
703	" "	17	SWNE	1840-11-10		A1
780	MCCULLEY, Mathew	14	NWSW	1835-09-14		A1
781	" "	14	SENW	1835-09-14		A1
847	MCDONALD, William	7	SWSW	1837-04-10		A1
844	" "	15	NWNE	1838-09-01		A1
846	" "	6	SENW	1838-09-01		A1
845	" "	6	NWSW	1850-08-10		A1
805	MCDOWELL, Ephraim	14	SWSW	1844-07-10		A1 G51
806	" "	15	S½SW	1844-07-10		A1 G51
777	MCELHEREN, Joseph	11	W½SW	1838-09-01		A1
653	MCGOWAN, George	3	W½SE	1838-09-01		A1
652	" "	3	NESE	1840-10-10		A1
791	MCGUIRE, Patrick	21	W½NE	1837-08-15		A1
790	" "	21	SENE	1838-09-01		A1
747	MCMULLEN, John	21	E½SW	1823-08-20		A1
749	" "	21	SWSW	1837-04-10		A1
748	" "	21	NWSW	1838-09-01		A1

ID	Individual in Patent	Sec.	Sec. Part	Date Issued	Other Counties	For More Info . . .
750	MESKIMEN, John	1	NWNW	1838-09-01		A1
720	MILLER, John B	10	NENE	1840-10-10		A1
784	MISKIMIN, Nelson	2	NENW	1835-09-08		A1
785	" "	2	NWNE	1835-09-08		A1
611	MISKIMINS, Abraham F	2	SWNE	1837-08-02		A1
704	MISKIMINS, James	2	NWSW	1838-09-01		A1
614	MORRISON, Alexander	2	SWSW	1842-08-01		A1
615	" "	3	SESE	1842-08-01		A1
646	MORROW, David	17	SWNW	1837-04-10		A1
705	MORROW, James	15	NWSW	1837-04-10		A1
706	" "	16	W½SW	1844-07-10		A1
851	MORROW, William	18	E½NW	1832-04-02		A1
848	" "	14	NESW	1835-09-14		A1
850	" "	17	NENE	1838-09-01		A1
849	" "	14	SENE	1840-10-10		A1
824	ORR, John	8	SWNE	1844-07-10		A1 G60
752	PATRICK, John	13	NWNE	1835-04-21		A1
751	" "	12	SESW	1837-08-10		A1
707	RANKIN, James	7	NESW	1835-10-05		A1
708	" "	7	SESW	1837-04-10		A1
619	" "	7	SWNW	1837-08-10		A1 G30
641	REED, William	9	SENW	1838-09-01		A1 G18
826	RIGDEN, John F	6	W½NW	1844-07-10		A1 G62
753	ROBERTSON, John	11	SE	1829-05-01		A1
758	ROBERTSON, Joseph	9	NESW	1840-11-10		A1 G37
709	RUTLEDGE, James	18	W½SE	1825-08-06		A1
827	RUTLEDGE, Thomas	22	W½NW	1827-10-20		A1
808	SCOTT, Samuel	24	N½NW	1837-08-10		A1
852	SCOTT, William	17	E½SE	1830-12-01		A1
655	SHERAR, George W	4	SENW	1840-10-10		A1
760	SIMMERMAN, John	1	SWSW	1840-10-10		A1
710	SNODGRASS, James	6	NENW	1840-11-10		A1
625	SOLINGER, James	11	E½SW	1844-07-10		A1 G35
626	" "	20	NWNE	1844-07-10		A1 G35
775	SPRAGUE, Jonathan	6	NWNE	1837-04-10		A1
774	" "	5	NWSW	1840-11-10		A1
766	STANBERRY, Jonas	18	W½NE	1832-04-02		A1
667	STANBERY, Howard	8	E½SE	1837-08-15		A1
666	" "	2	NESE	1842-08-01		A1
664	" "	13	S½SE	1844-07-10		A1
665	" "	17	NENW	1844-07-10		A1
772	STANBERY, Jonas	3	SENW	1835-04-21		A1 G94
768	" "	14	W½NE	1840-10-10		A1
769	" "	3	NWSW	1840-10-10		A1
770	" "	5	NWSE	1840-10-10		A1 G79
771	" "	5	SWSW	1840-10-10		A1 G79
767	" "	11	NENE	1844-07-10		A1
816	STURGES, Solomon	13	NWSE	1835-09-08		A1 G97
817	" "	13	NWSW	1835-09-08		A1 G97
818	" "	3	SWNE	1835-09-08		A1 G99
810	" "	1	NWSE	1842-08-01		A1
811	" "	1	SESE	1842-08-01		A1
812	" "	13	SWSW	1844-07-10		A1
813	" "	17	NESW	1844-07-10		A1
814	" "	17	NWSE	1844-07-10		A1
815	" "	17	SENE	1844-07-10		A1
782	TRACE, Matthias	17	NWNW	1837-04-10		A1
656	TRUSLER, Elias	4	SW	1840-11-10		A1 G110
657	" "	5	E½SE	1840-11-10		A1 G110
658	" "	6	NENE	1840-11-10		A1 G110
659	" "	7	NENW	1840-11-10		A1 G110
660	" "	7	NWNW	1840-11-10		A1 G111
656	TRUSLER, Goodhart	4	SW	1840-11-10		A1 G110
657	" "	5	E½SE	1840-11-10		A1 G110
658	" "	6	NENE	1840-11-10		A1 G110
659	" "	7	NENW	1840-11-10		A1 G110
660	" "	7	NWNW	1840-11-10		A1 G111
761	VOORHES, John	22	SWSE	1835-10-05		A1
801	VOORHES, Robert	19	NESW	1838-09-01		A1
714	WAGSTAFF, James	11	W½NE	1826-06-06		A1
712	" "	11	NENW	1835-04-21		A1
711	" "	10	SWSW	1837-04-10		A1
713	" "	11	SENW	1842-08-01		A1

ID	Individual in Patent	Sec.	Sec. Part	Date Issued	Other Counties	For More Info . . .
762	WAGSTAFF, John	20	E½NW	1830-12-01		A1
802	WAGSTAFF, Robert	10	SENE	1837-08-15		A1
645	WARDEN, David M	22	E½NW	1829-06-01		A1 G113
645	WARDEN, Jane	22	E½NW	1829-06-01		A1 G113
759	WARDEN, John S	23	E½NW	1838-09-01		A1
674	WATERS, John	9	NENW	1840-12-31		A1 G42
825	WEIR, Joseph	15	NESW	1844-07-10		A1 G61
778	" "	15	SENW	1844-07-10		A1
828	WEIR, Thomas	3	E½SW	1831-03-01		A1
772	" "	3	SENW	1835-04-21		A1 G94
853	WIER, William	15	E½NE	1824-04-17		A1
854	" "	15	SWNE	1837-04-10		A1
637	WILSON, Edward	9	SWSW	1835-09-14		A1 G20
715	WILSON, James	1	SESW	1840-11-10		A1
656	WISCARVER, Joseph	4	SW	1840-11-10		A1 G110
657	" "	5	E½SE	1840-11-10		A1 G110
658	" "	6	NENE	1840-11-10		A1 G110
659	" "	7	NENW	1840-11-10		A1 G110
660	WISCORVER, Joseph	7	NWNW	1840-11-10		A1 G111
855	YOUNG, William	24	E½NE	1825-08-06		A1
765	ZIMMERMAN, John	19	NWSE	1840-10-10		A1
763	" "	10	NWNW	1844-07-10		A1
764	" "	10	SWNW	1844-07-10		A1

Patent Map

T3-N R4-W
U.S. Military Survey Meridian

Map Group 6

Township Statistics

Parcels Mapped	:	246
Number of Patents	:	240
Number of Individuals	:	157
Patentees Identified	:	158
Number of Surnames	:	110
Multi-Patentee Parcels	:	37
Oldest Patent Date	:	1/10/1805
Most Recent Patent	:	7/1/1852
Block/Lot Parcels	:	1
Parcels Re - Issued	:	1
Parcels that Overlap	:	0
Cities and Towns	:	4
Cemeteries	:	6

MANYPENNY George W 1838	MISKIMIN Nelson 1835	MISKIMIN Nelson 1835	ATKINSON Robert 1837	MESKIMEN John 1838	HEDGE Israel 1837
JONES Hugh 1835	BUCKINGHAM Alvah 1837	MISKIMINS Abraham F 1837	BRUSH Daniel 1838	HEDGE Israel 1837	**1**

Section 2

MISKIMINS James 1838	**2**	STANBERY Howard 1842
MORRISON Alexander 1842	BRUSH [14] Daniel 1837	LAWRENCE Jacob 1832 LAWRENCE Jacob 1837

Section 1

HEDGE Israel 1837	HEDGE Joseph 1837	STURGES Solomon 1842	HEDGE Aaron 1837
SIMMERMAN John 1840	WILSON James 1840	COOK Robert 1840	STURGES Solomon 1842

Section 9

FERBRACHE John S 1840	HALE [42] Isaiah B 1840
	BRUSH [18] Daniel 1838
FERBRACHE John S 1840	FERBRACHE [37] John S 1840
BRUSH [20] Daniel 1835	DISALLUMS John 1840

Section 10

ZIMMERMAN John 1844	MARKEE James 1844	DAVIS John 1844	MILLER John B 1840
ZIMMERMAN John 1844	DAVIS John 1844	JONES Sarah 1852	WAGSTAFF Robert 1837
JACKSON Hosea 1844	HALL William 1844	**10**	
WAGSTAFF James 1837			

Section 12

DISALLUMS John 1835	DISALLUMS [36] Thomas 1835
CLARK William 1835	**12**
FERBRACHE Jacob N 1837	FERBRACHE Jacob N 1837
	PATRICK John 1837

Section 11

JACKSON Hosea 1844	WAGSTAFF James 1835	WAGSTAFF James 1826	STANBERY Jonas 1844
	WAGSTAFF James 1842		HELLYER John 1844
MCELHEREN Joseph 1838	DAVIS [35] Benjamin 1844	**11** ROBERTSON John 1829	

Section 19

	19		
	VOORHES Robert 1838	ZIMMERMAN John 1840	DAVIS Jabez 1840
BRUSH Daniel 1844	DAVIS Jabez 1840	CORBET Peter 1837	BUCKINGHAM [26] Alvah 1835

Section 20

		DAVIS [35] Benjamin 1844	GANT Richard 1837
FERBRACHE Thomas 1838	WAGSTAFF John 1830	GANT Richard 1838	
	20		
CULLEN James 1831	CULLEN James 1828	BOGLE Samuel 1827	BOGLE Samuel 1826

Section 22

RUTLEDGE Thomas 1827	WARDEN [113] David M 1829	JONES Enoch 1827	
	22		
BOYD John 1825	CORBET Peter 1837	LYONS James 1830	
	VOORHES John 1835		

Section 21

	HALL John 1837	MCGUIRE Patrick 1837	GALAGHER Hugh 1837
MAPLE Isaac 1830	MAPLE Isaac 1835		MCGUIRE Patrick 1838
MCMULLEN John 1838	MCMULLEN John 1823	COCKRAN William 1835	**21**
MCMULLEN John 1837		GALAGHER Hugh 1837	COCHRAN William 1821

Copyright 2009 Boyd IT, Inc. All Rights Reserved

Helpful Hints

1. This Map's INDEX can be found on the preceding pages.

2. Refer to Map "C" to see where this Township lies within Guernsey County, Ohio.

3. Numbers within square brackets [ ] denote a multi-patentee land parcel (multi-owner). Refer to Appendix "C" for a full list of members in this group.

4. Areas that look to be crowded with Patentees usually indicate multiple sales of the same parcel (Re-issues) or Overlapping parcels. See this Township's Index for an explanation of these and other circumstances that might explain "odd" groupings of Patentees on this map.

Legend

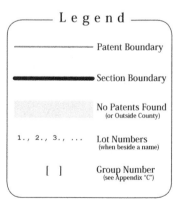

————————	Patent Boundary
▬▬▬▬▬▬▬	Section Boundary
	No Patents Found (or Outside County)
1., 2., 3., ...	Lot Numbers (when beside a name)
[ ]	Group Number (see Appendix "C")

Scale: Section = 1 mile X 1 mile
(generally, with some exceptions)

Road Map

T3-N R4-W
U.S. Military Survey Meridian

Map Group 6

Cities & Towns
Boden
Flat Ridge
Indian Camp
Mantua

Cemeteries
Flat Ridge Cemetery
Hawthorne Cemetery
Hopewell Methodist Episcopal
  Cemetery
Morrow Cemetery
Mount Herman Cemetery
Northfield Cemetery

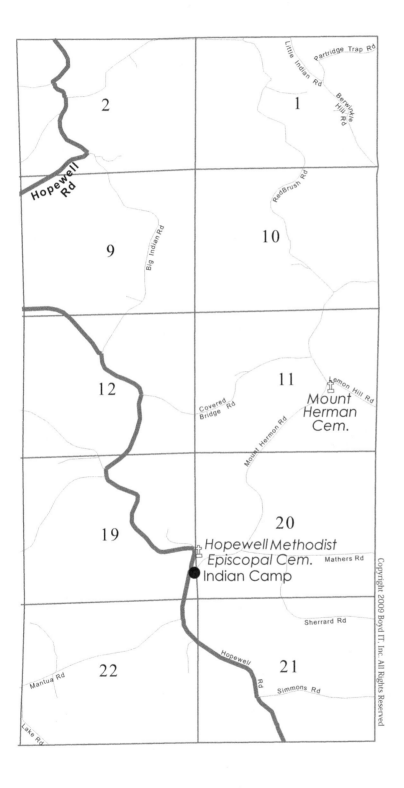

Helpful Hints

1. This road map has a number of uses, but primarily it is to help you: a) find the present location of land owned by your ancestors (at least the general area), b) find cemeteries and city-centers, and c) estimate the route/roads used by Census-takers & tax-assessors.

2. If you plan to travel to Guernsey County to locate cemeteries or land parcels, please pick up a modern travel map for the area before you do. Mapping old land parcels on modern maps is not as exact a science as you might think. Just the slightest variations in public land survey coordinates, estimates of parcel boundaries, or road-map deviations can greatly alter a map's representation of how a road either does or doesn't cross a particular parcel of land.

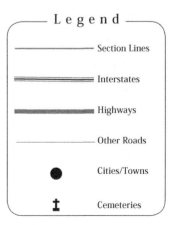

L e g e n d

——————	Section Lines
≡≡≡≡≡	Interstates
——————	Highways
————	Other Roads
●	Cities/Towns
☩	Cemeteries

Scale: Section = 1 mile X 1 mile
(generally, with some exceptions)

Historical Map

T3-N R4-W
U.S. Military Survey Meridian

Map Group 6

Cities & Towns
Boden
Flat Ridge
Indian Camp
Mantua

Cemeteries
Flat Ridge Cemetery
Hawthorne Cemetery
Hopewell Methodist Episcopal
 Cemetery
Morrow Cemetery
Mount Herman Cemetery
Northfield Cemetery

Two Mile Run

5	4	3
6	7	Flat ● 8 Ridge ⚑ *Flat Ridge Cem.*
15 Boden *Northfield Cem.* ⚑●	14	*Dry Run* 13
Hawthorne Cem. *Morrow Cem.* 16	17	18
25	*Indian Camp Run* 24	23 ● Mantua

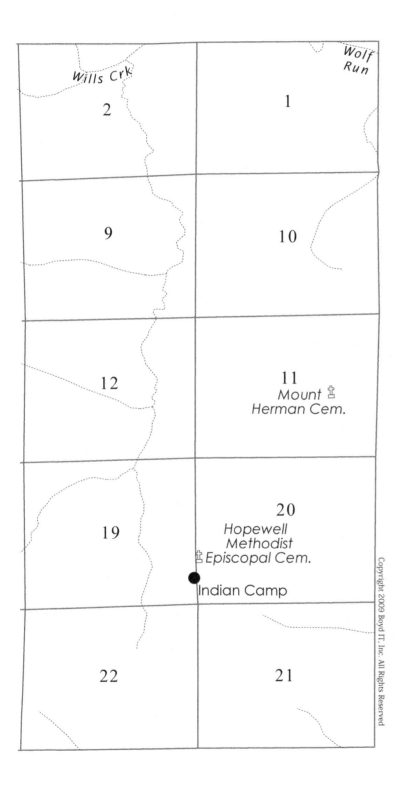

Wills Crk

Wolf Run

2

1

9

10

12

11
Mount ⚏
Herman Cem.

19

20
Hopewell
Methodist
⚏ Episcopal Cem.

Indian Camp

22

21

Helpful Hints

1. This Map takes a different look at the same Congressional Township displayed in the preceding two maps. It presents features that can help you better envision the historical development of the area: a) Water-bodies (lakes & ponds), b) Water-courses (rivers, streams, etc.), c) Railroads, d) City/ town center-points (where they were oftentimes located when first settled), and e) Cemeteries.

2. Using this "Historical" map in tandem with this Township's Patent Map and Road Map, may lead you to some interesting discoveries. You will often find roads, towns, cemeteries, and waterways are named after nearby landowners: sometimes those names will be the ones you are researching. See how many of these research gems you can find here in Guernsey County.

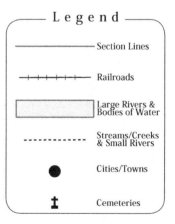

L e g e n d

——————— Section Lines

+–+–+–+–+ Railroads

Large Rivers &
Bodies of Water

- - - - - - - Streams/Creeks
& Small Rivers

● Cities/Towns

⚏ Cemeteries

Scale: Section = 1 mile X 1 mile
(there are some exceptions)

Map Group 7: Index to Land Patents

Township 3-North Range 3-West (U.S. Military Survey)

After you locate an individual in this Index, take note of the Section and Section Part then proceed to the Land Patent map on the pages immediately following. You should have no difficulty locating the corresponding parcel of land.

The "For More Info" Column will lead you to more information about the underlying Patents. See the *Legend* at right, and the "How to Use this Book" chapter, for more information.

```
                    LEGEND
        "For More Info . . . " column
A = Authority (Legislative Act, See Appendix "A")
B = Block or Lot (location in Section unknown)
C = Cancelled Patent
F = Fractional Section
G = Group  (Multi-Patentee Patent, see Appendix "C")
V = Overlaps another Parcel
R = Re-Issued (Parcel patented more than once)

(A & G items require you to look in the Appendixes referred
to above. All other Letter-designations followed by a number
require you to locate line-items in this index that possess
the ID number found after the letter).
```

ID	Individual in Patent	Sec.	Sec. Part	Date Issued	Other Counties	For More Info . . .
997	BELL, Hamilton	17	S½NW	1844-07-10		A1 G57
917	BELL, James	13	SWSE	1837-11-07		A1
960	BELL, Joseph	12	SWNE	1835-09-08		A1
959	" "	10	SWSW	1838-09-01		A1
979	BELL, Robert	14	SESW	1837-08-02		A1
994	" "	14	SESE	1837-11-07		A1 G96
980	" "	14	W½SW	1838-09-01		A1
972	BOGGS, James	19	E½NE	1823-08-20		A1 G65
936	BOGLE, John	25	E½NE	1821-09-08		A1
939	" "	25	W½SW	1825-08-06		A1
938	" "	25	SE	1828-05-30		A1
937	" "	25	NW	1831-02-10		A1
963	BOGLE, Joseph	24	E½NW	1823-08-20		A1
961	" "	16	E½SE	1825-03-10		A1
962	" "	16	W½SE	1831-02-10		A1
940	BOYLE, John	25	W½NE	1823-05-05		A1
919	BRADSHAW, James	10	SWNW	1837-11-07		A1
918	" "	10	SENW	1838-09-01		A1
942	BRITTON, John	7	NENW	1835-04-21		A1
941	" "	16	SWNW	1837-08-15		A1
871	BRUSH, Daniel	3	NENW	1835-09-14		A1 G12
870	" "	14	SWSE	1844-07-10		A1
860	BUCKINGHAM, Alvah	7	NWNE	1837-08-05		A1 G31
1001	COWAN, William	15	E½SW	1827-12-20		A1
958	" "	15	SENW	1837-08-10		A1 G81
907	CROW, Isaac	6	NWNE	1837-04-10		A1
906	" "	6	NENE	1840-10-10		A1
872	CULLY, Daniel	4	W½SW	1840-11-10		A1
873	DOUGLASS, David	3	SWNW	1835-10-05		A1
874	" "	4	NWSE	1837-04-10		A1
875	" "	5	NWNE	1837-04-10		A1
964	DOUGLASS, Joseph	10	NENW	1837-04-10		A1
876	DRAKE, David	1	NENW	1837-11-07		A1
956	" "	1	W½NE	1837-11-07		A1 G84
877	DULL, David	5	SWNE	1844-07-10		A1
1010	EVANS, David	16	N½NW	1844-07-10		A1 G109
920	FRAZIER, James	4	SESW	1837-04-10		A1
1002	FULLER, William	12	NWNE	1837-08-05		A1
943	GENTZLER, John	5	E½SW	1840-10-10		A1
944	" "	5	W½SE	1840-10-10		A1
965	GENTZLER, Joseph	6	NWNW	1840-10-10		A1
871	GIBSON, George	3	NENW	1835-09-14		A1 G12
1003	GIBSON, William	4	SWNE	1835-10-05		A1
1004	" "	4	SWNW	1837-04-10		A1
921	GILL, James	10	NWNW	1838-09-01		A1
966	GOODDE, Joseph	15	NENE	1844-07-10		A1

ID	Individual in Patent	Sec.	Sec. Part	Date Issued	Other Counties	For More Info . . .
922	GRIFFIN, James	10	SESE	1835-09-08		A1
923	" "	11	NENE	1835-09-08		A1
908	HAMMERSLEY, Isaac	2	NWNE	1835-09-14		A1
889	HAMMOND, John	25	E½SW	1837-08-15		A1 G95
864	HARRISS, Augustus C	14	W½NW	1844-07-10		A1
856	HEDGE, Aaron	5	SWSW	1837-04-10		A1
993	HEDGE, George M	5	NWSW	1838-09-01		A1 G102
945	HOSACK, John	13	E½SE	1829-04-01		A1 V887, 903
946	" "	19	SWSE	1835-04-21		A1
1005	HOSACK, William	1	W½NW	1825-03-10		A1
947	HUTCHESON, John	16	S½SW	1837-08-05		A1
949	KELL, John	20	E½SW	1831-02-10		A1
861	KENNEDY, Andrew	7	SENW	1844-07-10		A1
862	" "	7	SWNE	1844-07-10		A1
878	KINKEAD, David	1	E½NE	1840-11-10		A1
879	" "	1	N½SE	1840-11-10		A1
880	" "	1	NESW	1840-11-10		A1
881	" "	1	SENW	1840-11-10		A1
882	" "	2	NESE	1840-11-10		A1
883	" "	2	S½NE	1840-11-10		A1
884	" "	9	N½SW	1840-11-10		A1
885	" "	9	SENW	1840-11-10		A1
886	" "	9	W½NW	1840-11-10		A1
996	LEECH, Thomas	15	NENW	1844-07-10		A1
997	" "	17	S½NW	1844-07-10		A1 G57
895	LEEPER, George B	9	SESW	1837-04-10		A1
950	LEEPER, John	9	SWSW	1835-09-08		A1
975	LUCCOCK, Naphtali	4	S½SE	1837-04-10		A1
896	MARQUAND, George L	15	NWNE	1844-07-10		A1
952	MARQUAND, John	6	SESE	1835-09-08		A1
951	" "	15	SENE	1838-09-01		A1
903	MATHERS, Henry	13	SESE	1835-04-21		A1 V945
904	MATHEWS, Henry	16	SENW	1844-07-10		A1
905	MATTHEWS, Henry	16	W½NE	1835-04-02		A1
924	MCCARTNEY, James	12	E½NE	1827-10-20		A1
1006	MCCRACKEN, William	16	NESW	1837-08-05		A1
897	MCCULLEY, Gilbert	11	SESW	1835-09-08		A1
898	" "	11	W½SE	1835-09-08		A1
953	MCCUNE, John	11	SENE	1835-10-05		A1
998	MCKEE, Thomas	10	NESE	1837-08-10		A1
957	MCMILLAN, Joseph	10	SESW	1837-08-10		A1 G89
967	MCMULLAN, Joseph	10	NESW	1837-08-10		A1
968	" "	11	NESW	1837-08-15		A1
969	MCMULLEN, Joseph	11	W½NE	1838-09-01		A1
859	MILLER, Adam	19	E½SE	1823-08-20		A1
857	" "	10	W½SE	1825-03-10		A1
858	" "	13	NWSE	1835-10-05		A1
948	MILLER, John K	16	NWSW	1837-08-02		A1
972	MILLER, Joseph	19	E½NE	1823-08-20		A1 G65
971	" "	19	W½NE	1829-04-01		A1
970	" "	19	NWSE	1835-04-21		A1
892	MILLIKEN, Edward	4	NESW	1844-07-10		A1
974	MIRES, Mickel	17	NWNW	1852-07-01		A1
935	MITCHELL, George W	5	NESE	1835-09-14		A1 G67
901	MITCHELL, Hance	3	SW	1832-07-02		A1
902	" "	4	NESE	1837-04-10		A1
935	MITCHELL, John B	5	NESE	1835-09-14		A1 G67
863	NELSON, Archibald	22	SE	1823-08-20		A1
866	NEWELL, Charles	13	E½SW	1829-06-01		A1
867	" "	13	NWSW	1835-09-23		A1
869	" "	14	NESE	1838-09-01		A1
868	" "	13	SWSW	1842-08-01		A1
909	OLDHAM, Isaac	15	W½SE	1825-03-10		A1
982	OLDHAM, Robert	24	W½NW	1823-08-20		A1
893	PATTERSON, Elias	14	NWSE	1837-08-05		A1
894	" "	14	SWNE	1838-09-01		A1
981	PATTERSON, Robert M	3	SENW	1837-04-10		A1
954	PHILLIPS, John	14	NWNE	1835-09-08		A1
999	PHILLIPS, Thomas	3	NWNW	1837-04-10		A1
1007	PRESLEY, William	2	SESE	1835-09-23		A1
925	REA, James	1	S½SE	1837-04-10		A1
1008	REA, William	5	SESE	1840-10-10		A1
860	ROBERTS, Lewis	7	NWNE	1837-08-05		A1 G31

ID	Individual in Patent	Sec.	Sec. Part	Date Issued	Other Counties	For More Info . . .
983	ROBERTSON, Samuel	20	E½NW	1835-04-02		A1
984	" "	20	W½NW	1835-04-02		A1
985	" "	6	SENW	1837-08-15		A1
887	SARCHET, David	13	NESE	1835-04-21		A1 G75 V945
887	SARCHET, Moses	13	NESE	1835-04-21		A1 G75 V945
977	SARCHET, Peter	19	W½SW	1827-06-01		A1
976	" "	19	E½SW	1829-04-01		A1
887	" "	13	NESE	1835-04-21		A1 G75 V945
916	SCHWYHART, Jacob	1	SESW	1838-09-01		A1
865	SIGHTS, Casper	15	SWNW	1844-07-10		A1
888	SIGHTS, David	15	W½SW	1828-05-30		A1
890	SMITH, Ebenezer	3	W½SE	1832-07-02		A1
957	STANBERY, Jonas	10	SESW	1837-08-10		A1 G89
958	" "	15	SENW	1837-08-10		A1 G81
955	" "	16	E½NE	1837-08-15		A1
956	" "	1	W½NE	1837-11-07		A1 G84
889	STEETH, David	25	E½SW	1837-08-15		A1 G95
891	STEWART, Edie	9	NENW	1837-08-15		A1
926	STEWART, James	11	W½SW	1823-07-18		A1
928	" "	7	E½SE	1823-08-20		A1
927	" "	7	E½NE	1825-03-10		A1
929	" "	7	NESW	1835-09-08		A1
930	" "	7	SWSE	1837-04-10		A1
932	STEWART, James W	14	NESW	1840-08-19		A1
931	" "	14	NENW	1840-11-10		A1
987	STEWART, Samuel W	7	NWSE	1838-09-01		A1
1009	STEWART, William	10	NWSW	1838-09-01		A1
994	STURGES, Solomon	14	SESE	1837-11-07		A1 G96
993	" "	5	NWSW	1838-09-01		A1 G102
992	" "	4	NWNW	1844-07-10		A1
995	SWISHER, Stephen	5	E½NE	1840-11-10		A1
973	SWYHART, Joseph	14	SENW	1844-07-10		A1
1010	THOMAS, William	16	N½NW	1844-07-10		A1 G109
986	VANSICKEL, Samuel	15	NWNW	1844-07-10		A1
933	WALKER, James	21	SW	1830-12-01		A1
910	WARDAN, Isaac	7	W½NW	1838-09-01		A1
899	WARDEN, Hamilton	17	NENW	1837-08-15		A1
900	" "	17	NWNE	1837-08-15		A1
914	WARDEN, Isaac	7	W½SW	1823-08-20		A1
912	" "	17	SWNE	1835-09-08		A1
913	" "	7	SESW	1837-04-10		A1
911	" "	15	SWNE	1844-07-10		A1
988	WARDEN, Samuel	4	E½NE	1829-04-01		A1
991	" "	4	SENW	1837-04-10		A1
989	" "	4	NENW	1838-09-01		A1
990	" "	4	NWNE	1842-08-01		A1
915	WERDEN, Isaac	6	S½NE	1837-08-05		A1
934	WILSON, James	6	NENW	1840-11-10		A1
1000	WILSON, Thomas	3	E½SE	1825-03-10		A1
978	WIYRICK, Peter	2	NENE	1837-08-10		A1

Patent Map

T3-N R3-W
U.S. Military Survey Meridian

Map Group 7

Township Statistics

Parcels Mapped	:	155
Number of Patents	:	154
Number of Individuals	:	106
Patentees Identified	:	104
Number of Surnames	:	77
Multi-Patentee Parcels	:	13
Oldest Patent Date	:	9/8/1821
Most Recent Patent	:	7/1/1852
Block/Lot Parcels	:	0
Parcels Re - Issued	:	0
Parcels that Overlap	:	3
Cities and Towns	:	2
Cemeteries	:	3

Map

2

HAMMERSLEY
Isaac
1835

WIYRICK
Peter
1837

HOSACK
William
1825

DRAKE
David
1837

STANBERY [84]
Jonas
1837

KINKEAD
David
1840

KINKEAD
David
1840

KINKEAD
David
1840

1

KINKEAD
David
1840

KINKEAD
David
1840

KINKEAD
David
1840

PRESLEY
William
1835

SCHWYHART
Jacob
1838

REA
James
1837

KINKEAD
David
1840

STEWART
Edie
1837

KINKEAD
David
1840

9

GILL
James
1838

DOUGLASS
Joseph
1837

BRADSHAW
James
1837

BRADSHAW
James
1838

KINKEAD
David
1840

STEWART
William
1838

MCMULLAN
Joseph
1837

MILLER
Adam
1825

MCKEE
Thomas
1837

10

LEEPER
John
1835

LEEPER
George B
1837

BELL
Joseph
1838

STANBERY [89]
Jonas
1837

GRIFFIN
James
1835

FULLER
William
1837

MCCARTNEY
James
1827

GRIFFIN
James
1835

BELL
Joseph
1835

12

MCMULLEN
Joseph
1838

MCCUNE
John
1835

STEWART
James
1823

MCMULLAN
Joseph
1837

11

MCCULLEY
Gilbert
1835

MCCULLEY
Gilbert
1835

MILLER
Joseph
1829

MILLER [65]
Joseph
1823

ROBERTSON
Samuel
1835

19

ROBERTSON
Samuel
1835

20

SARCHET
Peter
1827

SARCHET
Peter
1829

MILLER
Joseph
1835

MILLER
Adam
1823

KELL
John
1831

HOSACK
John
1835

22

NELSON
Archibald
1823

WALKER
James
1830

21

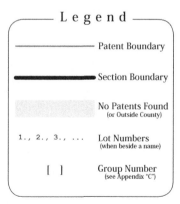

Helpful Hints

1. This Map's INDEX can be found on the preceding pages.

2. Refer to Map "C" to see where this Township lies within Guernsey County, Ohio.

3. Numbers within square brackets [ ] denote a multi-patentee land parcel (multi-owner). Refer to Appendix "C" for a full list of members in this group.

4. Areas that look to be crowded with Patentees usually indicate multiple sales of the same parcel (Re-issues) or Overlapping parcels. See this Township's Index for an explanation of these and other circumstances that might explain "odd" groupings of Patentees on this map.

Legend

———— Patent Boundary

━━━━ Section Boundary

▢ No Patents Found (or Outside County)

1., 2., 3., ...   Lot Numbers (when beside a name)

[ ]   Group Number (see Appendix "C")

Scale: Section = 1 mile X 1 mile (generally, with some exceptions)

Road Map

T3-N R3-W
U.S. Military Survey Meridian

Map Group 7

Cities & Towns
North Salem
Tyner

Cemeteries
Bells Cemetery
Kimbolton Cemetery
North Salem Cemetery

5	4	3
	Partridge Trap Rd	Weber Hill Rd
6	7	8
Norwalk Rd / Chestnut Hill Rd		Angus Rd
15	14	13
	Brush Run Rd	Tyner Rd
		Tyner ●
16	17	18
Lemon Hill Rd / Mathers Rd	Lutterus Ln	Tilton Ln / Salt Rd / Chambers Rd
25	24	23
Sherrard Rd / Simmons Rd		Smith Ln / Hutchison Ln

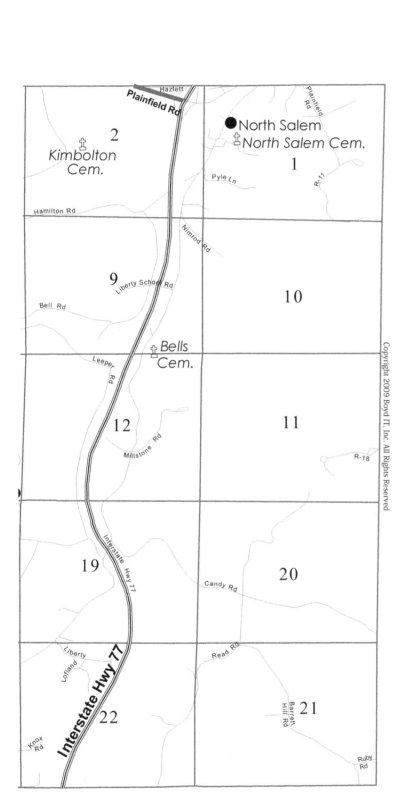

Helpful Hints

1. This road map has a number of uses, but primarily it is to help you: a) find the present location of land owned by your ancestors (at least the general area), b) find cemeteries and city-centers, and c) estimate the route/roads used by Census-takers & tax-assessors.

2. If you plan to travel to Guernsey County to locate cemeteries or land parcels, please pick up a modern travel map for the area before you do. Mapping old land parcels on modern maps is not as exact a science as you might think. Just the slightest variations in public land survey coordinates, estimates of parcel boundaries, or road-map deviations can greatly alter a map's representation of how a road either does or doesn't cross a particular parcel of land.

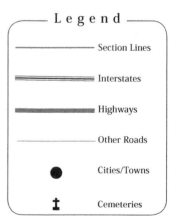

L e g e n d

	Section Lines
	Interstates
	Highways
	Other Roads
●	Cities/Towns
✝	Cemeteries

Scale: Section = 1 mile X 1 mile
(generally, with some exceptions)

Historical Map

T3-N R3-W
U.S. Military Survey Meridian

Map Group 7

Cities & Towns
North Salem
Tyner

Cemeteries
Bells Cemetery
Kimbolton Cemetery
North Salem Cemetery

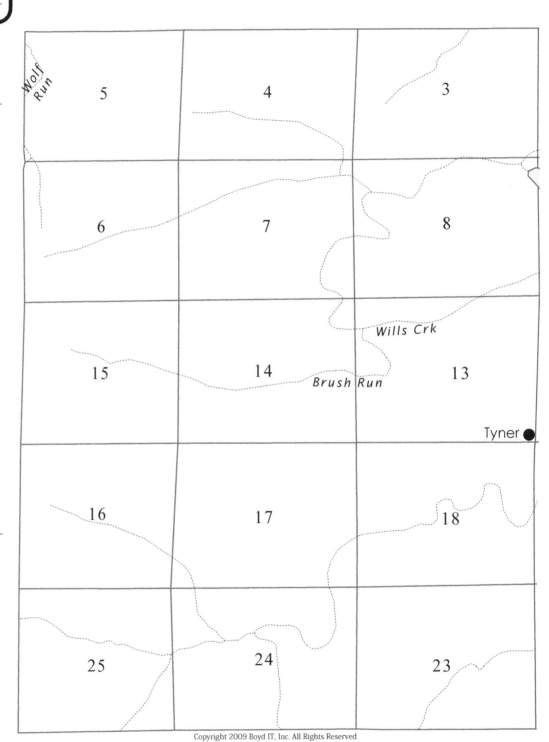

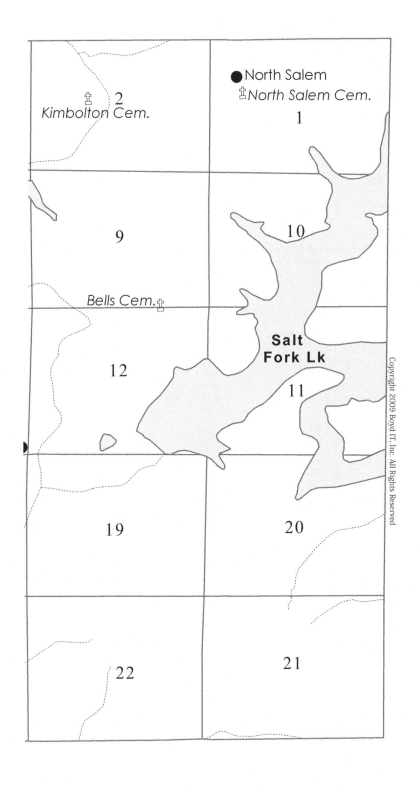

Helpful Hints

1. This Map takes a different look at the same Congressional Township displayed in the preceding two maps. It presents features that can help you better envision the historical development of the area: a) Water-bodies (lakes & ponds), b) Water-courses (rivers, streams, etc.), c) Railroads, d) City/town center-points (where they were oftentimes located when first settled), and e) Cemeteries.

2. Using this "Historical" map in tandem with this Township's Patent Map and Road Map, may lead you to some interesting discoveries. You will often find roads, towns, cemeteries, and waterways are named after nearby landowners: sometimes those names will be the ones you are researching. See how many of these research gems you can find here in Guernsey County.

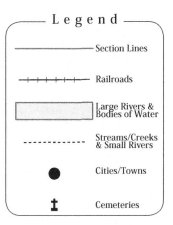

Legend

————————	Section Lines
+++++++++	Railroads
▭	Large Rivers & Bodies of Water
- - - - - - - -	Streams/Creeks & Small Rivers
●	Cities/Towns
☦	Cemeteries

Scale: Section = 1 mile X 1 mile
(there are some exceptions)

Map Group 8: Index to Land Patents

Township 3-North Range 2-West (U.S. Military Survey)

After you locate an individual in this Index, take note of the Section and Section Part then proceed to the Land Patent map on the pages immediately following. You should have no difficulty locating the corresponding parcel of land.

The "For More Info" Column will lead you to more information about the underlying Patents. See the *Legend* at right, and the "How to Use this Book" chapter, for more information.

```
                          LEGEND
              "For More Info . . . " column
A = Authority (Legislative Act, See Appendix "A")
B = Block or Lot (location in Section unknown)
C = Cancelled Patent
F = Fractional Section
G = Group  (Multi-Patentee Patent, see Appendix "C")
V = Overlaps another Parcel
R = Re-Issued (Parcel patented more than once)

(A & G items require you to look in the Appendixes referred
to above. All other Letter-designations followed by a number
require you to locate line-items in this index that possess
the ID number found after the letter).
```

ID	Individual in Patent	Sec.	Sec. Part	Date Issued	Other Counties	For More Info . . .
1075	ADAMS, John	5	E½NE	1824-04-17		A1
1074	" "	4	W½NW	1831-02-10		A1
1036	ALLEN, Francis B	4	26	1835-04-30		A1
1035	" "	4	25	1835-09-30		A1
1011	ARMSTRONG, Joseph	16	E½NW	1829-04-01		A1 G76
1012	" "	16	W½NE	1829-04-01		A1 G76
1114	" "	16	W½NW	1832-07-02		A1
1137	AYERS, Thomas	9	SESW	1835-09-23		A1
1076	BAIRD, John	15	E½NE	1835-04-02		A1
1122	BARNES, Nathan	1	SWNW	1837-04-10		A1
1124	BARNES, Reuben	14	NENW	1835-09-23		A1
1037	BEEMER, George	4	19	1804-05-26		A2
1038	" "	4	22	1806-05-22		A2
1104	BELT, John S	4	35	1804-12-19		A2
1105	" "	4	36	1804-12-19		A2
1106	" "	4	37	1804-12-19		A2
1151	BIGGS, Zaccheus	4	1	1804-06-27		A2
1155	" "	4	2	1804-06-27		A2
1152	" "	4	13	1804-12-19		A2
1153	" "	4	17	1804-08-21		A2
1154	" "	4	18	1804-08-21		A2
1156	" "	4	30	1804-08-21		A2
1157	" "	4	31	1804-08-21		A2
1158	" "	4	32	1804-08-21		A2
1159	" "	4	33	1804-06-27		A2
1160	" "	4	34	1804-06-27		A2
1125	BOSTON, Reuben	12	E½NW	1835-09-23		A1
1017	BOYD, Andrew	12	SWNE	1837-04-10		A1
1112	BOYD, Jonathan	12	NWNW	1840-11-10		A1
1115	BOYD, Joseph	8	W½NW	1821-09-08		A1
1077	BRACKIN, John	9	SWSE	1837-04-10		A1
1016	BUCKINGHAM, Alvah	18	NWNW	1837-08-10		A1
1071	BUNNEL, Jesse	13	W½SW	1837-08-10		A1
1058	CAMPBELL, James	2	NENE	1835-09-14		A1
1043	CASSIDY, Asa R	5	NWSW	1838-09-01		A1 G46
1018	CLARKE, Andrew	7	NWNW	1835-09-14		A1
1019	" "	7	SENW	1837-04-10		A1
1078	COLEMAN, John	4	7	1804-05-26		A2
1020	CONAN, Caleb	13	SWNE	1835-04-30		A1
1021	CONANN, Caleb	13	SENW	1837-08-05		A1
1079	CORBET, John	4	8	1804-05-28		A2
1025	COX, Church	10	E½SE	1824-04-17		A1
1081	CRAWFORD, John	14	E½SE	1835-09-08		A1
1080	" "	13	E½SW	1835-09-23		A1
1082	" "	14	SWSE	1835-09-23		A1
1083	" "	18	NENW	1835-09-23		A1

ID	Individual in Patent	Sec.	Sec. Part	Date Issued	Other Counties	For More Info . . .
1120	DAY, Lewis	12	NENE	1837-11-07		A1
1142	DUFFEY, William	2	W½NW	1829-05-01		A1
1059	DUFFY, James	3	E½SW	1824-04-17		A1
1040	FORD, George	8	W½NE	1825-03-10		A1
1039	" "	8	E½NE	1832-04-02		A1
1143	FRANEY, William	25	E½NW	1830-12-01		A1
1022	FRAZER, Charles	4	4	1804-02-20		A2
1070	GALLATIN, Jeremiah	4	E½NW	1829-06-01		A1
1144	GIBSON, William	10	SWSE	1835-04-30		A1
1145	" "	11	NWNE	1835-04-30		A1
1060	GILLASPIE, James	8	W½SW	1835-04-02		A1
1061	GILLESPIE, James	7	E½SE	1832-07-02		A1
1062	" "	7	NWSE	1835-04-21		A1
1084	GILLESPIE, John	13	NWNW	1835-04-30		A1
1085	GUNN, John	8	E½SW	1824-04-17		A1
1116	HAGAN, Joseph	11	E½NW	1835-09-14		A1
1043	HAVER, George W	5	NWSW	1838-09-01		A1 G46
1146	HELANNEN, William	4	27	1806-05-20		A2
1086	HENDERSON, John	16	E½NE	1826-06-06		A1
1048	HENRY, Harmon	12	SENE	1840-10-10		A1
1063	HENRY, James	25	W½NW	1830-12-01		A1
1087	HOWARD, John	4	6	1804-05-26		A2
1041	HUFFMAN, George	2	NESE	1837-04-10		A1
1042	" "	2	SENE	1837-04-10		A1
1057	HUFFMAN, Jacob	2	SESE	1835-09-23		A1
1056	" "	10	SWSW	1837-04-10		A1
1126	HUFFMAN, Robert F	10	NWSW	1837-08-15		A1
1033	JENKINS, Eleazar	10	NENE	1837-04-10		A1
1088	KEARNES, John	7	SESW	1837-04-10		A1
1089	KEARNS, John	7	NESW	1835-09-08		A1
1072	KEEN, Jesse	10	NWSE	1837-04-10		A1
1073	" "	10	S½NE	1837-04-10		A1
1090	KELL, John	16	W½SW	1831-02-10		A1
1013	KIMBLE, Adam	1	E½NW	1835-09-08		A1
1123	LACKEY, Philip	4	10	1804-11-09		A2
1092	LAKE, John	14	S½SW	1835-04-30		A1
1091	" "	14	NWSE	1840-11-10		A1
1053	LANING, Isaac	3	SE	1821-09-08		A1
1064	LEEPER, James	3	W½SW	1823-08-20		A1
1147	LITTLE, William	9	NESW	1835-09-08		A1
1148	" "	9	NWSE	1835-09-08		A1
1031	LUCY, Edward	2	W½NE	1829-04-01		A1
1149	LUPER, William	6	E½NW	1830-12-01		A1
1095	MARTIN, John	6	W½NW	1830-12-01		A1
1094	" "	5	W½NW	1835-04-02		A1
1093	" "	5	SWSW	1835-09-23		A1
1045	MCCULLEY, Gilbert	8	E½SE	1831-02-10		A1
1099	MCCULLOUGH, John	5	SWNE	1835-09-14		A1
1098	" "	5	SESW	1835-09-23		A1
1096	" "	5	NENW	1837-04-10		A1
1097	" "	5	SENW	1837-04-10		A1
1026	MCWILLIAMS, Daniel	5	NWNE	1835-09-30		A1
1054	MILLER, Isaac	4	16	1804-12-08		A2
1015	MILLIGAN, Alexander N	5	NESW	1835-09-23		A1
1135	MILLIGAN, John	7	S½NE	1838-09-01		A1 G106
1023	MORGAN, Charles	4	15	1805-05-14		A2
1117	MORRISON, Joseph	9	NESE	1837-04-10		A1
1118	" "	9	SESE	1837-04-10		A1
1050	MORTON, Hezekiah	4	20	1804-03-28		A2
1051	" "	4	21	1804-03-28		A2
1052	" "	4	3	1804-03-28		A2
1150	NORTHGRAVES, William	2	E½NW	1826-04-01		A1
1141	PARKE, Uriah	7	NENE	1835-09-23		A1 G72
1046	PICKERING, Greenberry	7	NWNE	1835-09-14		A1
1141	PICKERING, Greenbery	7	NENE	1835-09-23		A1 G72
1121	PICKERING, Lot	7	NENW	1835-10-05		A1
1024	PLEMLINE, Charles	4	23	1806-06-19		A2
1136	PORTER, Stewart	11	E½NE	1831-03-01		A1
1049	PULLEY, Henson	11	W½NW	1835-04-21		A1
1100	REILY, John	4	11	1804-06-27		A2
1101	" "	4	12	1804-06-27		A2
1102	" "	4	5	1804-06-27		A2
1065	ROBINSON, James	5	E½SE	1827-06-01		A1

ID	Individual in Patent	Sec.	Sec. Part	Date Issued	Other Counties	For More Info . . .
1066	ROBINSON, James (Cont'd)	7	NWSW	1835-09-08		A1
1067	" "	7	SWSW	1837-04-10		A1
1103	ROLINGSON, John	18	SENW	1835-04-30		A1
1011	SCOTT, Abraham	16	E½NW	1829-04-01		A1 G76
1012	" "	16	W½NE	1829-04-01		A1 G76
1107	SMITH, John	15	W½NE	1835-04-02		A1
1127	SPEERS, Robert	13	SWNW	1835-09-23		A1
1028	STACKEY, David	9	NWSW	1835-09-23		A1
1111	STANBERY, Jonas	13	NENE	1835-09-23		A1 G92
1111	STARKEY, David	13	NENE	1835-09-23		A1 G92
1029	" "	9	SWSW	1835-09-23		A1
1068	STEWART, James	14	SWNW	1838-09-01		A1
1113	STILES, Jonathan	14	N½SW	1837-08-10		A1
1134	STILES, Simon	18	SWNW	1835-09-14		A1
1138	STILES, Thomas	14	NWNW	1837-08-10		A1
1128	STOCKDALE, Robert	12	NWNE	1838-09-01		A1
1129	" "	13	SENE	1838-09-01		A1
1108	STULL, John	17	NE	1835-09-14		A1
1135	STURGES, Solomon	7	S½NE	1838-09-01		A1 G106
1131	TAYLOR, Samuel	13	NENW	1835-04-21		A1
1132	" "	13	NWNE	1837-04-10		A1
1014	TETIRICK, Adam	11	SWNE	1837-04-10		A1
1133	THOMAS, Samuel	10	NWNE	1835-09-08		A1
1034	TOPHAND, Ezekiel	4	28	1804-06-27		A2
1027	VAMPELT, Daniel	7	SWSE	1835-09-08		A1
1109	VAN CAMPEN, JOHN	12	SWNW	1837-11-07		A1
1110	WELCH, John	4	29	1804-06-27		A2
1119	WENTWORTH, Levi	4	14	1804-02-20		A2
1044	WHITAKER, George W	1	NWNW	1835-10-05		A1
1139	WHITEHILL, Thomas	6	E½SW	1824-04-17		A1
1140	" "	6	W½SE	1824-04-17		A1
1047	WILEY, Hans	6	W½SW	1832-07-02		A1
1032	WILLIS, Edward	2	W½SE	1832-07-02		A1
1055	WILLIS, Isaac	10	E½SW	1835-09-14		A1
1069	WILLIS, James	2	W½SW	1825-03-10		A1
1030	YARNEL, David	14	SENW	1835-09-14		A1
1130	YOUNG, Robert	7	SWNW	1835-09-30		A1

Patent Map

T3-N R2-W
U.S. Military Survey Meridian

Map Group 8

Township Statistics

Parcels Mapped	:	150
Number of Patents	:	140
Number of Individuals	:	111
Patentees Identified	:	108
Number of Surnames	:	97
Multi-Patentee Parcels	:	6
Oldest Patent Date	:	2/20/1804
Most Recent Patent	:	11/10/1840
Block/Lot Parcels	:	35
Parcels Re - Issued	:	0
Parcels that Overlap	:	0
Cities and Towns	:	2
Cemeteries	:	3

Section 5
MARTIN John 1835
MCCULLOUGH John 1837
MCWILLIAMS Daniel 1835
ADAMS John 1824
MCCULLOUGH John 1837
MCCULLOUGH John 1835
HAVER [46] George W 1838
MILLIGAN Alexander N 1835
MARTIN John 1835
MCCULLOUGH John 1835
ROBINSON James 1827

Section 4
ADAMS John 1831
GALLATIN Jeremiah 1829

Section 3
LEEPER James 1823
DUFFY James 1824
LANING Isaac 1821

Section 6
MARTIN John 1830
LUPER William 1830
WILEY Hans 1832
WHITEHILL Thomas 1824
WHITEHILL Thomas 1824

Section 7
CLARKE Andrew 1835
PICKERING Lot 1835
PICKERING Greenberry 1835
PARKE [72] Uriah 1835
YOUNG Robert 1835
CLARKE Andrew 1837
STURGES [106] Solomon 1838
ROBINSON James 1835
KEARNS John 1835
GILLESPIE James 1835
GILLESPIE James 1832
ROBINSON James 1837
KEARNES John 1837
VAMPELT Daniel 1835

Section 8
BOYD Joseph 1821
FORD George 1825
FORD George 1832
GILLASPIE James 1835
GUNN John 1824
MCCULLEY Gilbert 1831

Section 15
SMITH John 1835
BAIRD John 1835

Section 14
STILES Thomas 1837
BARNES Reuben 1835
STEWART James 1838
YARNEL David 1835
STILES Jonathan 1837
LAKE John 1840
CRAWFORD John 1835
LAKE John 1835
CRAWFORD John 1835

Section 13
GILLESPIE John 1835
TAYLOR Samuel 1835
TAYLOR Samuel 1837
STANBERY [92] Jonas 1835
SPEERS Robert 1835
CONANN Caleb 1837
CONAN Caleb 1835
STOCKDALE Robert 1838
BUNNEL Jesse 1837
CRAWFORD John 1835

Section 16
ARMSTRONG Joseph 1832
SCOTT [76] Abraham 1829
SCOTT [76] Abraham 1829
HENDERSON John 1826
KELL John 1831

Section 17
STULL John 1835

Section 18
BUCKINGHAM Alvah 1837
CRAWFORD John 1835
STILES Simon 1835
ROLINGSON John 1835

Section 25
HENRY James 1830
FRANEY William 1830

Section 24

Section 23

Map grid

DUFFEY William 1829	NORTHGRAVES William 1826 **2**	LUCY Edward 1829	CAMPBELL James 1835 / HUFFMAN George 1837	WHITAKER George W 1835 / BARNES Nathan 1837	KIMBLE Adam 1835	**1**
	WILLIS James 1825	WILLIS Edward 1832	HUFFMAN George 1837 / HUFFMAN Jacob 1835			

9

10: THOMAS Samuel 1835 | JENKINS Eleazar 1837 / KEEN Jesse 1837

| STACKEY David 1835 / STARKEY David 1835 | LITTLE William 1835 / AYERS Thomas 1835 | LITTLE William 1835 / BRACKIN John 1837 | MORRISON Joseph 1837 / MORRISON Joseph 1837 | HUFFMAN Robert F 1837 / HUFFMAN Jacob 1837 | WILLIS Isaac 1835 | KEEN Jesse 1837 / GIBSON William 1835 | COX Church 1824 |

12

| BOYD Jonathan 1840 / CAMPEN John Van 1837 | BOSTON Reuben 1835 | STOCKDALE Robert 1838 / BOYD Andrew 1837 | DAY Lewis 1837 / HENRY Harmon 1840 | PULLEY Henson 1835 | HAGAN Joseph 1835 | GIBSON William 1835 **11** / TETIRICK Adam 1837 | PORTER Stewart 1831 |

Lots-Sec. 4

```
1   BIGGS, Zaccheus    1804
2   BIGGS, Zaccheus    1804
3   MORTON, Hezekiah   1804
4   FRAZER, Charles    1804
5   REILY, John        1804
6   HOWARD, John       1804
7   COLEMAN, John      1804
8   CORBET, John       1804
10  LACKEY, Philip     1804
11  REILY, John        1804
12  REILY, John        1804
13  BIGGS, Zaccheus    1804
14  WENTWORTH, Levi    1804
15  MORGAN, Charles    1805
16  MILLER, Isaac      1804
17  BIGGS, Zaccheus    1804
18  BIGGS, Zaccheus    1804
19  BEEMER, George     1804
20  MORTON, Hezekiah   1804
21  MORTON, Hezekiah   1804
22  BEEMER, George     1806
23  PLEMLINE, Charles  1806
25  ALLEN, Francis B   1835
26  ALLEN, Francis B   1835
27  HELANNEN, William  1806
28  TOPHAND, Ezekiel   1804
29  WELCH, John        1804
30  BIGGS, Zaccheus    1804
31  BIGGS, Zaccheus    1804
32  BIGGS, Zaccheus    1804
33  BIGGS, Zaccheus    1804
34  BIGGS, Zaccheus    1804
35  BELT, John S       1804
36  BELT, John S       1804
37  BELT, John S       1804
```

4

Helpful Hints

1. This Map's INDEX can be found on the preceding pages.

2. Refer to Map "C" to see where this Township lies within Guernsey County, Ohio.

3. Numbers within square brackets [ ] denote a multi-patentee land parcel (multi-owner). Refer to Appendix "C" for a full list of members in this group.

4. Areas that look to be crowded with Patentees usually indicate multiple sales of the same parcel (Re-issues) or Overlapping parcels. See this Township's Index for an explanation of these and other circumstances that might explain "odd" groupings of Patentees on this map.

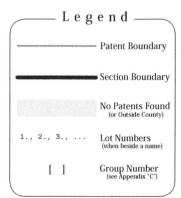

Legend

——————	Patent Boundary
▬▬▬▬▬	Section Boundary
(shaded)	No Patents Found (or Outside County)
1., 2., 3., ...	Lot Numbers (when beside a name)
[ ]	Group Number (see Appendix "C")

Scale: Section = 1 mile X 1 mile (generally, with some exceptions)

Road Map

T3-N R2-W
U.S. Military Survey Meridian

Map Group 8

Cities & Towns

Brady
Clio (historical)

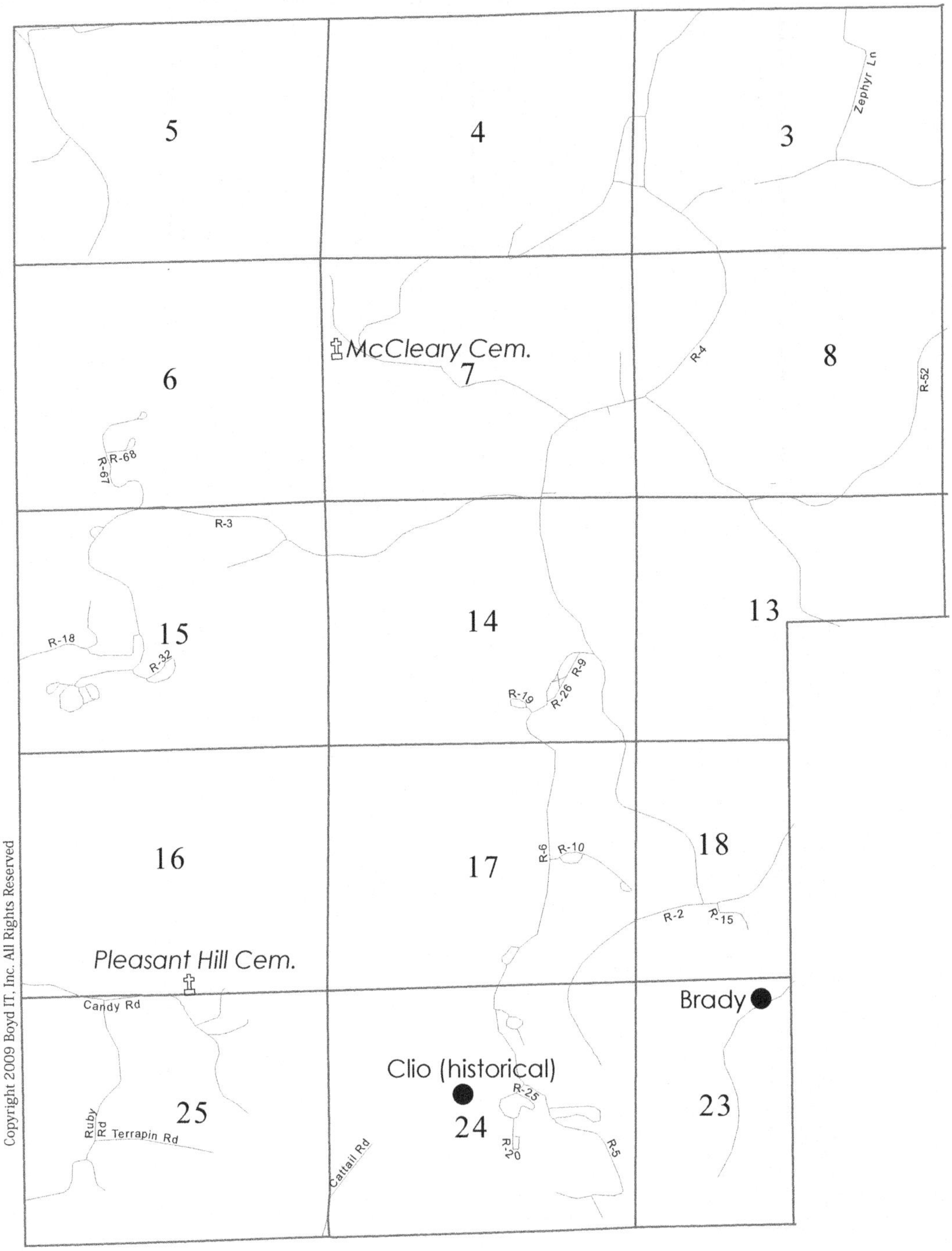

Cemeteries

Allen Cemetery
McCleary Cemetery
Pleasant Hill Cemetery

5	4	3
6	⚰ *McCleary Cem.* 7	8
15	14	13
16	17	18
Pleasant Hill Cem. 25	Clio (historical) 24	Brady ● 23

Zephyr Ln

R-4

R-52

R-67 R-68

R-3

R-18

R-32

R-19 R-26 R-9

R-6 R-10

R-2 R-15

Candy Rd

Ruby Rd Terrapin Rd

Cattail Rd

R-25

R-20

R-5

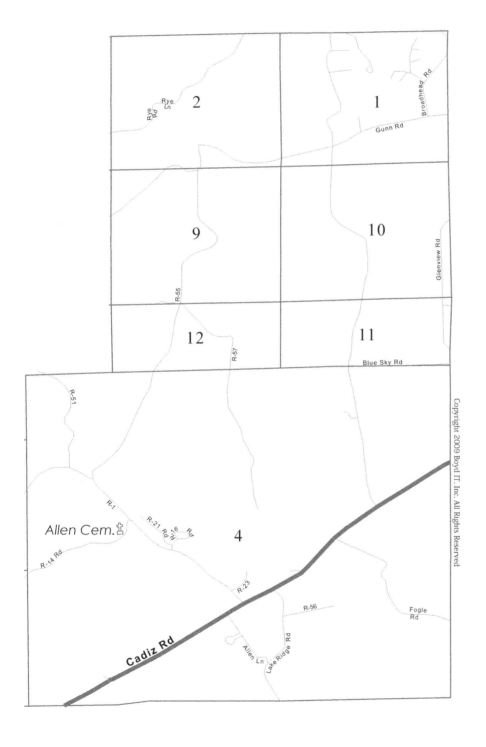

Helpful Hints

1. This road map has a number of uses, but primarily it is to help you: a) find the present location of land owned by your ancestors (at least the general area), b) find cemeteries and city-centers, and c) estimate the route/roads used by Census-takers & tax-assessors.

2. If you plan to travel to Guernsey County to locate cemeteries or land parcels, please pick up a modern travel map for the area before you do. Mapping old land parcels on modern maps is not as exact a science as you might think. Just the slightest variations in public land survey coordinates, estimates of parcel boundaries, or road-map deviations can greatly alter a map's representation of how a road either does or doesn't cross a particular parcel of land.

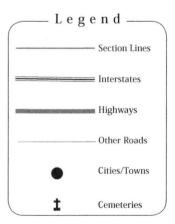

L e g e n d

———————— Section Lines

════════ Interstates

━━━━━━━━ Highways

———————— Other Roads

● Cities/Towns

✝ Cemeteries

Scale: Section = 1 mile X 1 mile
(generally, with some exceptions)

Historical Map

T3-N R2-W
U.S. Military Survey Meridian

Map Group 8

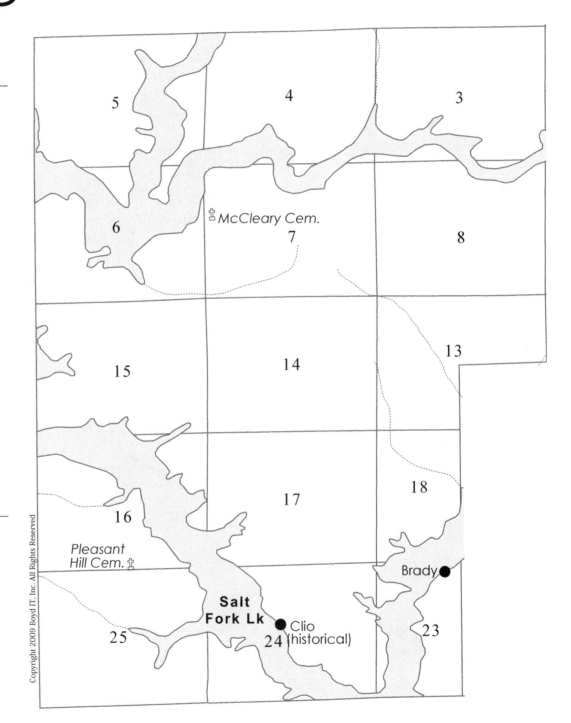

Cities & Towns
Brady
Clio (historical)

Cemeteries
Allen Cemetery
McCleary Cemetery
Pleasant Hill Cemetery

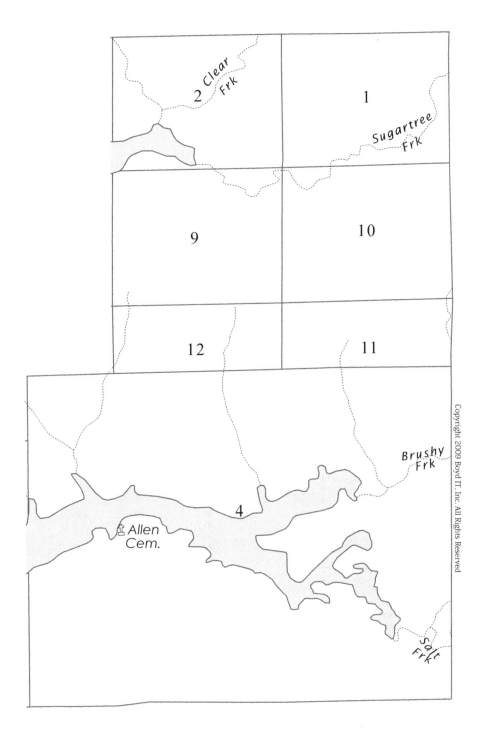

Helpful Hints

1. This Map takes a different look at the same Congressional Township displayed in the preceding two maps. It presents features that can help you better envision the historical development of the area: a) Water-bodies (lakes & ponds), b) Water-courses (rivers, streams, etc.), c) Railroads, d) City/ town center-points (where they were oftentimes located when first settled), and e) Cemeteries.

2. Using this "Historical" map in tandem with this Township's Patent Map and Road Map, may lead you to some interesting discoveries. You will often find roads, towns, cemeteries, and waterways are named after nearby landowners: sometimes those names will be the ones you are researching. See how many of these research gems you can find here in Guernsey County.

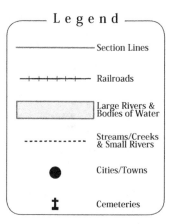

Legend

————	Section Lines
—+—+—+—	Railroads
▭	Large Rivers & Bodies of Water
- - - - - -	Streams/Creeks & Small Rivers
●	Cities/Towns
‡	Cemeteries

Scale: Section = 1 mile X 1 mile
(there are some exceptions)

Map Group 9: Index to Land Patents

Township 3-North Range 1-West (U.S. Military Survey)

After you locate an individual in this Index, take note of the Section and Section Part then proceed to the Land Patent map on the pages immediately following. You should have no difficulty locating the corresponding parcel of land.

The "For More Info" Column will lead you to more information about the underlying Patents. See the *Legend* at right, and the "How to Use this Book" chapter, for more information.

```
                              LEGEND
                  "For More Info . . . " column
A = Authority (Legislative Act, See Appendix "A")
B = Block or Lot (location in Section unknown)
C = Cancelled Patent
F = Fractional Section
G = Group  (Multi-Patentee Patent, see Appendix "C")
V = Overlaps another Parcel
R = Re-Issued (Parcel patented more than once)

(A & G items require you to look in the Appendixes referred
to above. All other Letter-designations followed by a number
require you to locate line-items in this index that possess
the ID number found after the letter).
```

ID	Individual in Patent	Sec.	Sec. Part	Date Issued	Other Counties	For More Info . . .
1187	BEVARD, Samuel	19	E½SE	1826-04-01		A1
1181	BIXLER, John	22	W½NE	1835-09-08		A1
1185	BOYD, Jonathan	19	W½NE	1832-04-02		A1
1192	BOYD, Thomas	22	W½SW	1830-12-01		A1
1191	" "	22	E½SW	1832-04-02		A1
1171	CALLENDINE, Henry	24	W½NW	1828-08-20		A1
1195	CARLILE, William	6	E½SW	1835-09-08		A1
1196	" "	6	SWNW	1835-09-08		A1 R1169
1182	COPELAND, John	20	E½SE	1828-05-30		A1
1164	COX, Church	5	W½SW	1824-04-17		A1
1166	DAYTON, Garrel	24	E½NW	1829-04-01		A1
1194	GILLET, Wheeler	7	SENW	1835-09-30		A1
1197	GRAY, William	12	SESW	1835-04-21		A1
1163	HAGEN, Charles	6	E½NE	1824-04-17		A1
1161	HUFFMAN, Benjamin	5	E½SW	1830-12-01		A1
1162	" "	5	SWSE	1837-04-10		A1
1165	KIRKPATRICK, David	7	W½SW	1835-09-08		A1
1188	LAWRENCE, Samuel	7	W½NW	1827-04-03		A1
1193	LENFESTEY, Thomas	5	E½SE	1835-09-14		A1
1172	MASTERS, Henry	4	E½SW	1832-04-02		A1
1173	" "	4	W½SW	1835-09-14		A1
1174	ONG, Jacob	2	E½NE	1823-08-20		A1
1186	PADGITT, Richard B	7	E½SW	1835-04-02		A1
1190	PORTER, Steward	12	E½SE	1828-02-20		A1
1189	POUNDS, Samuel	4	W½SE	1826-04-03		A1
1198	POUNDS, William	7	NENW	1835-04-30		A1
1183	RYAN, John	20	W½NW	1832-07-02		A1
1176	SMITH, James M	5	NWSE	1835-09-08		A1
1177	STOCKDALE, James	11	W½SW	1832-04-02		A1
1175	SUTTON, Jacob	22	E½NW	1835-09-08		A1
1167	TAYLOR, George	6	NWNW	1837-04-10		A1
1184	TROTT, John	19	W½SE	1835-09-08		A1
1178	WALKER, James	6	NENW	1835-09-14		A1
1179	" "	6	NWNE	1835-09-14		A1
1180	WARRACK, James	14	SW	1974-07-30		A1
1170	WINE, George	6	W½SW	1832-04-02		A1
1169	" "	6	SWNW	1835-04-21		A1 R1196
1168	" "	6	SWNE	1837-04-10		A1

Patent Map

T3-N R1-W
U.S. Military Survey Meridian

Map Group 9

Township Statistics

Parcels Mapped	:	38
Number of Patents	:	38
Number of Individuals	:	31
Patentees Identified	:	31
Number of Surnames	:	29
Multi-Patentee Parcels	:	0
Oldest Patent Date	:	8/20/1823
Most Recent Patent	:	7/30/1974
Block/Lot Parcels	:	0
Parcels Re - Issued	:	1
Parcels that Overlap	:	0
Cities and Towns	:	2
Cemeteries	:	3

5

COX
Church
1824

HUFFMAN
Benjamin
1830

SMITH
James M
1835

HUFFMAN
Benjamin
1837

LENFESTEY
Thomas
1835

4

MASTERS
Henry
1835

MASTERS
Henry
1832

POUNDS
Samuel
1826

3

TAYLOR
George
1837

CARLILE
William
1835

WINE
George
1835

WALKER
James
1835

WALKER
James
1835

WINE
George
1837

HAGEN
Charles
1824

LAWRENCE
Samuel
1827

POUNDS
William
1835

GILLET
Wheeler
1835

6

7

8

WINE
George
1832

CARLILE
William
1835

KIRKPATRICK
David
1835

PADGITT
Richard B
1835

15

14

WARRACK
James
1974

13

16

17

18

25

CALLENDINE
Henry
1828

DAYTON
Garrel
1829

24

23

1

12

GRAY
William
1835

PORTER
Steward
1828

STOCKDALE
James
1832

11

19

BOYD
Jonathan
1832

RYAN
John
1832

20

TROTT
John
1835

BEVARD
Samuel
1826

COPELAND
John
1828

22

SUTTON
Jacob
1835

BIXLER
John
1835

21

BOYD
Thomas
1830

BOYD
Thomas
1832

Helpful Hints

1. This Map's INDEX can be found on the preceding pages.

2. Refer to Map "C" to see where this Township lies within Guernsey County, Ohio.

3. Numbers within square brackets [ ] denote a multi-patentee land parcel (multi-owner). Refer to Appendix "C" for a full list of members in this group.

4. Areas that look to be crowded with Patentees usually indicate multiple sales of the same parcel (Re-issues) or Overlapping parcels. See this Township's Index for an explanation of these and other circumstances that might explain "odd" groupings of Patentees on this map.

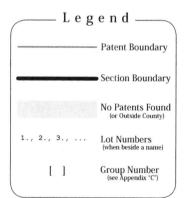

L e g e n d

——————— Patent Boundary

━━━━━━ Section Boundary

No Patents Found
(or Outside County)

1., 2., 3., ... Lot Numbers
(when beside a name)

[ ] Group Number
(see Appendix "C")

Scale: Section = 1 mile X 1 mile
(generally, with some exceptions)

Road Map

T3-N R1-W
U.S. Military Survey Meridian

Map Group 9

Cities & Towns
Antrim
Winterset

Cemeteries
Antrim Presbyterian Cemetery
Glenview Cemetery
Winterset Cemetery

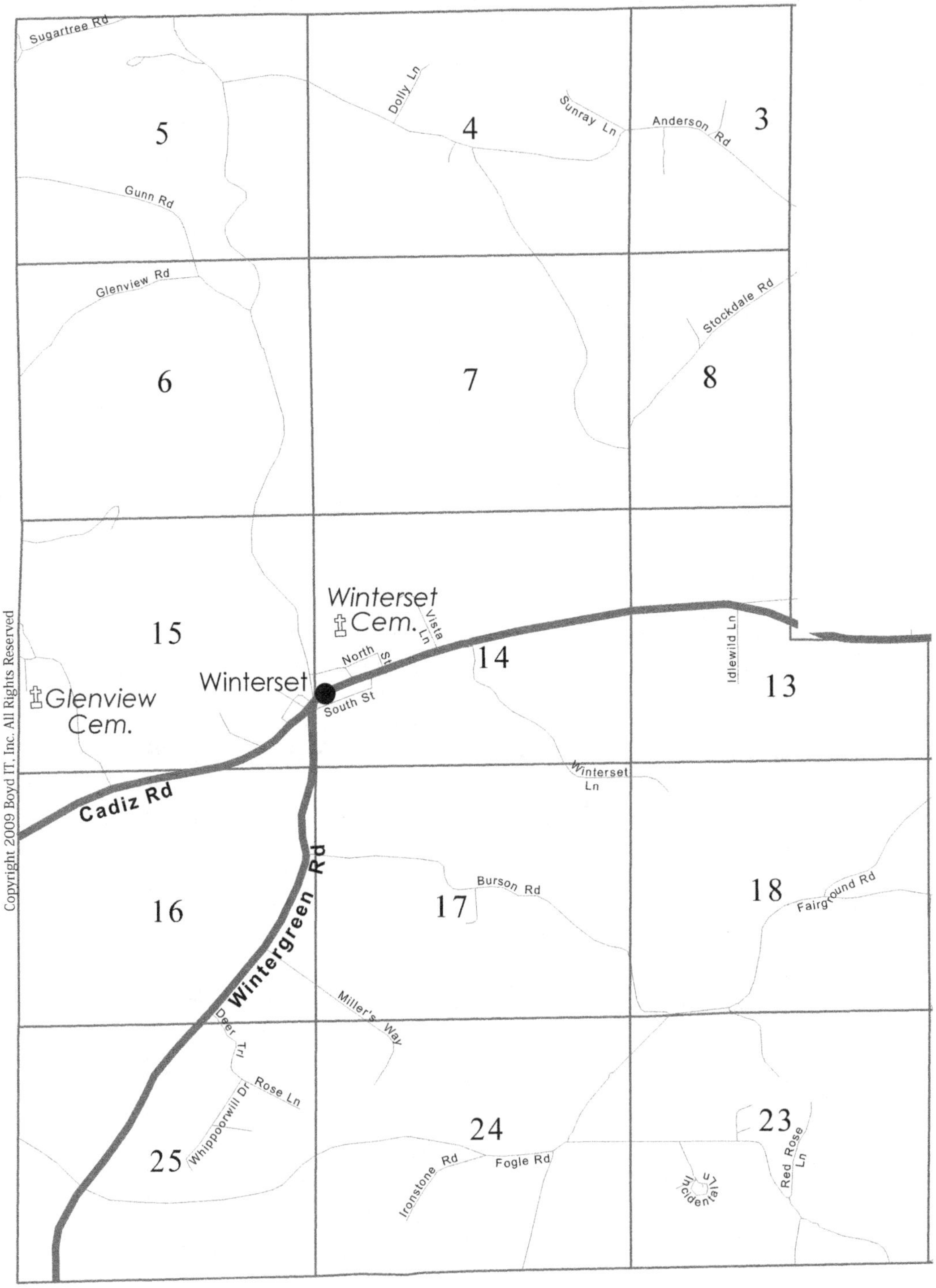

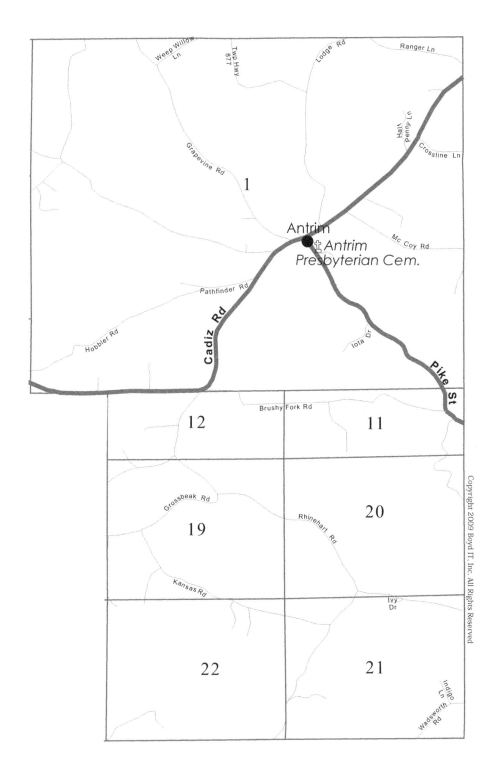

Helpful Hints

1. This road map has a number of uses, but primarily it is to help you: a) find the present location of land owned by your ancestors (at least the general area), b) find cemeteries and city-centers, and c) estimate the route/roads used by Census-takers & tax-assessors.

2. If you plan to travel to Guernsey County to locate cemeteries or land parcels, please pick up a modern travel map for the area before you do. Mapping old land parcels on modern maps is not as exact a science as you might think. Just the slightest variations in public land survey coordinates, estimates of parcel boundaries, or road-map deviations can greatly alter a map's representation of how a road either does or doesn't cross a particular parcel of land.

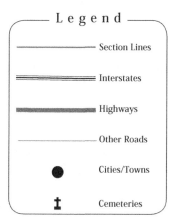

Legend

Section Lines
Interstates
Highways
Other Roads
Cities/Towns
Cemeteries

Scale: Section = 1 mile X 1 mile
(generally, with some exceptions)

Historical Map

T3-N R1-W
U.S. Military Survey Meridian

Map Group 9

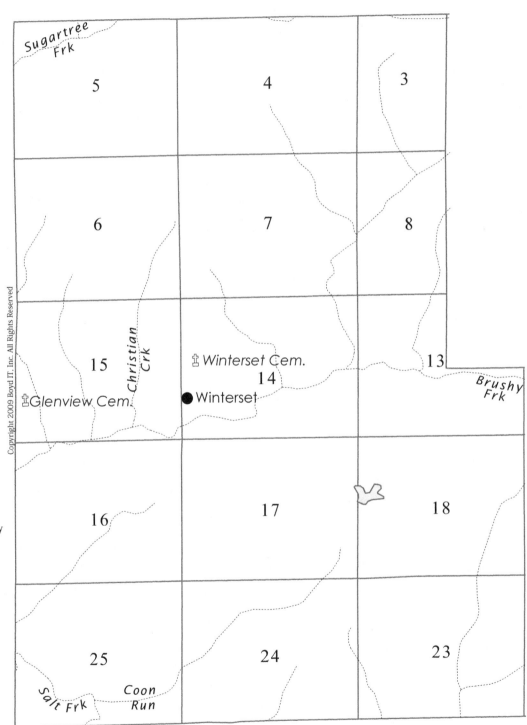

Cities & Towns
Antrim
Winterset

Cemeteries
Antrim Presbyterian Cemetery
Glenview Cemetery
Winterset Cemetery

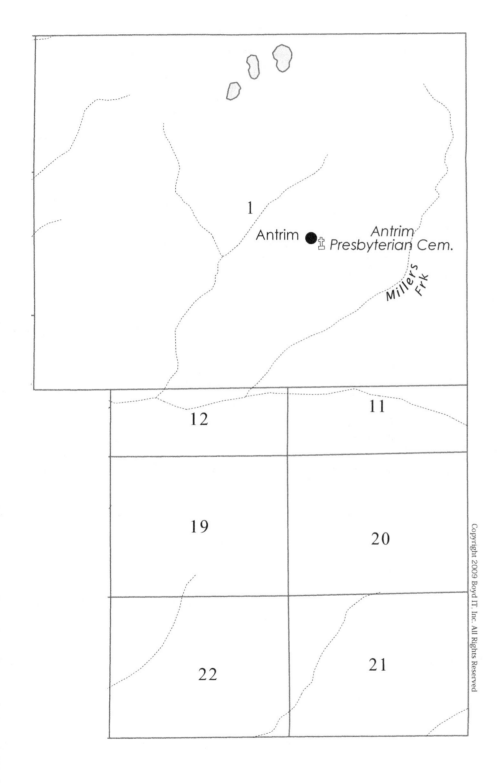

Helpful Hints

1. This Map takes a different look at the same Congressional Township displayed in the preceding two maps. It presents features that can help you better envision the historical development of the area: a) Water-bodies (lakes & ponds), b) Water-courses (rivers, streams, etc.), c) Railroads, d) City/town center-points (where they were oftentimes located when first settled), and e) Cemeteries.

2. Using this "Historical" map in tandem with this Township's Patent Map and Road Map, may lead you to some interesting discoveries. You will often find roads, towns, cemeteries, and waterways are named after nearby landowners: sometimes those names will be the ones you are researching. See how many of these research gems you can find here in Guernsey County.

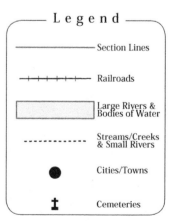

Scale: Section = 1 mile X 1 mile
(there are some exceptions)

Map Group 10: Index to Land Patents

Township 10-North Range 7-West (Ohio River Survey)

After you locate an individual in this Index, take note of the Section and Section Part then proceed to the Land Patent map on the pages immediately following. You should have no difficulty locating the corresponding parcel of land.

The "For More Info" Column will lead you to more information about the underlying Patents. See the *Legend* at right, and the "How to Use this Book" chapter, for more information.

```
                      LEGEND
              "For More Info . . . " column
A = Authority (Legislative Act, See Appendix "A")
B = Block or Lot (location in Section unknown)
C = Cancelled Patent
F = Fractional Section
G = Group  (Multi-Patentee Patent, see Appendix "C")
V = Overlaps another Parcel
R = Re-Issued (Parcel patented more than once)

(A & G items require you to look in the Appendixes referred
to above. All other Letter-designations followed by a number
require you to locate line-items in this index that possess
the ID number found after the letter).
```

ID	Individual in Patent	Sec.	Sec. Part	Date Issued	Other Counties	For More Info . . .
1210	BARKHURST, Joshua	22	E½NE	1823-09-01		A1
1211	" "	22	W½NW	1823-09-01		A1
1212	BOND, Larkin	12	W½NW	1825-03-10		A1
1202	CALDWELL, James	13	SW	1964-03-04		A1
1205	CAMPBELL, James	27	W½SE	1827-08-10		A1 G70
1200	CAROTHERS, Christopher	22	E½NW	1823-09-20		A1
1203	CAROTHERS, James	22	W½NE	1822-04-05		A1
1204	GARDINER, James	22	E½SE	1826-05-20		A1
1201	GRACEY, Jackson	15	W½SE	1823-09-20		A1
1215	GRIFFIN, Robert	5	NW	1967-01-05		A1
1216	GRIFFITH, Thomas	12	E½SW	1824-10-20		A1
1217	" "	12	W½SW	1827-04-10		A1
1214	MASTERS, Richard	24	E½SE	1826-08-12		A1 G63
1214	MASTERS, William	24	E½SE	1826-08-12		A1 G63
1218	MILLER, George	6	NE	1966-11-17		A1 G74
1205	NICHOLS, James	27	W½SE	1827-08-10		A1 G70
1199	PULLEY, Adam	22	W½SE	1822-04-30		A1
1218	RENNER, Tobias	6	NE	1966-11-17		A1 G74
1207	STEWART, John	17	NW	1958-09-08		A1
1208	TURKLE, John	15	NW	1822-04-05		A1
1209	TURKLE, Joseph	15	SW	1822-04-05		A1
1213	WELLS, Levi	15	E½SE	1822-04-30		A1
1206	WOODGET, Jared	12	E½NW	1827-03-06		A1

Patent Map

T10-N R7-W
Ohio River Survey Meridian

Map Group 10

Township Statistics

Parcels Mapped	:	20
Number of Patents	:	20
Number of Individuals	:	21
Patentees Identified	:	18
Number of Surnames	:	19
Multi-Patentee Parcels	:	3
Oldest Patent Date	:	4/5/1822
Most Recent Patent	:	1/5/1967
Block/Lot Parcels	:	0
Parcels Re - Issued	:	0
Parcels that Overlap	:	0
Cities and Towns	:	2
Cemeteries	:	6

36	30	24
		MASTERS [63] Richard 1826

35	29	23

34	28	22 — BARKHURST Joshua 1823 / CAROTHERS Christopher 1823 / CAROTHERS James 1822 / BARKHURST Joshua 1823 / PULLEY Adam 1822 / GARDINER James 1826

33	27 — NICHOLS [70] James 1827	21

32	26	20

31	25	19

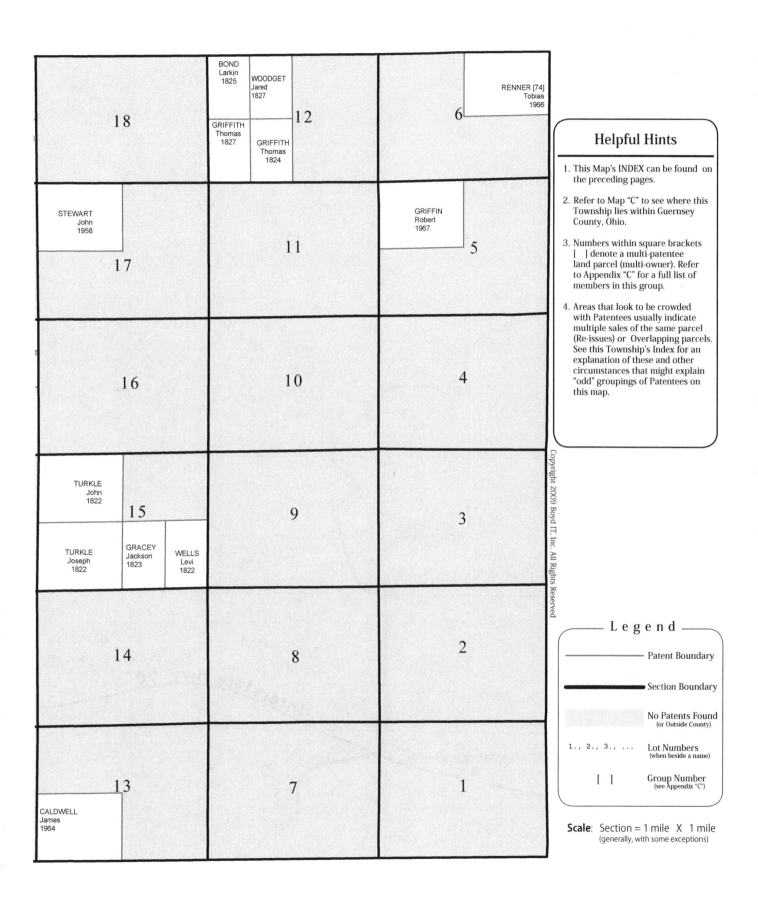

18

BOND
Larkin
1825

WOODGET
Jared
1827

12

GRIFFITH
Thomas
1827

GRIFFITH
Thomas
1824

6

RENNER [74]
Tobias
1966

STEWART
John
1958

17

11

GRIFFIN
Robert
1967

5

16

10

4

TURKLE
John
1822

15

TURKLE
Joseph
1822

GRACEY
Jackson
1823

WELLS
Levi
1822

9

3

14

8

2

13

CALDWELL
James
1964

7

1

Helpful Hints

1. This Map's INDEX can be found on the preceding pages.

2. Refer to Map "C" to see where this Township lies within Guernsey County, Ohio.

3. Numbers within square brackets [ ] denote a multi-patentee land parcel (multi-owner). Refer to Appendix "C" for a full list of members in this group.

4. Areas that look to be crowded with Patentees usually indicate multiple sales of the same parcel (Re-issues) or Overlapping parcels. See this Township's Index for an explanation of these and other circumstances that might explain "odd" groupings of Patentees on this map.

L e g e n d

―――――― Patent Boundary

━━━━━━ Section Boundary

No Patents Found
(or Outside County)

1., 2., 3., ... Lot Numbers
(when beside a name)

[ ] Group Number
(see Appendix "C")

Scale: Section = 1 mile X 1 mile
(generally, with some exceptions)

Road Map

T10-N R7-W
Ohio River Survey Meridian

Map Group 10

Cities & Towns
Fairview
Middlebourne

Cemeteries
Bond Cemetery
Bunfills Cemetery
Fairview Cemetery
McCoy Cemetery
Pisgah Cemetery
Salt Fork Baptist Cemetery

36

30

24

Millers Fork Rd

Reven Rd

Quiet Lane

Cocus Ln

Jasper Rd

Hatfield Ln

35

29

23

Marshall Rd

McCoy Rd

Davey Ln

Blaze Rd

Grassy Ln

34

28

22

Tyson Mill Rd

Stevens Ln

Turkle Rd

Kansas Rd

33

27

21

Baptist Rd

Salt Fork
Baptist Cem.

Hoover

Pike St

Hanna Rd

Pisgah Rd

Wadsworth Rd

20

32

26

Wrights Ln

Pisgah Cem.

Morris Ln

Wells Rd

Interstate Hwy 70

Horseshoe Ln

Fonner Ln

Middlebourne

Bridgewater Rd

Caldwell

Aaron

Benbow Ln

25

19

31

Rosedale Rd

Lydick Rd

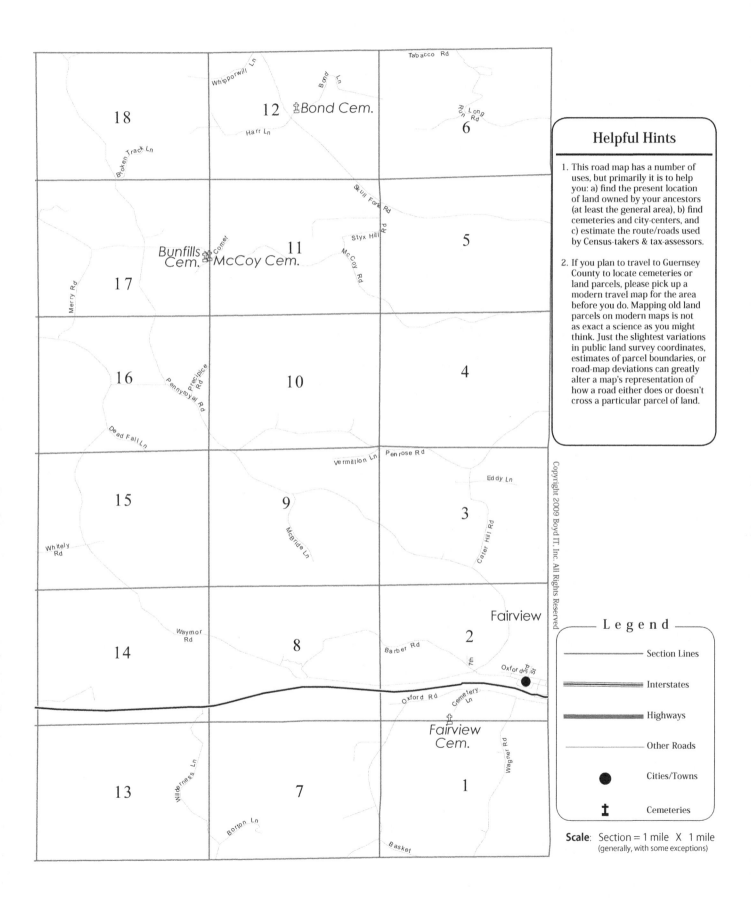

Helpful Hints

1. This road map has a number of uses, but primarily it is to help you: a) find the present location of land owned by your ancestors (at least the general area), b) find cemeteries and city-centers, and c) estimate the route/roads used by Census-takers & tax-assessors.

2. If you plan to travel to Guernsey County to locate cemeteries or land parcels, please pick up a modern travel map for the area before you do. Mapping old land parcels on modern maps is not as exact a science as you might think. Just the slightest variations in public land survey coordinates, estimates of parcel boundaries, or road-map deviations can greatly alter a map's representation of how a road either does or doesn't cross a particular parcel of land.

Legend

———	Section Lines
═══	Interstates
▬▬▬	Highways
———	Other Roads
●	Cities/Towns
✝	Cemeteries

Scale: Section = 1 mile X 1 mile
(generally, with some exceptions)

Historical Map

T10-N R7-W
Ohio River Survey Meridian

Map Group 10

Cities & Towns
Fairview
Middlebourne

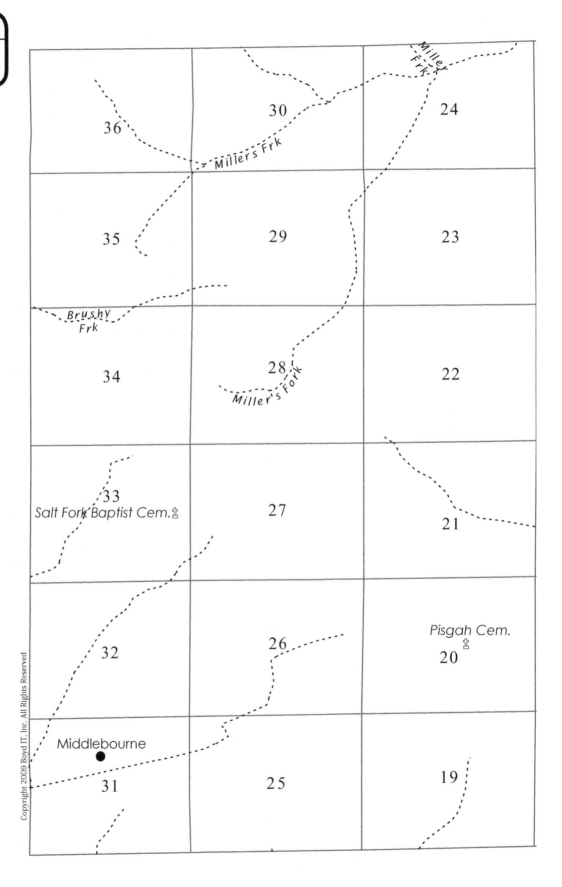

Cemeteries
Bond Cemetery
Bunfills Cemetery
Fairview Cemetery
McCoy Cemetery
Pisgah Cemetery
Salt Fork Baptist Cemetery

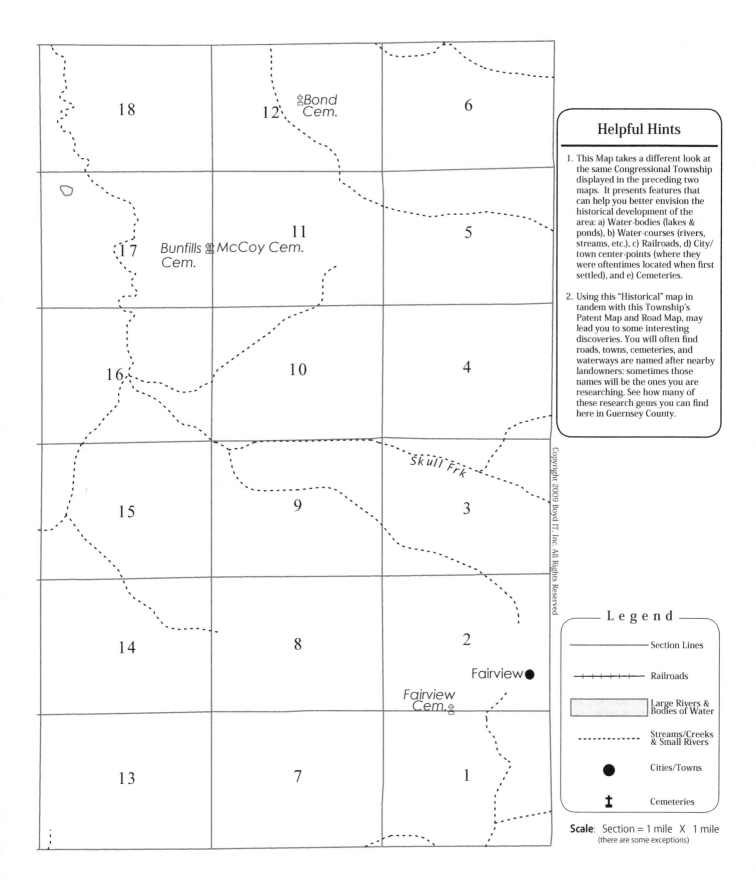

18

12 ⚰Bond Cem.

6

Helpful Hints

1. This Map takes a different look at the same Congressional Township displayed in the preceding two maps. It presents features that can help you better envision the historical development of the area: a) Water-bodies (lakes & ponds), b) Water-courses (rivers, streams, etc.), c) Railroads, d) City/ town center-points (where they were oftentimes located when first settled), and e) Cemeteries.

2. Using this "Historical" map in tandem with this Township's Patent Map and Road Map, may lead you to some interesting discoveries. You will often find roads, towns, cemeteries, and waterways are named after nearby landowners: sometimes those names will be the ones you are researching. See how many of these research gems you can find here in Guernsey County.

17   Bunfills ⚰McCoy Cem. Cem.

11

5

16

10

4

Skull Frk

15

9

3

14

8

2

Fairview ●

Fairview Cem. ✝

L e g e n d

————————	Section Lines
┼┼┼┼┼┼	Railroads
▭	Large Rivers & Bodies of Water
------------	Streams/Creeks & Small Rivers
●	Cities/Towns
✝	Cemeteries

13

7

1

Scale: Section = 1 mile X 1 mile
(there are some exceptions)

Map Group 11: Index to Land Patents

Township 2-North Range 4-West (U.S. Military Survey)

After you locate an individual in this Index, take note of the Section and Section Part then proceed to the Land Patent map on the pages immediately following. You should have no difficulty locating the corresponding parcel of land.

The "For More Info" Column will lead you to more information about the underlying Patents. See the *Legend* at right, and the "How to Use this Book" chapter, for more information.

```
                      LEGEND
            "For More Info . . . " column
A = Authority (Legislative Act, See Appendix "A")
B = Block or Lot (location in Section unknown)
C = Cancelled Patent
F = Fractional Section
G = Group (Multi-Patentee Patent, see Appendix "C")
V = Overlaps another Parcel
R = Re-Issued (Parcel patented more than once)

(A & G items require you to look in the Appendixes referred
to above. All other Letter-designations followed by a number
require you to locate line-items in this index that possess
the ID number found after the letter).
```

ID	Individual in Patent	Sec.	Sec. Part	Date Issued	Other Counties	For More Info . . .
1222	ANNETT, Arthur	20	E½NW	1823-08-20		A1
1248	" "	20	SWNW	1835-04-21		A1 G80
1228	BELL, Francis	2	E½NE	1830-12-01		A1
1230	BELL, George	13	W½SW	1823-08-20		A1
1236	BIGHAM, James	11	NWNE	1835-10-05		A1
1220	BLAIR, Alexander	12	W½SE	1829-04-01		A1
1273	BLAIR, William	12	SENE	1837-08-05		A1
1263	BRADEN, Samuel	20	NWNW	1837-04-10		A1
1237	BRADFORD, James	12	SWNE	1835-04-21		A1
1240	BRADING, John	12	E½SE	1837-04-10		A1
1242	BROWN, John	2	E½NW	1828-05-20		A1
1241	" "	1	SENW	1835-09-23		A1
1238	CLEMENTS, James	19	W½NE	1829-04-01		A1
1221	COCHRAN, Alexander	1	W½NW	1832-10-10		A1
1274	DARRAUGH, William	13	E½NE	1828-05-30		A1
1254	FORD, Robert	11	S½NE	1837-04-10		A1
1226	FRAZIER, David	13	W½NW	1831-02-10		A1
1275	FULTON, William	3	W½SE	1832-04-02		A1
1272	GIST, Thomas	2	W½SW	1830-12-01		A1
1233	HAINS, Jacob	11	NESE	1837-08-10		A1
1229	HAMMOND, John	12	N½NE	1835-09-23		A1 G77
1234	HEANS, Jacob	3	W½NE	1830-12-01		A1
1219	HERST, Aaron	1	NENW	1837-08-05		A1
1227	JACKSON, David	10	NW	1827-10-20		A1
1239	JOHNSTON, James	8	E½NE	1824-04-17		A1
1276	LAW, William	4	NW	1826-05-01		A1
1249	LINDLEY, Joseph	19	E½NE	1825-03-10		A1
1255	LISLE, Robert	3	E½NE	1831-02-10		A1
1253	MACKEY, Richard	8	W½NW	1831-02-10		A1
1256	MACKEY, Robert	8	E½NW	1826-10-02		A1
1257	" "	9	W½SW	1831-02-10		A1
1258	MCCRACKEN, Robert	12	NW	1823-08-20		A1
1259	" "	15	W½NE	1825-03-10		A1
1232	MCILYAR, Isaiah	11	W½SE	1827-12-20		A1
1279	MCILYAR, William	20	NENE	1835-04-21		A1
1277	" "	11	E½SW	1835-04-30		A1
1278	" "	11	SESE	1835-09-08		A1
1264	MCKNIGHT, Samuel	11	E½NW	1835-09-30		A1
1243	MCMICHAEL, John	13	E½SW	1823-08-20		A1
1245	MEHAFFEY, John	18	W½NW	1826-06-06		A1
1244	" "	18	E½NW	1826-10-02		A1
1260	MEHAFFEY, Robert	9	E½NE	1830-12-01		A1
1261	" "	9	W½NE	1831-02-10		A1
1266	MEHAFFEY, Samuel	9	E½NW	1828-01-30		A1
1267	" "	9	W½NW	1830-12-01		A1
1265	" "	10	E½SE	1831-03-01		A1

ID	Individual in Patent	Sec.	Sec. Part	Date Issued	Other Counties	For More Info . . .
1268	MEHAFFY, Samuel	10	W½SE	1831-06-01		A1
1269	MEHOFFY, Samuel	11	NENE	1835-09-23		A1
1246	NORRIS, John	8	W½NE	1831-02-10		A1
1251	PAXTON, Nathaniel	14	W½SW	1828-01-30		A1
1247	ROSE, John	9	E½SW	1827-04-03		A1
1229	SCOTT, Francis	12	N½NE	1835-09-23		A1 G77
1281	SHERRARD, William	10	W½SW	1832-04-02		A1
1280	" "	10	E½SW	1835-04-02		A1
1250	SIMPSON, Joseph	11	W½NW	1835-09-23		A1
1248	STANBERY, Jonas	20	SWNW	1835-04-21		A1 G80
1231	STEVENSON, George	15	E½NE	1827-06-01		A1
1252	SUIT, Philip C	20	SENE	1837-04-10		A1
1235	SUNAFRANK, Jacob	20	E½SE	1831-02-10		A1
1224	TONER, Charles	14	E½SE	1824-04-17		A1
1225	" "	14	W½SE	1826-10-02		A1
1262	VOORHES, Robert	2	NWNE	1835-04-30		A1
1270	WARD, Samuel	11	W½SW	1831-02-10		A1
1271	WELLS, Samuel	2	SWNE	1837-08-02		A1
1223	WHITE, Benjamin	13	W½SE	1831-02-10		A1

Patent Map

T2-N R4-W
U.S. Military Survey Meridian

Map Group 11

Township Statistics

Parcels Mapped	:	63
Number of Patents	:	63
Number of Individuals	:	53
Patentees Identified	:	52
Number of Surnames	:	47
Multi-Patentee Parcels	:	2
Oldest Patent Date	:	8/20/1823
Most Recent Patent	:	8/10/1837
Block/Lot Parcels	:	0
Parcels Re - Issued	:	0
Parcels that Overlap	:	0
Cities and Towns	:	3
Cemeteries	:	3

LAW
William
1826

5

4

HEANS
Jacob
1830

LISLE
Robert
1831

3

FULTON
William
1832

6

7

MACKEY
Richard
1831

MACKEY
Robert
1826

NORRIS
John
1831

JOHNSTON
James
1824

8

MCCRACKEN
Robert
1825

STEVENSON
George
1827

PAXTON
Nathaniel
1828

15

14

TONER
Charles
1826

TONER
Charles
1824

FRAZIER
David
1831

BELL
George
1823

MCMICHAEL
John
1823

13

WHITE
Benjamin
1831

DARRAUGH
William
1828

MEHAFFEY
John
1826

MEHAFFEY
John
1826

16

17

18

25

24

23

BROWN John 1828	VOORHES Robert 1835	BELL Francis 1830	COCHRAN Alexander 1832	HERST Aaron 1837		
	WELLS Samuel 1837			BROWN John 1835	**1**	
GIST Thomas 1830	**2**					
MEHAFFEY Samuel 1830	MEHAFFEY Robert 1831			JACKSON David 1827		
	MEHAFFEY Samuel 1828	MEHAFFEY Robert 1830		**10**		
MACKEY Robert 1831	**9**		SHERRARD William 1835			
	ROSE John 1827		SHERRARD William 1832	MEHAFFY Samuel 1831	MEHAFFEY Samuel 1831	

Helpful Hints

1. This Map's INDEX can be found on the preceding pages.

2. Refer to Map "C" to see where this Township lies within Guernsey County, Ohio.

3. Numbers within square brackets [ ] denote a multi-patentee land parcel (multi-owner). Refer to Appendix "C" for a full list of members in this group.

4. Areas that look to be crowded with Patentees usually indicate multiple sales of the same parcel (Re-issues) or Overlapping parcels. See this Township's Index for an explanation of these and other circumstances that might explain "odd" groupings of Patentees on this map.

MCCRACKEN Robert 1823	SCOTT [77] Francis 1835		SIMPSON Joseph 1835		BIGHAM James 1835	MEHOFFY Samuel 1835
	BRADFORD James 1835	BLAIR William 1837		MCKNIGHT Samuel 1835	FORD Robert 1837	
12			WARD Samuel 1831	**11**		HAINS Jacob 1837
	BLAIR Alexander 1829	BRADING John 1837	MCILYAR William 1835	MCILYAR Isaiah 1827		MCILYAR William 1835
	CLEMENTS James 1829		BRADEN Samuel 1837	ANNETT Arthur 1823		MCILYAR William 1835
		LINDLEY Joseph 1825	STANBERY [80] Jonas 1835	**20**		SUIT Philip C 1837
19						SUNAFRANK Jacob 1831
22			**21**			

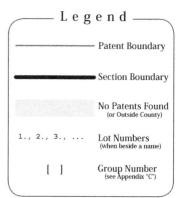

Legend

Patent Boundary

Section Boundary

No Patents Found (or Outside County)

1., 2., 3., ... Lot Numbers (when beside a name)

[ ] Group Number (see Appendix "C")

Scale: Section = 1 mile X 1 mile (generally, with some exceptions)

Road Map

T2-N R4-W
U.S. Military Survey Meridian

Map Group 11

Cities & Towns
Cassell
College Hill
Ridgewood Acres

Cemeteries
Ford Cemetery
Lebanon Cemetery
Sarchet Run Cemetery

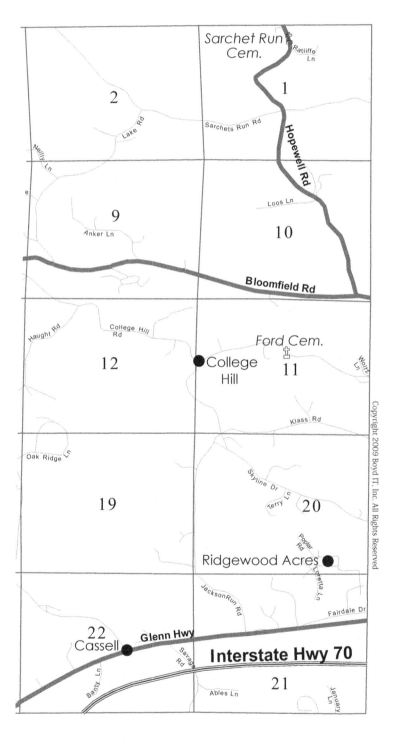

Sarchet Run Cem.

Ratliffe Ln

1

2

Lake Rd

Sarchets Run Rd

Nelly Ln

Hopewell Rd

Loos Ln

9

10

Anker Ln

Bloomfield Rd

Haught Rd

College Hill Rd

Ford Cem.

12

College Hill

11

Wolfz Ln

Klass Rd

Oak Ridge Ln

Skyline Dr

19

Terry Ln

20

Poplar Rd

Ridgewood Acres

Loretta Ln

JacksonRun Rd

Fairdale Dr

22

Glenn Hwy

Cassell

Savage Rd

Interstate Hwy 70

Banty Ln

21

Ables Ln

January Ln

Copyright 2009 Boyd IT, Inc. All Rights Reserved

Helpful Hints

1. This road map has a number of uses, but primarily it is to help you: a) find the present location of land owned by your ancestors (at least the general area), b) find cemeteries and city-centers, and c) estimate the route/roads used by Census-takers & tax-assessors.

2. If you plan to travel to Guernsey County to locate cemeteries or land parcels, please pick up a modern travel map for the area before you do. Mapping old land parcels on modern maps is not as exact a science as you might think. Just the slightest variations in public land survey coordinates, estimates of parcel boundaries, or road-map deviations can greatly alter a map's representation of how a road either does or doesn't cross a particular parcel of land.

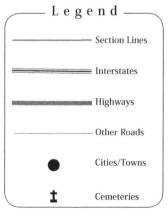

Legend

————————	Section Lines
════════════	Interstates
▬▬▬▬▬▬▬▬	Highways
————————	Other Roads
●	Cities/Towns
✝	Cemeteries

Scale: Section = 1 mile X 1 mile
(generally, with some exceptions)

Historical Map

T2-N R4-W
U.S. Military Survey Meridian

Map Group 11

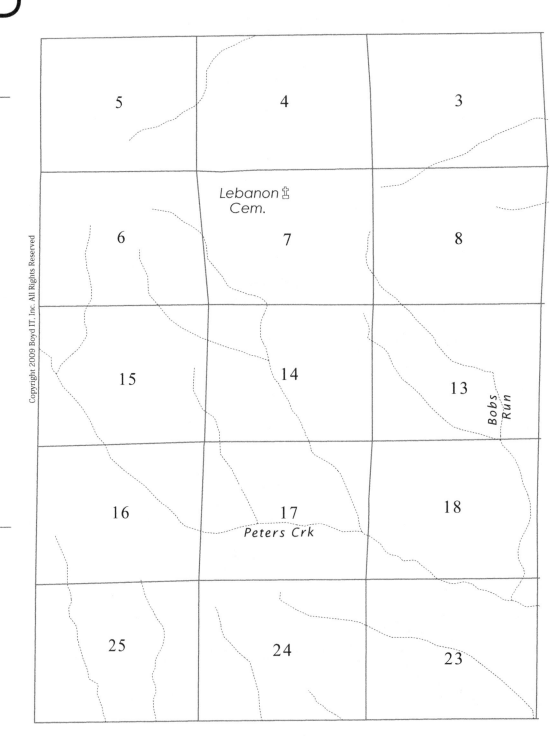

Cities & Towns
Cassell
College Hill
Ridgewood Acres

Cemeteries
Ford Cemetery
Lebanon Cemetery
Sarchet Run Cemetery

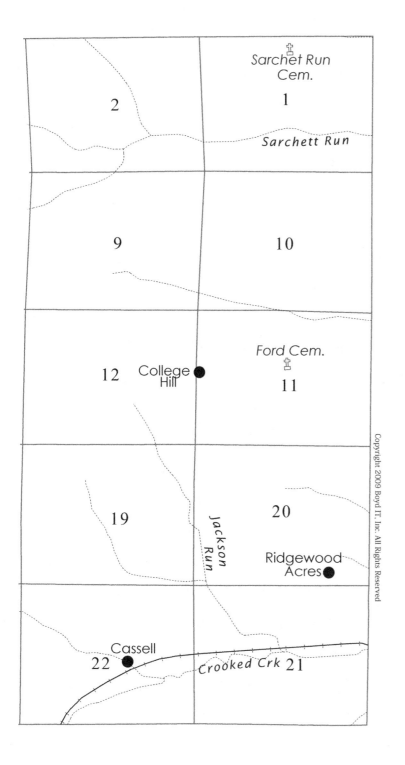

Helpful Hints

1. This Map takes a different look at the same Congressional Township displayed in the preceding two maps. It presents features that can help you better envision the historical development of the area: a) Water-bodies (lakes & ponds), b) Water-courses (rivers, streams, etc.), c) Railroads, d) City/town center-points (where they were oftentimes located when first settled), and e) Cemeteries.

2. Using this "Historical" map in tandem with this Township's Patent Map and Road Map, may lead you to some interesting discoveries. You will often find roads, towns, cemeteries, and waterways are named after nearby landowners: sometimes those names will be the ones you are researching. See how many of these research gems you can find here in Guernsey County.

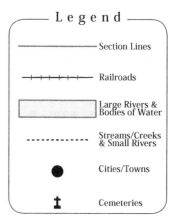

Legend

——————— Section Lines

-+-+-+-+- Railroads

Large Rivers & Bodies of Water

- - - - - - Streams/Creeks & Small Rivers

● Cities/Towns

✝ Cemeteries

Scale: Section = 1 mile X 1 mile
(there are some exceptions)

Map Group 12: Index to Land Patents

Township 2-North Range 3-West (U.S. Military Survey)

After you locate an individual in this Index, take note of the Section and Section Part then proceed to the Land Patent map on the pages immediately following. You should have no difficulty locating the corresponding parcel of land.

The "For More Info" Column will lead you to more information about the underlying Patents. See the *Legend* at right, and the "How to Use this Book" chapter, for more information.

LEGEND
"For More Info . . . " column
A = Authority (Legislative Act, See Appendix "A")
B = Block or Lot (location in Section unknown)
C = Cancelled Patent
F = Fractional Section
G = Group (Multi-Patentee Patent, see Appendix "C")
V = Overlaps another Parcel
R = Re-Issued (Parcel patented more than once)
(A & G items require you to look in the Appendixes referred to above. All other Letter-designations followed by a number require you to locate line-items in this index that possess the ID number found after the letter).

ID	Individual in Patent	Sec.	Sec. Part	Date Issued	Other Counties	For More Info . . .
1300	ASKINS, John	11	NWNW	1834-06-27		A1 G2
1300	ASKINS, Polly	11	NWNW	1834-06-27		A1 G2
1315	BEATTY, Zaccheus A	3		1801-11-06		A2 G7
1313	" "	14	NE	1950-07-24		A1 G5
1314	" "	14	NW	1950-07-24		A1 G5
1315	BIGGS, Zaccheus	3		1801-11-06		A2 G7
1313	" "	14	NE	1950-07-24		A1 G5
1314	" "	14	NW	1950-07-24		A1 G5
1283	BLAIR, Alexander	5	W½NW	1837-08-05		A1
1284	" "	7	NWNW	1837-08-05		A1
1290	BLAIR, James	11	E½NE	1825-03-10		A1
1285	DAVIS, Alexander	6	E½NW	1827-12-20		A1
1303	FERBACK, Thomas	2	E½SE	1829-06-01		A1
1304	FERBRACH, Thomas	9	E½NW	1825-03-10		A1
1309	FERGUSON, William	11	SWNW	1837-08-05		A1
1310	FOY, William	10	SW	1835-09-14		A1
1289	GOMBAR, Jacob	15	NW	1908-02-24		A1
1282	HERST, Aaron	7	SWNW	1837-04-10		A1
1301	HILL, Richard	10	E½SE	1830-12-01		A1
1305	LENFESTY, Thomas	11	E½NW	1827-07-30		A1
1291	MCCALL, James	6	NWNW	1837-04-10		A1 G64
1291	MCCALL, William M	6	NWNW	1837-04-10		A1 G64
1311	MCCLUNEY, William	4		1801-02-17		A2
1291	MCDOWEL, Mathew	6	NWNW	1837-04-10		A1 G64
1296	MCDOWL, Mathew	6	SWNW	1835-04-21		A1
1306	NEELEY, Thomas	6	E½SE	1828-08-20		A1
1307	NOBLE, Thomas	10	NWNE	1835-09-23		A1
1312	NOBLE, William	10	SWNE	1835-04-21		A1
1308	OLDHAM, Isaac	5	E½NW	1828-05-20		A1 G71
1308	OLDHAM, Thomas	5	E½NW	1828-05-20		A1 G71
1288	PATTERSON, David	6	W½SE	1835-04-02		A1
1297	REEVES, Menassah	10	E½NE	1831-03-01		A1
1286	ROBB, Andrew	1	E½NW	1823-08-20		A1
1287	" "	1	W½NW	1823-08-20		A1
1298	ROBERT, Paul	4	SE	1823-08-20		A1 V1311
1299	" "	7	E½NW	1824-04-17		A1
1295	ROLLINS, Jonathan	6	E½NE	1829-04-01		A1
1292	STEWART, James	10	NWSE	1835-04-21		A1
1293	" "	10	SWSE	1835-09-23		A1
1302	UNDERHILL, Samuel	6	W½NE	1835-09-23		A1
1294	WILLIAMS, John	11	W½NE	1835-09-30		A1

Patent Map

T2-N R3-W
U.S. Military Survey Meridian

Map Group 12

Township Statistics

Parcels Mapped	:	34
Number of Patents	:	34
Number of Individuals	:	33
Patentees Identified	:	29
Number of Surnames	:	28
Multi-Patentee Parcels	:	6
Oldest Patent Date	:	2/17/1801
Most Recent Patent	:	7/24/1950
Block/Lot Parcels	:	0
Parcels Re - Issued	:	0
Parcels that Overlap	:	1
Cities and Towns	:	19
Cemeteries	:	6

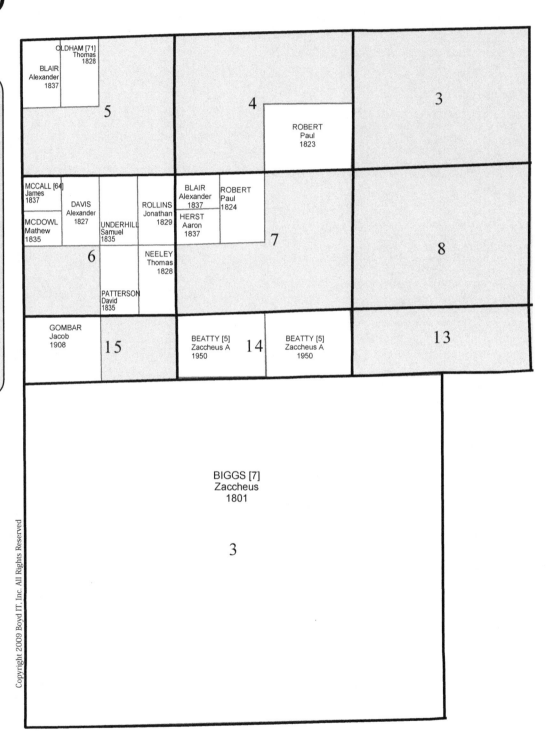

OLDHAM [71]
Thomas
1828

BLAIR
Alexander
1837

5

4

ROBERT
Paul
1823

3

MCCALL [64]
James
1837

DAVIS
Alexander
1827

MCDOWL
Mathew
1835

UNDERHILL
Samuel
1835

ROLLINS
Jonathan
1829

BLAIR
Alexander
1837

ROBERT
Paul
1824

HERST
Aaron
1837

7

8

6

NEELEY
Thomas
1828

PATTERSON
David
1835

GOMBAR
Jacob
1908

15

BEATTY [5]
Zaccheus A
1950

14

BEATTY [5]
Zaccheus A
1950

13

BIGGS [7]
Zaccheus
1801

3

ROBB
Andrew
1823

ROBB
Andrew
1823

2

1

FERBACK
Thomas
1829

NOBLE
Thomas
1835

REEVES
Menassah
1831

FERBRACH
Thomas
1825

9

NOBLE
William
1835

10

STEWART
James
1835

HILL
Richard
1830

FOY
William
1835

STEWART
James
1835

ASKINS [2]
Polly
1834

LENFESTY
Thomas
1827

WILLIAMS
John
1835

BLAIR
James
1825

12

FERGUSON
William
1837

11

MCCLUNEY
William
1801

4

Copyright 2009 Boyd IT, Inc. All Rights Reserved

Helpful Hints

1. This Map's INDEX can be found on the preceding pages.

2. Refer to Map "C" to see where this Township lies within Guernsey County, Ohio.

3. Numbers within square brackets [ ] denote a multi-patentee land parcel (multi-owner). Refer to Appendix "C" for a full list of members in this group.

4. Areas that look to be crowded with Patentees usually indicate multiple sales of the same parcel (Re-issues) or Overlapping parcels. See this Township's Index for an explanation of these and other circumstances that might explain "odd" groupings of Patentees on this map.

Legend

———— Patent Boundary

━━━━ Section Boundary

No Patents Found
(or Outside County)

1., 2., 3., ... Lot Numbers
(when beside a name)

[ ] Group Number
(see Appendix "C")

Scale: Section = 1 mile X 1 mile
(generally, with some exceptions)

Road Map

T2-N R3-W
U.S. Military Survey Meridian

Map Group 12

Cities & Towns

Abledell
Barton Manor
Black
Browns Heights
Cambridge
Cedar Hills
Coventry Estates
East Cambridge
Eastmoor
Fairdale
Fairmont
Five Forks
Georgetown
Henderson Heights
Meadow Village
Northgate
Oldham
Sunnymeade
Sycamore Hills

Cemeteries

Center Baptist Cemetery
Founders Cemetery
Guernsey Memorial Gardens
Mount Calvary Cemetery
Northwood Cemetery
Old City Cemetery

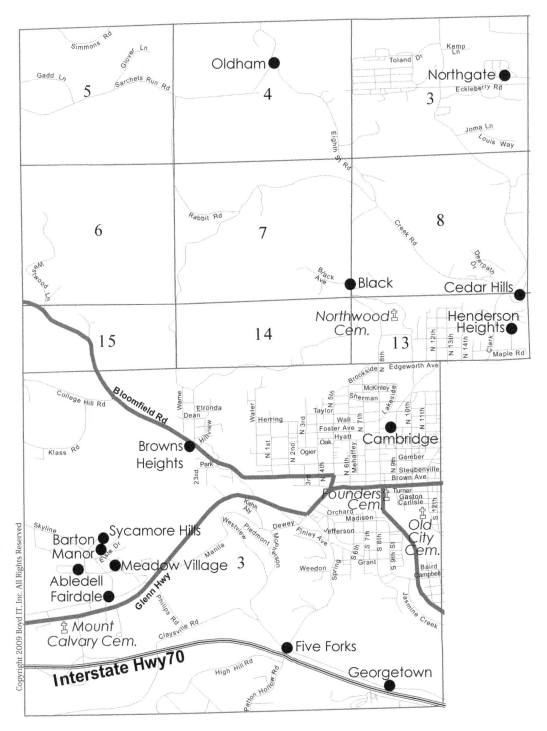

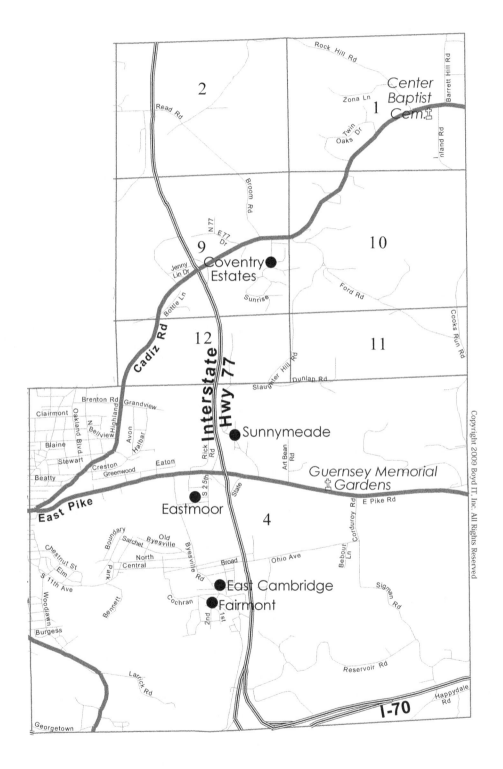

Helpful Hints

1. This road map has a number of uses, but primarily it is to help you: a) find the present location of land owned by your ancestors (at least the general area), b) find cemeteries and city-centers, and c) estimate the route/roads used by Census-takers & tax-assessors.

2. If you plan to travel to Guernsey County to locate cemeteries or land parcels, please pick up a modern travel map for the area before you do. Mapping old land parcels on modern maps is not as exact a science as you might think. Just the slightest variations in public land survey coordinates, estimates of parcel boundaries, or road-map deviations can greatly alter a map's representation of how a road either does or doesn't cross a particular parcel of land.

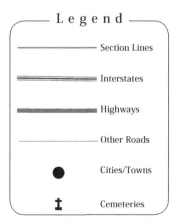

Legend

———————	Section Lines
═══════════	Interstates
▬▬▬▬▬▬▬	Highways
———————	Other Roads
●	Cities/Towns
✝	Cemeteries

Scale: Section = 1 mile X 1 mile
(generally, with some exceptions)

Historical Map

T2-N R3-W
U.S. Military Survey Meridian

Map Group 12

Cities & Towns
Abledell
Barton Manor
Black
Browns Heights
Cambridge
Cedar Hills
Coventry Estates
East Cambridge
Eastmoor
Fairdale
Fairmont
Five Forks
Georgetown
Henderson Heights
Meadow Village
Northgate
Oldham
Sunnymeade
Sycamore Hills

Cemeteries
Center Baptist Cemetery
Founders Cemetery
Guernsey Memorial Gardens
Mount Calvary Cemetery
Northwood Cemetery
Old City Cemetery

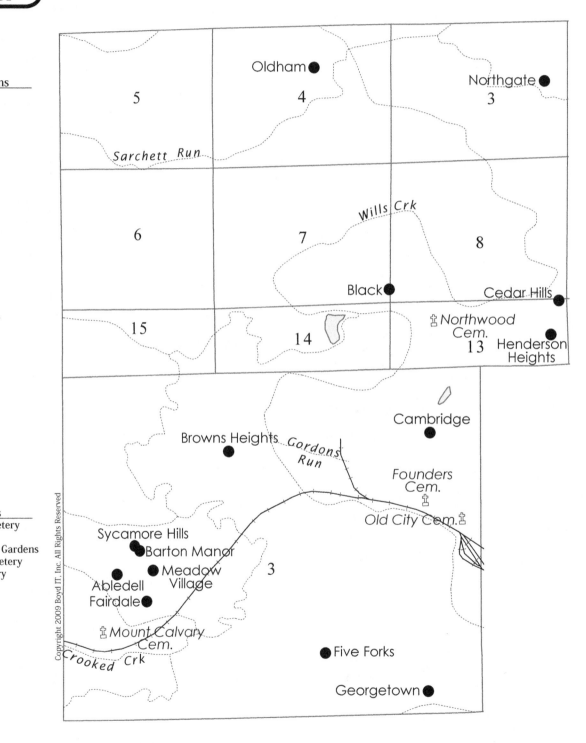

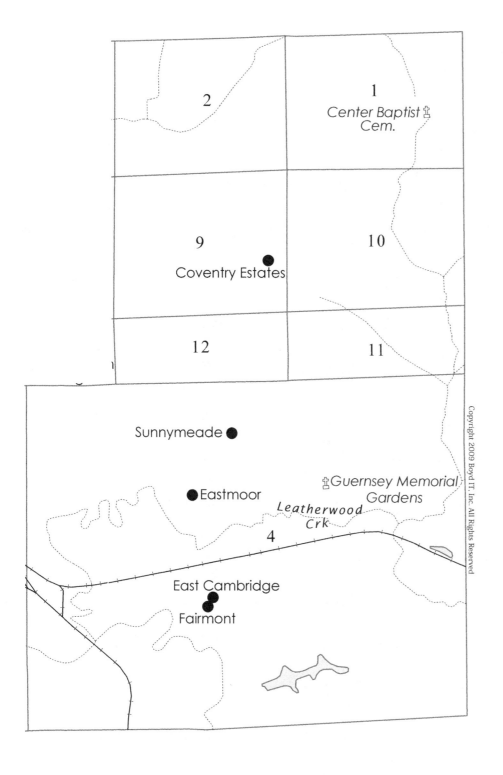

Helpful Hints

1. This Map takes a different look at the same Congressional Township displayed in the preceding two maps. It presents features that can help you better envision the historical development of the area: a) Water-bodies (lakes & ponds), b) Water-courses (rivers, streams, etc.), c) Railroads, d) City/town center-points (where they were oftentimes located when first settled), and e) Cemeteries.

2. Using this "Historical" map in tandem with this Township's Patent Map and Road Map, may lead you to some interesting discoveries. You will often find roads, towns, cemeteries, and waterways are named after nearby landowners: sometimes those names will be the ones you are researching. See how many of these research gems you can find here in Guernsey County.

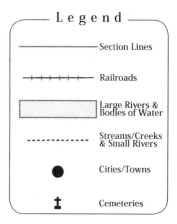

Legend

——————	Section Lines
┼┼┼┼┼┼	Railroads
▭	Large Rivers & Bodies of Water
------------	Streams/Creeks & Small Rivers
●	Cities/Towns
⚓	Cemeteries

Scale: Section = 1 mile X 1 mile
(there are some exceptions)

Map Group 13: Index to Land Patents

Township 2-North Range 2-West (U.S. Military Survey)

After you locate an individual in this Index, take note of the Section and Section Part then proceed to the Land Patent map on the pages immediately following. You should have no difficulty locating the corresponding parcel of land.

The "For More Info" Column will lead you to more information about the underlying Patents. See the *Legend* at right, and the "How to Use this Book" chapter, for more information.

```
                      LEGEND
            "For More Info . . ." column
A = Authority (Legislative Act, See Appendix "A")
B = Block or Lot (location in Section unknown)
C = Cancelled Patent
F = Fractional Section
G = Group  (Multi-Patentee Patent, see Appendix "C")
V = Overlaps another Parcel
R = Re-Issued (Parcel patented more than once)

(A & G items require you to look in the Appendixes referred
to above. All other Letter-designations followed by a number
require you to locate line-items in this index that possess
the ID number found after the letter).
```

ID	Individual in Patent	Sec.	Sec. Part	Date Issued	Other Counties	For More Info . . .
1350	BARBER, John	3	21	1803-03-29		A2
1346	BEAHAM, James	3	38	1801-09-21		A2
1332	BEYMER, George	3	15	1805-05-06		A2
1333	" "	3	16	1805-05-06		A2
1334	" "	3	17	1805-05-06		A2
1380	BEYMER, Philip	13	NE	1821-09-08		A1
1340	BEYNOR, George	11	NE	1907-07-17		A1 G6
1340	BEYNOR, Henry	11	NE	1907-07-17		A1 G6
1325	BICKHAM, Elizabeth	3	8	1805-09-14		A2
1326	" "	3	9	1805-09-14		A2
1385	BLACK, Samuel	7	W½NE	1832-04-02		A1
1363	BLAIR, John	6	E½SE	1823-08-20		A1 G50
1364	" "	6	W½SE	1827-01-30		A1 G50
1351	" "	15	E½NW	1829-05-01		A1
1352	" "	15	W½NW	1830-11-01		A1
1353	" "	6	NESW	1835-09-08		A1
1354	" "	6	SWSW	1835-10-05		A1
1347	BOYD, James	15	SWNE	1835-09-14		A1
1355	BRYANT, John	3	1	1805-05-06		A2
1320	BUCKINGHAM, Alvah	6	NWSW	1835-10-05		A1 G29
1396	CAMPBELL, William	7	W½SW	1827-04-03		A1
1317	CLEGG, Alexander	5	W½NW	1834-06-12		A1
1373	CLEGG, Matthew	4	W½SW	1831-02-10		A1
1374	" "	5	E½NW	1832-04-02		A1
1321	COARTS, Charles	4	E½SW	1831-02-10		A1
1316	COLE, Abner	3	28	1801-09-19		A2
1377	CROSBY, Nathan	3	27	1803-03-29		A2
1390	DYSON, Thomas	9	E½NE	1829-04-01		A1
1356	EAGLETON, John	14	NWNW	1835-09-14		A1
1341	EVANS, Henry H	1	E½SE	1825-08-06		A1
1342	" "	1	W½SE	1826-04-03		A1
1382	EWINGS, Robert	12	E½NW	1823-08-20		A1
1357	FINLEY, John	3	23	1801-09-22		A2
1358	" "	3	24	1801-09-22		A2
1318	FLEMING, Alexander	7	E½SE	1825-03-10		A1
1322	FORD, Charles E	3	18	1807-11-26		A2 G38
1323	" "	3	19	1807-11-26		A2 G38
1322	FORD, Chilion	3	18	1807-11-26		A2 G38
1323	" "	3	19	1807-11-26		A2 G38
1322	FORD, Emily A	3	18	1807-11-26		A2 G38
1323	" "	3	19	1807-11-26		A2 G38
1348	GREENLAND, James	3	30	1802-12-28		A2
1397	HAYS, William	7	E½NW	1829-04-01		A1
1343	HILGER, Henry	3	2	1806-06-04		A2
1359	HILL, John	15	E½NE	1826-06-06		A1
1360	HUFF, John	13	W½NW	1831-02-10		A1

ID	Individual in Patent	Sec.	Sec. Part	Date Issued	Other Counties	For More Info . . .
1392	HYDE, Thomas	13	W½SE	1826-04-01		A1
1391	" "	13	E½SE	1826-05-01		A1
1335	IRWIN, George	14	E½NW	1823-08-20		A1
1378	JACOBY, Nicholas	3	10	1806-05-30		A2
1393	JOHNSTON, Thomas	1	E½NE	1829-05-01		A1
1363	KELL, John	6	E½SE	1823-08-20		A1 G50
1364	" "	6	W½SE	1827-01-30		A1 G50
1361	" "	15	NWNE	1835-04-21		A1
1362	" "	6	SESW	1835-09-30		A1
1375	KERSHAW, Mitchel	3	33	1805-02-26		A2
1376	KERSHAW, Mitchell	3	35	1803-01-03		A2
1395	KNAPP, Uzal	3	31	1802-12-28		A2
1340	LANE, John	11	NE	1907-07-17		A1 G6
1340	LANE, Noah	11	NE	1907-07-17		A1 G6
1365	LAUGHLAND, John	23	W½NE	1826-06-16		A1
1320	LEARD, George	6	NWSW	1835-10-05		A1 G29
1319	MCCOLLUM, Alexander	7	W½NW	1826-06-06		A1
1344	MCCOLLUM, Isaac	7	W½SE	1826-06-06		A1
1394	MCCONN, Thomas	7	E½SW	1826-10-02		A1
1366	MCDOWELL, John	14	SWNW	1837-04-10		A1
1367	MCMULLIN, John	9	W½NE	1829-04-01		A1
1368	MILLER, John	3	22	1802-06-09		A2
1398	OCALLIS, William	3	13	1806-03-26		A2
1399	" "	3	14	1806-03-26		A2
1349	PATTERSON, James	6	SENW	1835-04-30		A1
1388	PATTERSON, Stout	6	NWNW	1835-04-21		A1
1389	" "	6	SWNW	1835-09-23		A1
1387	" "	6	NENW	1837-04-10		A1
1345	PRIOR, Isaac	3	32	1805-06-12		A2
1336	RICE, George	3	5	1805-05-06		A2
1337	" "	3	6	1805-05-06		A2
1338	" "	3	7	1805-05-06		A2
1386	RICH, Samuel	3	29	1801-09-21		A2
1383	ROWEN, Robert	12	E½SW	1823-08-20		A1
1339	SLASON, George	12	W½NW	1826-04-01		A1
1327	SNOW, Elizabeth	3	36	1801-09-21		A2
1371	STOKELY, Joseph	3	3	1810-10-26		A2
1372	" "	3	4	1810-10-26		A2
1369	" "	3	11	1810-11-16		A2
1370	" "	3	12	1810-11-16		A2
1400	TALBUT, William	3	20	1804-03-21		A2
1384	TIMMONS, Robert	3	34	1803-01-03		A2
1328	VERNON, Frederick	3	25	1802-12-31		A2
1329	" "	3	26	1802-12-31		A2
1330	" "	3	39	1802-12-31		A2
1331	" "	3	40	1802-12-31		A2
1324	WEST, Eber	1	SWNE	1835-09-23		A1
1381	WHITE, Philip	3	37	1801-09-19		A2
1379	WIRICK, Obediah G	1	NWNE	1837-08-10		A1
1401	WOODS, William	12	W½SW	1823-08-20		A1

Patent Map

T2-N R2-W
U.S. Military Survey Meridian

Map Group 13

Township Statistics

Parcels Mapped	:	86
Number of Patents	:	73
Number of Individuals	:	67
Patentees Identified	:	62
Number of Surnames	:	58
Multi-Patentee Parcels	:	6
Oldest Patent Date	:	9/19/1801
Most Recent Patent	:	7/17/1907
Block/Lot Parcels	:	40
Parcels Re - Issued	:	0
Parcels that Overlap	:	0
Cities and Towns	:	4
Cemeteries	:	2

Map parcels:

- **5** — CLEGG Alexander 1834; CLEGG Matthew 1832
- **4** — CLEGG Matthew 1831; COARTS Charles 1831
- **3**
- **6** — PATTERSON Stout 1835; PATTERSON Stout 1837; PATTERSON Stout 1835; PATTERSON James 1835; BUCKINGHAM [29] Alvah 1835; BLAIR John 1835; BLAIR John 1835; KELL John 1835; KELL [50] John 1827; KELL [50] John 1823
- **7** — MCCOLLUM Alexander 1826; HAYS William 1829; BLACK Samuel 1832; CAMPBELL William 1827; MCCONN Thomas 1826; MCCOLLUM Isaac 1826; FLEMING Alexander 1825
- **8**
- **15** — BLAIR John 1830; BLAIR John 1829; KELL John 1835; BOYD James 1835; HILL John 1826
- **14** — EAGLETON John 1835; IRWIN George 1823; MCDOWELL John 1837
- **13** — HUFF John 1831; BEYMER Philip 1821; HYDE Thomas 1826; HYDE Thomas 1826
- **18**
- **23** — LAUGHLAND John 1826

Lots-Sec. 3

1	BRYANT, John	1805	21	BARBER, John	1803	
2	HILGER, Henry	1806	22	MILLER, John	1802	
3	STOKELY, Joseph	1810	23	FINLEY, John	1801	
4	STOKELY, Joseph	1810	24	FINLEY, John	1801	
5	RICE, George	1805	25	VERNON, Frederick	1802	
6	RICE, George	1805	26	VERNON, Frederick	1802	
7	RICE, George	1805	27	CROSBY, Nathan	1803	
8	BICKHAM, Elizabeth	1805	28	COLE, Abner	1801	
9	BICKHAM, Elizabeth	1805	29	RICH, Samuel	1801	
10	JACOBY, Nicholas	1806	30	GREENLAND, James	1802	
11	STOKELY, Joseph	1810	31	KNAPP, Uzal	1802	
12	STOKELY, Joseph	1810	32	PRIOR, Isaac	1805	
13	OCALLIS, William	1806	33	KERSHAW, Mitchel	1805	
14	OCALLIS, William	1806	34	TIMMONS, Robert	1803	
15	BEYMER, George	1805	35	KERSHAW, Mitchell	1803	
16	BEYMER, George	1805	36	SNOW, Elizabeth	1801	
17	BEYMER, George	1805	37	WHITE, Philip	1801	
18	FORD, Charles E [38]	1807	38	BEAHAM, James	1801	
19	FORD, Charles E [38]	1807	39	VERNON, Frederick	1802	
20	TALBUT, William	1804	40	VERNON, Frederick	1802	

3

	2		1	WIRICK Obediah G 1837		JOHNSTON Thomas 1829
				WEST Eber 1835		
				EVANS Henry H 1826		EVANS Henry H 1825

	9	MCMULLIN John 1829	DYSON Thomas 1829	10
SLASON George 1826	EWINGS Robert 1823	12		11	BEYNOR [6] Henry 1907
WOODS William 1823	ROWEN Robert 1823			

| 19 | 20 |
| 22 | 21 |

Copyright 2009 Boyd IT, Inc. All Rights Reserved

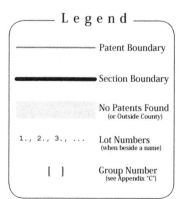

Legend ———

——— Patent Boundary

━━━ Section Boundary

░░░ No Patents Found
(or Outside County)

1., 2., 3., ...   Lot Numbers
(when beside a name)

[ ]   Group Number
(see Appendix "C")

Scale: Section = 1 mile X 1 mile
(generally, with some exceptions)

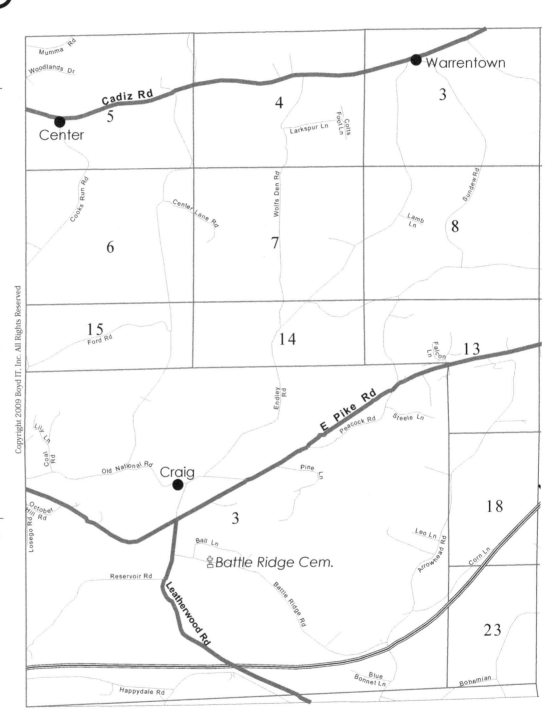

Road Map

T2-N R2-W
U.S. Military Survey Meridian

Map Group 13

Cities & Towns
Center
Craig
Old Washington
Warrentown

Cemeteries
Battle Ridge Cemetery
Old Washington Cemetery

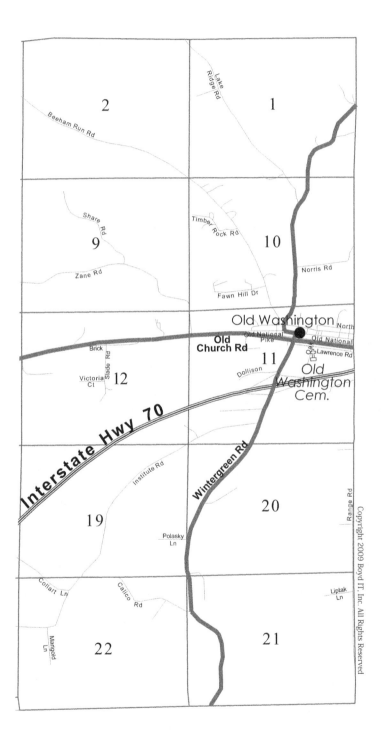

Helpful Hints

1. This road map has a number of uses, but primarily it is to help you: a) find the present location of land owned by your ancestors (at least the general area), b) find cemeteries and city-centers, and c) estimate the route/roads used by Census-takers & tax-assessors.

2. If you plan to travel to Guernsey County to locate cemeteries or land parcels, please pick up a modern travel map for the area before you do. Mapping old land parcels on modern maps is not as exact a science as you might think. Just the slightest variations in public land survey coordinates, estimates of parcel boundaries, or road-map deviations can greatly alter a map's representation of how a road either does or doesn't cross a particular parcel of land.

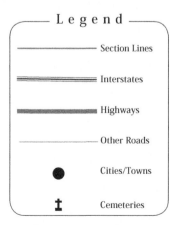

L e g e n d

— Section Lines
— Interstates
— Highways
— Other Roads
● Cities/Towns
† Cemeteries

Scale: Section = 1 mile X 1 mile
(generally, with some exceptions)

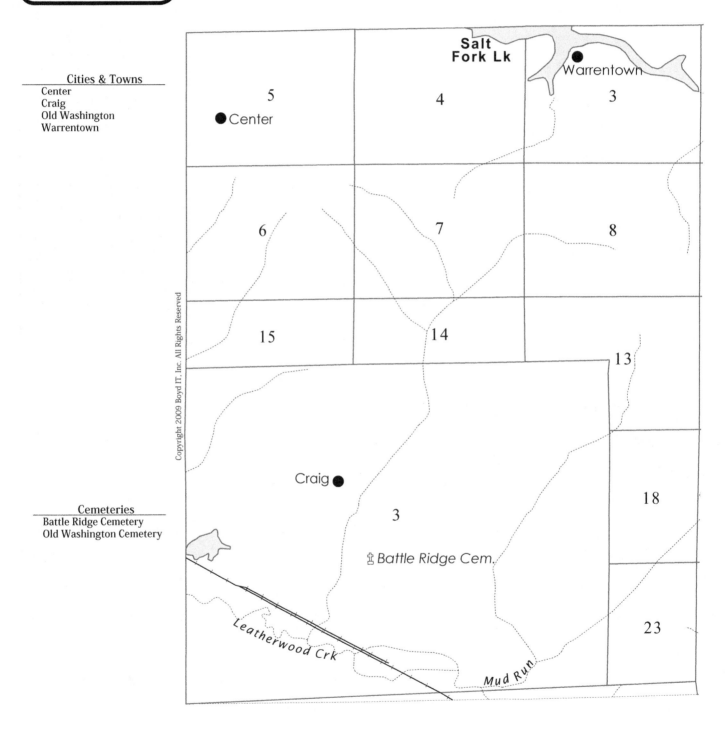

Historical Map

T2-N R2-W
U.S. Military Survey Meridian

Map Group 13

Cities & Towns
Center
Craig
Old Washington
Warrentown

Cemeteries
Battle Ridge Cemetery
Old Washington Cemetery

Salt Fork Lk

Warrentown

5

●Center

4

3

6

7

8

15

14

13

Craig ●

3

⚰ Battle Ridge Cem.

18

23

Leatherwood Crk

Mud Run

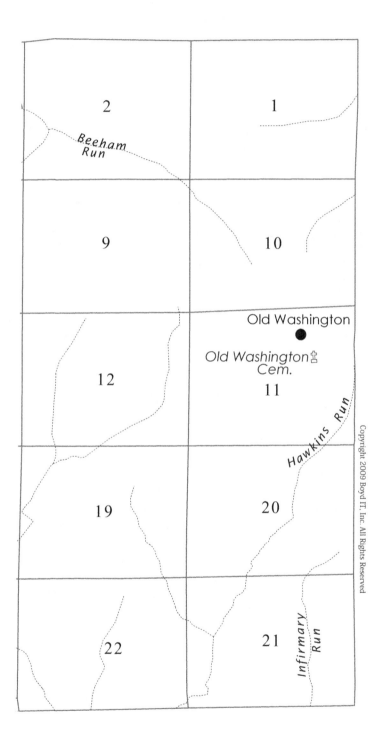

Helpful Hints

1. This Map takes a different look at the same Congressional Township displayed in the preceding two maps. It presents features that can help you better envision the historical development of the area: a) Water-bodies (lakes & ponds), b) Water-courses (rivers, streams, etc.), c) Railroads, d) City/town center-points (where they were oftentimes located when first settled), and e) Cemeteries.

2. Using this "Historical" map in tandem with this Township's Patent Map and Road Map, may lead you to some interesting discoveries. You will often find roads, towns, cemeteries, and waterways are named after nearby landowners: sometimes those names will be the ones you are researching. See how many of these research gems you can find here in Guernsey County.

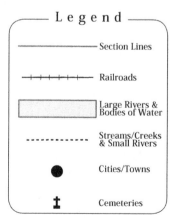

Scale: Section = 1 mile X 1 mile
(there are some exceptions)

Map Group 14: Index to Land Patents

Township 2-North Range 1-West (U.S. Military Survey)

After you locate an individual in this Index, take note of the Section and Section Part then proceed to the Land Patent map on the pages immediately following. You should have no difficulty locating the corresponding parcel of land.

The "For More Info" Column will lead you to more information about the underlying Patents. See the *Legend* at right, and the "How to Use this Book" chapter, for more information.

```
                    LEGEND
            "For More Info . . . " column
A = Authority (Legislative Act, See Appendix "A")
B = Block or Lot (location in Section unknown)
C = Cancelled Patent
F = Fractional Section
G = Group  (Multi-Patentee Patent, see Appendix "C")
V = Overlaps another Parcel
R = Re-Issued (Parcel patented more than once)

(A & G items require you to look in the Appendixes referred
to above. All other Letter-designations followed by a number
require you to locate line-items in this index that possess
the ID number found after the letter).
```

ID	Individual in Patent	Sec.	Sec. Part	Date Issued	Other Counties	For More Info . . .
1403	BEVARD, Charles	14	E½NE	1825-03-10		A1
1404	JOHNSON, James	1		1802-02-06		A2
1405	MCLAUGHLIN, Patrick	8	E½NW	1829-05-01		A1
1402	MOORE, Andrew	12	SE	1908-02-24		A1

Patent Map

T2-N R1-W
U.S. Military Survey Meridian

Map Group 14

Township Statistics

Parcels Mapped	:	4
Number of Patents	:	4
Number of Individuals	:	4
Patentees Identified	:	4
Number of Surnames	:	4
Multi-Patentee Parcels	:	0
Oldest Patent Date	:	2/6/1802
Most Recent Patent	:	2/24/1908
Block/Lot Parcels	:	0
Parcels Re - Issued	:	0
Parcels that Overlap	:	0
Cities and Towns	:	2
Cemeteries	:	5

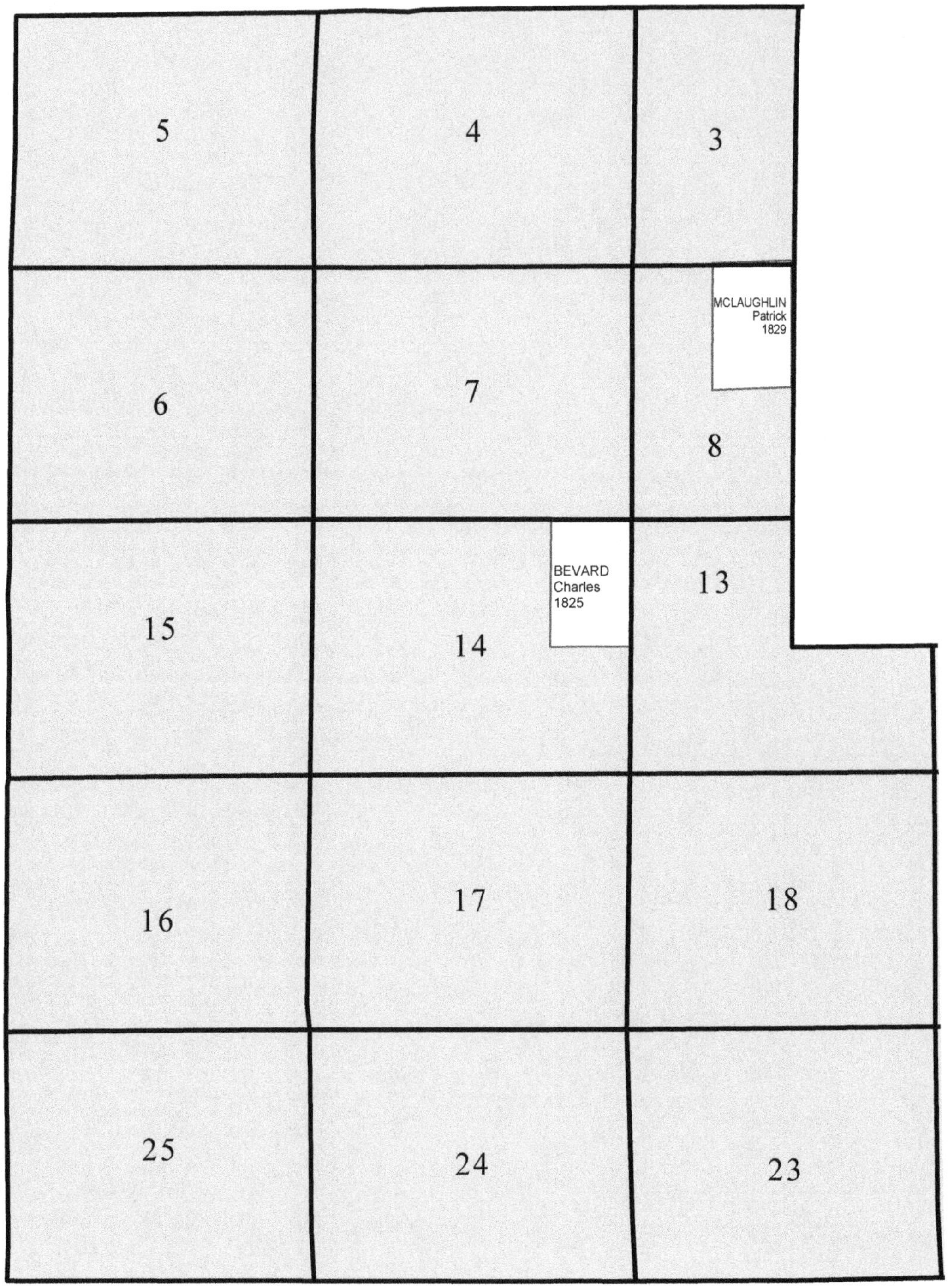

5

4

3

MCLAUGHLIN
Patrick
1829

6

7

8

BEVARD
Charles
1825

15

14

13

16

17

18

25

24

23

Copyright 2009 Boyd IT, Inc. All Rights Reserved

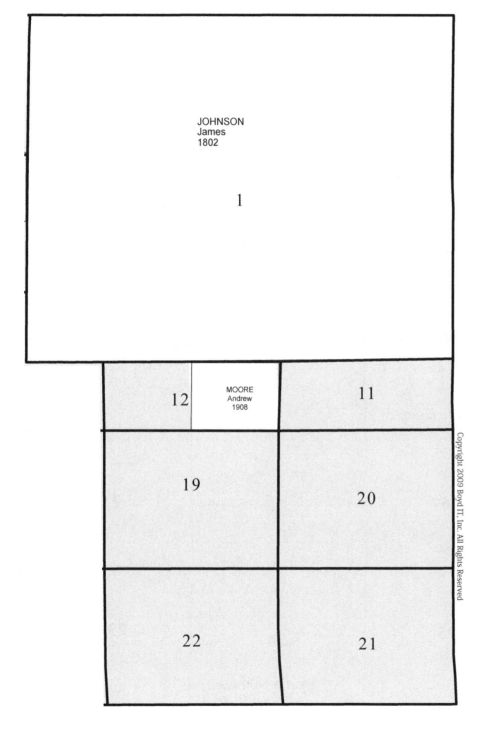

Helpful Hints

1. This Map's INDEX can be found on the preceding pages.

2. Refer to Map "C" to see where this Township lies within Guernsey County, Ohio.

3. Numbers within square brackets [ ] denote a multi-patentee land parcel (multi-owner). Refer to Appendix "C" for a full list of members in this group.

4. Areas that look to be crowded with Patentees usually indicate multiple sales of the same parcel (Re-issues) or Overlapping parcels. See this Township's Index for an explanation of these and other circumstances that might explain "odd" groupings of Patentees on this map.

Legend

——— Patent Boundary

═══ Section Boundary

No Patents Found (or Outside County)

1., 2., 3., ... Lot Numbers (when beside a name)

[ ] Group Number (see Appendix "C")

Scale: Section = 1 mile X 1 mile
(generally, with some exceptions)

Road Map

T2-N R1-W
U.S. Military Survey Meridian

Map Group 14

Cities & Towns
Easton
Elizabethtown

Cemeteries
Carlisle Cemetery
Elizabethtown Cemetery
Frame Number One Cemetery
Leatherwood Cemetery
McQuade Cemetery

Wintergreen Rd

5

Laughman Rd

4

3

Robinson Ln

Norris Rd

Thumb

6

Hitchcock Ln Fairground Rd

7

Slasor Rd

8

Bugos Ln

Elizabethtown Cem.

Old
National

Easton Rd

Old
Church

●Easton

Elizabethtown

15

14

13

Range Rd

Erie Rd

McQuade Cem.

16

County Home Rd

Shugert Ln

17

18

Putney
Ridge Rd

25

Polasky Rd

24

23

Nicholas Ln

Salem Rd

Tipton

*Frame Number
One Cem.*

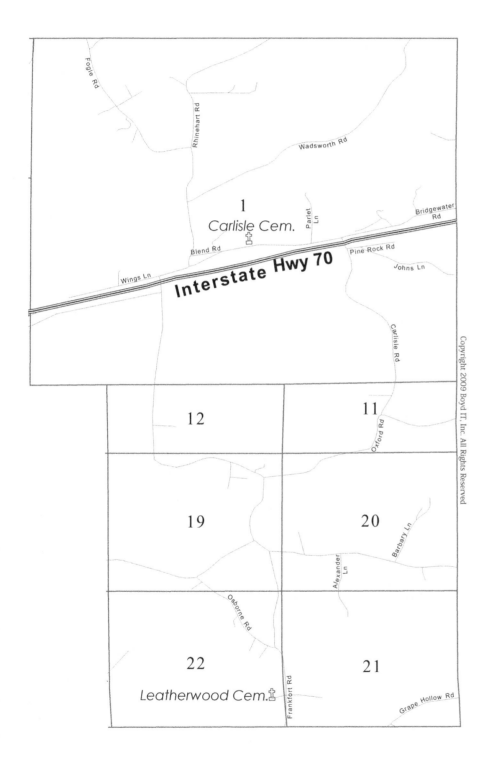

Helpful Hints

1. This road map has a number of uses, but primarily it is to help you: a) find the present location of land owned by your ancestors (at least the general area), b) find cemeteries and city-centers, and c) estimate the route/roads used by Census-takers & tax-assessors.

2. If you plan to travel to Guernsey County to locate cemeteries or land parcels, please pick up a modern travel map for the area before you do. Mapping old land parcels on modern maps is not as exact a science as you might think. Just the slightest variations in public land survey coordinates, estimates of parcel boundaries, or road-map deviations can greatly alter a map's representation of how a road either does or doesn't cross a particular parcel of land.

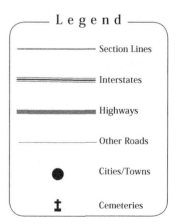

Legend

————	Section Lines
═══════	Interstates
▬▬▬▬	Highways
————	Other Roads
●	Cities/Towns
☦	Cemeteries

Scale: Section = 1 mile X 1 mile
(generally, with some exceptions)

Historical Map

T2-N R1-W
U.S. Military Survey Meridian

Map Group 14

Cities & Towns
Easton
Elizabethtown

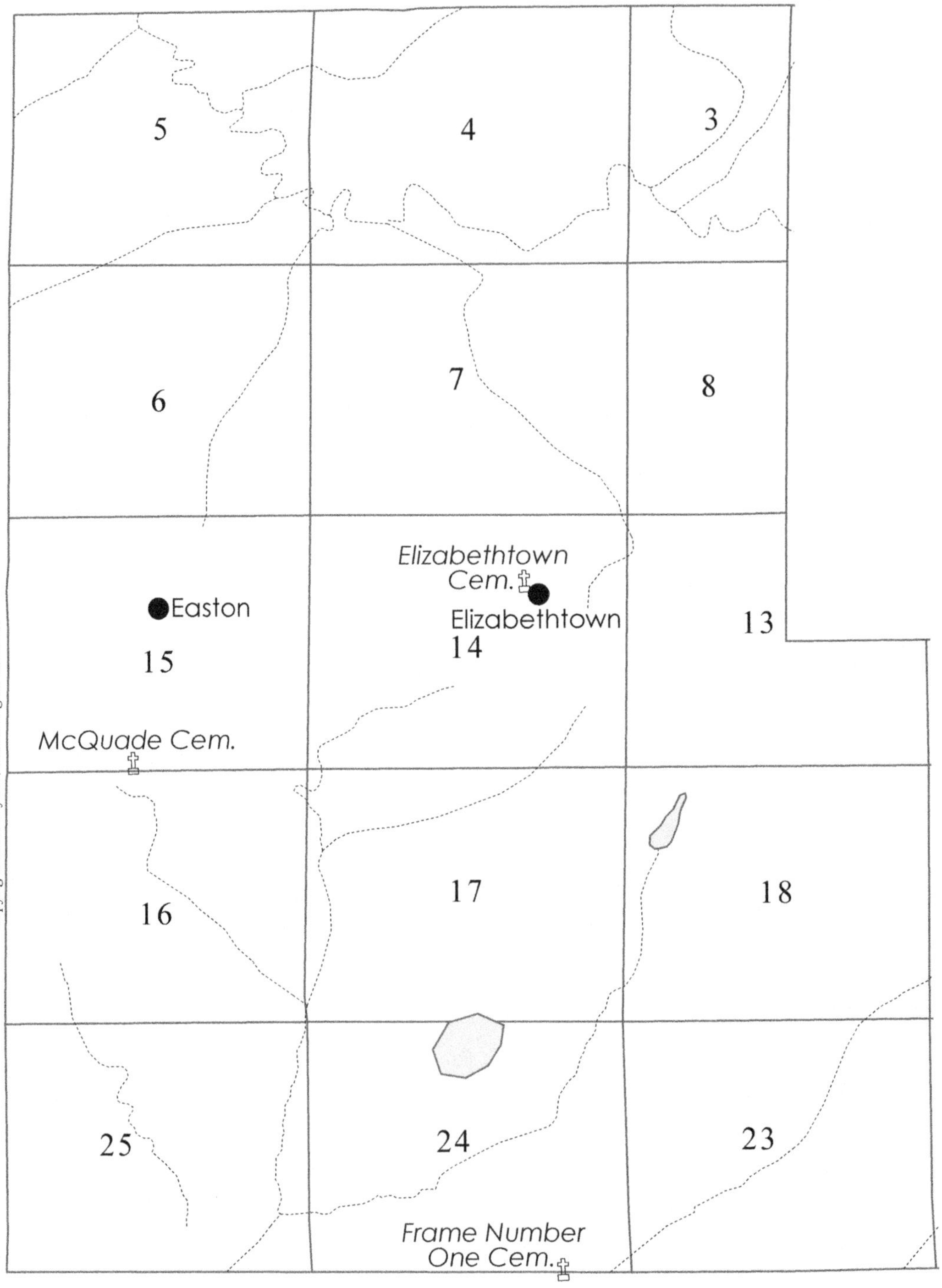

Cemeteries
Carlisle Cemetery
Elizabethtown Cemetery
Frame Number One Cemetery
Leatherwood Cemetery
McQuade Cemetery

5

4

3

6

7

8

●Easton

Elizabethtown Cem. ⚰

Elizabethtown

15

14

13

McQuade Cem.
⚰

16

17

18

25

24

23

Frame Number One Cem. ⚰

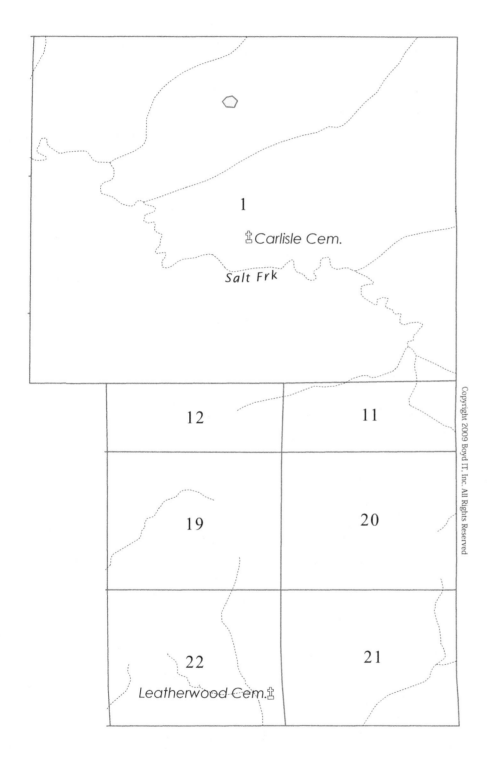

1

♱*Carlisle Cem.*

Salt Frk

12

11

19

20

22

21

Leatherwood Cem.♱

Helpful Hints

1. This Map takes a different look at the same Congressional Township displayed in the preceding two maps. It presents features that can help you better envision the historical development of the area: a) Water-bodies (lakes & ponds), b) Water-courses (rivers, streams, etc.), c) Railroads, d) City/ town center-points (where they were oftentimes located when first settled), and e) Cemeteries.

2. Using this "Historical" map in tandem with this Township's Patent Map and Road Map, may lead you to some interesting discoveries. You will often find roads, towns, cemeteries, and waterways are named after nearby landowners: sometimes those names will be the ones you are researching. See how many of these research gems you can find here in Guernsey County.

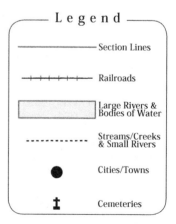

Legend

————	Section Lines
+++++	Railroads
▭	Large Rivers & Bodies of Water
- - - - - -	Streams/Creeks & Small Rivers
●	Cities/Towns
♱	Cemeteries

Scale: Section = 1 mile X 1 mile
(there are some exceptions)

Map Group 15: Index to Land Patents

Township 9-North Range 7-West (Ohio River Survey)

After you locate an individual in this Index, take note of the Section and Section Part then proceed to the Land Patent map on the pages immediately following. You should have no difficulty locating the corresponding parcel of land.

The "For More Info" Column will lead you to more information about the underlying Patents. See the *Legend* at right, and the "How to Use this Book" chapter, for more information.

```
                        LEGEND
                "For More Info . . . " column
A = Authority (Legislative Act, See Appendix "A")
B = Block or Lot (location in Section unknown)
C = Cancelled Patent
F = Fractional Section
G = Group  (Multi-Patentee Patent, see Appendix "C")
V = Overlaps another Parcel
R = Re-Issued (Parcel patented more than once)

(A & G items require you to look in the Appendixes referred
to above. All other Letter-designations followed by a number
require you to locate line-items in this index that possess
the ID number found after the letter).
```

ID	Individual in Patent	Sec.	Sec. Part	Date Issued	Other Counties	For More Info . . .
1421	ANDERSON, Humphrey	22	W½NW	1823-09-10		A1
1407	BAY, Andrew	35	W½SE	1824-10-20		A1
1406	" "	34	E½SW	1827-12-10		A1
1471	BAY, William	35	E½SE	1825-08-10		A1
1416	BEALL, Elijah	25	W½NW	1821-12-13		A1
1419	BRILL, George	26	W½NW	1831-04-02		A1
1420	" "	32	NENE	1833-11-18		A1
1439	BRILL, John	25	E½NW	1829-04-02		A1
1437	CHALFANT, Jesse	19	E½SE	1821-10-02		A1
1417	CLARY, Enoch	21	E½SE	1832-03-21		A1 G33
1460	CLARY, Nathaniel	9	W½NE	1826-06-23		A1
1458	" "	15	E½NE	1827-08-10		A1
1459	" "	15	E½NW	1831-12-06		A1
1417	CLARY, Samuel	21	E½SE	1832-03-21		A1 G33
1422	COLES, Isaac	9	E½NE	1831-12-06		A1
1462	CONDON, Perry	26	E½NE	1831-04-02		A1
1465	FARRA, Rees	19	W½SE	1821-10-02		A1
1464	" "	13	W½SE	1826-05-20		A1
1468	FOULKE, Samuel M	26	W½NE	1826-05-20		A1
1418	GALLOWAY, Enoch	15	W½NW	1825-08-10		A1
1429	GEORGE, James	33	W½NE	1827-08-10		A1
1428	GOSSET, Jacob	26	E½NW	1831-10-10		A1
1473	GRAHAM, William	31	E½SE	1827-12-10		A1
1472	" "	25	W½SW	1828-08-10		A1
1440	GRIER, John	15	W½SE	1823-09-01		A1
1456	HAGER, Kelion	1	E½NE	1826-06-23		A1
1410	HALL, Benjamin	9	W½SW	1832-11-12		A1
1411	HALL, Caleb	9	E½SW	1826-08-12		A1
1441	HALL, John	7	W½SE	1830-11-01		A1
1442	HARTLEY, John	20	W½NE	1827-05-22		A1
1451	HARTLEY, Joseph	19	E½NW	1830-12-02		A1
1461	HARTLEY, Noah	19	W½NW	1827-08-10		A1
1415	HAYES, Edmund	2	W½SW	1826-05-20		A1
1470	HAYS, Thomas	34	E½SE	1826-05-20		A1
1430	HOLT, James	22	SENE	1833-11-18		A1
1455	JAMES, Judah	9	W½NW	1827-08-10		A1
1409	JOHNSON, Archibald	2	W½NW	1826-08-12		A1
1408	" "	2	E½NW	1832-11-12		A1
1450	KESTER, Jonathan H	25	E½SE	1832-11-12		A1
1474	KESTER, William	20	E½NE	1827-02-20		A1
1463	LINGENFELTER, Peter	32	SENE	1833-11-18		A1
1452	MARSH, Joseph	21	E½NE	1830-12-02		A1
1469	MARSHALL, Samuel	15	E½SE	1824-05-11		A1
1475	MARSHALL, William	15	E½SW	1824-05-11		A1
1466	MCCORMICK, Robert	27	W½SW	1826-06-23		A1
1457	MCILVAIN, Mclain	1	W½NW	1826-05-20		A1

ID	Individual in Patent	Sec.	Sec. Part	Date Issued	Other Counties	For More Info . . .
1443	MCNEELY, John	27	SESW	1835-12-08		A1
1423	MOLAND, Isaac	15	NWSW	1834-09-10		A1
1424	" "	15	SWSW	1837-04-01		A1
1445	MORRISON, John	10	SWSW	1833-11-18		A1
1444	" "	10	NWSW	1837-04-01		A1
1476	MORRISON, William	21	W½SW	1831-12-06		A1
1446	OVERLEY, John	22	W½SW	1823-09-10		A1
1425	PEREGO, Isaac	10	E½SW	1826-06-23		A1
1426	" "	9	E½NW	1831-07-01		A1
1431	PEREGO, James	22	E½SE	1826-06-23		A1
1447	ROSE, John	27	NESW	1833-11-18		A1
1438	SCOTT, Jesse	25	W½SE	1833-01-01		A1
1467	SMITH, Robert	7	E½SW	1830-12-01		A1
1477	SMITH, William	22	E½NW	1826-05-20		A1
1478	" "	22	W½NE	1826-05-20		A1
1454	THOMAS, Josiah	21	W½NW	1830-12-01		A1
1413	THOMPSON, David	21	E½SW	1824-05-06		A1
1414	" "	21	W½SE	1824-05-06		A1
1448	TOWNSEND, John	7	E½SE	1824-05-11		A1
1412	WEBSTER, Charles P	25	SESW	1839-12-10		A1
1449	WEBSTER, John	13	E½SW	1826-05-30		A1
1453	WEBSTER, Joseph	25	NESW	1833-11-18		A1
1433	WHITCRAFT, James	21	W½NE	1823-09-25		A1
1435	" "	22	W½SE	1823-09-25		A1
1434	" "	22	E½SW	1826-06-23		A1
1432	" "	21	E½NW	1831-12-06		A1
1479	WINEBURNER, William	22	NENE	1833-11-18		A1
1427	WOOD, Israel	1	W½NE	1824-05-11		A1
1436	YOUNG, James	2	W½NE	1830-12-01		A1

Patent Map

T9-N R7-W
Ohio River Survey Meridian

Map Group 15

Township Statistics

Parcels Mapped	:	74
Number of Patents	:	74
Number of Individuals	:	60
Patentees Identified	:	59
Number of Surnames	:	45
Multi-Patentee Parcels	:	1
Oldest Patent Date	:	10/2/1821
Most Recent Patent	:	12/10/1839
Block/Lot Parcels	:	0
Parcels Re - Issued	:	0
Parcels that Overlap	:	0
Cities and Towns	:	3
Cemeteries	:	5

36	30	24
35 / BAY Andrew 1824 / BAY William 1825	29	23
34 / BAY Andrew 1827 / HAYS Thomas 1826	28	ANDERSON Humphrey 1823 / SMITH William 1826 / SMITH William 1826 / WINEBURNER William 1833 / HOLT James 1833 / 22 / OVERLEY John 1823 / WHITCRAFT James 1826 / WHITCRAFT James 1823 / PEREGO James 1826
33 / GEORGE James 1827	27 / MCCORMICK Robert 1826 / ROSE John 1833 / MCNEELY John 1835	THOMAS Josiah 1830 / WHITCRAFT James 1831 / WHITCRAFT James 1823 / MARSH Joseph 1830 / 21 / MORRISON William 1831 / THOMPSON David 1824 / THOMPSON David 1824 / CLARY [33] Enoch 1832
32 / BRILL George 1833 / LINGENFELTER Peter 1833 / BRILL George 1831 / GOSSET Jacob 1831 / FOULKE Samuel M 1826 / CONDON Perry 1831 / 26	20 / HARTLEY John 1827 / KESTER William 1827
31 / GRAHAM William 1827 / GRAHAM William 1828 / BEALL Elijah 1821 / WEBSTER Joseph 1833 / WEBSTER Charles P 1839 / BRILL John 1829 / 25 / SCOTT Jesse 1833 / KESTER Jonathan H 1832	HARTLEY Noah 1827 / HARTLEY Joseph 1830 / 19 / FARRA Rees 1821 / CHALFANT Jesse 1821

18	12	6
17	11	5

Helpful Hints

1. This Map's INDEX can be found on the preceding pages.

2. Refer to Map "C" to see where this Township lies within Guernsey County, Ohio.

3. Numbers within square brackets [ ] denote a multi-patentee land parcel (multi-owner). Refer to Appendix "C" for a full list of members in this group.

4. Areas that look to be crowded with Patentees usually indicate multiple sales of the same parcel (Re-issues) or Overlapping parcels. See this Township's Index for an explanation of these and other circumstances that might explain "odd" groupings of Patentees on this map.

Section 10 / 16

16	MORRISON John 1837 / MORRISON John 1833	PEREGO Isaac 1826	10	4

Section 15 / 9

GALLOWAY Enoch 1825	CLARY Nathaniel 1831	CLARY Nathaniel 1827	JAMES Judah 1827	PEREGO Isaac 1831	CLARY Nathaniel 1826	COLES Isaac 1831
MOLAND Isaac 1834 / MOLAND Isaac 1837	MARSHALL William 1824	GRIER John 1823	MARSHALL Samuel 1824	HALL Benjamin 1832	HALL Caleb 1826	9

15

3

Section 14 / 8 / 2

14	8	JOHNSON Archibald 1826	JOHNSON Archibald 1832	YOUNG James 1830
		HAYES Edmund 1826	2	

Section 13 / 7 / 1

13	7	MCILVAIN Mclain 1826	WOOD Israel 1824	HAGER Kelion 1826
FARRA Rees 1826	WEBSTER John 1826	SMITH Robert 1830	HALL John 1830	TOWNSEND John 1824	1

Legend

———————	Patent Boundary
▬▬▬▬▬▬▬	Section Boundary
(shaded)	No Patents Found (or Outside County)
1., 2., 3., ...	Lot Numbers (when beside a name)
[ ]	Group Number (see Appendix "C")

Scale: Section = 1 mile X 1 mile (generally, with some exceptions)

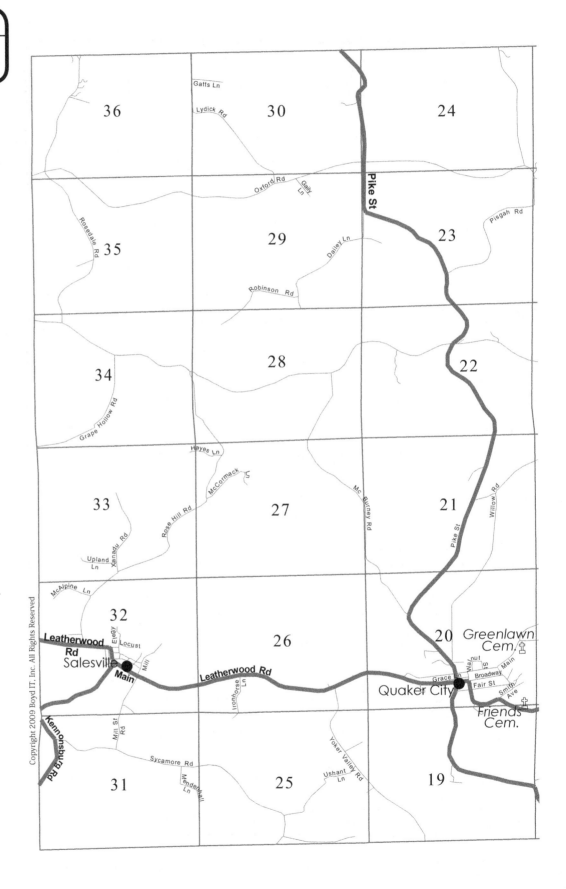

Road Map

T9-N R7-W
Ohio River Survey Meridian

Map Group 15

Cities & Towns
Quaker City
Salesville
Spencer Station

Cemeteries
Barker Cemetery
Eldon Cemetery
Fletcher Cemetery
Friends Cemetery
Greenlawn Cemetery

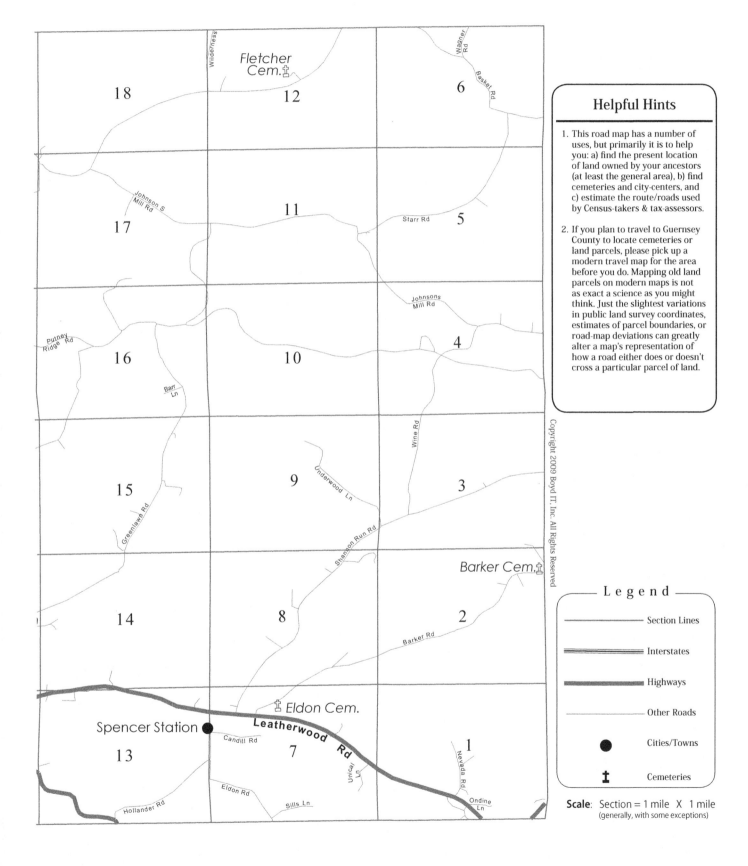

Helpful Hints

1. This road map has a number of uses, but primarily it is to help you: a) find the present location of land owned by your ancestors (at least the general area), b) find cemeteries and city-centers, and c) estimate the route/roads used by Census-takers & tax-assessors.

2. If you plan to travel to Guernsey County to locate cemeteries or land parcels, please pick up a modern travel map for the area before you do. Mapping old land parcels on modern maps is not as exact a science as you might think. Just the slightest variations in public land survey coordinates, estimates of parcel boundaries, or road-map deviations can greatly alter a map's representation of how a road either does or doesn't cross a particular parcel of land.

Legend

————	Section Lines
═══════	Interstates
━━━━━	Highways
————	Other Roads
●	Cities/Towns
☦	Cemeteries

Scale: Section = 1 mile X 1 mile
(generally, with some exceptions)

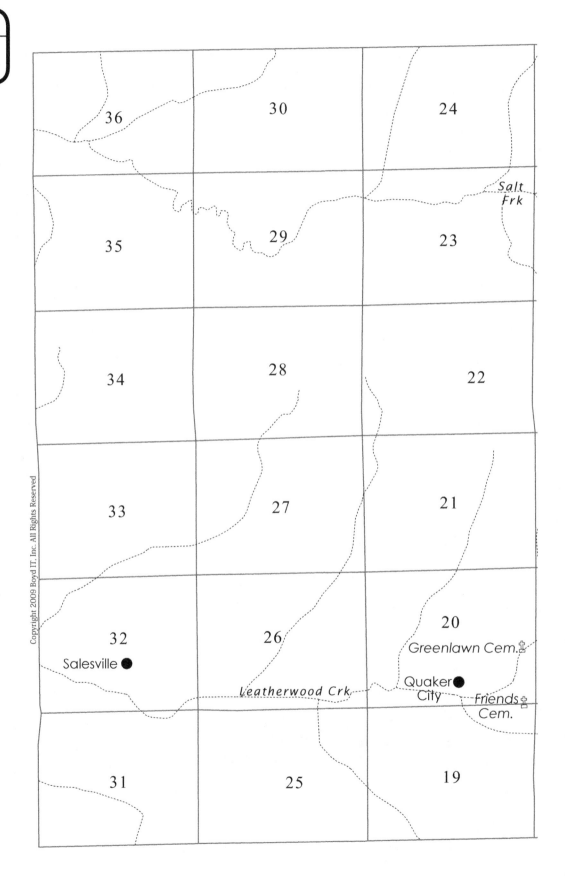

Historical Map

T9-N R7-W
Ohio River Survey Meridian

Map Group 15

Cities & Towns
Quaker City
Salesville
Spencer Station

Cemeteries
Barker Cemetery
Eldon Cemetery
Fletcher Cemetery
Friends Cemetery
Greenlawn Cemetery

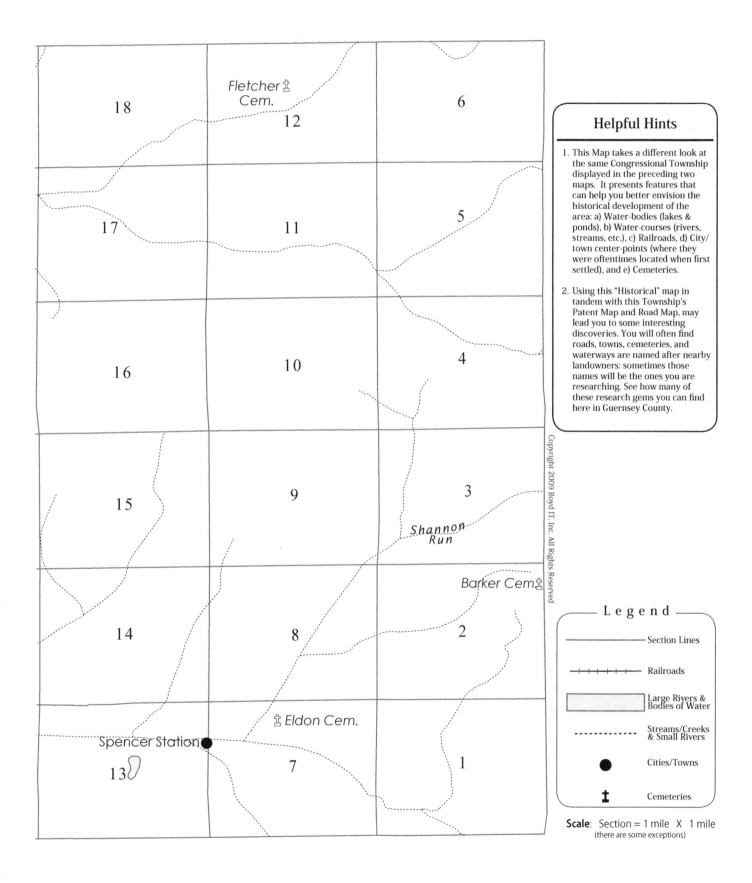

18

Fletcher ⚰
Cem.
12

6

17

11

5

16

10

4

15

9

3

Shannon
Run

Barker Cem⚰

14

8

2

⚰ Eldon Cem.

Spencer Station ●

13

7

1

Helpful Hints

1. This Map takes a different look at the same Congressional Township displayed in the preceding two maps. It presents features that can help you better envision the historical development of the area: a) Water-bodies (lakes & ponds), b) Water-courses (rivers, streams, etc.), c) Railroads, d) City/town center-points (where they were oftentimes located when first settled), and e) Cemeteries.

2. Using this "Historical" map in tandem with this Township's Patent Map and Road Map, may lead you to some interesting discoveries. You will often find roads, towns, cemeteries, and waterways are named after nearby landowners: sometimes those names will be the ones you are researching. See how many of these research gems you can find here in Guernsey County.

Legend

——————	Section Lines
—+—+—+—+—	Railroads
▭	Large Rivers & Bodies of Water
- - - - - - -	Streams/Creeks & Small Rivers
●	Cities/Towns
⚰	Cemeteries

Scale: Section = 1 mile X 1 mile
(there are some exceptions)

Map Group 16: Index to Land Patents

Township 1-North Range 4-West (U.S. Military Survey)

After you locate an individual in this Index, take note of the Section and Section Part then proceed to the Land Patent map on the pages immediately following. You should have no difficulty locating the corresponding parcel of land.

The "For More Info" Column will lead you to more information about the underlying Patents. See the *Legend* at right, and the "How to Use this Book" chapter, for more information.

```
┌─────────────────────────────────────────────────────┐
│                    LEGEND                           │
│        "For More Info . . ." column                 │
│ A = Authority (Legislative Act, See Appendix "A")   │
│ B = Block or Lot (location in Section unknown)      │
│ C = Cancelled Patent                                │
│ F = Fractional Section                              │
│ G = Group  (Multi-Patentee Patent, see Appendix "C")│
│ V = Overlaps another Parcel                         │
│ R = Re-Issued (Parcel patented more than once)      │
│                                                     │
│ (A & G items require you to look in the Appendixes referred │
│ to above. All other Letter-designations followed by a number │
│ require you to locate line-items in this index that possess │
│ the ID number found after the letter).              │
└─────────────────────────────────────────────────────┘
```

ID	Individual in Patent	Sec.	Sec. Part	Date Issued	Other Counties	For More Info . . .
1488	BARNDOLLAR, Jacob	21	NE	1821-09-08		A1 G3
1480	BOYD, Adam	13	E½SE	1825-08-06		A1
1503	CAMP, Robert	12	E½SE	1827-09-20		A1
1506	CAMP, Thomas	11	W½SW	1827-12-20		A1
1488	COULTER, Elizabeth	21	NE	1821-09-08		A1 G3
1484	"	21	W½NW	1824-04-17		A1
1485	"	22	E½NE	1849-12-01		A1
1495	CUMMING, John N	3		1800-03-29		A2
1493	FORDYCE, John	21	E½SE	1827-07-30		A1
1483	GALAWAY, Elijah	12	E½SW	1823-08-20		A1
1487	HARTMAN, George	20	E½NW	1829-04-01		A1
1494	HUNTER, John	19	E½SE	1832-04-02		A1 V1481
1509	HUNTER, William	22	E½SW	1826-06-06		A1
1510	"	22	W½NE	1826-06-06		A1
1511	"	22	W½NW	1826-06-06		A1
1512	"	22	W½SE	1826-06-06		A1
1507	"	19	W½SW	1826-06-16		A1
1508	"	21	W½SW	1828-08-20		A1
1486	JOHNSON, Frederick	19	W½NE	1835-09-08		A1
1499	JOHNSON, Margaret	22	E½SE	1821-09-08		A1
1497	KELLY, Joseph	22	W½SW	1826-04-01		A1
1502	LEAMON, Reuben	19	E½NE	1823-08-20		A1
1513	LEMON, William	20	W½SW	1823-08-20		A1
1490	MAGEE, James	13	SWSE	1835-09-30		A1
1489	"	13	NWSE	1838-09-01		A1
1514	MCCLUNEY, William	2		1801-02-17		A2
1481	MCILVAIN, Andrew	19	SE	1826-10-02		A1 V1494
1505	PAXTON, Samuel	21	E½NW	1823-08-20		A1
1504	POOLE, Robert V	12	W½SW	1826-11-01		A1
1501	SPENCER, Nathan	21	W½SE	1828-05-30		A1
1500	"	21	E½SW	1830-12-01		A1
1491	STEELL, James	20	W½SE	1831-02-10		A1
1482	STEVENS, Charles A	22	E½NW	1826-06-06		A1
1492	STULE, James	20	E½SW	1825-03-10		A1
1496	WALLER, John	19	NW	1825-08-06		A1
1498	WALLER, Joseph	20	SESE	1835-09-14		A1
1515	WALLER, William	11	E½SW	1827-12-20		A1
1516	"	20	NESE	1835-09-08		A1

Patent Map

T1-N R4-W
U.S. Military Survey Meridian

Map Group 16

Township Statistics

Parcels Mapped	:	37
Number of Patents	:	37
Number of Individuals	:	28
Patentees Identified	:	28
Number of Surnames	:	23
Multi-Patentee Parcels	:	1
Oldest Patent Date	:	3/29/1800
Most Recent Patent	:	12/1/1849
Block/Lot Parcels	:	0
Parcels Re - Issued	:	0
Parcels that Overlap	:	2
Cities and Towns	:	4
Cemeteries	:	3

MCCLUNEY
William
1801

2

CUMMING
John N
1800

3

1

Helpful Hints

1. This Map's INDEX can be found on the preceding pages.

2. Refer to Map "C" to see where this Township lies within Guernsey County, Ohio.

3. Numbers within square brackets [ ] denote a multi-patentee land parcel (multi-owner). Refer to Appendix "C" for a full list of members in this group.

4. Areas that look to be crowded with Patentees usually indicate multiple sales of the same parcel (Re-issues) or Overlapping parcels. See this Township's Index for an explanation of these and other circumstances that might explain "odd" groupings of Patentees on this map.

MAGEE
James
1838

BOYD
Adam
1825

MAGEE
James
1835

13

POOLE
Robert V
1826

GALAWAY
Elijah
1823

12

CAMP
Robert
1827

CAMP
Thomas
1827

WALLER
William
1827

11

WALLER
John
1825

JOHNSON
Frederick
1835

LEAMON
Reuben
1823

HARTMAN
George
1829

20

18

HUNTER
William
1826

19

MCILVAIN
Andrew

HUNTER
John
1832

LEMON
William
1823

STULE
James
1825

STEELL
James
1831

WALLER
William
1835

WALLER
Joseph
1835

23

HUNTER
William
1826

STEVENS
Charles A
1826

HUNTER
William
1826

COULTER
Elizabeth
1849

COULTER
Elizabeth
1824

PAXTON
Samuel
1823

21

BARNDOLLAR [3]
Jacob
1821

KELLY
Joseph
1826

22

HUNTER
William
1826

HUNTER
William
1826

JOHNSON
Margaret
1821

HUNTER
William
1828

SPENCER
Nathan
1830

SPENCER
Nathan
1828

FORDYCE
John
1827

Legend

Patent Boundary

Section Boundary

No Patents Found
(or Outside County)

1., 2., 3., ...   Lot Numbers
(when beside a name)

[ ]   Group Number
(see Appendix "C")

Scale: Section = 1 mile X 1 mile
(generally, with some exceptions)

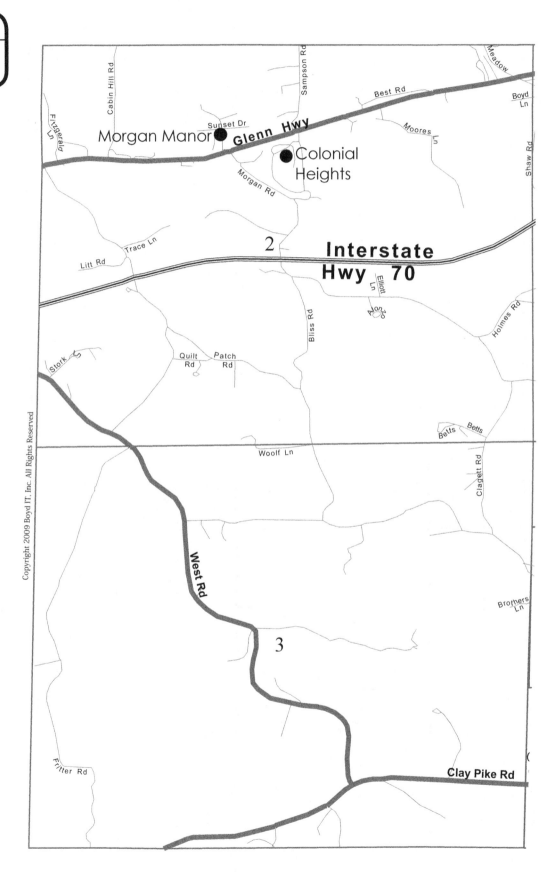

Road Map

T1-N R4-W
U.S. Military Survey Meridian

Map Group 16

Cities & Towns
Cassellview
Claysville
Colonial Heights
Morgan Manor

Cemeteries
Cedar Cemetery
East Union Cemetery
Zion Cemetery

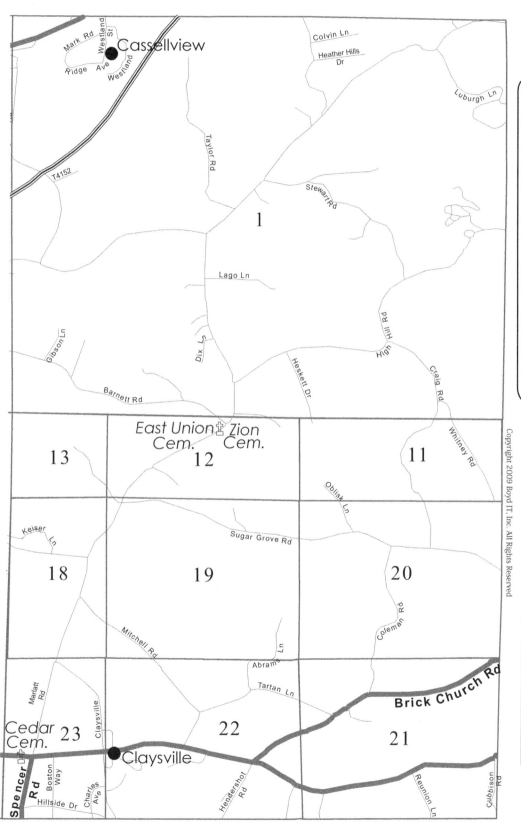

Cassellview

Mark Rd

Westland St

Ridge Ave

Westland

Colvin Ln

Heather Hills Dr

Luburgh Ln

T4152

Taylor Rd

Stewart Rd

1

Lago Ln

Gibson Ln

Dix Ln

High Hill Rd

Heskett Dr

Craig Rd

Barnett Rd

East Union Cem.

Zion Cem.

13

12

11

Whitney Rd

Keiser Ln

Sugar Grove Rd

Oblisk Ln

18

19

20

Mitchell Rd

Abrams Ln

Coleman Rd

Marlatt Rd

Claysville

Tartan Ln

Cedar Cem.

23

22

Brick Church Rd

21

Claysville

Spencer Rd

Boston Way

Charles Ave

Hillside Dr

Hendershot Rd

Reunion Ln

Cubbison Rd

Helpful Hints

1. This road map has a number of uses, but primarily it is to help you: a) find the present location of land owned by your ancestors (at least the general area), b) find cemeteries and city-centers, and c) estimate the route/roads used by Census-takers & tax-assessors.

2. If you plan to travel to Guernsey County to locate cemeteries or land parcels, please pick up a modern travel map for the area before you do. Mapping old land parcels on modern maps is not as exact a science as you might think. Just the slightest variations in public land survey coordinates, estimates of parcel boundaries, or road-map deviations can greatly alter a map's representation of how a road either does or doesn't cross a particular parcel of land.

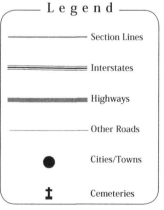

L e g e n d

———————— Section Lines

════════ Interstates

━━━━━━━━ Highways

———————— Other Roads

● Cities/Towns

✝ Cemeteries

Scale: Section = 1 mile X 1 mile
(generally, with some exceptions)

Historical Map

T1-N R4-W
U.S. Military Survey Meridian

Map Group 16

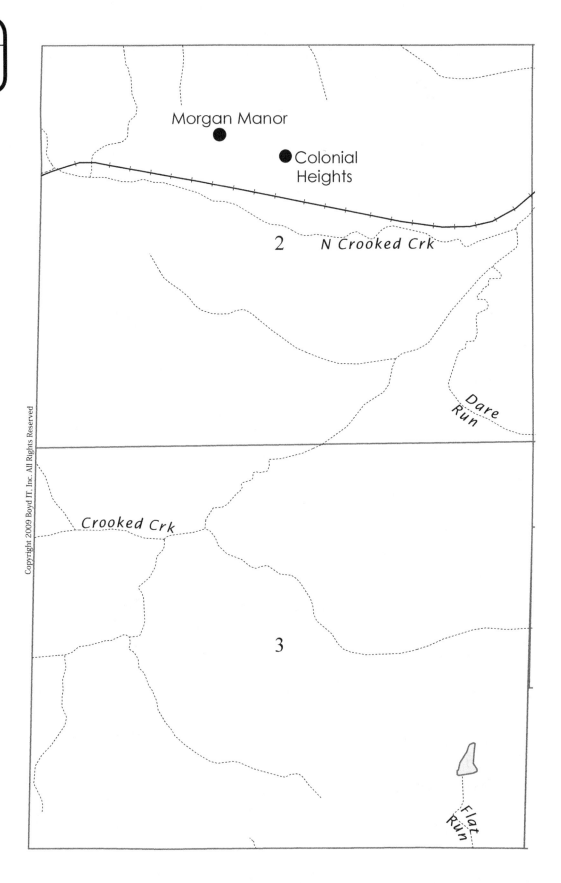

Morgan Manor

Colonial Heights

2

N Crooked Crk

Dare Run

Crooked Crk

3

Flat Run

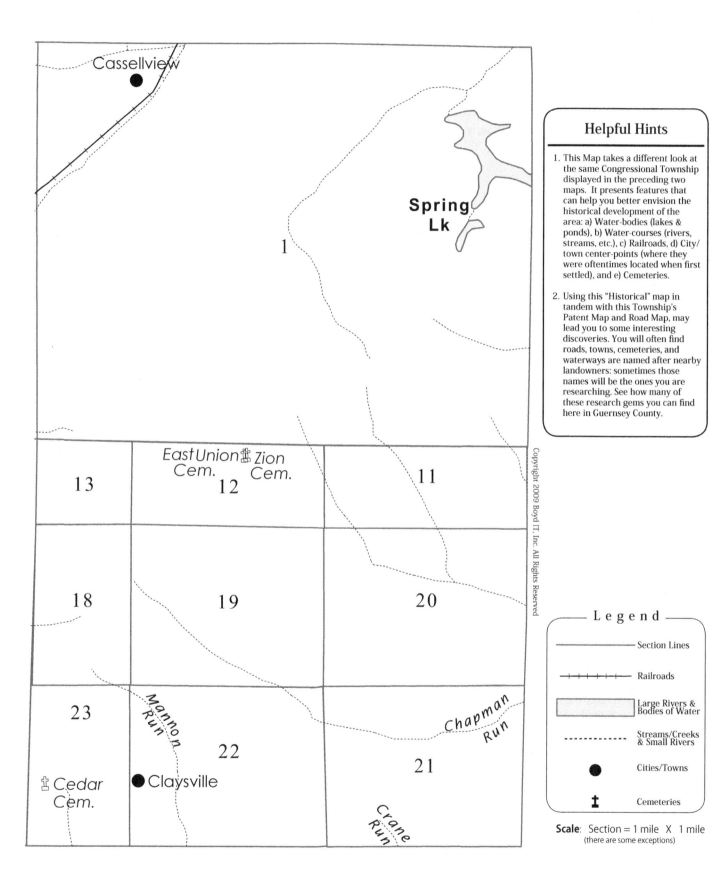

Cassellview

Spring
Lk

1

Helpful Hints

1. This Map takes a different look at the same Congressional Township displayed in the preceding two maps. It presents features that can help you better envision the historical development of the area: a) Water-bodies (lakes & ponds), b) Water-courses (rivers, streams, etc.), c) Railroads, d) City/ town center-points (where they were oftentimes located when first settled), and e) Cemeteries.

2. Using this "Historical" map in tandem with this Township's Patent Map and Road Map, may lead you to some interesting discoveries. You will often find roads, towns, cemeteries, and waterways are named after nearby landowners: sometimes those names will be the ones you are researching. See how many of these research gems you can find here in Guernsey County.

East Union Zion
Cem.   Cem.

13   12   11

18   19   20

23

Mannon Run

22   Chapman Run

21

Cedar Cem.   Claysville

Crane Run

Legend

——————	Section Lines
+–+–+–+–+	Railroads
▭	Large Rivers & Bodies of Water
- - - - -	Streams/Creeks & Small Rivers
●	Cities/Towns
✝	Cemeteries

Scale: Section = 1 mile X 1 mile
(there are some exceptions)

Map Group 17: Index to Land Patents

Township 1-North Range 3-West (U.S. Military Survey)

After you locate an individual in this Index, take note of the Section and Section Part then proceed to the Land Patent map on the pages immediately following. You should have no difficulty locating the corresponding parcel of land.

The "For More Info" Column will lead you to more information about the underlying Patents. See the *Legend* at right, and the "How to Use this Book" chapter, for more information.

```
                         LEGEND
               "For More Info . . . " column
A = Authority (Legislative Act, See Appendix "A")
B = Block or Lot (location in Section unknown)
C = Cancelled Patent
F = Fractional Section
G = Group  (Multi-Patentee Patent, see Appendix "C")
V = Overlaps another Parcel
R = Re-Issued (Parcel patented more than once)

(A & G items require you to look in the Appendixes referred
to above. All other Letter-designations followed by a number
require you to locate line-items in this index that possess
the ID number found after the letter).
```

ID	Individual in Patent	Sec.	Sec. Part	Date Issued	Other Counties	For More Info . . .
1595	AIKIN, John	14	E½NW	1825-03-10		A1
1551	AKIN, George	16	W½SE	1823-08-20		A1
1687	ALLEN, Samuel	22	W½NW	1835-09-08		A1
1577	ARBUCKLE, James	25	W½NE	1827-12-20		A1
1576	" "	13	SWNW	1835-10-05		A1
1636	AYERS, Jacob	21	NE	1907-07-17		A1 G112
1540	AZBILL, David	17	SESE	1835-10-05		A1
1541	" "	18	SWSW	1835-10-05		A1
1714	BEATTY, Zaccheus A	1	36	1808-12-14		A2
1715	" "	1	37	1808-12-14		A2
1712	" "	1	34	1809-01-26		A2
1713	" "	1	35	1809-01-26		A2
1716	" "	1	38	1809-09-14		A2
1711	" "	1	16	1815-04-15		A2
1564	BEETLY, Isaac	1	15	1803-04-13		A2
1524	BELL, Andrew	7	S½NW	1835-09-23		A1
1596	BELL, John	11	NESW	1835-09-23		A1
1597	" "	7	NWNW	1838-09-01		A1
1578	BICHARD, James	24	E½SE	1823-08-20		A1
1704	BIERCE, William	1	18	1805-05-06		A2
1703	BLISS, Washington	7	S½SE	1837-08-05		A1
1648	BOYD, Joseph	5	SESE	1837-04-10		A1
1705	BROWN, William	6	W½NW	1832-07-02		A1
1537	BRUSH, Daniel	18	NENE	1835-09-14		A1 G17
1535	" "	18	NESE	1835-09-14		A1
1536	" "	6	SESE	1837-08-05		A1 G8
1517	BRYSON, Abraham	5	NESW	1837-04-10		A1
1518	" "	5	NWSE	1837-04-10		A1
1538	BURT, Daniel	12	NWSW	1837-04-10		A1
1542	BURT, David	16	SENW	1835-04-30		A1
1532	CARRELL, Charles	25	NENW	1837-08-10		A1
1706	CARRY, William	6	SESW	1835-10-05		A1
1598	CHAPMAN, John	3	SWNW	1837-04-10		A1
1649	CLARK, Joseph	22	E½SE	1826-06-06		A1
1591	COLEMAN, Robert	1	24	1801-02-03		A2 G114
1592	" "	1	25	1801-02-03		A2 G114
1593	" "	1	40	1801-02-03		A2 G114
1600	COLLINS, John	22	SENW	1835-04-21		A1
1599	" "	22	NENW	1839-08-24		A1
1673	CONNER, Patrick	1	11	1802-06-08		A2
1645	COX, Joseph	7	SWSW	1835-04-30		A1 G82
1650	" "	14	NWNW	1835-09-30		A1
1525	CRAIG, Andrew	7	NENW	1838-09-01		A1
1526	" "	7	NWSW	1838-09-01		A1
1605	DE LARUE, JOHN	7	SESW	1835-04-21		A1
1604	" "	14	SWNE	1837-08-05		A1

ID	Individual in Patent	Sec.	Sec. Part	Date Issued	Other Counties	For More Info . . .
1692	DEEREN, Thomas	23	SWSE	1835-09-14		A1
1606	DELARUE, John	14	NWNE	1835-04-30		A1
1555	DENNIS, Henry	6	NESE	1837-04-10		A1
1536	" "	6	SESE	1837-08-05		A1 G8
1651	DENNIS, Joseph	15	SESW	1835-10-05		A1
1688	DENNIS, Samuel	16	NENW	1835-04-30		A1
1557	DENNISON, Henry	15	SWNE	1835-04-21		A1
1556	" "	15	SENE	1835-09-14		A1
1579	DUKE, James	5	SWSE	1835-04-30		A1
1679	FISHER, Philip	22	W½SW	1831-02-10		A1
1565	FOX, Isaac	18	NENW	1835-04-21		A1
1566	" "	18	NWNE	1835-04-30		A1
1580	FREEMAN, James	13	E½NW	1824-04-17		A1
1558	FREY, Henry F	23	W½NE	1828-08-20		A1
1559	FRY, Henry F	22	E½SW	1835-09-08		A1
1672	FRY, Noah S	19	SESW	1837-04-10		A1
1527	GALLIWAY, Benjamin	25	E½SE	1830-12-01		A1 G40
1528	" "	24	W½SW	1831-03-01		A1 G41 R1529
1529	" "	24	W½SW	1924-12-18		A1 G41 R1528
1560	GASS, Henry	1	6	1802-06-17		A2
1708	GRAHAM, William	25	W½SE	1827-06-01		A1
1707	" "	25	E½SW	1829-06-01		A1
1521	GRAY, Alexander	1	33	1809-01-26		A2
1552	GRIFFIN, George G	15	NWSW	1835-09-08		A1
1678	HAGAN, Peter	1	21	1802-06-21		A2
1607	HALL, John	4	NESE	1837-08-10		A1
1608	" "	4	SENE	1837-08-10		A1
1581	HANNA, James	12	E½SW	1826-04-01		A1
1527	HAWS, Ann	25	E½SE	1830-12-01		A1 G40
1528	HAWS, Anne	24	W½SW	1831-03-01		A1 G41 R1529
1529	" "	24	W½SW	1924-12-18		A1 G41 R1528
1609	HECKEL, John	23	E½NE	1829-04-01		A1
1554	HENRY, Gustavus	6	NESW	1835-09-08		A1
1570	HENRY, Jacob	6	E½NW	1832-04-02		A1
1690	" "	6	NWSE	1835-09-08		A1 G103
1691	" "	6	SWNE	1835-09-08		A1 G103
1661	HENRY, Margaret	6	NWNE	1835-10-05		A1
1659	HISKETT, Landon	25	E½NE	1831-02-10		A1 R1660
1660	" "	25	E½NE	1924-12-18		A1 R1659
1549	JENKINS, Edward	15	SENW	1837-08-15		A1
1586	KARR, James	24	E½NW	1823-08-20		A1
1587	" "	24	W½NE	1830-12-01		A1
1583	" "	17	W½SE	1835-04-21		A1
1582	" "	17	SESW	1835-09-23		A1
1584	" "	18	NESW	1838-09-01		A1
1585	" "	18	SESW	1838-09-01		A1
1523	KELLEY, Alfred	5	SENE	1838-09-01		A1
1668	KENNEDY, Nathaniel	4	NWSW	1837-08-05		A1
1669	" "	4	SWNW	1837-08-05		A1
1663	KLINE, Matthew	6	SWSW	1837-04-10		A1
1571	LONG, Jacob	3	NWNW	1837-08-10		A1
1572	" "	3	SENW	1837-08-15		A1
1531	LONGWORTH, Caleb	22	N½NE	1835-09-23		A1
1635	LONGWORTH, John W	22	S½NE	1835-09-23		A1
1681	LYANS, Robert	13	NWNW	1835-09-30		A1
1543	MAXWELL, David	4	NENW	1835-09-14		A1
1652	MAXWELL, Joseph	4	NWNW	1838-09-01		A1
1610	MCCONAUGHY, John	4	SESW	1837-04-10		A1
1611	" "	4	SWSE	1837-04-10		A1
1709	MCCONAUGHY, William	8	NWSW	1835-04-30		A1
1588	MCCOUGHY, James	11	N½SE	1835-09-23		A1
1563	MCCOY, Hugh	19	E½NW	1835-09-08		A1
1674	MCCROSSON, Patrick	1	22	1802-06-21		A2
1539	MCDONALD, Daniel	5	W½SW	1835-04-30		A1
1612	MCELROY, John	1	12	1802-06-09		A2
1544	MCKEE, David	6	NENE	1835-09-23		A1
1615	MCKEE, John	5	NWNE	1835-04-30		A1
1613	" "	18	SWNE	1837-08-05		A1
1614	" "	18	W½SE	1837-08-05		A1
1682	MCKEE, Robert	5	SESE	1835-09-14		A1
1693	MCKEE, Thomas	5	NENE	1835-10-05		A1
1694	MCKINNEY, Thomas	17	W½SW	1826-04-01		A1 R1695
1695	" "	17	W½SW	1924-12-18		A1 R1694

ID	Individual in Patent	Sec.	Sec. Part	Date Issued	Other Counties	For More Info . . .
1616	MCNAIR, John	1	10	1805-05-06		A2
1696	MOLLOY, Thomas	23	NW	1829-04-01		A1
1643	MORRIS, Abraham	18	SENE	1835-04-30		A1 G90
1519	" "	19	W½NW	1837-04-10		A1
1644	MORRIS, Isaac	18	SESE	1835-04-30		A1 G91
1537	" "	18	NENE	1835-09-14		A1 G17
1683	NELSON, Robert	14	SENE	1837-04-10		A1
1601	NEVIN, John D	14	NENE	1837-08-05		A1
1602	" "	4	NESW	1837-08-10		A1
1603	" "	4	NWSE	1837-08-10		A1
1617	NEWLAND, John	17	NESW	1835-04-21		A1
1618	NEWNOM, John	4	SESE	1835-04-30		A1
1619	" "	7	NENE	1835-09-14		A1
1620	" "	7	W½NE	1835-09-14		A1
1684	NICHOLSON, Robert	3	NESW	1837-04-10		A1
1685	" "	3	NWSW	1837-08-05		A1
1664	NOURSE, Michael	1	1	1804-11-20		A2
1665	" "	1	2	1804-11-20		A2
1666	" "	1	3	1804-11-20		A2
1667	" "	1	4	1805-08-16		A2
1621	OBNEY, John	6	NWSW	1835-09-30		A1
1622	OGIER, John	4	SENW	1835-04-30		A1
1697	PAXTON, Thomas	24	W½NW	1830-12-01		A1
1671	PEDWIN, Nicholas	25	NWNW	1835-09-08		A1
1623	ROBBINS, John	23	E½SE	1831-03-01		A1
1676	ROBERT, Paul	1	8	1835-09-30		A1
1677	" "	1	9	1835-09-30		A1
1675	ROBERTS, Patrick	1	13	1802-06-09		A2
1624	ROBINS, John	23	SESW	1837-04-10		A1
1698	RUSSELL, Thomas	23	NWSE	1835-04-21		A1
1553	SAVELY, George	24	E½NE	1835-04-02		A1
1625	SAVELY, John	17	NESE	1835-04-21		A1
1700	SCOTT, Thomas	23	W½SW	1832-07-02		A1
1699	" "	23	NESW	1835-04-30		A1
1561	SELDERS, Henry	5	NESE	1837-11-07		A1
1680	SHOFF, Philip	12	W½SE	1832-07-02		A1
1520	SHRIVER, Adam	19	NESW	1835-09-08		A1
1574	SHRIVER, Jacob	13	SESE	1835-04-21		A1
1573	" "	13	NESE	1837-04-10		A1
1710	SINES, William	15	W½SE	1832-04-02		A1
1575	SLATER, Jacob	22	W½SE	1826-10-02		A1
1701	SMALLY, Thomas	1	14	1803-04-13		A2
1626	SMITH, John	1	23	1805-03-28		A2
1627	" "	1	27	1805-03-28		A2
1628	" "	1	28	1805-03-28		A2
1643	STANBERY, Jonas	18	SENE	1835-04-30		A1 G90
1644	" "	18	SESE	1835-04-30		A1 G91
1645	" "	7	SWSW	1835-04-30		A1 G82
1646	" "	15	SWNW	1837-04-10		A1 G93
1640	" "	15	SWSW	1837-04-10		A1
1641	" "	6	SWSE	1837-08-05		A1
1642	" "	7	SENE	1837-08-05		A1
1638	" "	13	W½SE	1837-08-10		A1
1639	" "	15	NWNE	1837-08-10		A1
1630	STEPHENS, John	24	W½SE	1834-06-12		A1
1629	" "	18	NWSW	1835-04-30		A1
1550	STEVENS, Elijah	18	SENW	1835-04-21		A1
1631	STEVENS, John	24	E½SW	1835-04-02		A1
1646	STEWART, Thomas H	15	SWNW	1837-04-10		A1 G93
1653	STOKELY, Joseph	1	7	1810-11-16		A2
1546	STRAHL, David	25	SWNW	1835-04-21		A1
1545	" "	25	SENW	1835-09-14		A1
1654	STRONG, Joseph	1	19	1805-05-06		A2
1655	" "	1	20	1805-05-06		A2
1656	" "	1	29	1805-05-06		A2
1657	" "	1	30	1805-05-06		A2
1690	STURGES, Solomon	6	NWSE	1835-09-08		A1 G103
1691	" "	6	SWNE	1835-09-08		A1 G103
1632	TAYLOR, John	5	SWNE	1838-09-01		A1
1589	THARP, James	15	NENE	1837-04-10		A1
1633	TINGLE, John	18	W½NW	1825-03-10		A1
1634	TORODE, John	4	SWSW	1837-08-15		A1
1686	TOWNSHEND, Robert	6	SENE	1835-09-30		A1

ID	Individual in Patent	Sec.	Sec. Part	Date Issued	Other Counties	For More Info . . .
1534	VANCUREN, Cornelius	12	SESE	1835-09-14		A1
1533	" "	12	NESE	1837-08-10		A1
1647	VERREY, Jonathan	1	26	1803-04-13		A2
1522	WALLACE, Alexander	3	SESW	1835-09-08		A1
1636	WALLER, John	21	NE	1907-07-17		A1 G112
1658	WALLER, Joseph	25	W½SW	1825-08-06		A1
1662	WALLER, Margaret	4	NENE	1835-04-30		A1
1689	WALLER, Samuel	4	W½NE	1832-04-02		A1
1530	WIERS, Benjamin	14	SWNW	1835-09-14		A1
1547	WILLIAMS, David	8	E½SW	1825-03-10		A1
1548	" "	8	SWSW	1835-04-30		A1
1637	WILLIAMS, John	1	5	1802-06-09		A2
1670	WILLIAMS, Nehemiah	3	NENW	1835-04-21		A1
1590	WILLSON, James	15	NWNW	1838-09-01		A1
1594	WILLSON, Jesse	15	NENW	1835-09-30		A1
1568	WILSON, Isaac	16	E½SE	1830-12-01		A1
1569	" "	16	W½NW	1835-04-02		A1
1567	" "	15	NESW	1837-08-15		A1
1702	WILSON, Thomas	12	SWSW	1835-09-14		A1
1562	WOODROW, Henry	19	W½SW	1823-08-20		A1
1591	YATES, Jasper	1	24	1801-02-03		A2 G114
1592	" "	1	25	1801-02-03		A2 G114
1593	" "	1	40	1801-02-03		A2 G114

Patent Map

T1-N R3-W
U.S. Military Survey Meridian

Map Group 17

Township Statistics

Parcels Mapped	:	200
Number of Patents	:	188
Number of Individuals	:	141
Patentees Identified	:	142
Number of Surnames	:	116
Multi-Patentee Parcels	:	15
Oldest Patent Date	:	2/3/1801
Most Recent Patent	:	12/18/1924
Block/Lot Parcels	:	36
Parcels Re - Issued	:	3
Parcels that Overlap	:	0
Cities and Towns	:	6
Cemeteries	:	7

Section 5
MCKEE John 1835 · MCKEE Thomas 1835 · TAYLOR John 1838 · KELLEY Alfred 1838 · MCDONALD Daniel 1835 · BRYSON Abraham 1837 · BRYSON Abraham 1837 · SELDERS Henry 1837 · BOYD Joseph 1837 · DUKE James 1835 · MCKEE Robert 1835

Section 4
MAXWELL Joseph 1838 · MAXWELL David 1835 · WALLER Samuel 1832 · KENNEDY Nathaniel 1837 · OGIER John 1835 · KENNEDY Nathaniel 1837 · NEVIN John D 1837 · NEVIN John D 1837 · TORODE John 1837 · MCCONAUGHY John 1837 · MCCONAUGHY John 1837

Section 3
WALLER Margaret 1835 · LONG Jacob 1837 · WILLIAMS Nehemiah 1835 · HALL John 1837 · CHAPMAN John 1837 · LONG Jacob 1837 · HALL John 1837 · NICHOLSON Robert 1837 · NICHOLSON Robert 1837 · NEWNOM John 1835 · WALLACE Alexander 1835

Section 6
BROWN William 1832 · HENRY Jacob 1832 · HENRY Margaret 1835 · MCKEE David 1835 · STURGES [103] Solomon 1835 · TOWNSHEND Robert 1835 · OBNEY John 1835 · HENRY Gustavus 1835 · STURGES [103] Solomon 1835 · DENNIS Henry 1837 · BRUSH [8] Daniel 1837 · KLINE Matthew 1837 · KLINE Matthew 1837 · CARRY William 1835

Section 7
BELL John 1838 · CRAIG Andrew 1838 · BELL Andrew 1835 · CRAIG Andrew 1838 · STANBERY [82] Jonas 1835 · LARUE John De 1835 · NEWNOM John 1835 · NEWNOM John 1835 · STANBERY Jonas 1837 · BLISS Washington 1837

Section 8
MCCONAUGHY William 1835 · WILLIAMS David 1825 · WILLIAMS David 1835

Section 15
WILLSON James 1838 · WILLSON Jesse 1835 · STANBERY Jonas 1837 · THARP James 1837 · STANBERY [98] Jonas 1837 · JENKINS Edward 1837 · DENNISON Henry 1837 · DENNISON Henry 1835 · GRIFFIN George G 1835 · WILSON Isaac 1837 · STANBERY Jonas 1837 · DENNIS Joseph 1835 · SINES William 1832

Section 14
COX Joseph 1835 · AIKIN John 1825 · WIERS Benjamin 1835 · DELARUE John 1835 · NEVIN John D 1837 · LARUE John De 1837 · NELSON Robert 1837 · LYANS Robert 1835 · ARBUCKLE James 1835

Section 13
FREEMAN James 1824 · STANBERY Jonas 1837 · SHRIVER Jacob 1835

Section 16
WILSON Isaac 1835 · DENNIS Samuel 1835 · BURT David 1835 · AKIN George 1823 · WILSON Isaac 1830

Section 17
MCKINNEY Thomas 1924 · NEWLAND John 1835 · KARR James 1835 · SAVELY John 1835 · MCKINNEY Thomas 1826 · KARR James 1835 · AZBILL David 1835

Section 18
TINGLE John 1825 · FOX Isaac 1835 · FOX Isaac 1835 · BRUSH [17] Daniel 1835 · STEVENS Elijah 1835 · MCKEE John 1837 · STANBERY [90] Jonas 1835 · STEPHENS John 1835 · KARR James 1838 · MCKEE John 1837 · BRUSH Daniel 1835 · AZBILL David 1835 · KARR James 1838 · STANBERY [91] Jonas 1835

Section 25
PEDWIN Nicholas 1835 · CARRELL Charles 1837 · ARBUCKLE James 1827 · HISKETT Landon 1924 · HISKETT Landon 1831 · STRAHL David 1835 · STRAHL David 1835 · WALLER Joseph 1825 · GRAHAM William 1829 · GRAHAM William 1827 · GALLIWAY [40] Benjamin 1830

Section 24
GALLIWAY [41] Benjamin 1831 · PAXTON Thomas 1830 · KARR James 1823 · KARR James 1830 · SAVELY George 1835 · GALLIWAY [41] Benjamin 1924 · STEVENS John 1835 · STEPHENS John 1834 · BICHARD James 1823

Section 23
MOLLOY Thomas 1829 · FREY Henry F 1828 · HECKEL John 1829 · SCOTT Thomas 1832 · SCOTT Thomas 1835 · RUSSELL Thomas 1835 · ROBBINS John 1831 · ROBINS John 1837 · DEEREN Thomas 1835

Lots-Sec. 1

1	NOURSE, Michael	1804
2	NOURSE, Michael	1804
3	NOURSE, Michael	1804
4	NOURSE, Michael	1805
5	WILLIAMS, John	1802
6	GASS, Henry	1802
7	STOKELY, Joseph	1810
8	ROBERT, Paul	1835
9	ROBERT, Paul	1835
10	MCNAIR, John	1805
11	CONNER, Patrick	1802
12	MCELROY, John	1802
13	ROBERTS, Patrick	1802
14	SMALLY, Thomas	1803
15	BEETLY, Isaac	1803
16	BEATTY, Zaccheus A	1815
18	BIERCE, William	1805
19	STRONG, Joseph	1805
20	STRONG, Joseph	1805
21	HAGAN, Peter	1802
22	MCCROSSON, Patrick	1802
23	SMITH, John	1805
24	YATES, Jasper [114]	1801
25	YATES, Jasper [114]	1801
26	VERREY, Jonathan	1803
27	SMITH, John	1805
28	SMITH, John	1805
29	STRONG, Joseph	1805
30	STRONG, Joseph	1805
33	GRAY, Alexander	1809
34	BEATTY, Zaccheus A	1809
35	BEATTY, Zaccheus A	1809
36	BEATTY, Zaccheus A	1808
37	BEATTY, Zaccheus A	1808
38	BEATTY, Zaccheus A	1809
40	YATES, Jasper [114]	1801

1

Helpful Hints

1. This Map's INDEX can be found on the preceding pages.

2. Refer to Map "C" to see where this Township lies within Guernsey County, Ohio.

3. Numbers within square brackets [ ] denote a multi-patentee land parcel (multi-owner). Refer to Appendix "C" for a full list of members in this group.

4. Areas that look to be crowded with Patentees usually indicate multiple sales of the same parcel (Re-issues) or Overlapping parcels. See this Township's Index for an explanation of these and other circumstances that might explain "odd" groupings of Patentees on this map.

BURT Daniel 1837

HANNA James 1826

WILSON Thomas 1835

12

SHOFF Philip 1832

VANCUREN Cornelius 1837

VANCUREN Cornelius 1835

BELL John 1835

11

MCCOUGHY James 1835

MORRIS Abraham 1837

MCCOY Hugh 1835

19

WOODROW Henry 1823

SHRIVER Adam 1835

FRY Noah S 1837

20

ALLEN Samuel 1835

COLLINS John 1839

COLLINS John 1835

LONGWORTH Caleb 1835

LONGWORTH John W 1835

WALLER [112] John 1907

22

FISHER Philip 1831

FRY Henry F 1835

SLATER Jacob 1826

CLARK Joseph 1826

21

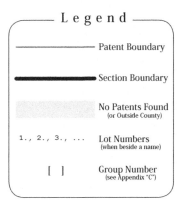

Legend

— Patent Boundary

━━ Section Boundary

No Patents Found (or Outside County)

1., 2., 3., ... Lot Numbers (when beside a name)

[ ] Group Number (see Appendix "C")

Scale: Section = 1 mile X 1 mile (generally, with some exceptions)

Road Map

T1-N R3-W
U.S. Military Survey Meridian

Map Group 17

Cities & Towns
Buckeyeville
Jackson Special
Lucasburg
Marysville
Oakwood
Spring Valley

Cemeteries
Beech Grove Chapel Cemetery
Enon Cemetery
Greenwood Cemetery
Harmony Cemetery
Mount Calvary Cemetery
Mount Zion Cemetery
Sigman Cemetery

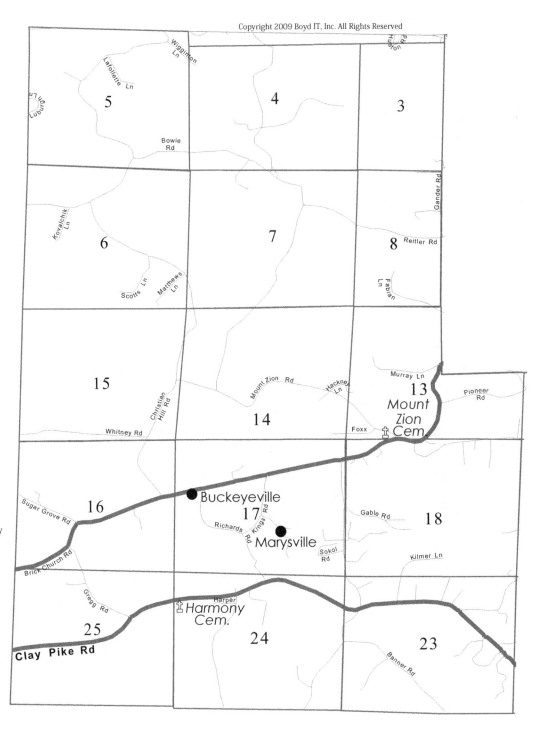

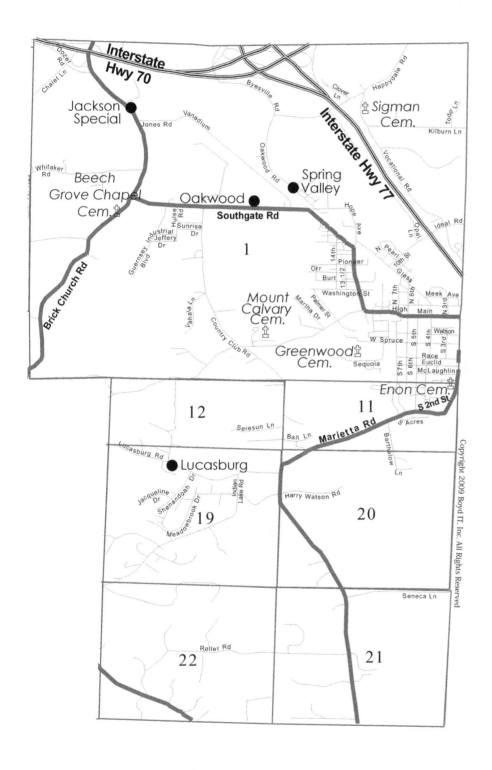

Helpful Hints

1. This road map has a number of uses, but primarily it is to help you: a) find the present location of land owned by your ancestors (at least the general area), b) find cemeteries and city-centers, and c) estimate the route/roads used by Census-takers & tax-assessors.

2. If you plan to travel to Guernsey County to locate cemeteries or land parcels, please pick up a modern travel map for the area before you do. Mapping old land parcels on modern maps is not as exact a science as you might think. Just the slightest variations in public land survey coordinates, estimates of parcel boundaries, or road-map deviations can greatly alter a map's representation of how a road either does or doesn't cross a particular parcel of land.

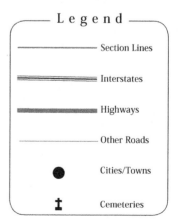

Legend

———	Section Lines
═══	Interstates
▬▬▬	Highways
———	Other Roads
●	Cities/Towns
✝	Cemeteries

Scale: Section = 1 mile X 1 mile
(generally, with some exceptions)

Historical Map

T1-N R3-W
U.S. Military Survey Meridian

Map Group 17

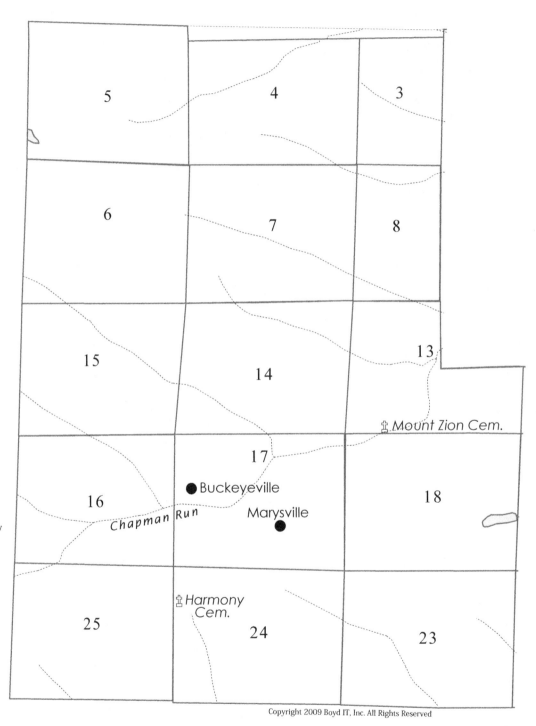

Cities & Towns
Buckeyeville
Jackson Special
Lucasburg
Marysville
Oakwood
Spring Valley

Cemeteries
Beech Grove Chapel Cemetery
Enon Cemetery
Greenwood Cemetery
Harmony Cemetery
Mount Calvary Cemetery
Mount Zion Cemetery
Sigman Cemetery

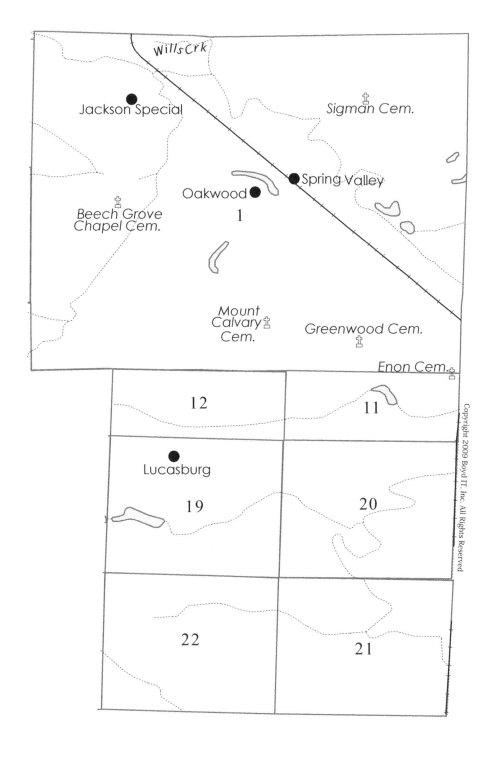

Willscrk

Jackson Special

Sigman Cem.

Oakwood ● ● Spring Valley

Beech Grove Chapel Cem.

1

Mount Calvary Cem.

Greenwood Cem.

Enon Cem.

12

11

Lucasburg

19

20

22

21

Copyright 2009 Boyd IT, Inc. All Rights Reserved

Helpful Hints

1. This Map takes a different look at the same Congressional Township displayed in the preceding two maps. It presents features that can help you better envision the historical development of the area: a) Water-bodies (lakes & ponds), b) Water-courses (rivers, streams, etc.), c) Railroads, d) City/ town center-points (where they were oftentimes located when first settled), and e) Cemeteries.

2. Using this "Historical" map in tandem with this Township's Patent Map and Road Map, may lead you to some interesting discoveries. You will often find roads, towns, cemeteries, and waterways are named after nearby landowners: sometimes those names will be the ones you are researching. See how many of these research gems you can find here in Guernsey County.

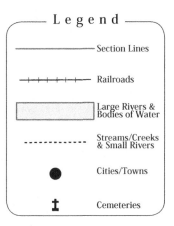

Legend

——————— Section Lines

+—+—+—+—+ Railroads

▭ Large Rivers & Bodies of Water

------------- Streams/Creeks & Small Rivers

● Cities/Towns

✝ Cemeteries

Scale: Section = 1 mile X 1 mile
(there are some exceptions)

Map Group 18: Index to Land Patents

Township 1-North Range 2-West (U.S. Military Survey)

After you locate an individual in this Index, take note of the Section and Section Part then proceed to the Land Patent map on the pages immediately following. You should have no difficulty locating the corresponding parcel of land.

The "For More Info" Column will lead you to more information about the underlying Patents. See the *Legend* at right, and the "How to Use this Book" chapter, for more information.

```
                    LEGEND
        "For More Info . . . " column
A = Authority (Legislative Act, See Appendix "A")
B = Block or Lot (location in Section unknown)
C = Cancelled Patent
F = Fractional Section
G = Group (Multi-Patentee Patent, see Appendix "C")
V = Overlaps another Parcel
R = Re-Issued (Parcel patented more than once)

(A & G items require you to look in the Appendixes referred
to above. All other Letter-designations followed by a number
require you to locate line-items in this index that possess
the ID number found after the letter).
```

ID	Individual in Patent	Sec.	Sec. Part	Date Issued	Other Counties	For More Info . . .
1739	ANDERSON, John	8	E½NW	1829-04-01		A1 R1728
1752	BELL, Joseph	15	NENE	1837-11-07		A1
1738	BIGHAM, James	2	W½SE	1829-05-01		A1
1740	BOTTS, John	8	E½SW	1823-08-20		A1
1741	" "	8	W½SW	1835-04-02		A1
1719	BUCKINGHAM, Alvah	15	SENE	1838-09-01		A1
1742	BURT, John	5	W½SW	1825-03-10		A1
1751	BYE, Jonathan	6	W½SW	1821-09-08		A1 G32
1750	" "	6	W½SE	1835-04-02		A1
1749	" "	6	SENE	1837-08-10		A1
1748	" "	6	E½SE	1837-11-07		A1
1755	CAMPBELL, Moses	12	E½SW	1826-05-01		A1
1760	CLARK, Samuel	4	SWSW	1837-04-10		A1
1758	" "	4	NWSW	1838-09-01		A1
1759	" "	4	SWNW	1838-09-01		A1
1766	CONDON, William	4	SENE	1837-04-10		A1 V1735
1770	DAVIES, Zadock	5	NW	1837-08-10		A1
1743	FRAME, John	14	W½NW	1835-04-02		A1
1767	GILPEN, William	5	NESE	1835-10-05		A1
1744	GILPIN, John	4	NENW	1835-04-21		A1
1747	GILPIN, Samuel	4	NWNW	1837-08-10		A1 G86
1737	GREEN, Jacob	5	NWSE	1835-09-23		A1
1751	HUNT, David	6	W½SW	1821-09-08		A1 G32
1768	ISRAEL, William	19	W½SW	1835-04-02		A1
1718	LAUGHLIN, Alexander	9	W½SW	1828-08-20		A1
1725	LAURENCE, David	6	W½NE	1832-04-02		A1
1757	LOWRY, Robert	13	E½NW	1831-02-10		A1
1761	LOWRY, Samuel	8	SESE	1835-04-21		A1
1720	MASTIN, Ann	14	E½NW	1837-04-10		A1
1764	MCCANN, Thomas	13	NWNW	1835-09-08		A1
1735	MCCREARY, Hugh	4	NE	1824-04-17		A1 V1766
1756	MCWILLIAMS, Philip	7	E½NW	1826-06-16		A1
1726	MORGAN, David	3		1800-05-21		A2
1717	PETERS, Abraham	7	W½SE	1826-06-16		A1
1724	PETERS, Daniel	7	E½SE	1835-09-08		A1
1734	REED, Hezekiah B	5	SWSE	1837-08-05		A1
1731	RIGGS, Evan	5	SESE	1837-11-07		A1
1753	RIGGS, Joseph T	12	W½SE	1828-05-30		A1
1727	ROBE, David	19	E½SW	1831-02-10		A1
1732	ROBINSON, Henry	3	E½NE	1826-04-01		A1 V1726
1745	ROBINSON, John	7	W½NW	1835-09-08		A1
1746	SIGMAN, John	5	E½SW	1835-04-02		A1
1733	SMITH, Henry	14	SENE	1837-04-10		A1
1754	SMITH, Mary	13	SWNW	1837-04-10		A1
1747	STANBERY, Jonas	4	NWNW	1837-08-10		A1 G86
1723	STUART, Charles	8	W½SE	1831-02-10		A1

ID	Individual in Patent	Sec.	Sec. Part	Date Issued	Other Counties	For More Info . . .
1722	STUART, Charles (Cont'd)	8	NESE	1837-08-05		A1
1721	THOMAS, Benjamin	6	NENE	1835-09-23		A1
1730	THOMAS, Enoch	4	E½SW	1825-08-06		A1
1729	" "	14	W½NE	1829-04-01		A1
1728	THOMPSON, David	8	E½NW	1832-04-02		A1 R1739
1736	WARDEN, Isaac J	12	E½SE	1835-04-21		A1
1763	WHITTEN, Sarah	6	E½SW	1826-04-01		A1
1762	" "	15	W½NE	1827-04-03		A1
1769	WILEY, William	14	NENE	1838-09-01		A1
1765	WILKINSON, Thomas	2	E½SE	1827-01-30		A1

Patent Map

T1-N R2-W
U.S. Military Survey Meridian

Map Group 18

Township Statistics

Parcels Mapped	:	54
Number of Patents	:	54
Number of Individuals	:	47
Patentees Identified	:	46
Number of Surnames	:	40
Multi-Patentee Parcels	:	2
Oldest Patent Date	:	5/21/1800
Most Recent Patent	:	9/1/1838
Block/Lot Parcels	:	0
Parcels Re - Issued	:	1
Parcels that Overlap	:	3
Cities and Towns	:	9
Cemeteries	:	4

5 — DAVIES Zadock 1837; BURT John 1825; SIGMAN John 1835; GREEN Jacob 1835; GILPEN William 1835; REED Hezekiah B 1837; RIGGS Evan 1837

4 — STANBERY [86] Jonas 1837; GILPIN John 1835; MCCREARY Hugh 1824; CONDON William 1837; CLARK Samuel 1838; CLARK Samuel 1838; CLARK Samuel 1837; THOMAS Enoch 1825

3 — ROBINSON Henry 1826

6 — LAURENCE David 1832; THOMAS Benjamin 1835; BYE Jonathan 1837; BYE [32] Jonathan 1821; WHITTEN Sarah 1826; BYE Jonathan 1835; BYE Jonathan 1837

7 — ROBINSON John 1835; MCWILLIAMS Philip 1826; PETERS Abraham 1826; PETERS Daniel 1835

8 — THOMPSON David 1832; ANDERSON John 1829; BOTTS John 1835; BOTTS John 1823; STUART Charles 1831; STUART Charles 1837; LOWRY Samuel 1835

15 — WHITTEN Sarah 1827; BELL Joseph 1837; BUCKINGHAM Alvah 1838; FRAME John 1835

14 — MASTIN Ann 1837; THOMAS Enoch 1829; WILEY William 1838; SMITH Henry 1837; MCCANN Thomas 1835; SMITH Mary 1837; LOWRY Robert 1831

13

18

23

3 — MORGAN David 1800

Copyright 2009 Boyd IT, Inc. All Rights Reserved

Map

2 BIGHAM James 1829 / WILKINSON Thomas 1827	1
9 LAUGHLIN Alexander 1828	10
12 CAMPBELL Moses 1826 / RIGGS Joseph T 1828 / WARDEN Isaac J 1835	11
19 ISRAEL William 1835 / ROBE David 1831	20
12	21

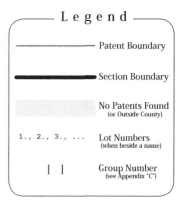

L e g e n d

Patent Boundary

Section Boundary

No Patents Found
(or Outside County)

1., 2., 3., ...   Lot Numbers
(when beside a name)

[ ]   Group Number
(see Appendix "C")

Scale: Section = 1 mile X 1 mile
(generally, with some exceptions)

Road Map

T1-N R2-W
U.S. Military Survey Meridian

Map Group 18

Cities & Towns
Blacktop
Byesville
Greenwood
Ideal
Kings Mine
Kipling
Lore City
Robins
Senecaville

Cemeteries
Bethel Methodist Protestant
  Cemetery
Lore City Cemetery
Saint Michael Cemetery
Senecaville Cemetery

Smiley Ln

2

1

Old Glory Rd

Range Rd

Leatherwood Rd

King
Queen Ave
High Ave

● Lore City

Division   Division

*Lore
City
Cem.*

Ideal
Rd

East

Goodyear Rd

9

Richland

10

Apache Ln

Hickory Tr

W Wind Ln

Eastener Ln

Jasmine Ln

12

Wintergreen Rd

11

Base Ln

Twp
Hwy 42

The Low Rd

Greenleaf
Ln

Richport Dr

Honey Bee Rd

19

20

Salem Rd

Gregg

Senecaville Cem.

N High

Rigby Rd

Tipton
Ln

Bridge
St

Royal Cherry

Brown

Grand
Ave

Fairway
Dr

Meadow
Ln

Mifflin

Church St

● Senecaville

Kiwi
Rd

12

Zanesville

Lashley Rd

Clay Pike Rd

Mill St

Hatchery Rd

21

● Greenwood

Helpful Hints

1. This road map has a number of uses, but primarily it is to help you: a) find the present location of land owned by your ancestors (at least the general area), b) find cemeteries and city-centers, and c) estimate the route/roads used by Census-takers & tax-assessors.

2. If you plan to travel to Guernsey County to locate cemeteries or land parcels, please pick up a modern travel map for the area before you do. Mapping old land parcels on modern maps is not as exact a science as you might think. Just the slightest variations in public land survey coordinates, estimates of parcel boundaries, or road-map deviations can greatly alter a map's representation of how a road either does or doesn't cross a particular parcel of land.

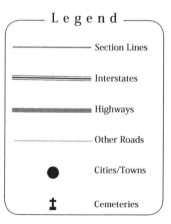

— L e g e n d —

———————	Section Lines
═══════════	Interstates
▬▬▬▬▬▬	Highways
———————	Other Roads
●	Cities/Towns
‡	Cemeteries

Scale: Section = 1 mile X 1 mile
(generally, with some exceptions)

Historical Map

T1-N R2-W
U.S. Military Survey Meridian

Map Group 18

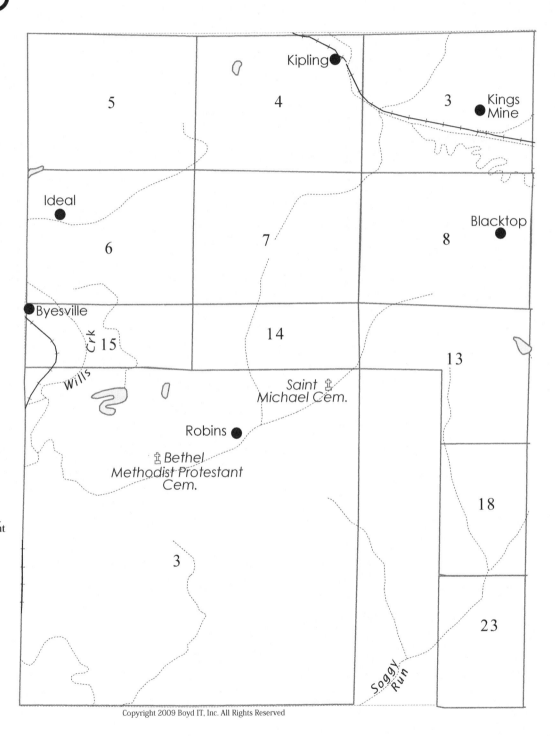

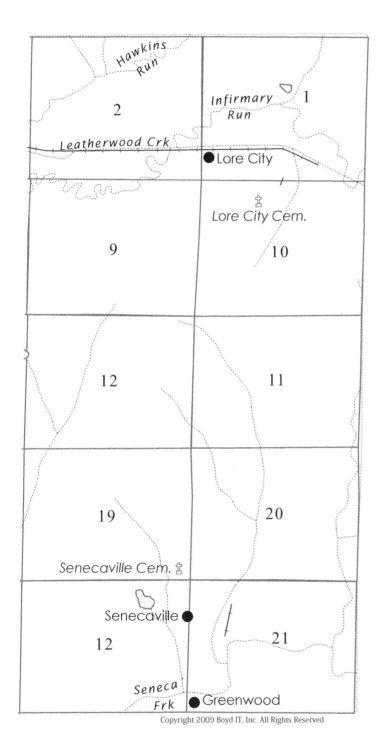

Hawkins Run

2

Infirmary Run

1

Leatherwood Crk

● Lore City

Lore City Cem.

9

10

12

11

19

20

Senecaville Cem. ‡

Senecaville ●

12

21

Seneca Frk

● Greenwood

Copyright 2009 Boyd IT, Inc. All Rights Reserved

Helpful Hints

1. This Map takes a different look at the same Congressional Township displayed in the preceding two maps. It presents features that can help you better envision the historical development of the area: a) Water-bodies (lakes & ponds), b) Water-courses (rivers, streams, etc.), c) Railroads, d) City/ town center-points (where they were oftentimes located when first settled), and e) Cemeteries.

2. Using this "Historical" map in tandem with this Township's Patent Map and Road Map, may lead you to some interesting discoveries. You will often find roads, towns, cemeteries, and waterways are named after nearby landowners: sometimes those names will be the ones you are researching. See how many of these research gems you can find here in Guernsey County.

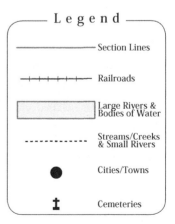

L e g e n d

——————— Section Lines

┼┼┼┼┼┼ Railroads

▭ Large Rivers & Bodies of Water

- - - - - - - Streams/Creeks & Small Rivers

● Cities/Towns

‡ Cemeteries

Scale: Section = 1 mile X 1 mile
(there are some exceptions)

Map Group 19: Index to Land Patents

Township 1-North Range 1-West (U.S. Military Survey)

After you locate an individual in this Index, take note of the Section and Section Part then proceed to the Land Patent map on the pages immediately following. You should have no difficulty locating the corresponding parcel of land.

The "For More Info" Column will lead you to more information about the underlying Patents. See the *Legend* at right, and the "How to Use this Book" chapter, for more information.

```
                        LEGEND
          "For More Info . . . " column
A = Authority (Legislative Act, See Appendix "A")
B = Block or Lot (location in Section unknown)
C = Cancelled Patent
F = Fractional Section
G = Group  (Multi-Patentee Patent, see Appendix "C")
V = Overlaps another Parcel
R = Re-Issued (Parcel patented more than once)

(A & G items require you to look in the Appendixes referred
to above. All other Letter-designations followed by a number
require you to locate line-items in this index that possess
the ID number found after the letter).
```

ID	Individual in Patent	Sec.	Sec. Part	Date Issued	Other Counties	For More Info . . .
1813	ARMSTRONG, Thomas	3	31	1806-03-05		A2
1789	ASKIN, John	3	10	1812-07-16		A2 G1
1790	BAKER, John	12	W½NE	1823-08-20		A1
1803	BAUM, Martin	3	39	1810-01-27		A2 G4
1804	" "	3	40	1810-01-27		A2 G4
1805	" "	3	6	1810-01-27		A2 G4
1822	BEATTY, Zaccheus A	3	24	1810-04-12		A2
1823	BIGGS, Zaccheus	2		1800-03-20		A2
1825	" "	3	8	1806-03-26		A2
1824	" "	3	37	1807-10-28		A2
1785	BLACK, James	3	25	1806-01-04		A2
1776	BLACKSHIRE, Ebenezer	3	7	1808-03-26		A2
1817	CARTER, William	3	14	1806-03-26		A2
1818	" "	3	15	1806-03-26		A2
1819	" "	3	16	1806-03-26		A2
1815	CARUTHERS, Thomas W	3	11	1806-03-26		A2
1816	" "	3	12	1806-03-26		A2
1778	DELONG, George	11	NW	1962-04-25		A1
1782	DEPEW, Isaac	10	W½NW	1826-06-06		A1
1786	DEPEW, James	23	E½SE	1827-07-30		A1
1787	" "	23	W½SE	1835-09-08		A1
1792	EMERSON, John	12	E½NE	1823-08-20		A1
1793	" "	12	E½SE	1825-08-06		A1
1791	" "	11	W½SW	1831-02-10		A1
1781	ENTROT, Henry	3	26	1815-04-10		A2
1806	FIELD, Reuben	3	17	1806-03-26		A2
1807	" "	3	18	1806-03-26		A2
1808	" "	3	19	1806-03-26		A2
1794	FLING, John	3	13	1806-03-05		A2
1788	FOREACRE, James	2	NW	1975-05-30		A1 V1823
1774	FOSTER, David	10	E½NW	1826-04-01		A1
1779	GOODERL, George	12	W½NW	1831-02-10		A1
1789	HUFF, Philip	3	10	1812-07-16		A2 G1
1780	MARINER, Gilbert	3	1	1814-03-29		A2
1771	MCBRIDE, Alexander	3	28	1806-03-05		A2
1809	MCBRIDE, Roger	3	2	1806-03-05		A2
1795	MCBURNEY, John	12	SW	1826-05-01		A1
1796	MEDEARIS, John	3	32	1802-06-21		A2
1797	" "	3	33	1802-06-21		A2
1798	" "	3	34	1802-06-21		A2
1783	MILLER, Jacob	3	21	1806-02-19		A2
1784	" "	3	22	1806-02-19		A2
1820	OHARA, William	3	29	1806-03-26		A2
1803	PERRY, Samuel	3	39	1810-01-27		A2 G4
1804	" "	3	40	1810-01-27		A2 G4
1805	" "	3	6	1810-01-27		A2 G4

ID	Individual in Patent	Sec.	Sec. Part	Date Issued	Other Counties	For More Info . . .
1821	PHILLIPS, William	11	E½SW	1831-02-10		A1
1810	PRATT, Rufus	12	W½SE	1821-09-08		A1
1799	ROGERS, John	3	20	1806-01-04		A2
1800	RUSSELL, John	3	3	1806-01-04		A2
1777	SANDERS, Edward	3	36	1806-01-04		A2
1812	STIERS, Samuel	11	W½SE	1828-05-30		A1
1811	" "	11	W½NE	1829-06-01		A1
1772	STIGLER, Benjamin	18	E½NE	1831-02-10		A1
1814	THOMPSON, Thomas	3	38	1810-01-04		A2
1773	WOLFORD, Daniel	11	E½SE	1835-04-02		A1
1775	WOLFORD, David	11	E½NE	1823-08-20		A1
1801	WOODSIDE, John	3	30	1806-01-04		A2
1802	" "	3	35	1806-01-04		A2

Patent Map

T1-N R1-W
U.S. Military Survey Meridian

Map Group 19

Township Statistics

Parcels Mapped	:	55
Number of Patents	:	45
Number of Individuals	:	40
Patentees Identified	:	38
Number of Surnames	:	37
Multi-Patentee Parcels	:	4
Oldest Patent Date	:	3/20/1800
Most Recent Patent	:	5/30/1975
Block/Lot Parcels	:	35
Parcels Re - Issued	:	0
Parcels that Overlap	:	1
Cities and Towns	:	9
Cemeteries	:	5

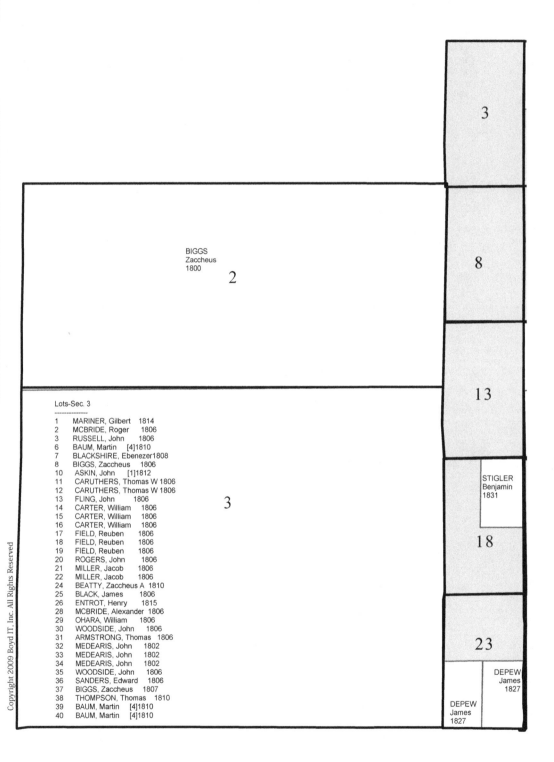

3

BIGGS
Zaccheus
1800

2

8

13

Lots-Sec. 3

1	MARINER, Gilbert		1814
2	MCBRIDE, Roger		1806
3	RUSSELL, John		1806
6	BAUM, Martin	[4]	1810
7	BLACKSHIRE, Ebenezer		1808
8	BIGGS, Zaccheus		1806
10	ASKIN, John	[1]	1812
11	CARUTHERS, Thomas W		1806
12	CARUTHERS, Thomas W		1806
13	FLING, John		1806
14	CARTER, William		1806
15	CARTER, William		1806
16	CARTER, William		1806
17	FIELD, Reuben		1806
18	FIELD, Reuben		1806
19	FIELD, Reuben		1806
20	ROGERS, John		1806
21	MILLER, Jacob		1806
22	MILLER, Jacob		1806
24	BEATTY, Zaccheus A		1810
25	BLACK, James		1806
26	ENTROT, Henry		1815
28	MCBRIDE, Alexander		1806
29	OHARA, William		1806
30	WOODSIDE, John		1806
31	ARMSTRONG, Thomas		1806
32	MEDEARIS, John		1802
33	MEDEARIS, John		1802
34	MEDEARIS, John		1802
35	WOODSIDE, John		1806
36	SANDERS, Edward		1806
37	BIGGS, Zaccheus		1807
38	THOMPSON, Thomas		1810
39	BAUM, Martin	[4]	1810
40	BAUM, Martin	[4]	1810

3

STIGLER
Benjamin
1831

18

23

DEPEW
James
1827

DEPEW
James
1827

Map

```
┌─────────────────────────┬───────────────────────────┐
│ ┌──────────┐            │                           │
│ │ FOREACRE │            │                           │
│ │ James    │            │           1               │
│ │ 1975     │            │                           │
│ └──────────┘  2         │                           │
│                         │                           │
├─────────────────────────┼─────────┬─────────────────┤
│                         │ DEPEW   │ FOSTER          │
│                         │ Isaac   │ David           │
│            9            │ 1826    │ 1826            │
│                         │         │        10       │
│                         ├─────────┴─────────────────┤
│  Guernsey               │                           │
├──────┬────┬──────┬──────┼──────────────┬──────┬─────┤
│GOODERL│   │BAKER │EMERSON│   DELONG     │STIERS│WOLFORD│
│George │   │John  │John   │   George     │Samuel│David │
│1831   │   │1823  │1823   │   1962       │1829  │1823  │
│      │ 12 │      │       │      11      │      ├─────┤
├──────┴────┼──────┼──────┼──────┬───────┼──────┤     │
│MCBURNEY   │PRATT │      │      │PHILLIPS│STIERS│WOLFORD│
│John       │Rufus │      │EMERSON│William│Samuel│Daniel│
│1826       │1821  │      │John   │1831   │1828  │1835  │
│           │      │      │1831   │       │      │     │
├───────────┴──────┴──────┼──────┴───────┴──────┴─────┤
│  Noble                  │                           │
│                         │                           │
│           19            │           20              │
│                         │                           │
├─────────────────────────┼───────────────────────────┤
│                         │                           │
│           22            │           21              │
│                         │                           │
└─────────────────────────┴───────────────────────────┘
```

Helpful Hints

1. This Map's INDEX can be found on the preceding pages.

2. Refer to Map "C" to see where this Township lies within Guernsey County, Ohio.

3. Numbers within square brackets [ ] denote a multi-patentee land parcel (multi-owner). Refer to Appendix "C" for a full list of members in this group.

4. Areas that look to be crowded with Patentees usually indicate multiple sales of the same parcel (Re-issues) or Overlapping parcels. See this Township's Index for an explanation of these and other circumstances that might explain "odd" groupings of Patentees on this map.

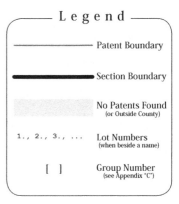

Legend

———————— Patent Boundary

━━━━━━━━ Section Boundary

░░░░░░░░ No Patents Found
(or Outside County)

1., 2., 3., ... Lot Numbers
(when beside a name)

[ ] Group Number
(see Appendix "C")

Scale: Section = 1 mile X 1 mile
(generally, with some exceptions)

Road Map

T1-N R1-W
U.S. Military Survey Meridian

Map Group 19

Cities & Towns
Chestnut Grove Cottage Area
Duch Addition
East Shore Cottage Area
Echo Point
Gibson
Hickory Grove Cottage Area
New Gottingen
Seneca Lake Estates
West Shore Cottage Area

Cemeteries
Gibson Station Cemetery
Saint Patricks Cemetery
Salem Baptist Cemetery
Sandhill Cemetery
Weaver Cemetery

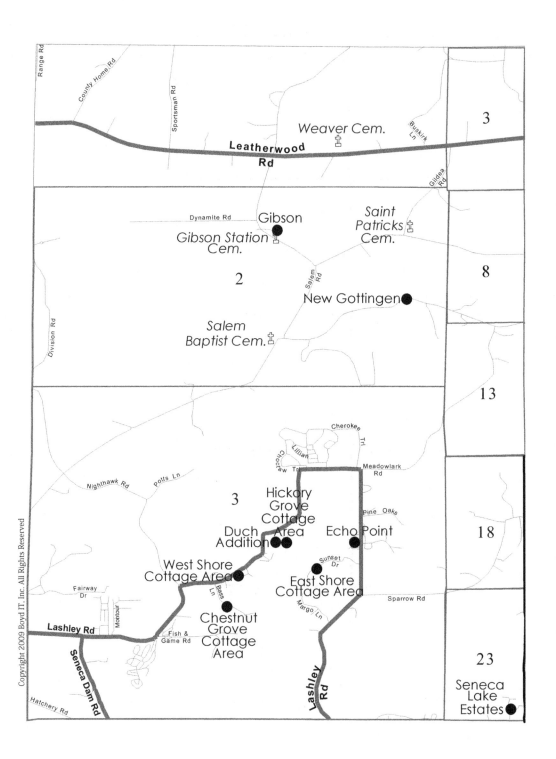

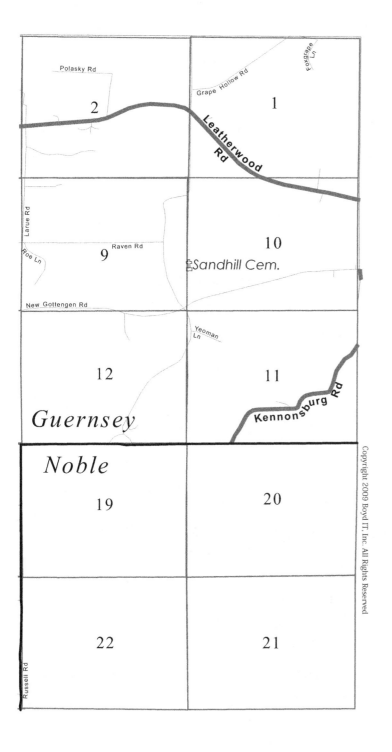

Helpful Hints

1. This road map has a number of uses, but primarily it is to help you: a) find the present location of land owned by your ancestors (at least the general area), b) find cemeteries and city-centers, and c) estimate the route/roads used by Census-takers & tax-assessors.

2. If you plan to travel to Guernsey County to locate cemeteries or land parcels, please pick up a modern travel map for the area before you do. Mapping old land parcels on modern maps is not as exact a science as you might think. Just the slightest variations in public land survey coordinates, estimates of parcel boundaries, or road-map deviations can greatly alter a map's representation of how a road either does or doesn't cross a particular parcel of land.

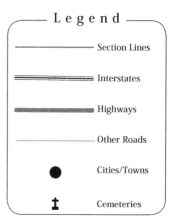

Legend

————	Section Lines
═══════	Interstates
━━━━━	Highways
————	Other Roads
●	Cities/Towns
✝	Cemeteries

Scale: Section = 1 mile X 1 mile
(generally, with some exceptions)

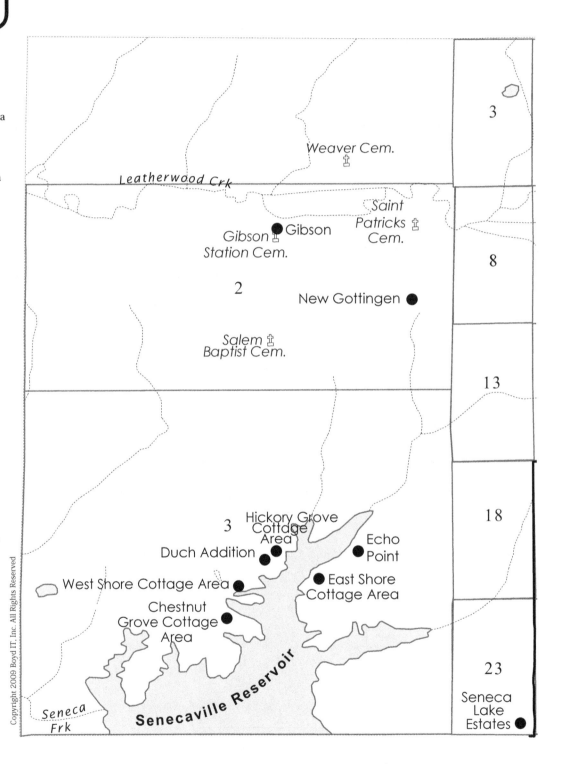

Historical Map

T1-N R1-W
U.S. Military Survey Meridian

Map Group 19

Cities & Towns
Chestnut Grove Cottage Area
Duch Addition
East Shore Cottage Area
Echo Point
Gibson
Hickory Grove Cottage Area
New Gottingen
Seneca Lake Estates
West Shore Cottage Area

Cemeteries
Gibson Station Cemetery
Saint Patricks Cemetery
Salem Baptist Cemetery
Sandhill Cemetery
Weaver Cemetery

Weaver Cem.

Leatherwood Crk

Gibson ● Gibson
Gibson
Station Cem.

Saint
Patricks
Cem.

2

New Gottingen ●

Salem
Baptist Cem.

3

8

13

18

23

Hickory Grove
Cottage
Area

Duch Addition ●
Echo
Point ●

3

West Shore Cottage Area ●
East Shore
Cottage Area ●

Chestnut
Grove Cottage
Area ●

Seneca
Frk

Senecaville Reservoir

Seneca
Lake
Estates ●

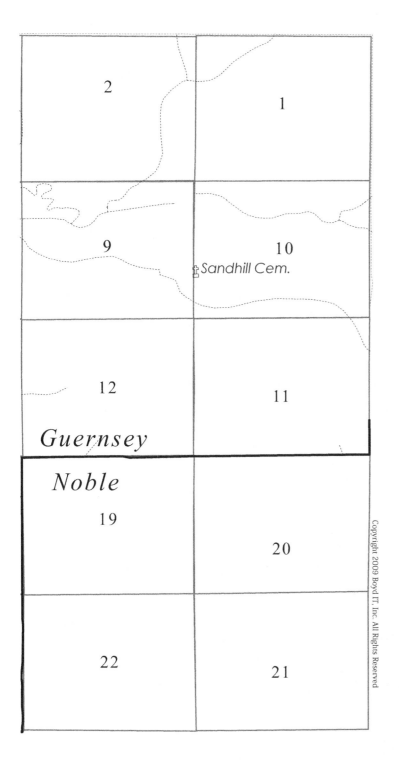

2

1

9

10

⚰ *Sandhill Cem.*

12

11

Guernsey

Noble

19

20

22

21

Helpful Hints

1. This Map takes a different look at the same Congressional Township displayed in the preceding two maps. It presents features that can help you better envision the historical development of the area: a) Water-bodies (lakes & ponds), b) Water-courses (rivers, streams, etc.), c) Railroads, d) City/town center-points (where they were oftentimes located when first settled), and e) Cemeteries.

2. Using this "Historical" map in tandem with this Township's Patent Map and Road Map, may lead you to some interesting discoveries. You will often find roads, towns, cemeteries, and waterways are named after nearby landowners: sometimes those names will be the ones you are researching. See how many of these research gems you can find here in Guernsey County.

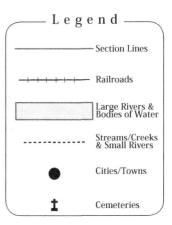

Legend

———————— Section Lines

+-+-+-+-+-+- Railroads

▭ Large Rivers & Bodies of Water

- - - - - - - Streams/Creeks & Small Rivers

● Cities/Towns

⚰ Cemeteries

Scale: Section = 1 mile X 1 mile
(there are some exceptions)

Map Group 20: Index to Land Patents

Township 9-North Range 10-West (Ohio River Survey)

After you locate an individual in this Index, take note of the Section and Section Part then proceed to the Land Patent map on the pages immediately following. You should have no difficulty locating the corresponding parcel of land.

The "For More Info" Column will lead you to more information about the underlying Patents. See the *Legend* at right, and the "How to Use this Book" chapter, for more information.

```
                    LEGEND
            "For More Info . . . " column
A = Authority (Legislative Act, See Appendix "A")
B = Block or Lot (location in Section unknown)
C = Cancelled Patent
F = Fractional Section
G = Group  (Multi-Patentee Patent, see Appendix "C")
V = Overlaps another Parcel
R = Re-Issued (Parcel patented more than once)

(A & G items require you to look in the Appendixes referred
to above. All other Letter-designations followed by a number
require you to locate line-items in this index that possess
the ID number found after the letter).
```

ID	Individual in Patent	Sec.	Sec. Part	Date Issued	Other Counties	For More Info . . .
1953	AIKINS, Robert	3	W½SE	1837-08-10		A1
1952	" "	25	SESE	1837-11-07		A1
1859	ARCHER, George	24	NWSW	1835-09-14		A1
1833	" "	23	NESE	1837-04-10		A1 G22
1862	ARCHER, Henry	24	NWSE	1835-09-14		A1
1834	" "	24	SWNE	1837-04-10		A1 G23
1827	ASHER, Abraham	2	SWSW	1835-04-21		A1
1970	BAY, William C	21	W½SW	1835-09-14		A1
1927	BELLEW, Joseph	10	NENW	1835-09-23		A1
1851	BISHOP, Eli	24	NWNE	1835-04-30		A1
1852	" "	24	SENE	1835-04-30		A1
1967	BOND, William	26	E½SE	1832-07-02		A1
1968	"	36	E½NW	1832-07-02		A1
1939	BROWN, Mason	19	W½NE	1825-03-10		A1
1969	BROWN, William	19	E½NE	1826-10-02		A1
1831	BUCKINGHAM, Alva	25	SWNE	1837-04-10		A1 G21
1832	BUCKINGHAM, Alvah	24	NWNW	1835-10-05		A1 G28
1833	" "	23	NESE	1837-04-10		A1 G22
1834	" "	24	SWNE	1837-04-10		A1 G23
1846	BURT, Ebenezer	23	NWSE	1835-04-21		A1
1928	BURT, Joseph	23	E½SW	1832-04-02		A1
1949	BURTON, Richard	1	SWSW	1835-04-21		A1
1883	CAEIRNS, James S	23	SWSE	1835-10-05		A1
1950	CARTER, Richard	1	SENE	1835-10-05		A1
1868	CLARK, Jacob	1	E½SE	1827-12-20		A1
1889	CONNER, John	27	SENE	1835-04-30		A1
1890	COWDEN, John	26	E½SW	1835-04-02		A1
1891	" "	26	W½SE	1835-04-02		A1
1972	CROW, William J	24	E½SE	1835-04-02		A1
1936	CULVER, Levi	10	W½NW	1826-06-06		A1
1863	DEAN, Henry	21	W½NW	1825-08-06		A1
1959	DEEREN, Thomas	1	NWNE	1835-09-14		A1
1842	DENNIS, David	9	SENE	1835-04-21		A1
1929	DOWNEY, Joseph	35	E½NW	1829-05-01		A1
1892	ELLIOTT, John	22	W½NW	1825-03-10		A1
1840	EVANS, Asahel	9	NENE	1835-09-30		A1
1973	EVANS, William J	36	SWNE	1837-08-05		A1
1946	FISHELL, Philip	12	E½NW	1827-09-20		A1
1947	FISHER, Philip	13	W½SW	1829-04-01		A1
1988	FOSTER, Wilson L	25	E½NW	1835-09-30		A1
1853	GILL, Elijah	13	NWNE	1835-09-30		A1
1860	GOINGS, George	23	NWSW	1835-10-05		A1
1925	GOINGS, Wesley	15	SWNE	1835-04-30		A1 G87
1861	GOWENS, George	21	E½NW	1832-04-02		A1
1930	GOWENS, Joel	21	E½NE	1825-08-06		A1 G68
1894	GRIMES, John	35	SWNE	1835-10-05		A1

ID	Individual in Patent	Sec.	Sec. Part	Date Issued	Other Counties	For More Info . . .
1893	GRIMES, John (Cont'd)	35	NWNE	1837-04-10		A1
1838	HAINELINE, Asa	10	E½SW	1826-12-01		A1
1888	HAINS, Joel	3	W½SW	1835-09-08		A1
1895	HALLY, John	36	NWSW	1835-10-05		A1
1877	HAMILTON, James	25	NESE	1837-08-10		A1
1878	" "	25	SWSE	1837-08-10		A1
1832	HAMMOND, Benjamin W	24	NWNW	1835-10-05		A1 G28
1879	HARR, James	1	E½NW	1837-04-10		A1
1869	HARTMAN, Jacob	25	SENE	1837-04-10		A1
1896	HARTMAN, John	23	SENE	1837-04-10		A1
1897	" "	24	SWNW	1837-04-10		A1
1830	HARTMAN, William	25	NWNE	1837-04-10		A1 G107
1971	HATFIELD, William	23	SWNE	1837-04-10		A1
1899	HAWS, John	3	E½NE	1830-12-01		A1
1898	" "	10	SWNE	1835-09-23		A1
1848	HESKETT, Elam	2	E½NE	1830-12-01		A1
1839	HINELINE, Asa	10	SENW	1835-04-21		A1
1850	HISKETT, Elam	1	W½NW	1830-12-01		A1
1849	" "	1	NWSW	1837-08-10		A1
1864	HOLLAND, Henry	15	NWNE	1837-04-10		A1
1940	HUFF, Nathan	3	NESE	1837-04-10		A1
1941	" "	3	SESE	1837-04-10		A1
1901	JOHNSON, John	14	E½NW	1823-08-20		A1
1900	" "	13	W½NW	1824-04-17		A1
1902	" "	15	SE	1825-03-10		A1
1938	JOHNSON, Margaret	15	W½SW	1826-06-06		A1
1974	JOHNSON, William	11	W½SE	1835-09-08		A1
1976	" "	13	NENW	1835-09-30		A1
1977	" "	13	SENW	1837-04-10		A1
1975	" "	13	NENE	1837-08-05		A1
1870	JONES, Jacob	36	E½SW	1831-06-01		A1
1871	" "	36	W½SE	1831-06-01		A1
1978	JONES, William	12	E½SW	1825-08-06		A1
1979	" "	13	E½SW	1832-07-02		A1
1926	" "	13	SWSE	1835-09-14		A1 G88
1980	" "	24	NESW	1837-04-10		A1
1981	" "	24	SENW	1837-04-10		A1
1933	JORDON, Joshua	4	E½NE	1835-04-21		A1
1934	" "	4	E½SE	1835-04-21		A1
1935	" "	4	SWNE	1835-04-21		A1
1903	KARR, John	1	NESW	1837-04-10		A1
1954	KELL, Robert	26	SWSW	1835-09-23		A1
1836	KELLS, Andrew	35	W½SE	1835-04-02		A1
1835	" "	35	SESE	1835-09-30		A1
1904	KENNEY, John	24	NENW	1835-10-05		A1
1945	LANGLOIS, Peter	12	W½SW	1823-08-20		A1
1857	LAZEARE, Francis	22	E½SW	1825-08-06		A1
1858	" "	22	W½SW	1825-08-06		A1 R1837
1944	LE PEDRIN, NICHOLAS	11	E½NE	1828-08-20		A1
1951	LETT, Richard	21	W½NE	1835-09-08		A1
1845	LINDLEY, Davidson	22	E½SE	1826-06-16		A1
1982	LLEWELLYN, William	10	W½SW	1838-09-01		A1
1955	LYLE, Robert	25	W½NW	1835-04-21		A1
1828	MACKEY, Alexander	8	W½SW	1823-08-20		A1
1872	MAPLE, Jacob	9	W½NE	1826-06-06		A1
1855	MARSHAL, Elizabeth	23	SWSW	1837-04-10		A1
1932	MARSHALL, Joseph W	35	E½SW	1832-04-02		A1
1866	MOORE, Isaac	23	NWNE	1837-04-10		A1
1905	MOORE, John	10	SENE	1835-04-30		A1
1930	MULLEN, Joseph	21	E½NE	1825-08-06		A1 G68
1931	NEWLAND, Joseph	23	NENE	1835-10-05		A1
1880	OGIER, James	11	E½SE	1825-03-10		A1
1961	OGIER, Thomas	11	SW	1823-08-20		A1
1962	" "	14	SW	1823-08-20		A1
1960	" "	10	E½SE	1824-04-17		A1
1963	" "	15	E½NE	1827-04-03		A1
1856	PARISH, Evans	36	W½NW	1832-07-02		A1
1847	PARRISH, Edward E	25	W½SW	1829-04-01		A1
1831	PARRISH, Evans	25	SWNE	1837-04-10		A1 G21
1826	PATTERSON, Abijah	25	NWSE	1837-04-10		A1
1937	PAXTON, Margaret F	14	W½NW	1831-03-01		A1
1956	PAXTON, Samuel	25	SESW	1837-08-10		A1
1964	PAXTON, Thomas	15	E½SW	1826-06-06		A1

ID	Individual in Patent	Sec.	Sec. Part	Date Issued	Other Counties	For More Info . . .
1966	PERRY, Walter G	13	SWNE	1835-09-14		A1
1965	PHILLIPS, Thomas	26	NWSW	1837-08-15		A1
1843	RANNELLS, David	26	E½NE	1835-04-02		A1
1907	ROBBINS, John	12	W½NW	1825-08-06		A1
1906	" "	11	E½NW	1828-05-30		A1
1914	ROBINS, John	12	W½NE	1821-09-08		A1
1913	" "	12	E½NE	1823-08-20		A1
1911	" "	11	W½NE	1827-12-20		A1
1912	" "	11	W½NW	1827-12-20		A1
1917	" "	2	E½NW	1830-12-01		A1
1919	" "	2	W½NE	1832-07-02		A1
1920	" "	2	W½NW	1832-07-02		A1
1916	" "	13	SENE	1835-04-30		A1
1910	" "	10	N½NE	1835-09-30		A1
1908	" "	1	SWNE	1837-04-10		A1
1915	" "	13	NESE	1837-04-10		A1
1909	" "	1	W½SE	1837-08-05		A1
1918	" "	2	NWSW	1837-08-15		A1
1882	ROBINSON, James	21	W½SE	1826-04-01		A1
1854	ROOSE, Elisha	4	NWNE	1835-09-14		A1
1957	RUSSELL, Samuel	3	W½NW	1835-09-08		A1
1865	SCOTT, Hugh	1	NENE	1835-10-05		A1
1886	SCOTT, James	2	W½SE	1824-04-17		A1
1884	" "	2	E½SE	1828-05-30		A1
1885	" "	2	E½SW	1835-09-14		A1
1844	SHARP, David	36	E½NE	1837-04-10		A1
1874	SHRIVER, Jacob	22	E½NW	1825-03-10		A1
1875	" "	22	W½NE	1825-03-10		A1
1876	" "	24	NENE	1835-09-30		A1
1873	" "	13	SESE	1835-10-05		A1
1881	SHRIVER, James P	13	NWSE	1835-09-30		A1
1829	SINES, Absalom	25	NENE	1837-04-10		A1 G108
1948	SMITH, Ransom	3	E½NW	1835-09-08		A1
1887	SPILMAN, James	21	E½SW	1826-04-01		A1
1925	STANBERY, Jonas	15	SWNE	1835-04-30		A1 G87
1926	" "	13	SWSE	1835-09-14		A1 G88
1923	" "	36	E½SE	1837-04-10		A1
1922	" "	23	SESE	1837-08-15		A1
1924	" "	36	NWNE	1837-08-15		A1
1983	STEVENS, William	4	W½SE	1835-04-21		A1
1984	STRAKE, William	3	E½SW	1835-09-08		A1
1958	STURGES, Solomon	25	NESW	1837-08-15		A1
1829	TEEL, Alexander	25	NENE	1837-04-10		A1 G108
1830	" "	25	NWNE	1837-04-10		A1 G107
1985	TULLOUGH, William	24	S½SW	1837-08-15		A1
1986	" "	24	SWSE	1837-08-15		A1
1867	VAN HORNE, ISAAC	3	W½NE	1832-07-02		A1
1841	VANDVORT, Barnat	8	E½SW	1825-08-06		A1
1942	WEST, Nathan	27	NENE	1835-09-23		A1
1943	" "	35	NESE	1835-09-30		A1
1837	WHARTON, Andrew	22	W½SE	1825-08-06		A1 R1858
1921	WHARTON, John	21	E½SE	1825-08-06		A1
1987	WINN, William	36	SWSW	1837-04-10		A1

Patent Map

T9-N R10-W
Ohio River Survey Meridian

Map Group 20

Township Statistics

Parcels Mapped	:	163
Number of Patents	:	162
Number of Individuals	:	116
Patentees Identified	:	115
Number of Surnames	:	96
Multi-Patentee Parcels	:	9
Oldest Patent Date	:	9/8/1821
Most Recent Patent	:	9/1/1838
Block/Lot Parcels	:	0
Parcels Re - Issued	:	1
Parcels that Overlap	:	0
Cities and Towns	:	4
Cemeteries	:	2

6

5

4
ROOSE
Elisha
1835
JORDON
Joshua
1835
JORDON
Joshua
1835
STEVENS
William
1835
JORDON
Joshua
1835

7

8
MACKEY
Alexander
1823
VANDVORT
Barnat
1825

9
MAPLE
Jacob
1826
EVANS
Asahel
1835
DENNIS
David
1835

18

17

16

19
BROWN
Mason
1825
BROWN
William
1826

20

21
DEAN
Henry
1825
GOWENS
George
1832
LETT
Richard
1835
MULLEN [68]
Joseph
1825
BAY
William C
1835
SPILMAN
James
1826
ROBINSON
James
1826
WHARTON
John
1825

30

29

28

31

32

33

RUSSELL Samuel 1835	SMITH Ransom 1835	HORNE Isaac Van 1832	HAWS John 1830	ROBINS John 1832	ROBINS John 1830	ROBINS John 1832	HESKETT Elam 1830	HISKETT Elam 1830	HARR James 1837	DEEREN Thomas 1835	SCOTT Hugh 1835

Helpful Hints

1. This Map's INDEX can be found on the preceding pages.

2. Refer to Map "C" to see where this Township lies within Guernsey County, Ohio.

3. Numbers within square brackets [ ] denote a multi-patentee land parcel (multi-owner). Refer to Appendix "C" for a full list of members in this group.

4. Areas that look to be crowded with Patentees usually indicate multiple sales of the same parcel (Re-issues) or Overlapping parcels. See this Township's Index for an explanation of these and other circumstances that might explain "odd" groupings of Patentees on this map.

Legend

Patent Boundary

Section Boundary

No Patents Found (or Outside County)

1., 2., 3., ... Lot Numbers (when beside a name)

[ ] Group Number (see Appendix "C")

Scale: Section = 1 mile X 1 mile (generally, with some exceptions)

Road Map

T9-N R10-W
Ohio River Survey Meridian

Map Group 20

Cities & Towns
Bluebell
Cumberland
Helena
Opperman

Cemeteries
Bethel Methodist Episcopal
  Cemetery
Cumberland Cemetery

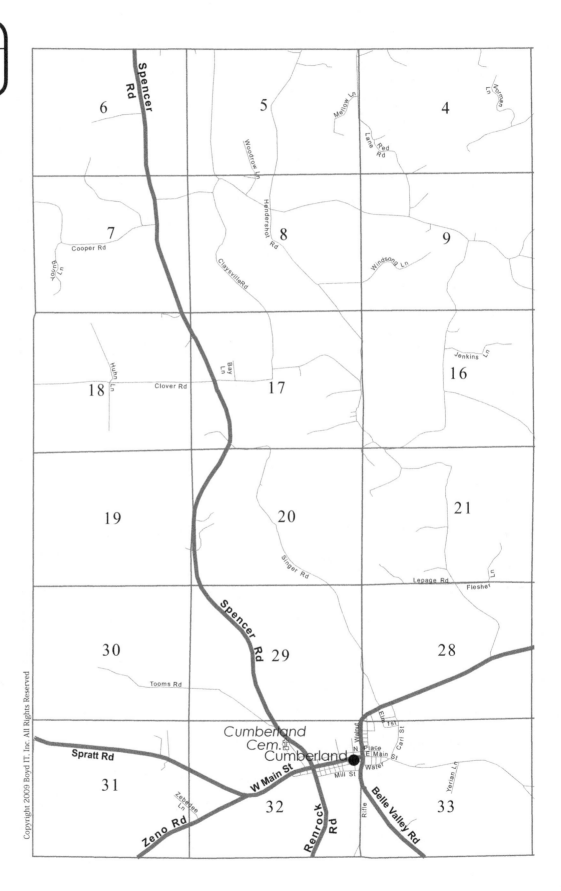

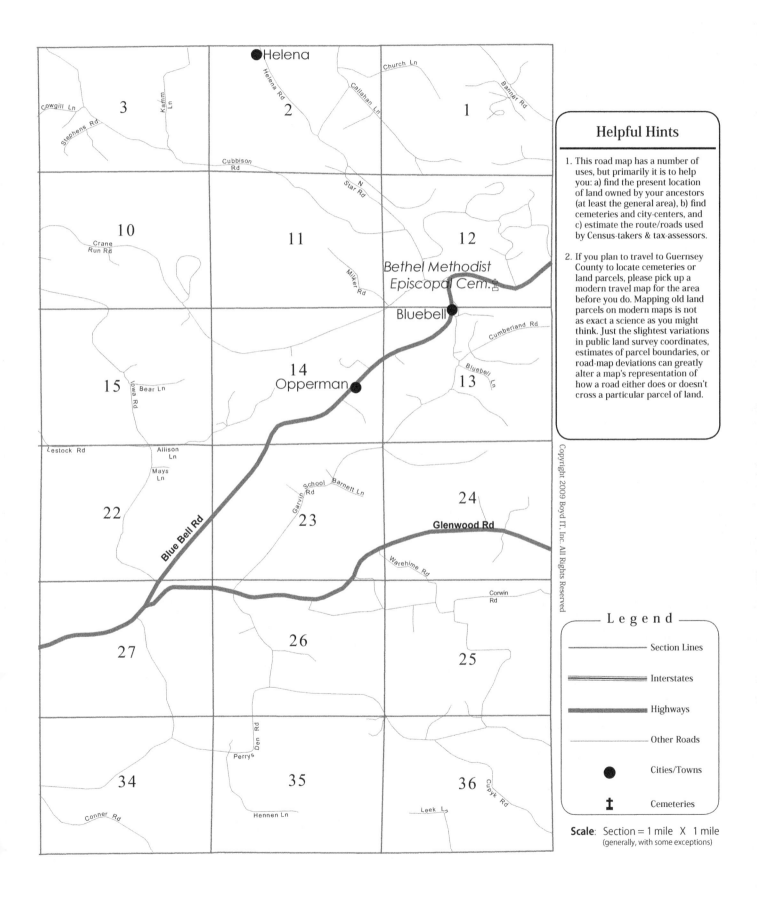

Helpful Hints

1. This road map has a number of uses, but primarily it is to help you: a) find the present location of land owned by your ancestors (at least the general area), b) find cemeteries and city-centers, and c) estimate the route/roads used by Census-takers & tax-assessors.

2. If you plan to travel to Guernsey County to locate cemeteries or land parcels, please pick up a modern travel map for the area before you do. Mapping old land parcels on modern maps is not as exact a science as you might think. Just the slightest variations in public land survey coordinates, estimates of parcel boundaries, or road-map deviations can greatly alter a map's representation of how a road either does or doesn't cross a particular parcel of land.

Legend

————	Section Lines
════	Interstates
▬▬▬▬	Highways
————	Other Roads
●	Cities/Towns
‡	Cemeteries

Scale: Section = 1 mile X 1 mile
(generally, with some exceptions)

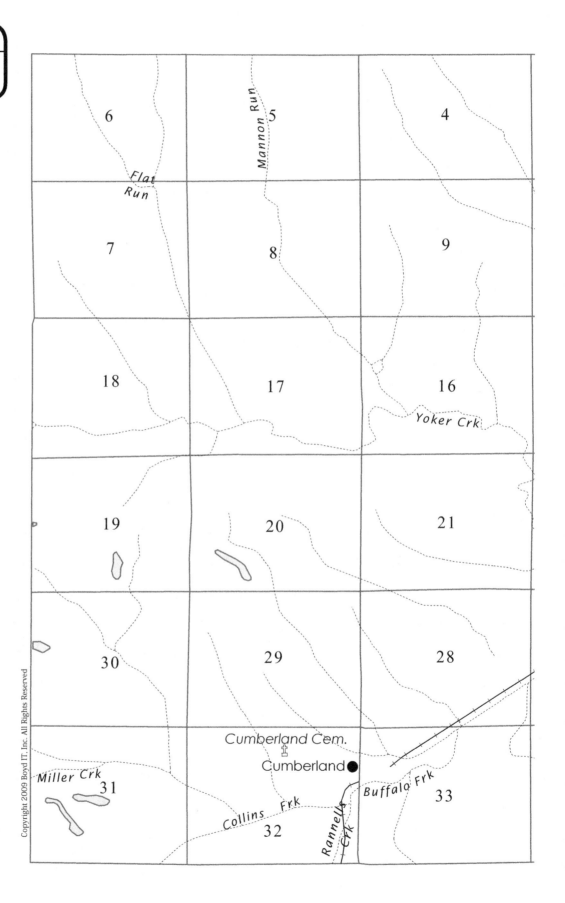

Historical Map

T9-N R10-W
Ohio River Survey Meridian

Map Group 20

Cities & Towns
Bluebell
Cumberland
Helena
Opperman

Cemeteries
Bethel Methodist Episcopal
 Cemetery
Cumberland Cemetery

6

5   *Mannon Run*

4

Flat Run

7

8

9

18

17

16

Yoker Crk

19

20

21

30

29

28

Cumberland Cem.

Cumberland ●

Miller Crk
31

Collins Frk

32

Rannells Crk

Buffalo Frk

33

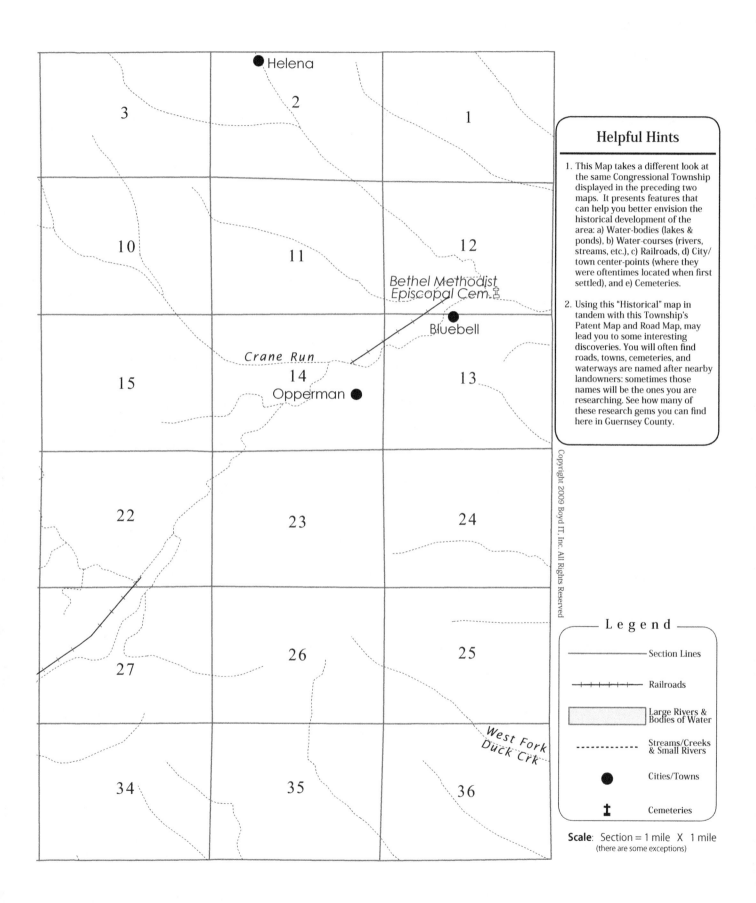

Helena

3

2

1

Helpful Hints

1. This Map takes a different look at the same Congressional Township displayed in the preceding two maps. It presents features that can help you better envision the historical development of the area: a) Water-bodies (lakes & ponds), b) Water-courses (rivers, streams, etc.), c) Railroads, d) City/town center-points (where they were oftentimes located when first settled), and e) Cemeteries.

2. Using this "Historical" map in tandem with this Township's Patent Map and Road Map, may lead you to some interesting discoveries. You will often find roads, towns, cemeteries, and waterways are named after nearby landowners: sometimes those names will be the ones you are researching. See how many of these research gems you can find here in Guernsey County.

10

11

12

Bethel Methodist Episcopal Cem. ‡

Bluebell

Crane Run

15

14

13

Opperman ●

22

23

24

Legend

— Section Lines

+ + + + + Railroads

Large Rivers & Bodies of Water

- - - - - Streams/Creeks & Small Rivers

● Cities/Towns

‡ Cemeteries

27

26

25

West Fork Duck Crk

34

35

36

Scale: Section = 1 mile X 1 mile
(there are some exceptions)

Map Group 21: Index to Land Patents

Township 8-North Range 9-West (Ohio River Survey)

After you locate an individual in this Index, take note of the Section and Section Part then proceed to the Land Patent map on the pages immediately following. You should have no difficulty locating the corresponding parcel of land.

The "For More Info" Column will lead you to more information about the underlying Patents. See the *Legend* at right, and the "How to Use this Book" chapter, for more information.

```
                         LEGEND
              "For More Info . . . " column
A = Authority (Legislative Act, See Appendix "A")
B = Block or Lot (location in Section unknown)
C = Cancelled Patent
F = Fractional Section
G = Group  (Multi-Patentee Patent, see Appendix "C")
V = Overlaps another Parcel
R = Re-Issued (Parcel patented more than once)

(A & G items require you to look in the Appendixes referred
to above. All other Letter-designations followed by a number
require you to locate line-items in this index that possess
the ID number found after the letter).
```

ID	Individual in Patent	Sec.	Sec. Part	Date Issued	Other Counties	For More Info . . .
1990	BURT, David	9	NESW	1835-04-30		A1
1999	FINLEY, John	12	NWSW	1837-08-05		A1
2003	FINLEY, Joseph	12	NESW	1835-09-23		A1
2004	" "	12	SENW	1835-09-23		A1 R2006
2006	FINLEY, Samuel	12	SENW	1837-08-05		A1 R2004
2007	" "	12	SWSE	1837-08-05		A1
1992	FOREMAN, Hiram	12	NENW	1837-08-15		A1 G39
2000	GILL, John	10	SWSW	1837-04-10		A1
1994	HUGHS, Isaac	10	W½SE	1823-08-20		A1
1995	LAFOLLETT, James	10	E½SW	1837-08-05		A1
1996	" "	10	NWSW	1837-08-15		A1
1993	MCCOY, Hugh	6	E½NW	1829-04-01		A1
1991	MCVICKER, Dennis	9	W½SW	1826-11-01		A1
1997	NEEDLER, James	12	NWSE	1835-09-23		A1 G73
1997	REED, James	12	NWSE	1835-09-23		A1 G73
1989	RIGGS, Daniel	12	W½NW	1837-08-05		A1
2001	SECRIST, John	9	E½SE	1835-04-02		A1
2005	SPAID, Michael	9	W½SE	1837-08-05		A1
2009	SPAID, William	9	SESW	1837-08-05		A1
2002	STANBERY, Jonas	6	W½NW	1837-04-10		A1
1992	" "	12	NENW	1837-08-15		A1 G39
2008	STRONG, Thomas F	12	SWSW	1835-04-30		A1
1998	THOMPSON, James	10	E½SE	1825-08-06		A1

Patent Map

T8-N R9-W
Ohio River Survey Meridian

Map Group 21

Township Statistics

Parcels Mapped	:	21
Number of Patents	:	21
Number of Individuals	:	19
Patentees Identified	:	18
Number of Surnames	:	16
Multi-Patentee Parcels	:	2
Oldest Patent Date	:	8/20/1823
Most Recent Patent	:	8/15/1837
Block/Lot Parcels	:	0
Parcels Re - Issued	:	1
Parcels that Overlap	:	0
Cities and Towns	:	5
Cemeteries	:	3

Note: the area contained in this map amounts to far less than a full Township. Therefore, its contents are completely on this single page (instead of a "normal" 2-page spread).

Legend

— Patent Boundary

— Section Boundary

No Patents Found (or Outside County)

1., 2., 3., ... Lot Numbers (when beside a name)

[ ] Group Number (see Appendix "C")

Scale: Section = 1 mile X 1 mile (generally, with some exceptions)

--- Map grid ---

Section 6: STANBERY Jonas 1837 / MCCOY Hugh 1829

Section 7

Section 18

Section 5

Section 8

Section 17

Section 4

Guernsey / Noble

Section 9: MCVICKER Dennis 1826 / BURT David 1835 / SPAID William 1837 / SPAID Michael 1837 / SECRIST John 1835

Section 16

Section 3

Section 10: LAFOLLETT James 1837 / GILL John 1837 / LAFOLLETT James 1837 / HUGHS Isaac 1823 / THOMPSON James 1825

Section 15

Section 2

Section 11

Section 14

Section 1

Section 12: RIGGS Daniel 1837 / STRONG Thomas F 1835 / FINLEY John 1837 / FINLEY Joseph 1835 / FOREMAN [39] Hiram 1837 / FINLEY Samuel 1837 / FINLEY Joseph 1835 / FINLEY James 1835 / REED [73] / FINLEY Samuel 1837

Section 13

221

Road Map

T8-N R9-W
Ohio River Survey Meridian

Map Group 21

Note: the area contained in this map amounts to far less than a full Township. Therefore, its contents are completely on this single page (instead of a "normal" 2-page spread).

Cities & Towns

Buffalo
Derwent
Fairview
Pleasant City
Walhonding

Cemeteries

Buffalo Cemetery
Old Hartford Cemetery
Pleasant City Protestant Cemetery

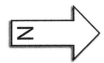

Legend

——————— Section Lines

═══════ Interstates

━━━━━━ Highways

——————— Other Roads

● Cities/Towns

✝ Cemeteries

Scale: Section = 1 mile X 1 mile
(generally, with some exceptions)

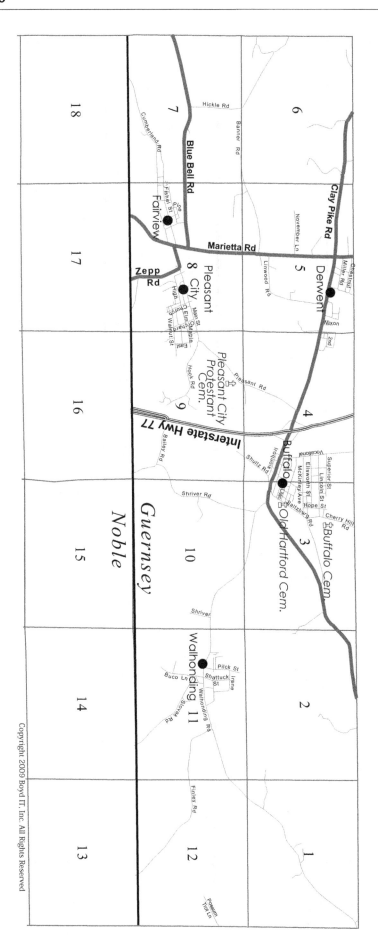

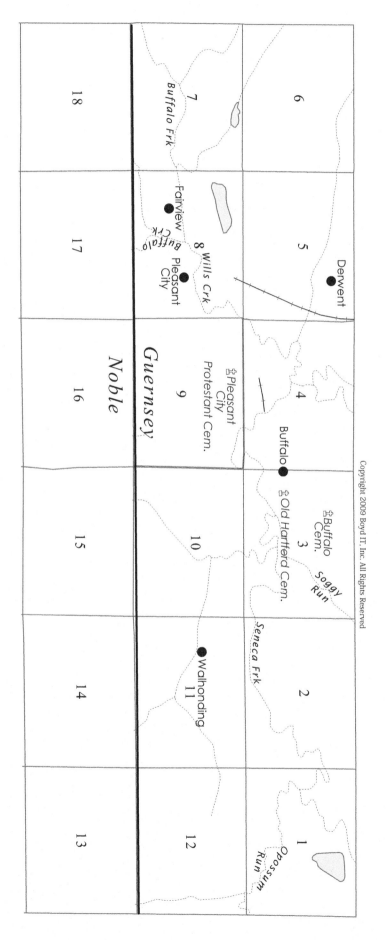

Historical Map

T8-N R9-W
Ohio River Survey Meridian

Map Group 21

Note: the area contained in this map amounts to far less than a full Township. Therefore, its contents are completely on this single page (instead of a "normal" 2-page spread).

Cities & Towns

Buffalo
Derwent
Fairview
Pleasant City
Walhonding

Cemeteries

Buffalo Cemetery
Old Hartford Cemetery
Pleasant City Protestant
  Cemetery

Legend

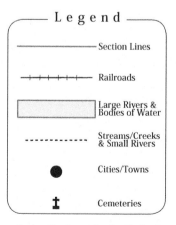

——————— Section Lines

╈╈╈╈╈╈ Railroads

▭ Large Rivers & Bodies of Water

- - - - - - - Streams/Creeks & Small Rivers

● Cities/Towns

✝ Cemeteries

Scale: Section = 1 mile X 1 mile
(there are some exceptions)

Appendices

Appendix A - Acts of Congress Authorizing the Patents Contained in this Book

The following Acts of Congress are referred to throughout the Indexes in this book. The text of the Federal Statutes referred to below can usually be found on the web. For more information on such laws, check out the publishers's web-site at *www.arphax.com,* go to the "Research" page, and click on the "Land-Law" link.

Ref. No.	Date and Act of Congress	Number of Parcels of Land
1	April 24, 1820: Sale-Cash Entry (3 Stat. 566)	1842
2	June 1, 1796: United Brethren Warrant Act (1 Stat. 480)	167

Appendix B - Section Parts (Aliquot Parts)

The following represent the various abbreviations we have found thus far in describing the parts of a Public Land Section. Some of these are very obscure and rarely used, but we wanted to list them for just that reason. A full section is 1 square mile or 640 acres.

Section Part	Description	Acres
\<none\>	Full Acre (if no Section Part is listed, presumed a full Section)	640
\<1-??\>	A number represents a Lot Number and can be of various sizes	?
E½	East Half-Section	320
E½E½	East Half of East Half-Section	160
E½E½SE	East Half of East Half of Southeast Quarter-Section	40
E½N½	East Half of North Half-Section	160
E½NE	East Half of Northeast Quarter-Section	80
E½NENE	East Half of Northeast Quarter of Northeast Quarter-Section	20
E½NENW	East Half of Northeast Quarter of Northwest Quarter-Section	20
E½NESE	East Half of Northeast Quarter of Southeast Quarter-Section	20
E½NESW	East Half of Northeast Quarter of Southwest Quarter-Section	20
E½NW	East Half of Northwest Quarter-Section	80
E½NWNE	East Half of Northwest Quarter of Northeast Quarter-Section	20
E½NWNW	East Half of Northwest Quarter of Northwest Quarter-Section	20
E½NWSE	East Half of Northwest Quarter of Southeast Quarter-Section	20
E½NWSW	East Half of Northwest Quarter of Southwest Quarter-Section	20
E½S½	East Half of South Half-Section	160
E½SE	East Half of Southeast Quarter-Section	80
E½SENE	East Half of Southeast Quarter of Northeast Quarter-Section	20
E½SENW	East Half of Southeast Quarter of Northwest Quarter-Section	20
E½SESE	East Half of Southeast Quarter of Southeast Quarter-Section	20
E½SESW	East Half of Southeast Quarter of Southwest Quarter-Section	20
E½SW	East Half of Southwest Quarter-Section	80
E½SWNE	East Half of Southwest Quarter of Northeast Quarter-Section	20
E½SWNW	East Half of Southwest Quarter of Northwest Quarter-Section	20
E½SWSE	East Half of Southwest Quarter of Southeast Quarter-Section	20
E½SWSW	East Half of Southwest Quarter of Southwest Quarter-Section	20
E½W½	East Half of West Half-Section	160
N½	North Half-Section	320
N½E½NE	North Half of East Half of Northeast Quarter-Section	40
N½E½NW	North Half of East Half of Northwest Quarter-Section	40
N½E½SE	North Half of East Half of Southeast Quarter-Section	40
N½E½SW	North Half of East Half of Southwest Quarter-Section	40
N½N½	North Half of North Half-Section	160
N½NE	North Half of Northeast Quarter-Section	80
N½NENE	North Half of Northeast Quarter of Northeast Quarter-Section	20
N½NENW	North Half of Northeast Quarter of Northwest Quarter-Section	20
N½NESE	North Half of Northeast Quarter of Southeast Quarter-Section	20
N½NESW	North Half of Northeast Quarter of Southwest Quarter-Section	20
N½NW	North Half of Northwest Quarter-Section	80
N½NWNE	North Half of Northwest Quarter of Northeast Quarter-Section	20
N½NWNW	North Half of Northwest Quarter of Northwest Quarter-Section	20
N½NWSE	North Half of Northwest Quarter of Southeast Quarter-Section	20
N½NWSW	North Half of Northwest Quarter of Southwest Quarter-Section	20
N½S½	North Half of South Half-Section	160
N½SE	North Half of Southeast Quarter-Section	80
N½SENE	North Half of Southeast Quarter of Northeast Quarter-Section	20
N½SENW	North Half of Southeast Quarter of Northwest Quarter-Section	20
N½SESE	North Half of Southeast Quarter of Southeast Quarter-Section	20

Section Part	Description	Acres
N½SESW	North Half of Southeast Quarter of Southwest Quarter-Section	20
N½SESW	North Half of Southeast Quarter of Southwest Quarter-Section	20
N½SW	North Half of Southwest Quarter-Section	80
N½SWNE	North Half of Southwest Quarter of Northeast Quarter-Section	20
N½SWNW	North Half of Southwest Quarter of Northwest Quarter-Section	20
N½SWSE	North Half of Southwest Quarter of Southeast Quarter-Section	20
N½SWSE	North Half of Southwest Quarter of Southeast Quarter-Section	20
N½SWSW	North Half of Southwest Quarter of Southwest Quarter-Section	20
N½W½NW	North Half of West Half of Northwest Quarter-Section	40
N½W½SE	North Half of West Half of Southeast Quarter-Section	40
N½W½SW	North Half of West Half of Southwest Quarter-Section	40
NE	Northeast Quarter-Section	160
NEN½	Northeast Quarter of North Half-Section	80
NENE	Northeast Quarter of Northeast Quarter-Section	40
NENENE	Northeast Quarter of Northeast Quarter of Northeast Quarter	10
NENENW	Northeast Quarter of Northeast Quarter of Northwest Quarter	10
NENESE	Northeast Quarter of Northeast Quarter of Southeast Quarter	10
NENESW	Northeast Quarter of Northeast Quarter of Southwest Quarter	10
NENW	Northeast Quarter of Northwest Quarter-Section	40
NENWNE	Northeast Quarter of Northwest Quarter of Northeast Quarter	10
NENWNW	Northeast Quarter of Northwest Quarter of Northwest Quarter	10
NENWSE	Northeast Quarter of Northwest Quarter of Southeast Quarter	10
NENWSW	Northeast Quarter of Northwest Quarter of Southwest Quarter	10
NESE	Northeast Quarter of Southeast Quarter-Section	40
NESENE	Northeast Quarter of Southeast Quarter of Northeast Quarter	10
NESENW	Northeast Quarter of Southeast Quarter of Northwest Quarter	10
NESESE	Northeast Quarter of Southeast Quarter of Southeast Quarter	10
NESESW	Northeast Quarter of Southeast Quarter of Southwest Quarter	10
NESW	Northeast Quarter of Southwest Quarter-Section	40
NESWNE	Northeast Quarter of Southwest Quarter of Northeast Quarter	10
NESWNW	Northeast Quarter of Southwest Quarter of Northwest Quarter	10
NESWSE	Northeast Quarter of Southwest Quarter of Southeast Quarter	10
NESWSW	Northeast Quarter of Southwest Quarter of Southwest Quarter	10
NW	Northwest Quarter-Section	160
NWE½	Northwest Quarter of Eastern Half-Section	80
NWN½	Northwest Quarter of North Half-Section	80
NWNE	Northwest Quarter of Northeast Quarter-Section	40
NWNENE	Northwest Quarter of Northeast Quarter of Northeast Quarter	10
NWNENW	Northwest Quarter of Northeast Quarter of Northwest Quarter	10
NWNESE	Northwest Quarter of Northeast Quarter of Southeast Quarter	10
NWNESW	Northwest Quarter of Northeast Quarter of Southwest Quarter	10
NWNW	Northwest Quarter of Northwest Quarter-Section	40
NWNWNE	Northwest Quarter of Northwest Quarter of Northeast Quarter	10
NWNWNW	Northwest Quarter of Northwest Quarter of Northwest Quarter	10
NWNWSE	Northwest Quarter of Northwest Quarter of Southeast Quarter	10
NWNWSW	Northwest Quarter of Northwest Quarter of Southwest Quarter	10
NWSE	Northwest Quarter of Southeast Quarter-Section	40
NWSENE	Northwest Quarter of Southeast Quarter of Northeast Quarter	10
NWSENW	Northwest Quarter of Southeast Quarter of Northwest Quarter	10
NWSESE	Northwest Quarter of Southeast Quarter of Southeast Quarter	10
NWSESW	Northwest Quarter of Southeast Quarter of Southwest Quarter	10
NWSW	Northwest Quarter of Southwest Quarter-Section	40
NWSWNE	Northwest Quarter of Southwest Quarter of Northeast Quarter	10
NWSWNW	Northwest Quarter of Southwest Quarter of Northwest Quarter	10
NWSWSE	Northwest Quarter of Southwest Quarter of Southeast Quarter	10
NWSWSW	Northwest Quarter of Southwest Quarter of Southwest Quarter	10
S½	South Half-Section	320
S½E½NE	South Half of East Half of Northeast Quarter-Section	40
S½E½NW	South Half of East Half of Northwest Quarter-Section	40
S½E½SE	South Half of East Half of Southeast Quarter-Section	40

Section Part	Description	Acres
S½E½SW	South Half of East Half of Southwest Quarter-Section	40
S½N½	South Half of North Half-Section	160
S½NE	South Half of Northeast Quarter-Section	80
S½NENE	South Half of Northeast Quarter of Northeast Quarter-Section	20
S½NENW	South Half of Northeast Quarter of Northwest Quarter-Section	20
S½NESE	South Half of Northeast Quarter of Southeast Quarter-Section	20
S½NESW	South Half of Northeast Quarter of Southwest Quarter-Section	20
S½NW	South Half of Northwest Quarter-Section	80
S½NWNE	South Half of Northwest Quarter of Northeast Quarter-Section	20
S½NWNW	South Half of Northwest Quarter of Northwest Quarter-Section	20
S½NWSE	South Half of Northwest Quarter of Southeast Quarter-Section	20
S½NWSW	South Half of Northwest Quarter of Southwest Quarter-Section	20
S½S½	South Half of South Half-Section	160
S½SE	South Half of Southeast Quarter-Section	80
S½SENE	South Half of Southeast Quarter of Northeast Quarter-Section	20
S½SENW	South Half of Southeast Quarter of Northwest Quarter-Section	20
S½SESE	South Half of Southeast Quarter of Southeast Quarter-Section	20
S½SESW	South Half of Southeast Quarter of Southwest Quarter-Section	20
S½SESW	South Half of Southeast Quarter of Southwest Quarter-Section	20
S½SW	South Half of Southwest Quarter-Section	80
S½SWNE	South Half of Southwest Quarter of Northeast Quarter-Section	20
S½SWNW	South Half of Southwest Quarter of Northwest Quarter-Section	20
S½SWSE	South Half of Southwest Quarter of Southeast Quarter-Section	20
S½SWSE	South Half of Southwest Quarter of Southeast Quarter-Section	20
S½SWSW	South Half of Southwest Quarter of Southwest Quarter-Section	20
S½W½NE	South Half of West Half of Northeast Quarter-Section	40
S½W½NW	South Half of West Half of Northwest Quarter-Section	40
S½W½SE	South Half of West Half of Southeast Quarter-Section	40
S½W½SW	South Half of West Half of Southwest Quarter-Section	40
SE	Southeast Quarter Section	160
SEN½	Southeast Quarter of North Half-Section	80
SENE	Southeast Quarter of Northeast Quarter-Section	40
SENENE	Southeast Quarter of Northeast Quarter of Northeast Quarter	10
SENENW	Southeast Quarter of Northeast Quarter of Northwest Quarter	10
SENESE	Southeast Quarter of Northeast Quarter of Southeast Quarter	10
SENESW	Southeast Quarter of Northeast Quarter of Southwest Quarter	10
SENW	Southeast Quarter of Northwest Quarter-Section	40
SENWNE	Southeast Quarter of Northwest Quarter of Northeast Quarter	10
SENWNW	Southeast Quarter of Northwest Quarter of Northwest Quarter	10
SENWSE	Souteast Quarter of Northwest Quarter of Southeast Quarter	10
SENWSW	Southeast Quarter of Northwest Quarter of Southwest Quarter	10
SESE	Southeast Quarter of Southeast Quarter-Section	40
SESENE	SoutheastQuarter of Southeast Quarter of Northeast Quarter	10
SESENW	Southeast Quarter of Southeast Quarter of Northwest Quarter	10
SESESE	Southeast Quarter of Southeast Quarter of Southeast Quarter	10
SESESW	Southeast Quarter of Southeast Quarter of Southwest Quarter	10
SESW	Southeast Quarter of Southwest Quarter-Section	40
SESWNE	Southeast Quarter of Southwest Quarter of Northeast Quarter	10
SESWNW	Southeast Quarter of Southwest Quarter of Northwest Quarter	10
SESWSE	Southeast Quarter of Southwest Quarter of Southeast Quarter	10
SESWSW	Southeast Quarter of Southwest Quarter of Southwest Quarter	10
SW	Southwest Quarter-Section	160
SWNE	Southwest Quarter of Northeast Quarter-Section	40
SWNENE	Southwest Quarter of Northeast Quarter of Northeast Quarter	10
SWNENW	Southwest Quarter of Northeast Quarter of Northwest Quarter	10
SWNESE	Southwest Quarter of Northeast Quarter of Southeast Quarter	10
SWNESW	Southwest Quarter of Northeast Quarter of Southwest Quarter	10
SWNW	Southwest Quarter of Northwest Quarter-Section	40
SWNWNE	Southwest Quarter of Northwest Quarter of Northeast Quarter	10
SWNWNW	Southwest Quarter of Northwest Quarter of Northwest Quarter	10

Section Part	Description	Acres
SWNWSE	Southwest Quarter of Northwest Quarter of Southeast Quarter	10
SWNWSW	Southwest Quarter of Northwest Quarter of Southwest Quarter	10
SWSE	Southwest Quarter of Southeast Quarter-Section	40
SWSENE	Southwest Quarter of Southeast Quarter of Northeast Quarter	10
SWSENW	Southwest Quarter of Southeast Quarter of Northwest Quarter	10
SWSESE	Southwest Quarter of Southeast Quarter of Southeast Quarter	10
SWSESW	Southwest Quarter of Southeast Quarter of Southwest Quarter	10
SWSW	Southwest Quarter of Southwest Quarter-Section	40
SWSWNE	Southwest Quarter of Southwest Quarter of Northeast Quarter	10
SWSWNW	Southwest Quarter of Southwest Quarter of Northwest Quarter	10
SWSWSE	Southwest Quarter of Southwest Quarter of Southeast Quarter	10
SWSWSW	Southwest Quarter of Southwest Quarter of Southwest Quarter	10
W½	West Half-Section	320
W½E½	West Half of East Half-Section	160
W½N½	West Half of North Half-Section (same as NW)	160
W½NE	West Half of Northeast Quarter	80
W½NENE	West Half of Northeast Quarter of Northeast Quarter-Section	20
W½NENW	West Half of Northeast Quarter of Northwest Quarter-Section	20
W½NESE	West Half of Northeast Quarter of Southeast Quarter-Section	20
W½NESW	West Half of Northeast Quarter of Southwest Quarter-Section	20
W½NW	West Half of Northwest Quarter-Section	80
W½NWNE	West Half of Northwest Quarter of Northeast Quarter-Section	20
W½NWNW	West Half of Northwest Quarter of Northwest Quarter-Section	20
W½NWSE	West Half of Northwest Quarter of Southeast Quarter-Section	20
W½NWSW	West Half of Northwest Quarter of Southwest Quarter-Section	20
W½S½	West Half of South Half-Section	160
W½SE	West Half of Southeast Quarter-Section	80
W½SENE	West Half of Southeast Quarter of Northeast Quarter-Section	20
W½SENW	West Half of Southeast Quarter of Northwest Quarter-Section	20
W½SESE	West Half of Southeast Quarter of Southeast Quarter-Section	20
W½SESW	West Half of Southeast Quarter of Southwest Quarter-Section	20
W½SW	West Half of Southwest Quarter-Section	80
W½SWNE	West Half of Southwest Quarter of Northeast Quarter-Section	20
W½SWNW	West Half of Southwest Quarter of Northwest Quarter-Section	20
W½SWSE	West Half of Southwest Quarter of Southeast Quarter-Section	20
W½SWSW	West Half of Southwest Quarter of Southwest Quarter-Section	20
W½W½	West Half of West Half-Section	160

Appendix C - Multi-Patentee Groups

The following index presents groups of people who jointly received patents in Guernsey County, Ohio. The Group Numbers are used in the Patent Maps and their Indexes so that you may then turn to this Appendix in order to identify all the members of the each buying group.

Group Number 1
ASKIN, John; HUFF, Philip

Group Number 2
ASKINS, Polly; ASKINS, John

Group Number 3
BARNDOLLAR, Jacob; COULTER, Elizabeth

Group Number 4
BAUM, Martin; PERRY, Samuel

Group Number 5
BEATTY, Zaccheus A; BIGGS, Zaccheus

Group Number 6
BEYNOR, Henry; BEYNOR, George; LANE, Noah; LANE, John

Group Number 7
BIGGS, Zaccheus; BEATTY, Zaccheus A

Group Number 8
BRUSH, Daniel; DENNIS, Henry

Group Number 9
BRUSH, Daniel; DUFF, James

Group Number 10
BRUSH, Daniel; FORREST, Thomas S

Group Number 11
BRUSH, Daniel; FULLER, Thomas R

Group Number 12
BRUSH, Daniel; GIBSON, George

Group Number 13
BRUSH, Daniel; JONES, Hugh

Group Number 14
BRUSH, Daniel; LAWRENCE, Jacob

Group Number 15
BRUSH, Daniel; MAPLE, William B

Group Number 16
BRUSH, Daniel; MARLATT, John

Group Number 17
BRUSH, Daniel; MORRIS, Isaac

Group Number 18
BRUSH, Daniel; REED, William

Group Number 19
BRUSH, Daniel; SPARKS, Eli

Group Number 20
BRUSH, Daniel; WILSON, Edward

Group Number 21
BUCKINGHAM, Alva; PARRISH, Evans

Group Number 22
BUCKINGHAM, Alvah; ARCHER, George

Group Number 23
BUCKINGHAM, Alvah; ARCHER, Henry

Group Number 24
BUCKINGHAM, Alvah; ATTWOOD, Cornelius

Group Number 25
BUCKINGHAM, Alvah; BROWN, John

Group Number 26
BUCKINGHAM, Alvah; CULLEN, William

Group Number 27
BUCKINGHAM, Alvah; HAMILTON, William

Group Number 28
BUCKINGHAM, Alvah; HAMMOND, Benjamin W

Group Number 29
BUCKINGHAM, Alvah; LEARD, George

Group Number 30
BUCKINGHAM, Alvah; RANKIN, James

Group Number 31
BUCKINGHAM, Alvah; ROBERTS, Lewis

Group Number 32
BYE, Jonathan; HUNT, David

Group Number 33
CLARY, Enoch; CLARY, Samuel

Group Number 34
COOK, Ellis; MCCUNE, James

Group Number 35
DAVIS, Benjamin; SOLINGER, James

Group Number 36
DISALLUMS, Thomas; DISALLUMS, John

Group Number 37
FERBRACHE, John S; ROBERTSON, Joseph

Group Number 38
FORD, Charles E; FORD, Emily A; FORD, Chilion

Group Number 39
FOREMAN, Hiram; STANBERY, Jonas

Group Number 40
GALLIWAY, Benjamin; HAWS, Ann

Group Number 41
GALLIWAY, Benjamin; HAWS, Anne

Group Number 42
HALE, Isaiah B; WATERS, John

Group Number 43
HALL, John; DEW, David

Group Number 44
HALL, John; DUFF, David

Group Number 45
HALL, John; WILSON, William M

Group Number 46
HAVER, George W; CASSIDY, Asa R

Group Number 47
HAWES, Welles; DUFF, Alexander

Group Number 48
HAWES, Welles; NORMAN, Benjamin B

Group Number 49
KANADY, John; FITZPATRICK, Bernard

Group Number 50
KELL, John; BLAIR, John

Group Number 51
KELL, Samuel; MCDOWELL, Ephraim

Group Number 52
KIMBLE, William; BEAL, George

Group Number 53
KREIDER, Henry; BRUSH, Daniel

Group Number 54
LEACH, Thomas; MURPHY, Michael

Group Number 55
LEACH, Thomas; PAYLOR, Samuel

Group Number 56
LEACH, Thomas; WILLIAMS, Samuel

Group Number 57
LEECH, Thomas; BELL, Hamilton

Group Number 58
LEECH, Thomas; EVANS, David

Group Number 59
LEECH, Thomas; MCCONNAUGHEY, David P

Group Number 60
LEECH, Thomas; ORR, John

Group Number 61
LEECH, Thomas; WEIR, Joseph

Group Number 62
LUCK, Thomas; RIGDEN, John F

Group Number 63
MASTERS, Richard; MASTERS, William

Group Number 64
MCCALL, James; MCCALL, William M; MCDOWEL, Mathew

Group Number 65
MILLER, Joseph; BOGGS, James

Group Number 66
MISKIMEN, James; CARMICHAEL, James

Group Number 67
MITCHELL, John B; MITCHELL, George W

Group Number 68
MULLEN, Joseph; GOWENS, Joel

Group Number 69
NEILL, William; STANBERY, Jonas

Group Number 70
NICHOLS, James; CAMPBELL, James

Group Number 71
OLDHAM, Thomas; OLDHAM, Isaac

Group Number 72
PARKE, Uriah; PICKERING, Greenbery

Group Number 73
REED, James; NEEDLER, James

Group Number 74
RENNER, Tobias; MILLER, George

Group Number 75
SARCHET, David; SARCHET, Moses; SARCHET, Peter

Group Number 76
SCOTT, Abraham; ARMSTRONG, Joseph

Group Number 77
SCOTT, Francis; HAMMOND, John

Group Number 78
SHAFFER, Samuel; SHAFFER, Christopher

Group Number 79
STANBERY, Jonas; ACHESON, John R

Group Number 80
STANBERY, Jonas; ANNETT, Arthur

Group Number 81
STANBERY, Jonas; COWAN, William

Group Number 82
STANBERY, Jonas; COX, Joseph

Group Number 83
STANBERY, Jonas; DILDINE, Harmon

Group Number 84
STANBERY, Jonas; DRAKE, David

Group Number 85
STANBERY, Jonas; FURNEY, Solomon

Group Number 86
STANBERY, Jonas; GILPIN, Samuel

Group Number 87
STANBERY, Jonas; GOINGS, Wesley

Group Number 88
STANBERY, Jonas; JONES, William

Group Number 89
STANBERY, Jonas; MCMILLAN, Joseph

Group Number 90
STANBERY, Jonas; MORRIS, Abraham

Group Number 91
STANBERY, Jonas; MORRIS, Isaac

Group Number 92
STANBERY, Jonas; STARKEY, David

Group Number 93
STANBERY, Jonas; STEWART, Thomas H

Group Number 94
STANBERY, Jonas; WEIR, Thomas

Group Number 95
STEETH, David; HAMMOND, John

Group Number 96
STURGES, Solomon; BELL, Robert

Group Number 97
STURGES, Solomon; CLARK, John

Group Number 98
STURGES, Solomon; DAVOULT, William

Group Number 99
STURGES, Solomon; DUFF, Robert

Group Number 100
STURGES, Solomon; FURNEY, John

Group Number 101
STURGES, Solomon; GIBSON, John

Group Number 102
STURGES, Solomon; HEDGE, George M

Group Number 103
STURGES, Solomon; HENRY, Jacob

Group Number 104
STURGES, Solomon; JOHNSON, Charles

Group Number 105
STURGES, Solomon; MCCARTNEY, William

Group Number 106
STURGES, Solomon; MILLIGAN, John

Group Number 107
TEEL, Alexander; HARTMAN, William

Group Number 108
TEEL, Alexander; SINES, Absalom

Group Number 109
THOMAS, William; EVANS, David

Group Number 110
TRUSLER, Goodhart; TRUSLER, Elias; WISCARVER, Joseph

Group Number 111
TRUSLER, Goodhart; TRUSLER, Elias; WISCORVER, Joseph

Group Number 112
WALLER, John; AYERS, Jacob

Group Number 113
WARDEN, David M; WARDEN, Jane

Group Number 114
YATES, Jasper; COLEMAN, Robert

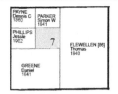

Extra! Extra! (about our Indexes)

We purposefully do not have an all-name index in the back of this volume so that our readers do not miss one of the best uses of this book: finding misspelled names among more specialized indexes.

Without repeating the text of our "How-to" chapter, we have nonetheless tried to assist our more anxious researchers by delivering a short-cut to the two county-wide Surname Indexes, the second of which will lead you to all-name indexes for each Congressional Township mapped in this volume :

For your convenience, the "How To Use this Book" Chart on page 2 is repeated on the reverse of this page.

We should be releasing new titles every week for the foreseeable future. We urge you to write, fax, call, or email us any time for a current list of titles. Of course, our web-page will always have the most current information about current and upcoming books.

Arphax Publishing Co.
2210 Research Park Blvd.
Norman, Oklahoma 73069
(800) 681-5298 toll-free
(405) 366-6181 local
(405) 366-8184 fax
info@arphax.com

www.arphax.com

How to Use This Book - A Graphical Summary

Part I
"The Big Picture"

Map A ▸ *Counties in the State*

Map B ▸ *Surrounding Counties*

Map C ▸ *Congressional Townships (Map Groups) in the County*

Map D ▸ *Cities & Towns in the County*

Map E ▸ *Cemeteries in the County*

Surnames in the County ▸ *Number of Land-Parcels for Each Surname*

Surname/Township Index ▸ Directs you to Township Map Groups in Part II

The <u>Surname/Township Index</u> can direct you to any number of **Township Map Groups**

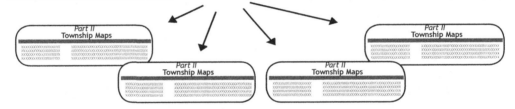

Part II
Township Map Groups
(1 for each Township in the County)

Each Township Map Group contains all four of of the following tools . . .

Land Patent Index ▸ *Every-name Index of Patents Mapped in this Township*

Land Patent Map ▸ *Map of Patents as listed in above Index*

Road Map ▸ *Map of Roads, City-centers, and Cemeteries in the Township*

Historical Map ▸ *Map of Railroads, Lakes, Rivers, Creeks, City-Centers, and Cemeteries*

Appendices

Appendix A ▸ *Congressional Authority enabling Patents within our Maps*

Appendix B ▸ *Section-Parts / Aliquot Parts (a comprehensive list)*

Appendix C ▸ *Multi-patentee Groups (Individuals within Buying Groups)*

Made in the USA
Coppell, TX
28 October 2024

39332273R00136